Between the Lines 12

Author

Richard Davies

Contributing Authors

Gillian Bartlett

Marg Hogan

Ross Laing

NELSON

NELSON

Between the Lines 12
Richard Davies

Director of Publishing
David Steele

Publisher
Mark Cressman

Program Manager
Norma Kennedy

Project Manager
Caron MacMenamin

Developmental Editor
Susan McNish

Senior Managing Editor
Nicola Balfour

Senior Production Editor
Carol Martin

Production Manager
Renate McCloy

Production Coordinator
Helen Locsin

Permissions and Photo Research
Cindy Howard

Interior Design
Suzanne Peden

Cover Design
Peter Papayanakis

Composition Manager
Marnie Benedict

Composition
Erich Falkenberg

Reviewers
The publishers gratefully acknowledge the contributions of the following educators:

Linda May Bell, ON
Nancy Daoust, ON
Owen Davis, ON
Barbara Davison, NS
Doug Gregory, AB
Irene Heffel, AB
Wayne J. Hurley, NF
Phyllis Kereliuk, BC
S.B. Kirby, NF
Roy Lalonde, ON
Elaine Leslie, ON
Colleen Lindsay, BC
Mary Anne MacArthur, ON
C. Mayne, AB
Mary McCarthy-Doyle, NF
A.J. Miller, BC
Jenelle Mitchell, BC
Mary Mullen, PEI
Karen Nieman, ON
Vince O'Brien, ON
Christopher Stoesser, ON
Terry Swift, MB
Lenard Wyatt, BC
Pamela Young, AB

Dedication
Richard Davies thanks his main teaching influences—Brian Kells, George Brown, and Betty Shaw (of Winnipeg) and R. Glenn Martin, Stephen Arnold, and David Wangler (of Edmonton).

**National Library of Canada
Cataloguing in Publication Data**

Davies, Richard
   Between the lines 12

(Nelson English)
For use in grade 12.
ISBN 0-17-619741-9 (bound)—
ISBN 0-17-619739-7 (pbk.)

1. English language—Study and teaching (Secondary) 2. Language arts (Secondary) I. Title. II. Series.

PE1112.D39 2002   428
C2002-900690-2

CONTENTS

UNIT 5: MEMORABLE MOMENTS AND INFLUENCES

UNIT 6: VALUES, BELIEFS, AND CHOICES

UNIT 7: INDIVIDUALS AND SOCIETY

To the Student—

Welcome to *Between the Lines 12*, an exciting new anthology for graduating high-school students!

This book contains several popular themes, each having to do with discovering the world around us. Most of the selections are contemporary and Canadian, with many other cultures and countries also represented.

You will encounter well-known writers such as Ray Bradbury, Robert Frost, Ellen Goodman, Wayson Choy, Maxine Tynes, and Ernest Buckler, and a blend of popular and classic literary works, including "The Hockey Song," "Cold Missouri Waters," "There Will Come Soft Rains," "Two Fishermen," and "Warren Pryor."

Along with drama, poetry, and short stories, you will find a variety of texts such as cartoons, newspaper and Web articles, interviews and editorials, photographs, advertisements, lyrics, and self-help segments.

Many of the topics in this book will be familiar to you. They include the generation gap and peer-group influence; gender equality; scientific advances in cloning, stem-cell research, robotics, and space travel; ecological concerns; issues relating to communication technologies—TV, movies, video games, and cellphones; and preparing for work and life after graduation.

Each of the eight units begins with a brief introduction to the theme, along with relevant quotations and questions to help you focus as you read and view. Each selection is followed by additional questions and activities to help you read between the lines, and most include additional notes and author information.

At the back of the book, there is a useful glossary of terms to help you talk, write, and think about the book's selections.

I hope you enjoy *Between the Lines 12*. It is a book specially designed for you, your needs, and your interests.

Wishing you a successful year in English,
Richard Davies

Something to think about ...

Small Bridges

Kihara Koichi

Since the very day that I was born
I have been learning only this:
to build bridges in the world   as many bridges as I can.

Against the morning light
I build a bridge across the narrow space between two buildings.
I build a bridge over the gap   between the hearts
of people who aimlessly rush by,
but
no one's hand can connect the distance
between hearts that are torn apart.

Under the infrared rays of the evening
I build a bridge between the passing moment and the upcoming moment.
I build a bridge between the love and hatred of a person
who is walking with his head drooping, without reason.
And I dream of completing a bridge someday
between human and human, between time and place
which no storms can destroy.

Ever since the very moment I was born
I have lived with only this thought:
to build bridges in the world   as many bridges as I can.

The wave of the future is coming and there is no fighting it.
— *Anne Morrow Lindbergh*

The present is great with the future.
— *Gottfried Wilhelm Leibnitz*

The future depends on the nobility of our imaginings.
— *Barbara Grizzuti Harrison*

FUTURE CONSIDERATIONS

This unit focuses on the future and, especially, on the impact of technology on humanity.

In writer Anne Morrow Lindbergh's words, change is inevitable and we should adjust ourselves to that reality.

At the same time, the German philosopher Leibnitz points out that, in a sense, the future is already here, and we need to pay attention to the changes and trends of our age.

The future offers many challenges, and American writer Barbara Grizzuti Harrison rightly emphasizes the "nobility of our imaginings." We will require moral judgement and imagination to deal with the serious problems ahead of us, such as threats to the planet's ecology and to the survival of our species.

As you read this unit, think about the following:

1) Are the various changes and technologies described good or bad in your opinion?

2) How will your future life be affected by these changes? What challenges do they present?

3) What might be some solutions to the problems that face us in the new millennium?

Shape of Things to Come

FROM MISCELLANEOUS SOURCES

LIST

Notes

holographic: using holograms (three-dimensional pictures)

immunotherapy: use of vaccines to help the body's immune system fight disease

imminent: happening soon

in vitro fertilization: fertilization of ova and sperm in an artificial environment, such as a test tube

nanotechnology: the technology of working with extremely small components, such as individual molecules and atoms

This list appeared in *Time* (Winter 1997–1998).

These robots (from Sega Corp.) have "emotion circuits" that allow them to show anger, love, and sadness.

Here's what scientific progress has in store for us.

2000 New advances in genetics enable doctors to combine gene therapy with immunotherapy to create more effective cancer treatments.

2001 Wall-mounted, 1-m-long flat screens show television programs or videos, and when not in use display works of art.

2003 Mobile phones with video cameras and screens enable people to watch films or play computer games from their home or office.

2005 Video vacation postcards, postcard-sized film screens that display 10 seconds of holiday sights and sounds, are introduced onto the market.

2005 The active contact lens, linked to the Internet, allows the wearer to read e-mail and surf the World Wide Web without even opening his or her eyes.

2006 Smart construction materials, with electronic sensors built into their molecular structures, detect excessive stress and warn of potential collapse. Clothes made from smart fabrics automatically warm up the wearer in cold weather and cool him or her down in hot weather.

2007 New cars are equipped with anti-collision radar, thermal imaging systems to improve visibility, on-board computers that detect and warn drivers about imminent faults, and satellite-based automatic global positioning systems.

2010 Robotic pets, programmed to recognize their owner's voice and face, operate and control all the computerized functions of the household.

2015 The genetic roots of all diseases are identified.

2016 The holographic telephone projects a life-size holographic image of the person being called.

2017 Human beings land on Mars. A permanent colony is established on the planet around 2044.

2020 Flying-wing aircraft are able to carry 1000 passengers up to a distance of 9000 km at average speeds of 900 km/h.

2022 Fetuses conceived in vitro mature to term in extra-uterine incubators and are born without ever having been inside a human womb.

2025 Computers connected directly to the brain are able to recognize and respond to thoughts, obviating the need for the manual input of data and commands.

2030 Following on the development of artificial lungs, kidneys, and livers, doctors can now create artificial legs and fully functional artificial eyes.

2030 Human hibernation is used for the first time in long-distance space travel.

2040 Nuclear fusion is harnessed to generate electricity.

2044 Microscopic robots capable of reproducing themselves are devised using nanotechnology.

2500 From an average of 78 years, human life spans are extended to 140 years.

You take it from here ...

Responding

1. Discuss in a Small Group   With two or three other students, compare and discuss the lists you made before reading. Then, review your understanding of the predictions by talking about them, what they mean, and what they might lead to.

2. Respond Personally   Write a journal response stating which predictions seem the most possible to you and which seem the most far-fetched. Give reasons to support your opinions.

3. Read Between the Lines   Why do you think the dates of the last two entries on the chart jump from 2044 to 2500? Compare ideas with a partner.

Extending

4. Make a Personalized Chart   Create a chart based on at least four
   entries from "Shape of Things to Come." For each entry, indicate what
   age you will be, predict what you may be doing in your personal life at
   that point, and then indicate how you think that specific scientific
   development might influence your life.

Year	My age	What I predict I'll be doing then	Predicted scientific development	Influence of the scientific development on my life

5. Make Predictions   Choose an area that interests you (e.g., entertainment,
   fashion, travel, the environment) and do some research to identify
   current trends and future possibilities in that field. Use your findings to
   write an article that makes some predictions about what will happen in
   this area in the future. Include a list of sources you consulted.

6. Assess Success of Early Predictions   This set of predictions was
   originally published in the 1990s. Choose a prediction for a year that
   has passed and do some research to assess how accurate the prediction
   was. Report on your findings in a small group.

The Fun They Had

He smiled at her and gave her an apple, then took the teacher apart.

Short Story by Isaac Asimov

Notes

Isaac Asimov (1920–1992), a Russian-born American writer, is considered one of the great science-fiction authors. He wrote more than 500 books covering virtually all areas of knowledge.

Margie even wrote it that night in her diary. On the page headed May 17, 2155, she wrote, "Today Tommy found a real book!"

It was a very old book. Margie's grandfather once said that when he was a little boy *his* grandfather told him there was a time all stories were printed on paper.

They turned the pages, which were yellow and crinkly, and it was awfully funny to read words that stood still instead of moving the way they were supposed to—on a screen, you know. And then, when they turned back to the page before, it had the same words on it that it had had when they read it the first time.

"Gee," said Tommy, "what a waste. When you're through with the book, you just throw it away, I guess. Our television screen must have had a million books on it and it's good for plenty more. I wouldn't throw it away."

"Same with mine," said Margie. She was 11 and hadn't seen as many telebooks as Tommy had. He was 13.

She said, "Where did you find it?"

"In my house." He pointed without looking, because he was busy reading. "In the attic."

"What's it about?"

"School."

Margie was scornful. "School? What's there to write about school? I hate school." Margie always hated school, but now she hated it more than ever. The mechanical teacher had been giving her test after test in geography and she had been doing worse and worse until her mother had shaken her head sorrowfully and sent for the County Inspector.

He was a round little man with a red face and a whole box of tools with dials and wires. He smiled at her and gave her an apple, then took the teacher apart. Margie had hoped he wouldn't know how to put it together again, but he knew how all right and after an hour or so, there it was again, large and black and ugly with a big screen on which all the lessons were shown and the questions were asked. That wasn't so bad. The part she hated most was the slot where she had to put homework and test papers. She always had to write them out in a punch code they made her learn when she was six years old, and the mechanical teacher calculated the mark in no time.

The Inspector had smiled after he was finished and patted her head. He said to her mother, "It's not the little girl's fault, Mrs. Jones. I think the geography sector was geared a little too quick. Those things happen sometimes. I've slowed it up to an average 10-year level. Actually, the overall pattern of her progress is quite satisfactory." And he patted Margie's head again.

Margie was disappointed. She had been hoping they would take the teacher away altogether. They had once taken Tommy's teacher away for nearly a month because the history sector had blanked out completely.

So she said to Tommy, "Why would anyone write about school?"

Tommy looked at her with very superior eyes. "Because it's not our kind of school, stupid. This is the old kind of school that they had hundreds and hundreds of years ago." He added loftily, pronouncing the word carefully, "*Centuries* ago."

Margie was hurt. "Well, I don't know what kind of school they had all that time ago." She read the book over his shoulder for a while, then said, "Anyway, they had a teacher."

"Sure they had a teacher, but it wasn't a *regular* teacher. It was a man."

"A man? How could a man be a teacher?"

"Well, he just told the boys and girls things and gave them homework and asked them questions."

"A man isn't smart enough."

"Sure he is. My father knows as much as my teacher."

"He can't. A man can't know as much as a teacher."

"He knows almost as much, I betcha."

Margie wasn't prepared to dispute that. She said, "I wouldn't want a strange man in my house to teach me."

Tommy screamed with laughter. "You don't know much, Margie. The teachers didn't live in the house. They had a special building and all the kids went there."

"And all the kids learned the same thing?"

"Sure, if they were the same age."

"But my mother says a teacher has to be adjusted to fit the mind of each boy and girl it teaches and that each kid has to be taught differently."

"Just the same they didn't do it that way then. If you don't like it, you don't have to read the book."

"I didn't say I didn't like it," Margie said quickly. She wanted to read about those funny schools.

They weren't even half finished when Margie's mother called, "Margie! School!"

Margie looked up. "Not yet, Mamma."

"Now," said Mrs. Jones. "And it's probably time for Tommy, too."

Margie said to Tommy, "Can I read the book some more with you after school?"

"Maybe," he said nonchalantly. He walked away whistling, the dusty old book tucked beneath his arm.

Margie went into the schoolroom. It was right next to her bedroom, and the mechanical teacher was on and waiting for her. It was always on at the same time every day except Saturday and Sunday, because her mother said little girls learned better if they learned at regular hours.

The screen was lit up, and it said: "Today's arithmetic lesson is on the addition of proper fractions. Please insert yesterday's homework in the proper slot."

Margie did so with a sigh. She was thinking about the old schools they had when her grandfather's grandfather was a little boy. All the kids from the whole neighbourhood came, laughing and shouting in the schoolyard, sitting together in the schoolroom, going home together at the end of the day. They learned the same things so they could help one another on the homework and talk about it.

And the teachers were people....

The mechanical teacher was flashing on the screen: "When we add the fractions $\frac{1}{2}$ and $\frac{1}{4}$—"

Margie was thinking about how the kids must have loved it in the old days. She was thinking about the fun they had.

You take it from here ...

Responding

1. Respond Personally   Write one or two paragraphs comparing your early school experiences with Margie's. How would you feel about attending a school without classmates and with mechanical teachers? What would be some of the advantages of this type of education? What would be some of the disadvantages?

2. Examine Characters   Do you think that Margie and Tommy are believable 11- and 13-year-olds? Discuss your opinion with a partner and provide examples from the text to support it.

3. Evaluate Your Own Experience   What do you think of when you hear the expression "traditional schools"? Could any aspect of your own education be considered untraditional? Share your views in a small-group discussion.

Extending

4. Use an Interview as a Research Tool   Prepare a list of specific questions to ask, and then interview someone who went to school a number of years ago. Your aim is to discover how this person's educational experiences compare with your own. If the person you are interviewing agrees, tape-record the interview and present a portion of it to the class.

5. Write a Children's Story   Adapt and rewrite this story for an audience of six- to eight-year-olds. You could illustrate it yourself, or perhaps work with a younger child who could provide illustrations for your manuscript. Share your adaptations in small groups.

> **PEER ASSESSMENT**
> * Was the language level appropriate for the intended audience?
> * Did the illustrations work well with the story?
> * Was the adaptation carefully proofread, with no spelling or grammatical errors?

Before you read, choose a time and place where you can read this entire story uninterrupted.

As you read, try not to break your concentration.

Supertoys Last All Summer Long

"I'm no good, Teddy. Let's run away!"

Short Story by Brian Aldiss

Notes

Brian Aldiss (1925–) was born in Norfolk, England. A prolific author, he is best known for his many works of science fiction. This story inspired the 2001 Steven Spielberg movie *A.I.*

perpetual: continuing without interruption

impeccable: flawless, perfect

lambent: softly bright (like the moon)

unostentatious: not pretentious, modest

ardently: passionately

de-opaqued: made transparent

In Mrs. Swinton's garden, it was always summer. The lovely almond trees stood about it in perpetual leaf. Monica Swinton plucked a saffron-coloured rose and showed it to David.

"Isn't it lovely?" she said.

David looked up at her and grinned without replying. Seizing the flower, he ran with it across the lawn and disappeared behind the kennel where the mowervator crouched, ready to cut or sweep or roll when the moment dictated. She stood alone on her impeccable plastic gravel path.

She had tried to love him.

When she made up her mind to follow the boy, she found him in the courtyard floating the rose in his paddling pool. He stood in the pool engrossed, still wearing his sandals.

"David, darling, do you have to be so awful? Come in at once and change your shoes and socks."

He went with her without protest, his dark head bobbing at the level of her waist. At the age of five, he showed no fear of the ultrasonic dryer in the kitchen. But before his mother could reach for a pair of slippers, he wriggled away and was gone into the silence of the house.

He would probably be looking for Teddy.

Monica Swinton, 29, of graceful shape and lambent eye, went and sat in her living room, arranging her limbs with taste. She began by sitting and thinking; soon she was just sitting. Time waited on her shoulder with the manic sloth it reserves for children, the insane, and wives whose husbands are away improving the world. Almost by reflex, she reached out and changed the wavelength of her windows. The garden faded; in its place, the city centre rose by her left hand, full of crowding people, blow-boats, and buildings—but she kept the sound

down. She remained alone. An overcrowded world is the ideal place in which to be lonely.

❧

The directors of Synthank were eating an enormous luncheon to celebrate the launching of their new product. Some of them wore plastic facemasks popular at the time. All were elegantly slender, despite the rich food and drink they were putting away. Their wives were elegantly slender, despite the food and drink they too were putting away. An earlier and less sophisticated generation would have regarded them as beautiful people, apart from their eyes. Their eyes were hard and calculating.

Henry Swinton, Managing Director of Synthank, was about to make a speech.

"I'm sorry your wife couldn't be with us to hear you," his neighbour said.

"Monica prefers to stay at home thinking beautiful thoughts," said Swinton, maintaining a smile.

"One would expect such a beautiful woman to have beautiful thoughts," said the neighbour.

Take your mind off my wife, you bastard, thought Swinton, still smiling.

He rose to make his speech amid applause.

After a couple of jokes, he said, "Today marks a real breakthrough for the company. It is now almost 10 years since we put our first synthetic life forms on the world market. You all know what a success they have been, particularly the miniature dinosaurs. But none of them had intelligence.

"It seems like a paradox that in this day and age we can create life but not intelligence. Our finest selling line, the Crosswell Tape, sells best of all, and is the most stupid of all."

Everyone laughed.

"Though three-quarters of our overcrowded world is starving, we are lucky here to have more than enough, thanks to population control. Obesity's our problem, not malnutrition. I guess there's nobody round this table who doesn't have a Crosswell working for him in the small intestine, a perfectly safe parasite tapeworm that enables its host to eat up to 50 percent more food and still keep his or her figure. Right?"

General nods of agreement.

"Our miniature dinosaurs are almost equally stupid. Today, we launch an intelligent synthetic life form—a full-size serving-man.

"Not only does he have intelligence, he has a controlled amount of intelligence. We believe people would be afraid of a being with a human brain. Our serving-man has a small computer in his cranium.

"There have been mechanicals on the market with mini-computers for brains—plastic things without life, supertoys—but we have at last found a way to link computer circuitry with synthetic flesh."

David sat by the long window of his nursery, wrestling with paper and pencil. Finally, he stopped writing and began to roll the pencil up and down the slope of the desk lid.

"Teddy!" he said.

Teddy lay on the bed against the wall, under a book with moving pictures and a giant plastic soldier. The speech pattern of his master's voice activated him and he sat up.

"Teddy, I can't think what to say!"

Climbing off the bed, the bear walked stiffly over to cling to the boy's leg. David lifted him and set him on the desk.

"What have you said so far?"

"I've said—" He picked up his letter and stared hard at it. "I've said, 'Dear Mummy, I hope you're well just now. I love you.'"

There was a long silence, until the bear said, "That sounds fine. Go downstairs and give it to her."

Another long silence.

"It isn't quite right. She won't understand."

Inside the bear, a small computer worked through its program of possibilities. "Why not do it again in crayon?"

David was staring out of the window. "Teddy, you know what I was thinking? How do you tell what are real things from what aren't real things?"

The bear shuffled its alternatives. "Real things are good."

"I wonder if time is good. I don't think Mummy likes time very much. The other day, lots of days ago, she said that time went by her. Is time real, Teddy?"

"Clocks tell the time. Clocks are real. Mummy has clocks so she must like them. She has a clock on her wrist next to her dial."

David had started to draw an airliner on the back of his letter. "You and I are real, Teddy, aren't we?"

The bear's eyes regarded the boy unflinchingly. "You and I are real, David." It specialized in comfort.

Monica walked slowly about the house. It was almost time for the afternoon post to come over the wire. She punched the O.L. number on the dial on her wrist, but nothing came through. A few minutes more.

She could take up her painting. Or she could dial her friends. Or she could wait till Henry came home. Or she could go up and play with David....

She walked out into the hall and to the bottom of the stairs.

"David!"

No answer. She called again and a third time.

"Teddy!" she called, in sharper tones.

"Yes, Mummy!" After a moment's pause, Teddy's head of golden fur appeared at the top of the stairs.

"Is David in his room, Teddy?"

"David went into the garden, Mummy."

"Come down here, Teddy!"

She stood impassively, watching the little furry figure as it climbed down from step to step on its stubby limbs. When it reached the bottom, she picked it up and carried it into the living room. It lay unmoving in her arms, staring up at her. She could feel just the slightest vibration from its motor.

"Stand there, Teddy. I want to talk to you." She set him down on a tabletop, and he stood as she requested, arms set forward and open in the eternal gesture of embrace.

"Teddy, did David tell you to tell me he had gone into the garden?"

The circuits of the bear's brain were too simple for artifice.

"Yes, Mummy."

"So you lied to me."

"Yes, Mummy."

"Stop calling me Mummy! Why is David avoiding me? He's not afraid of me, is he?"

"No. He loves you."

"Why can't we communicate?"

"Because David's upstairs."

The answer stopped her dead. Why waste time talking to this machine? Why not simply go upstairs and scoop David into her arms and talk to him, as a loving mother should to a loving son? She heard the sheer weight of silence in the house, with a different quality of silence issuing from every room. On the upper landing, something was moving very silently—David, trying to hide away from her....

He was nearing the end of his speech now. The guests were attentive; so was the Press, lining two walls of the banqueting chamber, recording Henry's words and occasionally photographing him.

"Our serving-man will be, in many senses, a product of the computer. Without knowledge of the genome, we could never have worked through the sophisticated biochemics that go into synthetic flesh. The serving-man will also be an extension of the computer—for he will contain a computer in his own head, a microminiaturized computer capable of dealing with almost any situation he may encounter in the home. With reservations, of course."

Laughter at this; many of those present knew the heated debate that had engulfed the Synthank boardroom before the decision had finally been taken to leave the serving-man neuter under his flawless uniform.

"Amid all the triumphs of our civilization—yes, and amid the crushing problems of overpopulation too—it is sad to reflect how many millions of people suffer from increasing loneliness and isolation. Our serving-man will be a boon to them; he will always answer, and the most vapid conversation cannot bore him.

"For the future, we plan more models, male and female—some of them without the limitations of this first one, I promise you!—of more advanced design, true bioelectronic beings.

"Not only will they possess their own computers, capable of individual programming: they will be linked to the Ambient, the World Data Network. Thus everyone will be able to enjoy the equivalent of an Einstein in their own homes. Personal isolation will then be banished forever!"

He sat down to enthusiastic applause. Even the synthetic serving-man, sitting at the table dressed in an unostentatious suit, applauded with gusto.

Dragging his satchel, David crept round the side of the house. He climbed onto the ornamental seat under the living-room window and peeped cautiously in.

His mother stood in the middle of the room. Her face was blank; its lack of expression scared him. He watched, fascinated. He did not move; she did not move. Time might have stopped, as it had stopped in the garden. Teddy looked round, saw him, tumbled off the table, and came over to the window. Fumbling with his paws, he eventually got it open.

They looked at each other.

"I'm no good, Teddy. Let's run away!"

"You're a very good boy. Your mummy loves you."

Slowly, he shook his head. "If she loves me, then why can't I talk to her?"

"You're being silly, David. Mummy's lonely. That's why she had you."

"She's got Daddy. I've got nobody 'cept you, and I'm lonely."

Teddy gave him a friendly cuff over the head. "If you feel so bad, you'd better go to the psychiatrist again."

"I hate that old psychiatrist—he makes me feel I'm not real." He started to run across the lawn. The bear toppled out of the window and followed as fast as its stubby legs would allow.

Monica Swinton was up in the nursery. She called to her son once and then stood there, undecided. All was silent.

Crayons lay on his desk. Obeying a sudden impulse, she went over to the desk and opened it. Dozens of pieces of paper lay inside. Many of them were written in crayon in David's clumsy writing, with each letter picked out in a colour different from the letter preceding it. None of the messages was finished.

MY DEAR MUMMY, HOW ARE YOU REALLY, DO YOU LOVE ME AS MUCH

DEAR MUMMY, I LOVE YOU AND DADDY AND THE SUN IS SHINING

DEAR DEAR MUMMY, TEDDY'S HELPING ME TO WRITE TO YOU. I LOVE YOU AND TEDDY

DARLING MUMMY, I'M YOUR ONE AND ONLY SON AND I LOVE YOU SO MUCH THAT SOME TIMES

DEAR MUMMY, YOU'RE REALLY MY MUMMY AND I HATE TEDDY

DARLING MUMMY, GUESS HOW MUCH I LOVE

DEAR MUMMY, I'M YOUR LITTLE BOY NOT TEDDY AND I LOVE YOU BUT TEDDY

DEAR MUMMY, THIS IS A LETTER TO YOU JUST TO SAY HOW MUCH HOW EVER SO MUCH

Monica dropped the pieces of paper and burst out crying. In their gay inaccurate colours the letters fanned out and settled on the floor.

Henry Swinton caught the express in high spirits, and occasionally said a word to the synthetic serving-man he was taking home with him. The serving-man answered politely and punctually, although his answers were not always entirely relevant by human standards.

The Swintons lived in one of the ritziest city blocks. Embedded in other apartments, their apartment had no windows onto the outside; nobody wanted to see the overcrowded external world. Henry unlocked the door with his retina-pattern-scanner and walked in, followed by the serving-man.

At once, Henry was surrounded by the friendly illusion of gardens set in eternal summer. It was amazing what Whologram could do to create huge mirages in small spaces. Behind its roses and wisteria stood their house: the deception was complete: a Georgian mansion appeared to welcome him.

"How do you like it?" he asked the serving-man.

"Roses occasionally suffer from black spot."

"These roses are guaranteed free from any imperfections."

"It is always advisable to purchase goods with guarantees, even if they cost slightly more."

"Thanks for the information," Henry said dryly. Synthetic life forms were less than 10 years old, the old android mechanicals less than 16; the faults of their systems were still being ironed out, year by year.

He opened the door and called to Monica.

She came out of the sitting room immediately and flung her arms round him, kissing him ardently on cheek and lips. Henry was amazed.

Pulling back to look at her face, he saw how she seemed to generate light and beauty. It was months since he had seen her so excited. Instinctively, he clasped her tighter.

"Darling, what's happened?"

"Henry, Henry—oh, my darling, I was in despair.... But I've dialled the afternoon post and—you'll never believe it! Oh, it's wonderful!"

"For heaven's sake, woman, what's wonderful?"

He caught a glimpse of the heading on the stat in her hand, still warm from the wall-receiver: Ministry of Population. He felt the colour drain from his face in sudden shock and hope.

"Monica ... oh.... Don't tell me our number's come up!"

"Yes, my darling, yes, we've won this week's parenthood lottery! We can go ahead and conceive a child at once!"

He let out a yell of joy. They danced round the room. Pressure of population was such that reproduction had to be strictly controlled. Childbirth required government permission. For this moment they had waited four years. Incoherently they cried their delight.

They paused at last, gasping, and stood in the middle of the room to laugh at each other's happiness. When she had come down from the nursery, Monica had de-opaqued the windows, so that they now revealed the vista of garden beyond. Artificial sunlight was growing long and golden across the lawn—and David and Teddy were staring through the window at them.

Seeing their faces, Henry and his wife grew serious.

"What do we do about *them*?" Henry asked.

"Teddy's no trouble. He works well enough."

"Is David malfunctioning?"

"His verbal communication centre is still giving him trouble. I think he'll have to go back to the factory again."

"Okay. We'll see how he does before the baby's born. Which reminds me—I have a surprise for you: help just when help is needed! Come into the hall and see what I've got."

As the two adults disappeared from the room, boy and bear sat down beneath the standard roses.

"Teddy—I suppose Mummy and Daddy are real, aren't they?"

Teddy said, "You ask such silly questions, David. Nobody knows what 'real' really means. Let's go indoors."

"First I'm going to have another rose!" Plucking a bright pink flower, he carried it with him into the house. It could lie on the pillow as he went to sleep. Its beauty and softness reminded him of Mummy.

You take it from here ...

Responding

1. Reflect on the Reading Process   In your journal, make notes on your reading of the story. Did you want to put it aside? Did you feel compelled to continue to the end? As you read, at what points did you check back to clarify the twists and turns of plot and character development? Is there anything about the story that you still find mystifying? When you have finished writing, compare notes with a partner.

2. Examine Character   Where did you first begin to question the truth about David? In a one-page response, explain the complexities of his character: who he is, what he needs or wants, his relationships with others, his status at the end of the story, and how you feel about him.

3. Deliberate on the Surprise Ending   Working in a small group, discuss the twist ending of the story. Review the story and identify clues (*foreshadowing*) that were there all the time, clearly pointing to the ending. Share your findings with another group.

4. Explain the Title   With a partner, discuss the meaning of the title. What does it say about the society of this story? How does it connect to the story's theme?

Extending

5. Form an Opinion   Write an essay examining the world of the future shown in this story. Is it ideal (utopian) or far less than ideal (dystopian)? Include a detailed discussion of the story to support both views, but in the end, decide whether this future world is a place in which you would want to live.

6. View the Movie   View the movie *A.I.*, which is based on this story. Write a report comparing the story and the movie, focusing on the character of David.

Before you read, discuss and list three or four things good cartoons have in common.

As you read, be aware of how you view the cartoon—what do you notice first, next, and so on?

Which One Is Yours?

Cartoon by Ben Wicks

Notes

Ben Wicks (1926–2000) was a London-born Canadian cartoonist whose work was published in over 200 newspapers. Poverty forced him to leave school at the age of 14, and he eventually arrived in Canada after the Second World War with only $25 to his name. His own lack of formal education led Wicks to become an advocate for literacy and other charitable causes.

"Which one is yours?"

You take it from here ...

Responding

1. Discuss Meaning   In a class discussion, identify what new technology this cartoon is satirizing.

2. Analyze the Cartoon   Reading a cartoon involves looking at the drawing and the caption, examining all the different parts, and then putting it back together. Work with a partner to comment on the following:
   a) What do you see first when you look at the cartoon?
   b) How does the cartoonist use a mixture of design and empty space to achieve his purpose?
   c) What is the effect of having the nurse off to one side? Why is she wearing a mask? (Think of symbolic as well as practical reasons.)
   d) Does this cartoon meet the criteria you identified for an effective cartoon? Did the cartoonist achieve his purpose by making you both laugh and think? How?

3. Respond to Issues   Write a paragraph identifying some of the concerns that the "children" in the cartoon may have as they grow up.

Extending

4. Write Dialogue   Work with a partner to write what you imagine will be the dialogue when one of the "children" in the cartoon is old enough to ask Mom or Dad, "Where did I come from?" Be prepared to read your dialogue aloud, in character, to the class.

5. Draw a Cartoon   Create a cartoon exploring your own idea of a futuristic answer to the age-old question, "Where do babies come from?" Remember that good cartoons use humour to make a strong comment or criticism.

Before you read, think about what you have heard about cloning. Do you already have an opinion about this controversial subject?

As you read, flag at least two ideas that you want to clarify or discuss further.

"What about cloning a Hitler or Michael Jordan?"

A Clone of Our Own

by Gunjan Sinha
(with Hank Greely)

INTERVIEW

Notes

genomics: the study of how to manipulate genetic material

Dolly: a sheep, the first successful clone from an adult mammal. Her birth in Scotland in 1997 caused concern that attempts would soon be made to clone humans as well.

Will humans be the next clones? The technology, called nuclear transfer, still has a long way to go before it's considered safe to try on humans. But even if it were safe, would it be right? Gunjan Sinha, Associate Editor of *Popular Science*, spoke with Hank Greely, who sits on an advisory committee on human cloning for the state of California. Greely is a professor of law and co-director of a program in Genomics, Ethics, and Society at Stanford University in California.

GS: When will we clone a human?

Greely: That's not a simple question. I think we have to ask ourselves, is there something about the technology that is so wrong or so evil that it shouldn't be used at all? Or should it be weighed based on its intended uses?

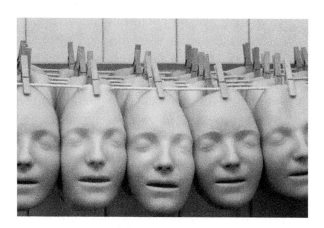

GS: What are justifiable uses?

Greely: We really need to distinguish between reproductive cloning and nonreproductive human cloning. If we use nuclear transfer to grow a new liver, I don't think many people will have problems with that—as long as it's growing a liver and not taking the liver from a cloned person. Human reproductive cloning is much trickier.

GS: Why?

Greely: Safety. There's still a very low success rate. With Dolly, more than 200 sheep eggs underwent nuclear transfer and 29 were implanted in the uteri of sheep to get one Dolly. We don't worry too much about sheep miscarriages or about deformed lambs being born. But we would with humans. And we wouldn't know if a human clone would be healthy.

GS: Dolly appears to be healthy. Why wouldn't a human clone be so?

Greely: There may be mutations that are initially invisible and only show themselves as the clone ages. There's also the telomere problem. We know that Dolly's telomeres [the ends of chromosomes in cells, which shorten until the cells can no longer reproduce] are shorter than those of other sheep her age, and we don't know what that means yet.

GS: Suppose human cloning was safe. In what situations do you see cloning being used?

Greely: As a fertility aid. We let people do all sorts of things to have a child that's genetically related, in-vitro fertilization for one.

GS: Are there other situations where it might be ethically justified to create a human clone?

63 percent believe scientists will clone a human within 25 years

71 percent think cloning a human is unethical, but 40 percent say it's okay to help infertile couples

Greely: A situation where parents want to create a new child to be a bone marrow donor for an older sick child. That's a real tough one. But this issue might never arise if we succeed in growing bone marrow outside the body. Another situation is cloning a child who has accidentally died. I think that's creepy. But I've never been in that position [of having a child die] and so I don't feel comfortable saying whether that's a good application or a bad application of the technology.

GS: What about cloning a Hitler or Michael Jordan?

Greely: I think we can dismiss those as bad or even silly applications.

GS: Is there anything else you'd like to say about the future of human cloning?

Greely: Even if cloning humans were safe and we as a society had decided it was ethically justifiable for reproductive purposes, I don't think we'd see a lot of clones. The old-fashioned way of making babies has a lot going for it: It's easy, traditional, well understood, and occasionally even pleasant. People are not going to give up sex anytime soon.

You take it from here ...

Responding

1. Understand Content   With two or three other students, review your understanding of this interview by answering the following questions in your own words:

   • According to Greely, why is it difficult to give a simple answer to the question "When will we clone a human?"

A Clone of Our Own

- What is the difference between reproductive cloning and nonreproductive cloning?
- What are Greely's doubts about human cloning?
- Why is human reproductive cloning trickier than reproductive cloning of other animals?
- According to Greely, what applications of human cloning would be good? questionable? silly?
- What tone does Greely take in his last answer?

2. Evaluate the Question-and-Answer Format   As a class, discuss how the question-and-answer format affects the readability of this interview. In your opinion, does it make the information easier or more difficult to understand? In what ways might this format impose limitations on an article? Does the interviewer's final question effectively address these potential limitations?

3. Extend the Inquiry   Write down two additional questions you would ask if you were interviewing Hank Greely. Exchange your questions with a partner and respond to your partner's questions as you think Greely might. (If answering the question would require further research, respond by suggesting sources where the questioner might find the information.) When you have finished, compare and discuss your questions and responses with another student pair.

Extending

4. Research a Topic on the Internet   Use Internet and library resources to find out more about human cloning. Make a list of the most useful resources to share with the class, and prepare a brief presentation on one of them (e.g., a book, article, documentary, or Web site).

5. Write an Editorial   Using the information in this interview and in other sources, write an editorial stating your opinion as to whether research on cloning should be funded in the future. Remember to give reasons for your arguments and to support them with examples where you can.

Before you read, consider how medical research has changed our lives over the years. What advances have been made in the past 100 years? What cures and treatments are still being sought?

As you read, keep in mind the main question: "What is all the excitement about?"

Most of the studies have only been done on lab animals.

Stem Cells Q and A

by Amina Ali and Owen Wood

WEB SITE ARTICLE

Notes

This article appeared on the CBC Web site at www.cbc.ca. You can search the site to find this article and many useful related links.

Scientists have been all abuzz in the last couple of years over something called stem cells—cellular magicians that promise to dazzle and amaze.

In December 1999, the editors of *Science*, the journal devoted to scientific and medical matters, went as far as calling stem-cell research the "Breakthrough of the Year."

Here's a quick overview of what all the excitement is about.

What are stem cells?

Stem cells can be thought of as blank slates or cells that have yet to become specialized. They have the ability to become any type of cell to form skin, bones, organs, or other body parts.

Are there different kinds of stem cells?

Yes. Stem cells come in three forms: embryonic stem cells, embryonic germ cells, and adult stem cells. Embryonic stem cells come from embryos,

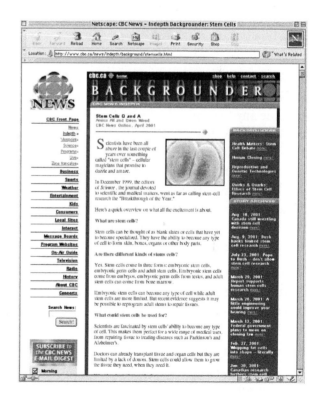

embryonic germ cells from testes, and adult stem cells can come from bone marrow.

Embryonic stem cells can become any type of cell while adult stem cells are more limited. But recent evidence suggests it may be possible to reprogram adult stems to repair tissues.

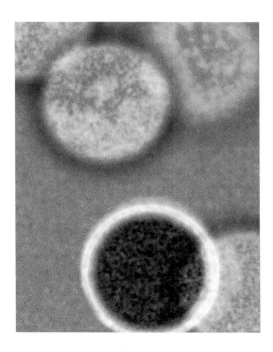

What could stem cells be used for?

Scientists are fascinated by stem cells' ability to become any type of cell. This makes them perfect for a wide range of medical uses, from repairing tissue to treating diseases such as Parkinson's and Alzheimer's.

Doctors can already transplant tissue and organ cells, but they are limited by a lack of donors. Stem cells could allow them to grow the tissue they need, when they need it.

What has been done so far?

Stem-cell research has shown benefits in many areas of health, but most of the studies have only been done on lab animals. Some examples:

- Improved stroke recovery was shown in rats.
- Embryonic stem cells were used to treat a Parkinson's-like condition in mice and rats.
- Scientists caused new brain cells to grow from adult stem cells in birds.
- Canadian and Italian scientists transplanted adult stem cells from the brains of mice into the bone marrow of other rodents. The stem cells changed behaviour and began making blood cells.
- Movement was restored in paralyzed mice and rats by injecting stem cells into the spinal fluid.

In one of the few stem-cell studies involving humans, some people who failed to benefit from cataract surgery improved when they received corneal stem-cell transplants.

What do stem cells have to do with cloning?

When people think of cloning they usually think of copying people from head to toe. But human cloning also includes making copies of just cells.

Researchers don't necessarily need to clone stem cells, but cloning would make their work a whole lot easier. Instead of having to collect the millions of stem cells needed to grow a patch of skin for a patient who suffered a severe burn, for example, doctors could collect only a few stem cells and make millions of copies.

What are the ethical issues involved?

Currently, the best source for stem cells is a human embryo. But using human material, such as aborted fetuses, in research is a contentious issue because it can be construed as the sacrifice of human life for scientific progress.

So far, there are no federal laws in Canada to ban the use of human embryonic tissue in research. Although members of the medical community are still debating what should and shouldn't be allowed, the overall consensus seems to be that stem-cell research should go ahead, but with strict limitations.

In March 2001, the Canadian Institute of Health Research suggested guidelines for the use of stem cells. The guidelines limit scientists to using leftover embryos created to help couples conceive, and only if the couples agree. The embryos also wouldn't be allowed to exceed 14 days.

This Web site includes links to related information, including

Backgrounders

Health Matters: Stem-Cell Debate
Human Cloning
Reproductive and Genetic Technologies
Quirks & Quarks: Ethics of Stem-Cell Research

Story Archives

Aug. 9, 2001: Bush approves limited stem-cell research

July 23, 2001: Pope to Bush—don't allow stem-cell research

Mar. 29, 2001: Report supports human stem-cell research

Mar. 26, 2001: A little engineering could improve your hearing

Mar. 12, 2001: Federal government plans to move on cloning law

Feb. 27, 2001: Whipping fat cells into shape—literally

Jan. 30, 2001: Canadian research furthers stem-cell growth

Jan. 26, 2001: Province pours research funding into Ottawa

Dec. 28, 2000: Blood discovery furthers stem-cell research

Nov. 6, 2000: Dead brains become source for new cells

Aug. 23, 2000: U.S. gives go-ahead to human embryonic cell research

Aug. 16, 2000: UK scientists say human cloning should be allowed

Aug. 15, 2000: Cloning first—scientists transplant embryonic stem cells in mice

Mar. 17, 2000: Retina cells discovery may cure damaged eyes

Dec. 16, 1999: Stem-cell research year's biggest story: Science

Feb. 17, 1999: McGill researchers unlock secret of cell programming

Jan. 21, 1999: Scientists turn brain cells to blood cells

Dec. 8, 1998: Canadian parents bank on cord blood

You take it from here ...

Responding

1. Identify Key Ideas   Work with a partner to list the main ideas presented in this article. Then, individually, use the list to write a one- or two-paragraph response to the question "Why are scientists all abuzz over stem cells?" Include your thoughts on how stem-cell research might be used in the treatment of people with debilitating conditions.

2. Formulate Questions   Using this article's overview as a starting point, write three further questions concerning stem-cell research that you would like to ask an expert. Then list three specific sources (e.g., Web sites, library resources, individuals) where you could begin to search for answers to your questions.

TIP

To help you focus on possible uses of stem-cell research, consider the work of such high-profile advocates as
- Christopher Reeve (spinal injury)
- Michael J. Fox (Parkinson's disease)
- Mary Tyler Moore (diabetes)

3. Relate Form and Style   This article was designed to make a complex subject accessible to a wide audience. Work with one or two other students to analyze how effectively this has been accomplished. You might begin by looking at such features as

- the type of language used (e.g., word choice, general tone)
- the length of sentences and paragraphs
- the overall structure (e.g., the question-and-answer format, the links to more detailed information)

Identify as many other features as you can, and share them in a class discussion. In terms of understandability, how does this article compare with other informational articles or Web sites you have seen?

Extending

4. Work in a Study Group   Form a study group with two or three other students. Using the Internet, magazines, and news sources, find several articles reporting on the latest developments in stem-cell research, including ethical and legal issues. Have each group member present a different article and lead a group discussion on the topic it covers.

5. Create a Multimedia Presentation   Still working in your study group, use this selection, the articles you studied in Activity 4, and other Internet and library resources to develop a list of topics related to stem-cell research. Together, choose one topic to research in depth, and put together a multimedia presentation.

GROUP ASSESSMENT
- Did all group members have an equal chance to contribute and suggest what direction the research should take?
- Did all members of the group share the work equally?

"I can plug into any kind of sensor to monitor anything."

Smart Shirt

by Priya Giri

MAGAZINE ARTICLE

Notes

Harry Winston: a famous Beverly Hills jeweller

That basic T-shirt isn't only the most comfortable thing in your closet. Soon it will be the smartest.

Using plastic optical fibres woven into a T-shirt, engineers at the Georgia Institute of Technology have come up with a "wearable motherboard," which can monitor heart rate, temperature, respiration, and other bodily functions. Some vital signs can be monitored directly by sensors woven into the shirt; for other functions, a person fastens sensors to his or her body—the kind used in electrocardiograms, for example—and attaches them to the T-shirt with snaps. The signals can be transmitted to a receiver in a watch or bounced to a satellite and then back down to anywhere on Earth.

The smart shirt was developed for the armed services as a way of tracking the health of soldiers on the battlefield. Medics miles away can find out immediately when a soldier goes down and how bad his injury is. Sensors can locate a gunshot wound and monitor vital signs while medics travel to the scene. Tiny microphones in the shirt can instantly put caregivers in contact with the injured.

Dr. Sundaresan Jayaraman, head of the research team at Georgia Tech, hopes to infiltrate civilian society with this technology within five years. A postoperative patient could continuously be monitored as he recovers at home. Attendants in nursing homes could keep a closer watch on multiple patients. And law enforcement officers could wear the T-shirts while on their beats and be monitored back at headquarters.

"I can plug into any kind of sensor to monitor anything," says Jayaraman, suggesting applications for athletes concerned about stress or for parents concerned about sudden infant death syndrome. "This could be as ubiquitous as a home-alarm system."

The cost of the shirt? Astonishingly, Jayaraman says, it won't be more than $35 (sensors not included). For those with a taste for something more expensive, there's the Harry Winston "Heartthrob" brooch. Sensors in the rubies make the gems glow with every heartbeat. Price tag: a cool $500 000.

You take it from here ...

Responding

1. **Extend Ideas**   Working with a partner, think of up to 10 additional smart products that could soon be on the market.

2. **Examine Style**   As a class, discuss the following:
   a) why you think the writer chose to write two sentences, rather than one, in the first paragraph
   b) what the word "infiltrate" in paragraph 4 suggests
   c) what the word "ubiquitous" in paragraph 5 means
   d) why you think the writer ends with the reference to the Harry Winston brooch

> **TIP**
> • Read between the lines and try to discover the author's interests, attitudes, and so on.

3. **Form an Impression of the Author**   Reread the article and write a sentence or two commenting on the type of person you think the writer is. Share your impressions with a partner.

Extending

4. **Write with a Different Slant**   The writer uses examples to persuade us that the smart shirt will improve our lives. What if, instead, the article were to begin as follows: "That basic T-shirt isn't only the most comfortable thing in your closet. Soon it will be the scariest." Write the next two or three paragraphs of an article entitled "Scary Shirt." Remember to provide specific examples, and write to persuade your reader.

> **TIP**
> • Visuals can be hand-drawn, or you can use images cut from old magazines or from clip art.

5. **Design a Print Ad**   Create a print ad to promote the smart shirt. Include visuals, a caption or slogan, and a written description (advertising copy). Share your design with the class and invite others' comments.

> **PEER ASSESSMENT**
> • What techniques did others use to make their ads eye-catching?
> • How persuasive were the slogans and advertising copy?

Before you read, react to the statement "Life is not life without risk!"

As you read, decide which position best represents your own point of view.

Risk

Most of the unfrozen people
seemed to like this new world.

Short Short Story by Joanna Russ

Notes

Joanna Russ (1937–) is an American feminist and science-fiction writer who is known for her wit. Her works include *The Hidden Side of the Moon* (1987), *How to Suppress Women's Writing* (1983), and *The Female Man* (1975).

bubonic plague: highly contagious, deadly bacterial disease accompanied by chills, fever, and swelling

cryogenics: area of physics dealing with the effects of very low temperatures; also associated with the still unproven idea that frozen humans can one day be restored to life

Medical advances had made it impossible to die of anything....

He didn't like this future world, oh no he didn't, our old friend John Hemingway London Rockne Knievel Dickey Wayne. It wasn't risky enough. He had been a racing-car driver way back then (before he was frozen) and he couldn't stand cars that protected you in head-on collisions and roads that wouldn't let you collide with anything in the first place. Nor did he like the medical advances that had made it impossible to die of anything (except extreme old age), or the sports they practised for health and fun (but never for danger). Nor was it possible to be better at something than anybody else. That is, you could be, but who cared? He wanted to go deep-sea diving, glider crashing, mountain climbing, alligator wrestling, lion shooting, novel writing, and even

worse things. So he went before a parliament of these sensitive-but-bland men and women who had resurrected him from the cryogenic chambers of an earlier day and said loudly, legs planted far apart:

"LIFE IS NOT LIFE WITHOUT RISK!"

Then he said, even louder:

"MANKIND—IDENTITY—EVEN LIFE ITSELF—DEMANDS THE CONSTANT TEST OF DANGER!"

They said, "Oh dear." Their eyes got very round. They murmured worriedly among themselves. He thought he might have to throw a temper tantrum (the kind he used to put on so well in front of the news cameras), but that proved unnecessary. They debated politely. They put their hands over their faces. They said most of the unfrozen people seemed to like this new world. They said there really was no accounting for tastes, was there, after all.

But finally they said, "Very well; you shall have your Risk."

And they inoculated him with bubonic plague.

You take it from here ...

Responding

1. Identify Clues to Character   In a class discussion, identify the larger-than-life figures after whom the main character is named. Describe how his behaviour reflects these names.

2. Express an Opposing Perspective   The main character vehemently declares his position to the men and women in the parliament: "Life is not life without risk!" and "Mankind—identity—even life itself—demands the constant test of danger!" Write two equally strong responses expressing the opposite point of view.

3. Respond Personally   Examine the details given about the future world in this story, and write a personal journal entry reflecting on how you would feel if you were placed in this future world. Work an understanding of yourself into your response, considering your likes and dislikes, strengths and weaknesses.

4. **Define Utopia and Dystopia**   Look up the words "utopia" and "dystopia" in a dictionary, and explain how they apply to the story. Could the two possibly exist in the same place at the same time? Write a *thematic statement* that expresses this idea in terms of this story.

TIP

• A *thematic statement* summarizes a story's message in a single sentence.

Extending

5. **Write a Short Short Story**   Create a character who is a composite of four to six famous personalities, and write a one-page story placing the character in a futuristic setting. Remember, the character's name provides clues to his or her conflict and behaviour.

6. **Write a Poem**   Write a poem beginning with the line, "Life is not life without risk!" If you wish, you could find or draw an appropriate illustration to accompany it. Share your work with the class or in small groups.

TIP

• You can look for ideas for creating your story's futuristic setting by scanning one or more of the nonfiction articles in this unit.

Your car reads your e-mail and you dictate replies.

When Cars Drive You

by Keith Naughton

MAGAZINE ARTICLE

It's 2050, and one quintessential North American passion has withstood the test of time: we like to drive. So you decide to hit the open road and cruise across country. First you must unplug your car from your house. That's right: cars now run on electric fuel cells, those hydrogen-powered devices found only in rockets back in the 20th century. Your fuel cell throws off so much juice that it can fill the electrical needs of both home and car. Or, as Pete Beardmore, director of Ford's research lab, describes it: "Your car becomes the brain stem for controlling your house." (You'll have a home backup system when you take a trip.)

You ease into your personalized driver's seat—which in a crash whisks you out of harm's way, eliminating the need for airbags—and you grab hold of the joystick. Steering wheels and pedals have gone the way of the buggy whip. All the movements of your car—accelerating, turning, braking—are now controlled by a joystick familiar to generations weaned on computer games. Consider it a giant mouse to point and drive your car. You weave through traffic with confidence. And why not? Your car is programmed with special radar to sense a crash before it happens and automatically hit the brakes. That frees you to respond to e-mail, but your hand never leaves the joystick. In a

The CIRCA

To see the future, auto designer Greg Howell took a peek into the past. The spare, industrial look of the CIRCA—a product of Detroit's Center for Creative Studies—is inspired by the streamlined locomotives of the 1930s. Yet this car is packed with futuristic features, such as a system that controls the car with electronic impulses instead of gears.

Design: The low-slung silhouette cuts down on drag.

Features of the future

Part home office, part home theatre, cars will comply with our voice commands to send e-mails or check stocks—while the kids play videogames in the back seat. But auto futurists say that this won't make the roads more hazardous: cars will have collision-avoiding radar for drivers who get distracted. Here's a look at some of the other new auto technologies:

Speed and style

Fuel cell: Gas engines will give way to hydrogen-powered fuel cells, but the conversion will be costly.

(1) Compressor: Sends pressurized air to the fuel cell.

(2) Fuel cell: Combines hydrogen with oxygen (from air) to make electricity.

(3) Traction inverter module: Converts electricity for the motor.

(4) Motor: Converts electrical to mechanical energy.

The cockpit: CIRCA's interior mixes high tech with fun. The centre console snaps out and serves as a cooler, and the jet throttle-like lever above the console controls the electronic gearshift. There's an on-board computer with liquid crystal display, and a specially tinted windshield keeps the interior climate controlled.

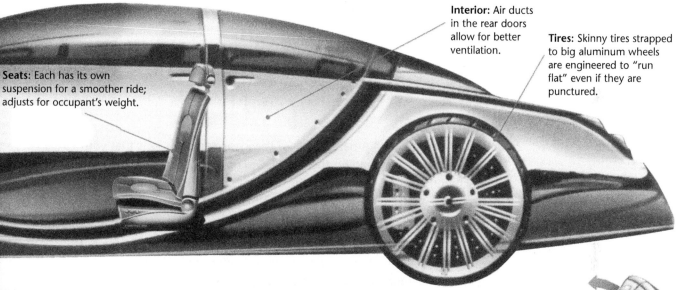

Seats: Each has its own suspension for a smoother ride; adjusts for occupant's weight.

Interior: Air ducts in the rear doors allow for better ventilation.

Tires: Skinny tires strapped to big aluminum wheels are engineered to "run flat" even if they are punctured.

Night vision: Perfect for baby boomers' failing eyesight, Cadillac already offers this feature (left) on its 2000 De Ville ($1995 extra). Using Gulf War infrared technology, drivers can see up to five times farther than with headlights alone. The infrared image is projected close to the outer edge of the hood, which keeps the driver's eyes focused on the road.

Joy ride: A joystick (detail, right) might replace steering wheels, as well as brake and gas pedals. In tests, drivers brake more quickly with joysticks.

Turn signal, lights, horn

Acceleration, brake sensor

Steering sensor

Motor

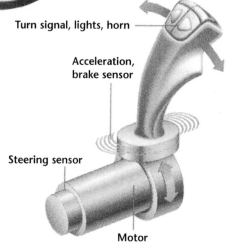

friendly voice, your car reads your e-mail and you dictate replies.

Suddenly an ear-splitting warning erupts inside your car and your seat begins to vibrate. The biofeedback sensor in your dashboard has measured your pupils and determined that you are getting drowsy. Alerted by this cattle-prod safety feature, you merge into the "nap lane." You lay a course on your satellite-guided navigation system, flip the autopilot switch, and hop into the back seat to sink into a deep slumber. The driving is left to a car that can read a road embedded with computer chips.

This is not science fiction or fantasy. Right now, automakers are spending billions researching all of these futuristic features. General Motors tested an "intelligent highway" in California that allows cars to be driven on autopilot. DaimlerChrysler outfits prototype cars with joysticks and finds that many drivers operate them better than steering wheels. Every carmaker in the world is rushing to replace the internal-combustion engine with fuel cells. And satellite-navigation systems that talk to you are already on the road. In fact, today's cars have more computing power than the Apollo 11 moon shot. Not too far down the road, it will be hard to tell whether you or your car is in the driver's seat.

You take it from here ...

Responding

1. Discuss Ideas   With a partner, share the ideas and questions that you jotted down while reading the article. Discuss your reaction when you reached the final paragraph of the article, which brings the fantasy described earlier into the realm of possibility.

2. Think Locally   Develop a list of any features of your own region (e.g., geography, climate) that could present a special challenge to designers of futuristic automobiles. For each feature, offer some suggestions (perhaps including hand-drawn diagrams or other illustrations) on how designers might meet the challenges.

3. Appreciate Writing Style   Scan the article and notice the techniques the author uses to make the writing exciting and energetic. Work with a partner to list as many techniques as you can, considering such things as word choice, sentence structure, and use of images and examples.

4. Examine the Visuals   With a partner, examine the photographs and illustrations that accompany the article. Explain how each visual is placed, the balance between pictures or diagrams and text, the use of space, and so on. Suggest some alternative ways of organizing the text and visuals, and/or suggest some additional visuals that might be included.

Extending

5. **Research Automobile Features** Choose an automobile that appeals to you and research what fairly new or first-time features the latest model offers. What features, once themselves new, are now standard? Try to find out when features such as power windows and air conditioning were first introduced. Present your findings in a form of your choice (e.g., report, sales brochure, poster, radio or TV commercial).

6. **Write a Similar Article** Using the style and structure of "When Cars Drive You" as a model, write your own article (it can be fictional) about something that interests you (e.g., travel, the workplace, the home, entertainment, education). Begin by presenting a future scenario in the present tense, and then end the article with an overview of current research (either real or imaginary) that might eventually make the scenario a reality.

TIP

- Consider using a word-processing or page-layout program to prepare your final copy.

"Hi, I'm a complete stranger from next door."

Logged On to the Guy Next Door

by Scott McKeen

NEWSPAPER ARTICLE

The view of Internet fanatics as antisocial loners is being seriously undermined by research on a Toronto suburb where computers linked neighbours—and made them more neighbourly.

Not only did families in this wired community get to know more of their neighbours, but they talked over the phone and visited each other more often than a control group of nonwired families.

Dubbed Netville by researchers, the neighbourhood was wired with a super high-speed computer network. In a community of 109 homes, 64 were wired together.

The network was tricked-up with all kinds of toys, including an online jukebox, videophones, and direct access to health-care professionals. But a local e-mail list service was by far the most utilized feature, said University of Toronto researcher Keith Hampton, who lived in Netville for two years of the three-year study.

"The irony in this research was twofold," says Hampton, a sociologist and Edmonton native. "First, these people had a wonderful broadband network, but used the lowest band application, e-mail. Secondly, the Internet is supposed to be a global communications medium, but it actually connects people on this very local level."

In Netville, people posted e-mail to a list service, which distributed the posting to all the wired homes. New neighbours were easily brought into the fold with information exchanges on such mundane topics as where to find good local pizza. The Internet acted as a community-wide icebreaker, said Hampton.

"Yes, these people were inside their houses, yes they were sitting at their computers, but what they were not doing was isolating themselves," says Hampton.

Modern lifestyles and modern communities are isolating as it is and create all sorts of barriers to social interaction, he says.

Just walking up to a new neighbour's door is a social challenge.

"You have to pass all these barriers in terms of fences and steps and then knock on that door and say 'Hi, I'm a complete stranger from next door'," says Hampton.

A local e-mail list service allows even shy people to communicate easily, at everyone's convenience.

Neighbours in Netville quickly found out about each other's hobbies, kids, occupations— what academics call social capital—via the Net. The computer link also facilitated collective and political action, says Hampton. People organized buying co-ops and a baby-sitting network and debated a local teachers' strike. They also organized strategies for dealing with complaints against the neighbourhood developer.

Hampton won't name the community, but previous press accounts identified it as a suburb near Newmarket.

When the study concluded in early 1999, the wired neighbourhood even banded together to try and keep the technology provided by a consortium of private and government interests.

Some other wired communities are being developed in Seattle and California. Telus is part of Toronto's CityPlace, billed as the most technologically advanced neighbourhood in Canada. It will provide high-speed Internet access to all residents, including Web-camera building security.

But, the final irony about the lessons from Netville is that the most popular option, a neighbourhood e-mail list, might not be commercially viable, according to Hampton.

Why? There are some privacy issues to overcome, as well as trying to identify a neighbourhood's true boundaries.

But, more important, any neighbourhood or group can simply go onto an Internet site, such as eGroups (www.egroups.com) and establish its own e-mail list service, for free.

In fact, that's exactly what the residents of Netville did when their fancy computer network was removed.

Netville, Canada

Facts about Netville neighbours linked by a local high-speed computer network:

- Recognized three times as many neighbours and talked to twice as many as their nonwired counterparts.
- Made five times as many local phone calls as the nonwired folk.
- Knew more of their neighbours living elsewhere in the suburb, rather than just close neighbours.
- Organized more social events with neighbours, such as parties and barbecues.
- Collectively organized to purchase goods and protest housing concerns.

You take it from here ...

Responding

1. Discuss Ideas   In groups of two or three, exchange ideas about how the local e-mail list described in this article could be adapted to your own school community. What benefits might result? What disadvantages might there be?

Logged On to the Guy Next Door   **37**

2. **Respond Personally** Answer the following in one or two paragraphs: Would you have been interested in being part of the Netville research project? Why or why not?

3. **Examine Newspaper Style** This article was written in typical newspaper style. With this in mind, consider the following:
   a) Does the introductory sentence encourage you to read on?
   b) At what point do we understand who is involved, what has happened, and where and when it has occurred?
   c) Where does the information answering the why question appear?
   d) What is the function of the sidebar? Did you read it first or later?
   e) How well does the headline reflect the content of the article? Suggest one or two alternatives.

Extending

4. **Hold a Debate** In a small group, debate the following statement: "By reducing the need for face-to-face contact, technologies such as e-mail are diminishing our collective social skills." Jot down the main arguments and share them with the class at the conclusion of the debate.

> **GROUP ASSESSMENT**
> - Did everyone in the group have a chance to be heard?
> - Did group members listen respectfully to one another's opinions?

5. **Create a Cartoon** Create a cartoon visual that might accompany this article. Remember that cartoons capture your attention and make you chuckle as well as think.

6. **Role-Play a Conversation** Imagine that you have a summer job going door-to-door selling memberships in Neighbours Together, an online company that will hook up entire neighbourhoods, as in the Netville pilot project. Working with a partner, develop your sales pitch and the dialogue you will have with whoever opens the door at a particular house (you must first decide on some details about that person).

> **PEER ASSESSMENT**
> - Were the dialogues convincing and carefully thought-out?
> - Was the language used appropriate to the characters?
> - Which dialogue did you find most interesting? Why?

There Will Come Soft Rains

At ten o'clock the house began to die.

Short Story by Ray Bradbury

Notes

Ray Bradbury (1920–), who lives in Los Angeles, is the author of hundreds of science-fiction stories, including *Something Wicked This Way Comes* (1962), *Fahrenheit 451* (1953), *The Martian Chronicles* (1950), and the stories of the *Ray Bradbury Theater* television series (1980s and 1990s).

Matisse, Picasso: two famous 20th-century abstract painters

Sara Teasdale (1884–1933): popular St. Louis poet who wrote rhyming lyric poems about love, marriage, suffering, and strength

In the living room the voice-clock sang. *Tick-tock, seven o'clock, time to get up, time to get up, seven o'clock!* as if it were afraid that nobody would. The morning house lay empty. The clock ticked on, repeating and repeating its sounds into the emptiness. *Seven-nine, breakfast time, seven-nine!*

In the kitchen the breakfast stove gave a hissing sigh and ejected from its warm interior eight pieces of perfectly browned toast, eight eggs sunny side up, sixteen slices of bacon, two coffees, and two cool glasses of milk.

"Today is August 4, 2026," said a second voice from the kitchen ceiling, "in the city of Allendale, California." It repeated the date three times for memory's sake. "Today is Mr. Featherstone's birthday. Today is the anniversary of Tilita's marriage. Insurance is payable, as are the water, gas, and light bills."

Somewhere in the walls, relays clicked, memory tapes glided under electric eyes.

Eight-one, tick-tock, eight-one o'clock, off to school, off to work, run, run, eight-one! But no doors slammed, no carpets took the soft tread of rubber heels. It was raining outside. The weather box on the front door sang quietly: "Rain, rain, go away; rubbers, raincoats for today...." And the rain tapped on the empty house, echoing.

Outside, the garage chimed and lifted its door to reveal the waiting car. After a long wait the door swung down again.

At eight-thirty the eggs were shrivelled and the toast was like stone. An aluminum wedge scraped them into the sink, where hot water whirled them down a metal throat which digested and flushed them away to the distant sea. The dirty dishes were dropped into a hot washer and emerged twinkling dry.

Nine-fifteen, sang the clock, *time to clean.*

Out of warrens in the wall, tiny robot mice darted. The rooms were acrawl with the small cleaning animals, all rubber and metal. They thudded against chairs, whirling their moustached runners, kneading the rug nap, sucking gently at hidden dust. Then, like mysterious invaders, they popped into their burrows. Their pink electric eyes faded. The house was clean.

Ten o'clock. The sun came out from behind the rain. The house stood alone in a city of rubble and ashes. This was the one house left standing. At night the ruined city gave off a radioactive glow which could be seen for miles.

Ten-fifteen. The garden sprinklers whirled up in golden founts, filling the soft morning air with scatterings of brightness. The water pelted windowpanes, running down the charred west side where the house had been burned evenly free of its white paint. The entire west face of the house was black, save for five places. Here the silhouette in paint of a man mowing a lawn. Here, as in a photograph, a woman bent to pick flowers. Still farther over, their images burned on wood in one titanic instant, a small boy, hands flung into the air; higher up, the image of a thrown ball, and opposite him a girl, hands raised to catch a ball which never came down.

The five spots of paint—the man, the woman, the children, the ball—remained. The rest was a thin charcoaled layer.

The gentle sprinkler rain filled the garden with falling light.

Until this day, how well the house had kept its peace. How carefully it had inquired, "Who goes there? What's the password?" and, getting no answer from lonely foxes and whining cats, it had shut up its windows and drawn shades in an old-maidenly preoccupation with self-protection which bordered on a mechanical paranoia.

It quivered at each sound, the house did. If a sparrow brushed a window, the shade snapped up. The bird, startled, flew off! No, not even a bird must touch the house!

The house was an altar with ten thousand attendants, big, small, servicing, attending, in choirs. But the gods had gone away, and the ritual of the religion continued senselessly, uselessly.

Twelve noon.

A dog whined, shivering, on the front porch.

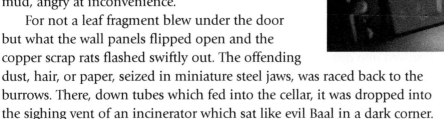

The front door recognized the dog voice and opened. The dog, once huge and fleshy, but now gone to bone and covered with sores, moved in and through the house, tracking mud. Behind it whirred angry mice, angry at having to pick up mud, angry at inconvenience.

For not a leaf fragment blew under the door but what the wall panels flipped open and the copper scrap rats flashed swiftly out. The offending dust, hair, or paper, seized in miniature steel jaws, was raced back to the burrows. There, down tubes which fed into the cellar, it was dropped into the sighing vent of an incinerator which sat like evil Baal in a dark corner.

The dog ran upstairs, hysterically yelping to each door, at last realizing, as the house realized, that only silence was here.

It sniffed the air and scratched the kitchen door. Behind the door, the stove was making pancakes which filled the house with a rich baked odour and the scent of maple syrup.

The dog frothed at the mouth, lying at the door, sniffing, its eyes turned to fire. It ran wildly in circles, biting at its tail, spun in a frenzy, and died. It lay in the parlour for an hour.

Two o'clock, sang a voice.

Delicately sensing decay at last, the regiments of mice hummed out as softly as blown grey leaves in an electrical wind.

Two-fifteen.

The dog was gone.

In the cellar, the incinerator glowed suddenly and a whirl of sparks leaped up the chimney.

Two-thirty-five.

Bridge tables sprouted from patio walls. Playing cards fluttered onto pads in a shower of pips. Martinis manifested on an oaken bench with egg-salad sandwiches. Music played.

But the tables were silent and the cards untouched.

At four o'clock the tables folded like great butterflies back through the panelled walls.

∽

Four-thirty.

The nursery walls glowed.

Animals took shape: yellow giraffes, blue lions, pink antelopes, lilac panthers cavorting in crystal substance. The walls were glass. They looked out upon colour and fantasy. Hidden films clocked through well-oiled sprockets, and the walls lived. The nursery floor was woven to resemble a crisp cereal meadow. Over this ran aluminum roaches and iron crickets, and in the hot still air butterflies of delicate red tissue wavered among the sharp aroma of animal spoors! There was the sound like a great matted yellow hive of bees within a dark bellows, the lazy bumble of a purring lion. And there was the patter of okapi feet and the murmur of a fresh jungle rain, like other hoofs, falling upon the summer-starched grass. Now the walls dissolved into distances of parched weed, mile on mile, and warm endless sky. The animals drew away into thorn brakes and water holes.

∾

It was the children's hour.

∾

Five o'clock. The bath filled with clear hot water.

Six, seven, eight o'clock. The dinner dishes manipulated like magic tricks, and in the study *a click.* In the metal stand opposite the hearth where a fire now blazed up warmly, a cigar popped out, half an inch of soft grey ash on it, smoking, waiting.

Nine o'clock. The beds warmed their hidden circuits, for nights were cool here.

Nine-five. A voice spoke from the study ceiling:

"Mrs. McClellan, which poem would you like this evening?"

The house was silent.

The voice said at last, "Since you express no preference, I shall select a poem at random." Quiet music rose to back the voice. "Sara Teasdale. As I recall, your favourite....

"There will come soft rains and the smell of the ground,
And swallows circling with their shimmering sound;

And frogs in the pools singing at night,
And wild plum-trees in tremulous white;

Robins will wear their feathery fire
Whistling their whims on a low fence-wire;

And not one will know of the war, not one
Will care at last when it is done.

Not one would mind, either bird nor tree
If mankind perished utterly;

And Spring herself, when she woke at dawn,
Would scarcely know that we were gone."

The fire burned on the stone hearth and the cigar fell away into a mound of quiet ash on its tray. The empty chairs faced each other between the silent walls, and the music played.

At ten o'clock the house began to die.

The wind blew. A falling tree bough crashed through the kitchen window. Cleaning solvent, bottled, shattered over the stove. The room was ablaze in an instant!

"Fire!" screamed a voice. The house lights flashed, water pumps shot water from the ceilings. But the solvent spread on the linoleum, licking, eating under the kitchen door, while the voices took it up in chorus: "Fire, fire, fire!"

The house tried to save itself. Doors sprang tightly shut, but the windows were broken by the heat and the wind blew and sucked upon the fire.

The house gave ground as the fire in 10 billion angry sparks moved with flaming ease from room to room and then up the stairs. While scurrying water rats squeaked from the walls, pistolled their water, and ran for more. And the wall sprays let down showers of mechanical rain.

But too late. Somewhere, sighing, a pump shrugged to a stop. The quenching rain ceased. The reserve water supply which had filled baths and washed dishes for many quiet days was gone.

The fire crackled up the stairs. It fed upon Picassos and Matisses in the upper halls, like delicacies, baking off the oily flesh, tenderly crisping the canvases into black shavings.

Now the fire lay in beds, stood in windows, changed the colours of drapes!

And then, reinforcements.

From attic trapdoors, blind robot faces peered down with faucet mouths gushing green chemical.

The fire backed off, as even an elephant must at the sight of a dead snake. Now there were 20 snakes whipping over the floor, killing the fire with a clear cold venom of green froth.

But the fire was clever. It had sent flame outside the house, up through the attic to the pumps there. An explosion! The attic brain which

directed the pumps was shattered into bronze shrapnel on the beams.

The fire rushed back into every closet and felt of the clothes hung there.

The house shuddered, oak bone on bone, its bared skeleton cringing from the heat, its wire, its nerves revealed as if a surgeon had torn the skin off to let the red veins and capillaries quiver in the scalded air. Help, help! Fire! Run, run! Heat snapped mirrors like the first brittle winter ice. And the voices wailed Fire, fire, run, run, like a tragic nursery rhyme, a dozen voices, high, low, like children dying in a forest, alone, alone. And the voices fading as the wires popped their sheathings like hot chestnuts. One, two, three, four, five voices died.

In the nursery the jungle burned. Blue lions roared, purple giraffes bounded off. The panthers ran in circles, changing colour, and 10 million animals, running before the fire, vanished off toward a distant steaming river....

Ten more voices died. In the last instant under the fire avalanche, other choruses, oblivious, could be heard announcing the time, playing music, cutting the lawn by remote-control mower, or setting an umbrella frantically out and in the slamming and opening front door, a thousand things happening, like a clock shop when each clock strikes the hour insanely before or after the other, a scene of maniac confusion, yet unity; singing, screaming, a few last cleaning mice darting bravely out to carry the horrid ashes away! And one voice, with sublime disregard for the situation, read poetry aloud in the fiery study, until all the film spools burned, until all the wires withered and the circuits cracked.

The fire burst the house and let it slam flat down, puffing out skirts of spark and smoke.

In the kitchen, an instant before the rain of fire and timber, the stove could be seen making breakfasts at a psychopathic rate, ten dozen eggs, six loaves of toast, twenty dozen bacon strips, which, eaten by fire, started the stove working again, hysterically hissing!

The crash. The attic smashing into kitchen and parlour. The parlour into cellar, cellar into sub-cellar. Deep freeze, armchair, film tapes, circuits, beds, and all like skeletons thrown in a cluttered mound deep under.

Smoke and silence. A great quantity of smoke.

Dawn showed faintly in the east. Among the ruins, one wall stood alone. Within the wall, a last voice said, over and over again and again, even as the sun rose to shine upon the heaped rubble and steam:

"Today is August 5, 2026, today is August 5, 2026, today is...."

You take it from here ...

Responding

1. Discuss Initial Reactions   Share in a class discussion the moments as you were reading the story when you had sudden insights—even feelings of shock—about what was happening.

2. Locate Details   Working with a partner, list details from the story that tell us that the catastrophe happened some time ago. What difference would it make to the story if the catastrophe had just happened?

3. Put Yourself into the Story   Imagine that you were a member of the family that lived in the house before the catastrophe. Write two or three paragraphs describing what you think your life would have been like, supporting your ideas with clues from the story.

4. Discuss Personification   *Personification* is the technique of attributing human characteristics to inanimate objects or to nonhuman creatures. Identify several examples of personification in this story, and comment on why Bradbury might have used this technique so extensively.

5. Consider Theme   In a class discussion, speculate on why Bradbury wrote this story. Consider the time when it was first published (1950) and what was happening in the world then that might have influenced his choice of subject.

Extending

6. Create a Collage   In this story Bradbury uses many descriptive details and images (words that appeal to our senses); some of these are exquisitely beautiful and others are tremendously sad. List several of these images and find (or draw) pictures to represent them. Use these to create a collage that expresses the contrasts in the story. Be prepared to present and explain your collage to the class.

7. Write a Poem   Select some words and phrases from the story that you find particularly descriptive. Combine these with your own words to create a free-verse poem inspired by Bradbury's story.

Before you read, as a class, discuss any theories you have heard for how the world might end. Which are the most common?

As you read, decide whether the speaker really feels that the end of the world is imminent, or whether he is speaking on an abstract level.

Fire and Ice

Poem by Robert Frost

Notes

Robert Frost (1874–1963) was a popular New England poet. He wrote such famous works as "The Road Not Taken," "Stopping by Woods on a Snowy Evening," "Mending Wall," and "The Tuft of Flowers." Frost won the Pulitzer Prize for Poetry four times and was considered America's unofficial poet laureate.

Some say the world will end in fire,

Some say in ice.

From what I've tasted of desire

I hold with those who favor fire.

But if it had to perish twice,

I think I know enough of hate

To say that for destruction ice

Is also great

And would suffice.

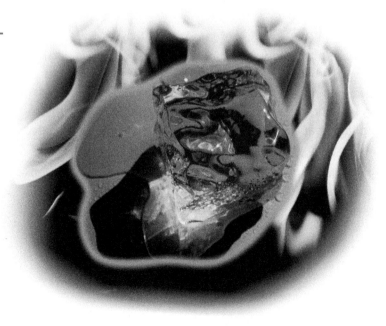

You take it from here ...

Responding

1. Understand the Poem   Work through the poem with a partner or in a small group and answer the following questions:

   • In the title and lines 1 and 2, what might "fire" and "ice" allude to?
   • In lines 3 and 4, what is the poet's opinion? What emotion or aspect of human behaviour might fire symbolize?
   • Comment on the idea about the world's ending that arises in line 5.
   • In lines 6 through 9, what is the poet's opinion? What emotion or aspect of human behaviour might ice symbolize?
   • As you consider the poem's tone, do you think the poet is mainly interested in raising alarm about the end of the world, or is he more interested in discussing two extremes of human behaviour? Defend your answer.

2. Go Beyond the Obvious   This poem may be more about how to live life than about how life will end. As you interpret the symbols, consider what the poet's choice of fire over ice suggests about him and the way he lives his life. Share your thoughts with a partner.

3. Explain the Main Idea   What emotional or behavioural extremes do fire and ice represent? What is the poet saying by linking these ideas to the ending of the world? Write a paragraph in which you explain and respond to the main idea of this poem. In a class discussion, share your interpretations.

Extending

4. Study Other Works   Find and read two other poems by Robert Frost mentioned in the Notes next to this poem. Analyze these poems closely and compare them with "Fire and Ice." In what ways are they similar and in what ways are they different? Present your comparison in chart form.

5. Write a Personal Response   Reflect back on Activity 3, which focuses on the emotional extremes or extremes of human behaviour fire and ice represent. Write a reflective journal response in which you examine a major decision that you have made in your life, and analyze whether you made your choice more influenced by "fire" or "ice." What do you think we have to do to keep these two extremes balanced in our lives?

Notes

Bruce Cockburn (1945–) is a Canadian folk singer and activist whose many hits include "Wonderin' Where the Lions Are," "Lovers in a Dangerous Time," and "Waiting for a Miracle." Cockburn has said of "If a Tree Falls" that he wasn't just thinking of Brazil, but also about the destruction of forests on the western coast of Canada.

If a tree falls: an old philosophical question— "If a tree falls in the forest and there's no one to hear it, does it make a sound?"

cortege: funeral procession

lobotomy: brain operation once used to treat patients with severe mental problems

refuse (n.): waste; useless matter

If a Tree Falls

Lyrics by Bruce Cockburn

rain forest
mist and mystery
teeming green
green brain facing lobotomy
climate control centre for the world
ancient cord of coexistence
hacked by parasitic greedhead scam—
from Sarawak to Amazonas
Costa Rica to mangy B.C. hills—
cortege rhythm of falling timber.

What kind of currency grows in these new deserts,
these brand new flood plains?

If a tree falls in the forest does anybody hear?
If a tree falls in the forest does anybody hear?
Anybody hear the forest fall?

Cut and move on
Cut and move on
take out trees
take out wildlife at a rate of a species every single day
take out people who've lived with this for 100,000 years—
inject a billion burgers worth of beef—
grain eaters—methane dispensers—

through thinning ozone,

waves fall on wrinkled earth—

gravity, light, ancient refuse of stars,

speak of a drowning—

but this, this is something other

busy monster eats dark holes in the spirit world

where wild things have to go

to disappear

forever

If a tree falls in the forest does anybody hear?

If a tree falls in the forest does anybody hear?

Anybody hear the forest fall?

You take it from here ...

Responding

1. Reflect on First Impressions   Review the lyrics and take jot notes, identifying which words and phrases convey to you a sense of beauty. Which convey criticism and/or anger? Which do you think are the most effective? Why?

2. Understand the Lyrics   Summarize your understanding of Cockburn's lyrics by stating, in point form, what he says about the value of the rain forests and what he sees as the problems that result from clearing them. Share your ideas with one or two other students.

3. Clarify Meanings in Context   Working with a partner, write an explanation of what the following lines mean in the context of the song. Look up any unfamiliar terms in a dictionary.

   • rain forest / mist and mystery / teeming green
   • green brain facing lobotomy
   • cortege rhythm of falling timber
   • gravity, light, ancient refuse of stars, / speak of a drowning—/ but this, this is something other
   • busy monster eats dark holes in the spirit world

   When you have finished, share your interpretations in a class discussion.

4. Consider Rhetorical Questions   A rhetorical question is one that is asked only for effect and to which no answer is expected. As a class, consider the meaning of the rhetorical question in the chorus: "If a tree falls in the forest does anybody hear?" What is the effect of asking this question in the chorus?

Extending

5. Make a Visual Presentation   Find or create a photograph or painting that addresses the issues and questions in this song. Identify specifically how the illustration conveys these ideas, and prepare an oral presentation of your analysis.

6. Express Your Views   Overall, do you think technological advancements have been mostly harmful or mostly beneficial for people and the planet? Or have the results been mixed? Write an opinion piece expressing your views on the relative costs and benefits of scientific and technological research.

7. Learn about the Artist   Find out more about Bruce Cockburn, his music, and the causes he supports. As you explore, select two items you find especially interesting (e.g., a song, a magazine article, a Web link to an environmental organization), and share them with a small group.

TIP

- While you can choose to consider the costs and benefits in general terms, you might prefer to focus on a particular issue, such as the environment, health, hunger, poverty, education, or security.

TIP

- The Cockburn Project Web Site— www.cockburnproject. net—brings together a great deal of information on Bruce Cockburn and his work.

Before you read, have a class discussion about what we as individuals can do to protect the environment.

As you read, identify the things you already do in your home and neighbourhood to promote a clean and healthy environment.

A drip from a leaky faucet can waste almost 200 litres a day.

Simple Ways You Can Help Save the Earth

by THE EARTHWORKS GROUP

MAGAZINE FEATURE

Adapted from *50 Simple Things You Can Do to Save the Earth*

A wise man once said, "Nobody made a greater mistake than he who did nothing because he could do so little." It's easy to let news reports about enormous environmental problems overwhelm and paralyze you. In fact, each of us *can* do something, every day, to make the planet more livable for ourselves and for future generations.

The 1990s ushered in a new understanding that government and business can't repair the waste and pollution damage that comes from the actions of millions of people. But remember: As much as we are the source of the problem, we are also the beginning of its solution.

The good news is that conservation can be accomplished by simple, cost-effective measures that require little change in how you live. Here are some ways you can help save the earth:

Give your home a checkup. If your heating system is inefficient, up to 50 percent of the energy it uses is wasted. A simple tune-up can increase the efficiency of an oil furnace by 5 percent.

The second-largest energy user is your water heater. Many people keep their water heaters at 60°—hotter than necessary. Turn yours down to 55°—still hot enough to kill bacteria—and you reduce energy use by 6 percent.

Nearly half of the energy used in homes leaks out windows, attics, or cracks. If you have insulation, check if you have enough. Attic insulation alone can save more than 5 percent on heating costs and 15 percent on air-conditioning bills.

Monitor your appliances. The pilot light on a gas stove should be burning with a blue, cone-shaped flame. If it's yellow, you're wasting energy; burners and ports are clogged or need adjustment. If you are buying a new gas stove, those with electronic ignition systems use about 40 percent less gas than a pilot light. (Always go for the most energy-efficient models when you purchase appliances.)

If your refrigerator and freezer are 5° colder than necessary, your energy consumption will increase up to 25 percent. The refrigerator temperature should be between 3° and 6°; the freezer between –18° and –15°.

Up to 90 percent of the energy used for washing clothes goes to heating the water. A warm wash and cold rinse will work just as well as hot water. Washers use up to 225 litres a load; to save water, wait until you have a full load of washing.

Light it right. Conserve energy by turning lights off when they are not being used and choose your light bulbs with conservation in mind.

For example, a 100-watt bulb puts out almost as much light as two 60-watt bulbs and takes less energy. (Remember, a "long-life" incandescent bulb is less energy efficient than a standard bulb.) Look for compact fluorescent bulbs. They give off light like a traditional bulb, yet are big energy savers. They cost more, but save money in the long run because they use less electricity. Substituting a compact fluorescent for an incandescent will keep a half-tonne of carbon dioxide out of the atmosphere over the life of the bulb.

Don't waste water. Do you leave the water running while brushing your teeth, shaving, or washing dishes? That's not a drop in the bucket. It's more than 50 litres every time you brush, 75 litres each time you shave, and 110 litres for every load of dishes. A household can save more than 75 000 litres of water each year just by getting a grip on its faucets.

You can also conserve an amazing amount of water by installing a few inexpensive devices in your home—low-flow shower heads and shut-off valves. The shower heads alone can cut hot-water use by as much as 2500 litres a month for a family of four.

If you put a small, water-filled plastic bottle in your toilet tank, each flush will save 4 to 8 litres of water out of the normal 20 to 25 litres used.

Fix those leaks. A drip from a leaky faucet can waste almost 200 litres a day; a leaky toilet wastes 170 000 litres in six months.

Don't forget the outdoors. Washing the car with a running hose uses up to 550 litres of water; a sponge and bucket takes 55 litres, a self-service car wash less than 40 litres.

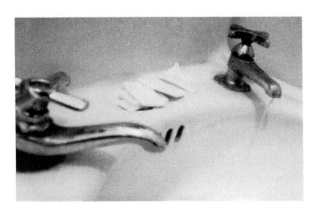

Beware of toxic wastes. Many of us are unaware that common household and garage items are hazardous wastes: paints and thinners; oven, drain, and toilet-bowl cleaners; car batteries; brake and transmission fluid; antifreeze; pesticides. We may innocently dump these toxic substances down the drain or into the sewer system. Result: serious water contamination.

Car batteries, paint thinners, and some solvents can be refined for reuse. If there's no recycling in your area, call your local government authority for information on disposal.

Recycle it away. Recycling saves landfill space, and making new products from old uses much less energy than making them from scratch. It won't take much time if you set up separate bins in your home for different products.

Be a gas miser. Cars give off nearly 2.5 kilograms of carbon dioxide—the key ingredient in the greenhouse effect—for every litre of gas consumed. So a car that gets 11 kilometres per litre will emit a tonne of carbon dioxide every 4400 kilometres. Cars also cause acid rain by emitting nitrogen oxides and also produce tree-killing, lung-damaging ozone smog by emitting hydrocarbons. Again, this is directly related to the amount of fuel consumed.

The easiest way to make your car more fuel efficient is to keep it tuned. A well-tuned car uses up to 9 percent less gasoline than one that's poorly tuned. That means 9 percent fewer toxic emissions. Hydrocarbons help create ozone smog when they evaporate. So when you fill your tank, try to keep the vapours from escaping into the atmosphere. Keeping tires properly inflated preserves their life (preventing premature wear from overflexing and overheating) and saves gas since underinflation can waste up to 5 percent of a car's fuel by increasing rolling resistance.

Carpooling is especially practical if you commute to an urban area. Carpooling just 13 kilometres twice a day will save thousands of auto kilometres per person every year.

If you change your oil yourself, recycle it. When used motor oil is poured into the ground, it can seep into the groundwater and contaminate drinking water. A single litre of motor oil can pollute 945 000 litres of drinking water. Pouring oil into the sewer is like pouring it directly into a stream or river. Tossing it into the trash is essentially the same as pouring it out. The oil will be dumped in a landfill, where it will eventually seep into the ground.

Most communities have gas stations or oil-changing outlets that recycle their oil and will accept yours for a small fee. Most recycled oil is reprocessed and sold as fuel for ships and industrial boilers. The rest is processed into lubricating and industrial oils.

Be kind to a beach. Plastic waste kills up to a million seabirds, 100 000 sea mammals, and countless fish each year. If you live near a beach, next time you visit, be sure to take along a trash bag and spend a few minutes picking up litter.

Snip each circle of your plastic six-pack rings with scissors before you toss them into the garbage. They are a hazard to birds and marine life, whether left on the beach or dumped into the ocean with other refuse. They are virtually invisible underwater, and marine animals can't avoid them.

Finally, spread the word. One person can help protect the environment; two can do even more. As you inspire friends and family, they'll inspire others. So share what you have learned—and watch the impact grow. It all begins with you.

You take it from here ...

Responding

1. **Share Experience and Ideas** With a partner or in a small group, share what you are currently doing to promote a healthy environment. Work together to create a list of new ideas from the article that you could easily incorporate into your own life.

2. **Check Out Your Household** Create a checklist of at least 10 points from this article that you would like to check at home, and use it to conduct a brief survey to see whether your household is doing what it can for the environment.

3. **Reflect on a Quotation** Reread the famous quotation at the beginning of this selection (a statement made by British statesman and philosopher Edmund Burke): "Nobody made a greater mistake than he who did nothing because he could do so little." With a partner, discuss how this quotation could apply to another social issue, such as homelessness, hunger, or child labour.

Extending

TIP

- Your municipal department in charge of waste management can be a good source of information. You might be able to arrange an interview or tour of the recycling facilities.

4. **Investigate Community Recycling** Working in a small group, investigate your own community's recycling program. Choose a specific area to focus on (e.g., the economic benefits and costs of recycling, products made from recycled material), and organize your findings into a written or oral report.

5. **Create a Poster** In keeping with the article's advice to "spread the word," design a poster to encourage individual actions to protect the environment. Before you begin, decide what message you want to convey and who your target audience will be.

6. **Research New Appliances** Many households have at least five home appliances: stove, fridge, dishwasher, washer, and dryer. Working in a group of five, each select one appliance and research how the latest models are more ecologically friendly than earlier ones. Report your findings to the group.

Before you read, write one or two sentences predicting what the story will be about, based on the title.

As you read, pay close attention to the details and try to picture the creatures and settings clearly.

Zoo

"My ship can remain here only six hours."

Short Short Story by Edward D. Hoch

Notes

Edward D. Hoch (1930–) is a well-known American writer. A past president of Mystery Writers of America, he has won the organization's Edgar Award for best short story, among other honours.

The children were always good during the month of August, especially when it began to get near the twenty-third. It was on this day that the great silver spaceship carrying Professor Hugo's Interplanetary Zoo settled down for its annual six-hour visit to the Chicago area.

Before daybreak the crowds would form, long lines of children and adults both, each one clutching his or her dollar, and waiting with wonderment to see what race of strange creatures the Professor had brought this year.

In the past they had sometimes been treated to three-legged creatures from Venus, or tall, thin men from Mars, or even snake-like horrors from somewhere more distant. This year, as the great round ship settled slowly to Earth in the huge tri-city parking area just outside of Chicago, they watched with awe as the sides slowly slid up to reveal the familiar barred cages. In them were some wild breed of nightmare—small, horse-like animals that moved with quick, jerking motions and constantly chattered in a high-pitched tongue. The citizens of Earth clustered around as Professor Hugo's crew quickly collected the waiting dollars, and soon the good Professor himself made an appearance, wearing his many-coloured rainbow cape and top hat. "Peoples of Earth," he called into his microphone.

The crowd's noise died down and he continued. "Peoples of Earth, this year you see a real treat for your single dollar—the little-known horse-spider people of Kaan—brought to you across a million miles of space at great expense. Gather around, see them, study them, listen to them, tell your friends about them. But hurry! My ship can remain here only six hours!"

And the crowds slowly filed by, at once horrified and fascinated by these strange creatures that looked like horses but ran up the walls of their cages like spiders. "This is certainly worth a dollar," one man remarked, hurrying away. "I'm going home to get the wife."

All day long it went like that, until ten thousand people had filed by the barred cages set into the side of the spaceship. Then, as the six-hour limit ran out, Professor Hugo once more took microphone in hand. "We must go now, but we will return next year on this date. And if you enjoyed our zoo this year, phone your friends in other cities about it. We will land in New York tomorrow, and next week on to London, Paris, Rome, Hong Kong, and Tokyo. Then on to other worlds!"

He waved farewell to them, and as the ship rose from the ground the Earth peoples agreed that this had been the very best Zoo yet....

Some two months and three planets later, the silver ship of Professor Hugo settled at last onto the familiar jagged rocks of Kaan, and the queer horse-spider creatures filed quickly out of their cages. Professor Hugo was there to say a few parting words, and then they scurried away in a hundred different directions, seeking their homes among the rocks.

In one, the she-creature was happy to see the return of her mate and offspring. She babbled a greeting in the strange tongue and hurried to embrace them. "It was a long time you were gone. Was it good?"

And the he-creature nodded. "The little one enjoyed it especially. We visited eight worlds and saw many things."

The little one ran up the wall of the cave. "On the place called Earth it was the best. The creatures there wear garments over their skins, and they walk on two legs."

"But isn't it dangerous?" asked the she-creature.

"No," her mate answered. "There are bars to protect us from them. We remain right in the ship. Next time you must come with us. It is well worth the 19 compocs it costs."

And the little one nodded. "It was the very best Zoo ever...."

You take it from here ...

Responding

1. React to the Surprise Ending   The ending of this story is effective because it reverses our expectations. In a paragraph, write your reaction to the story. Did you see the ending coming, or were you caught off guard? What is the irony of the ending?

2. Dig into Character   List what we are told about Professor Hugo, and also what you figure out by reading between the lines (interpreting what you read). Then write a one- or two-paragraph interpretation of his character.

3. Respond to Descriptive Writing   As you read, were you able to create a clear picture in your mind of the creatures, the ship, and Professor Hugo? Use the images you created to describe or draw an illustration that might accompany this story if it were in a children's book.

4. Examine Deeper Issues   Write a journal response examining some of the deeper issues that this story makes you think about. When you have finished writing, share your ideas with one or two other students.

Extending

5. Create a Flyer for the Kaan Tourist Market   Suppose that you run a travel agency on Kaan and are advertising your next tour to other worlds, including Earth. Create an imaginative one-page flyer that you will send out to other agencies trying to sell tickets for this excursion.

6. Write a Pair of Diary Entries   Create a pair of diary entries, one written by a child from Earth who stood in line to see Professor Hugo's Interplanetary Zoo, and the other written by a child from Kaan who was on board the ship. Try to capture the experience of strangeness and, of course, other details that each would write about in a diary. Perhaps you could set up an ironic situation for your reader to recognize and enjoy.

Reflecting on the Unit

Responding

1. Evaluate the Selections   Briefly review the selections studied in this unit and choose three that provided you with new insights or that you found surprising. For each selection, write a paragraph stating why you chose it, what you learned from it, and how you foresee the issue affecting your life in the future. Then share, compare, and discuss your beliefs with two other students.

2. Write an Essay   Reread the introduction to the unit, including the quotations. Think about how the quotations relate to the individual selections. Choose a quotation that most agrees with your views and use it as the first sentence of an essay. Expand on the quotation, making reference to three selections and incorporating your personal interpretations.

Extending

3. Review a Movie   As a class, brainstorm a list of movies that are set in the future. Watch one, and then write a review of the film focusing on the feasibility of the future presented. Connect the movie you chose with relevant selections in this unit by identifying parallels and differences. Is the perception of various aspects of our future the same in the movie as is presented in the selections?

4. Research a Topic of Interest   In pairs, choose a topic from one of these categories: ethical issues related to medical research or population control; technological advancements; interplanetary exploration. Using magazines, online resources, and other sources, research and justify your answers to the following questions: How will continued research in this field affect us, both individually and globally? What are the risks, and are they worth taking? Present your research to the class.

> **SELF-ASSESSMENT**
>
> The main focus of this unit is the future and technological change. Identify
> - the most significant thing you learned in terms of your own future
> - the most confusing aspect or concept in this unit that could use further clarification
>
> Write your response as a journal entry.

Work in some form or other is the appointed lot of us all.
– *Anna Jameson*

Dedication to one's work in the world is the only possible satisfaction.
– *Cynthia Ozick*

To love what you do and feel that it matters—how could anything be more fun?
– *Katharine Graham*

The World of Work

Unit 2, like the previous unit, is about the future, but more specifically about your own future as you begin to contemplate and enter the world of work.

In the words of art critic Anna Jameson, work is a reality for all of us and, for this reason, requires serious consideration.

American writer Cynthia Ozick presents the view that work is very important in terms of personal fulfillment. Making the right job choices is very important for your own satisfaction.

The famous publisher Katharine Graham, who inherited a newspaper to run, speaks from personal experience when she says that work can be fun if you enjoy it and feel it is meaningful.

As you read this unit, think about the following:

1) How are school and the working world related?
2) What do you have to do in order to find a job?
3) How important are aptitude and personal goals and values in selecting meaningful work?
4) What interesting work options are available to people?

Zits

Cartoon by Jerry Scott and Jim Borgman

Notes

Zits, the popular comic strip about the life and times of 15-year-old Jeremy Duncan, began in 1997 and runs in over 1000 newspapers worldwide. It has been voted the Best Comic Strip twice by the National Cartoonists Society.

Jerry Scott, writer and co-creator of *Zits*, began his career by taking over the *Nancy* strip. He then co-created *Baby Blues* (which is based on his experiences with his second daughter) before going on to do *Zits*.

Jim Borgman, Pulitzer Prize-winning cartoonist, was raised in blue-collar neighbourhoods of Cincinnati. He was hired by the *Cincinnati Enquirer* one week after graduation to start work cartooning.

Jim Borgman and Jerry Scott

You take it from here ...

Responding

1. Assess Reactions   Most cartoons are intended to be humorous. Did you find this one humorous? Write a paragraph explaining why or why not.

2. Explore Satire   Satire usually pokes fun at a person, a group, or a thing. Often, satire aims to promote some kind of change. As a class, discuss the ways in which this cartoon could be considered satirical. What type of change might it be suggesting?

3. Imagine a Response   The teacher in the cartoon is silent. Write a dialogue bubble showing his thoughts or words to indicate
   a) a sympathetic response
   b) a sarcastic response

Extending

4. Write an Article   Write an article for a Web site or magazine aimed at high-school and college students. In it, offer advice about setting up an ideal study environment based on what works for you. Include as many details as you can, such as the best type of furniture and lighting, good reference resources to have available, best type of music to play (if any), and best snacks and drinks to have on hand. Include an illustration for your article.

> **TIP**
> • You could begin with a short description of some of the best and worst places you've studied. Then go on to describe your ideal environment.

5. Examine Alternatives   While the typical workday runs from 9:00 A.M. to 5:00 P.M., research has shown that many people do their best work at different times of day, such as in the early morning or late evening. Search the Internet for sites dealing with alternative work schedules and write a summary of the information from one source.

> **TIPS**
> • Begin your search for relevant Web sites by typing "alternative work schedules" (including quotation marks) into a search engine.
> • In your report, be sure to include the Web address of the site you are reporting on.

Deportation at Breakfast

I could smell my eggs starting to burn.

Short Short Story by Larry Fondation

Notes

Larry Fondation, who lives in California, works with community organizations focusing on such issues as raising the minimum wage, building affordable housing, providing leadership training, and increasing political participation in ethnic neighbourhoods.

The signs on the windows lured me inside. For a dollar I could get two eggs, toast, and potatoes. The place looked better than most—family-run and clean. The signs were hand-lettered and neat. The paper had yellowed some, but the black letters remained bold. A green-and-white awning was perched over the door, where the name "Clara's" was stencilled.

Inside, the place had an appealing and old-fashioned look. The air smelled fresh and homey, not greasy. The menu was printed on a chalkboard. It was short and to the point. It listed the kinds of toast you could choose from. One entry was erased from the middle of the list. By deduction, I figured it was rye. I didn't want rye toast anyway.

Because I was alone, I sat at the counter, leaving the empty tables free for other customers that might come in. At the time, business was quiet. Only two tables were occupied, and I was alone at the counter. But it was still early—not yet seven-thirty.

Behind the counter was a short man with dark black hair, a mustache, and a youthful beard, one that never grew much past stubble. He was dressed immaculately, all in chef's white—pants, shirt, and apron, but no hat. He had a thick accent. The name "Javier" was stitched on his shirt. I ordered coffee, and asked for a minute to choose between the breakfast special for a dollar and the cheese omelette for $1.59. I selected the omelette.

The coffee was hot, strong, and fresh. I spread my newspaper on the counter and sipped at the mug as Javier went to the grill to cook my meal.

The eggs were spread out on the griddle, the bread plunged inside the toaster, when the authorities came in. They grabbed Javier quickly and without a word, forcing his hands behind his back. He, too, said nothing. He did not resist, and they shoved him out the door and into their waiting car.

On the grill, my eggs bubbled. I looked around for another employee—maybe out back somewhere, or in the washroom. I leaned over the counter and called for someone. No one answered. I looked behind me toward the tables. Two elderly men sat at one, two elderly women at the other. The two women were talking. The men were reading the paper. They seemed not to have noticed Javier's exit.

I could smell my eggs starting to burn. I wasn't quite sure what to do about it. I thought about Javier and stared at my eggs. After some hesitation, I got up from my red swivel stool and went behind the counter. I grabbed a spare apron, then picked up the spatula and turned my eggs. My toast had popped up, but it was not browned, so I put it down again. While I was cooking, the two elderly women came to the counter and asked to pay. I asked what they had had. They seemed surprised that I didn't remember. I checked the prices on the chalkboard and rang up their order. They paid slowly, fishing through large purses, and went out, leaving me a dollar tip. I took my eggs off the grill and slid them onto a clean plate. My toast had come up. I buttered it and put it on my plate beside my eggs. I put the plate at my spot at the counter, right next to my newspaper.

As I began to come back from behind the counter to my stool, six new customers came through the door. "Can we pull some tables together?" they asked. "We're all one party." I told them yes. Then they ordered six coffees, two decaffeinated.

I thought of telling them I didn't work there. But perhaps they were hungry. I poured their coffee. Their order was simple: six breakfast specials, all with scrambled eggs and wheat toast. I got busy at the grill.

Then the elderly men came to pay. More new customers began arriving. By eight-thirty, I had my hands full. With this kind of business, I couldn't understand why Javier hadn't hired a waitress. Maybe I'd take out a help-wanted ad in the paper tomorrow. I had never been in the restaurant business. There was no way I could run this place alone.

You take it from here ...

Responding

1. Consider Assumptions   Compare with another student the lists of questions you made while reading. What assumptions must the reader make? Discuss why the author does not give all the answers to the reader.

2. Connect Setting and Character   In the first sentence of the story, the narrator claims to have been "lured" into the restaurant. Make a list of words or expressions at the beginning of the story that suggest why the restaurant appeals to the narrator. In a paragraph, explain what you can infer about the narrator from the choice of restaurant.

3. Analyze Irony   *Situational irony* occurs when events develop in a way that is unexpected in a particular situation. In one or two paragraphs, explain the situational irony in this story and evaluate how realistic the narrator's response is at the end of the story.

4. Reflect on an Issue   This story touches on the issue of illegal immigration. As a class, consider why people sometimes want to leave their country of origin, even if they have to do so illegally. What risks do illegal immigrants face? Why might they be willing to accept such risks?

Extending

TIPS
- Provide background detail to help your audience understand the situation.
- Add suspense.
- Focus on taking responsibility.
- Finish with an interesting conclusion.

5. Make an Informal Oral Presentation   Recall or invent a specific situation where you or someone else had to step in and take responsibility. Tell your story to the class.

6. Develop a Storyboard   Using the descriptive details in the story, develop a storyboard of about five to seven frames showing key shots that could be used to create a video. Be sure to include dialogue between the characters.

7. Write from a Different Perspective   Write a diary entry from Javier's point of view reflecting on the events of the day and on what might happen next to him and his job.

Before you read, as a class, discuss what our appearance says about us as individuals.

As you read, decide which side of the issue you support more strongly.

In some cases people just remove their jewellery for work.

Sporting That Strangely Piercing Look

by SHARON LINDORES

NEWSPAPER ARTICLE

Notes

Sharon Lindores is a staff writer for the *Kingston Whig-Standard*.

"The company has a reputation and image as a forward-thinking company and obviously style, trends, and fashion help make for a dynamic workforce. So we wouldn't think of discriminating against that."
– Jeff Welke, Telus manager of external communications

Sean Greene was hired by Telus Planet, long-distance over the phone, sight unseen.

But the fact that the computer analyst wears silver barbell facial jewellery to work doesn't matter, because Telus has a fairly progressive attitude.

"The company has a reputation and image as a forward-thinking company and obviously style, trends, and fashion help make for a dynamic workforce," said Jeff Welke, Telus manager of external communications. "So we wouldn't think of discriminating against that."

Facial jewellery is becoming more and more status quo in the under-35 age group.

But companies faced with employees wearing rings on their eyebrows or lips are still grappling with public perception.

Shawn Paulson, Telus human resources representative, agreed pierced faces wouldn't be an issue in terms of hiring. He hinted that people dealing with the public may have to use discretion in some departments.

But Greene, 32, wears a silver barbell through the top of his nose bridge and another barbell lengthwise through his left ear at work.

He's offered to lose the potentially more offensive ear barbell if he gets an internal transfer. (You can't see his nose barbell when he wears his glasses.)

"If something's at stake like a job, I want as much on my side as possible," Greene said. "I don't want to possibly offend anyone."

He was told it wasn't necessary to remove the jewellery.

That's also what Danika Dennis, 18, was told when she forgot to take her eyebrow ring out for work at a local car dealership.

She thought it was great to be able to wear it at work.

Dennis, who works in the back shop, was originally hired as a work experience student from Queen Elizabeth Composite High School. The school's coordinator told her to take the ring out when she went for her job interview. Dennis did and she took it out for work as well until she discovered that nobody cared if she did wear it.

The firm's service manager was hesitant about the topic and asked that his name not be used in this article. He said piercings don't bother him personally.

"But I don't think we'd allow it (employees with pierced eyebrows or lips) in front of the public," he said. "We don't have a set policy in place for ear piercing or whatever."

The military does.

And now that Dennis has joined the military, she'll have to start taking her eyebrow ring out again.

Women are restricted to wearing only one earring per ear.

"They're very strict," Dennis said.

Representatives from companies such as Interprovincial Pipe Line Ltd. and EPCOR were ambiguous about their policies. Employees are expected to dress "appropriately" and to respect any company safety concerns.

Jewellery is not dealt with under employment standards.

But in some cases, it might be covered by human rights legislation.

"Human rights legislation is intended to protect things people can't change, like colour and where people come from," said Marie Riddle, director of the Human Rights and Citizenship Commission.

If wearing jewellery was truly an aspect of a religion, like hair length and beards sometimes are, it could be covered, she said.

So, if someone thought they were discriminated against on the basis of facial piercings, it would have to be dealt with on an individual basis.

"Employers do have the right to establish appearance, grooming, and dress standards they believe are necessary," Riddle said.

Many chains don't approve of pierced faces.

In some cases people just remove their jewellery for work.

That's not a problem for Lisa Spitkouski, 22. A body piercer at Ritualistics, she has 28 piercings on her face. She thinks piercings, especially singular piercings, should be accepted in the workplace.

"I really don't think the person ordering two Big Macs cares," Spitkouski said. "You shouldn't judge a book by its cover. Especially if a person's getting paid minimum wage."

Karen Kent, human resources associate at the Kingsway Bay, said a person's qualifications and personality easily outweigh appearance in the grand scheme of things.

"If they're a friendly, people-person overall, what they have done to their eyebrow doesn't matter," Kent said.

"If they had a football attached to their nose, it might be taken into consideration," she said.

"A lot of nose rings are very nice. And if it's a nice little diamond, it's not a big issue."

Some employers might even like employees with piercings, said Shaliza Shorey, Hire-A-Student representative.

The organization, which sees some pierced students looking for work, doesn't advise them to remove jewellery.

"Some places like M.A.C. at the Bay might even prefer it, but it probably wouldn't go over well in a federal government office," Shorey said.

You take it from here ...

Responding

1. **Summarize Opinions** Make a two-column chart to record the opinions of the people quoted in the article. Which side of the argument makes the more convincing points? In one sentence, summarize the argument of the side you selected.

Body jewellery should be allowed at work because ...	Body jewellery should not be allowed at work because ...

2. **Interpret Meanings** With one or two other students, discuss why some companies and organizations have strict policies about body piercings while others do not. What reasons might some companies have for creating policies to ensure that their employees dress appropriately?

3. **Discuss Form and Organization** With a partner, list the specific features of this selection that are common to most newspaper articles.

TIPS

Be sure you refer to
- the use of names throughout the article
- layout and organization
- both visual and textual information

Extending

4. Prepare a Debate Have a class debate on one of the following topics:

   - In the workplace, qualifications and personality outweigh appearance as factors in success.
   - The rights of the employee should be above the rights of the employer.
   - No one should be required to wear a uniform in school or in the workplace.

5. Write a Policy With a partner, imagine that you are employers. Identify the type of work your company does, and develop an appropriate policy for the personal appearance of your employees.

SELF-ASSESSMENT

   - Did you find this task challenging?
   - Did you present valid ideas to your partner and listen with an open mind to your partner's ideas?
   - Did you share responsibilities equally with your partner?
   - Were you pleased with the end result?

Before you read, in small groups, talk about any jobs you have had in the past and how you were hired.

As you read, make note of any information in the article that repeats or emphasizes what was talked about in your small group.

First impressions are often lasting impressions.

Four Minutes That Get You Hired

by CONNIE BROWN GLASER
AND BARBARA STEINBERG SMALLEY

ADAPTED FROM *MORE POWER TO YOU!*

Notes

Connie Brown Glaser and Barbara Steinberg Smalley are American writers who have collaborated on a number of books about how to succeed in business.

The 28-year-old had spent six years working nights and going to college during the day. "I've always wanted to be a teacher," she says, "and I worked hard to earn my degree. When I finally graduated, I was very optimistic." She had her eye on a teaching position at an elementary school in a Boston suburb.

With the help of friends who teach at the school, she landed an interview with the principal. "I noticed a tiny run in my stockings that morning," she recalls. "I thought about changing, but I knew I'd be late if I did. By the time I got to the interview, the run stretched from my ankle to my knee. I walked in and immediately apologized for not looking my best. I spent the rest of the time trying to sit in a way that he couldn't see the run."

The would-be teacher didn't get the job. In fact, one of her friends told her the principal's only comment was, "If a person doesn't take the time to present her best image at an interview, what kind of teacher is she going to be?"

First impressions are often lasting impressions. Indeed, if you play your cards right, you can enjoy the benefits of what sociologists call the halo effect. This means that if you're viewed positively within the critical first four minutes, the person you've met will likely assume everything you do is positive.

Four minutes! Studies tell us that's the amount of time we have to make an impression on someone we've just met. And within a mere *10 seconds*, that person will begin to make judgements about our professionalism, social class, morals, and intelligence. People tend to focus on what they see (dress, eye contact, movement), on what they hear (how fast or slow we talk, our voice tone and volume), and on our actual words.

Bungle a first encounter, and in many cases the interviewer will mistakenly assume you have a slew of other negative traits. Worse, he or she may not take the time to give you a second chance.

Most employers believe that those who look as if they care about themselves are more likely to care about their jobs. We know "it's what's inside that counts," but research shows that physically attractive people are generally perceived by prospective employers as more intelligent, likable, and credible. Your goal should be to come across in the best possible light—attractive in the way you dress, in your gestures and facial expressions, and in your speech.

Here's how to make those crucial four minutes count:

Look your best. It signals success. Studies have linked clothing consciousness to higher self-esteem and job satisfaction. And one study funded by the Clairol Corporation found that it pays, literally, to project a professional image. Judith Waters, a professor at Fairleigh Dickinson University in New Jersey, sent out identical résumés with either a "before" or an "after" photograph of hypothetical job candidates to more than 300 companies. (No company received both "before" and "after" photos of the same person.) Waters asked them to determine a starting salary for each "candidate." The result? Salaries were 8 to 20 percent higher for those whose résumés had been accompanied by the photo with an upgraded image.

Yet many people fail to understand the importance of projecting a professional image. For example, a 32-year-old in Washington worked for 10 years as an administrative assistant in a large accounting firm. When the office manager retired last year, she applied for the position. She wasn't even granted an interview.

"I thought it was an oversight, so I asked the director of personnel what happened," she says. "He told me I didn't fit the image of an office manager. He suggested I revamp my wardrobe—get rid of my neon-coloured skirts and dangling earrings—before I applied again for another position. I was shocked. I do a great job, and the way I dress shouldn't have any bearing. My clothes reflect my personal style."

Forget about personal style. At work, your clothes must convey the message that you are competent, reliable, and authoritative.

Dress for the job you *want*, not the job you have. If you're scheduled for an interview at a company you've never visited and aren't sure what to wear, send for a copy of its annual report and study what the employees pictured are wearing, or drop by ahead of time to see how they dress.

Monitor your body language. How you move and gesture will greatly influence an interviewer's first impression of you. In a landmark study of communications, psychologist Albert Mehrabian discovered that 7 percent of any message about our feelings and attitudes comes from the words we use, 38 percent from our voice, and a startling 55 percent from our facial expressions. In fact, when our facial expression or tone of voice conflicts with our words, the listener will typically put more weight on the nonverbal message.

Start your first encounter with a firm handshake. If the interviewer doesn't initiate the gesture, offer your hand first. Whenever you have a choice of seats, select a chair beside his or her desk, as opposed to one across from it.

That way there are no barriers between the two of you and the effect is somewhat less confrontational. If you must sit facing the desk, shift your chair slightly as you sit down, or angle your body in the chair so you're not directly in front of your interviewer.

Monitor your body language to make sure you don't seem too desperate for the job or too eager to please. When a 26-year-old telemarketing specialist in Athens, Georgia, applied for a promotion, her interview went so well she was offered a job on the spot. "I was ecstatic," she recalls. "But I reacted to the offer with too much enthusiasm. Once the boss sensed how excited I was, he knew I wasn't going to turn him down. Consequently, he offered me a lower salary than I'd hoped for. I'm convinced I could have got more had I contained myself."

Keep a poker face in business situations. Audrey Nelson-Schneider, a communications consultant in Boulder, Colorado, says that inappropriate smiling is the most common example of a nonverbal behaviour that undercuts verbal messages—making you appear weak and unassertive.

Good eye contact is also important. One study found that job applicants who make more eye contact are perceived as more alert, dependable, confident, and responsible.

Say what you mean. Your goal is to exude confidence and be believed. Clinch that favourable first impression by making your words consistent with your body language and appearance. If they aren't in sync, your mixed messages are bound to confuse your interviewer.

Open and close your conversation on a positive note. For example, if you've studied the company's annual report—and you should have!—consider remarking on any substantial progress the firm has made within the past year,

or cite an area of company involvement that interests you. When you leave, summarize why you're the best candidate for the job and thank the person for his interest.

Use a person's name when talking. It's the best way to get—and keep—his or her attention. And avoid verbal clutter. As business consultant Marian Woodall puts it: "Poor communicators tend to talk in paragraphs. Successful communicators talk in short sentences."

Master the art of small talk. Most people who *appear* comfortable with strangers in social and business situations will tell you they've worked hard to look that way. Their advice? Read a weekly newsmagazine and at least one daily newspaper—especially the sports section—so you can hold your own in a conversation.

Ask questions. Too often when people meet, they feel awkward about what to say after the introductions. Almost everyone likes to be asked questions, so don't be afraid to be the initiator.

Finally, there is the question of *how* you speak. Any voice coach will tell you that you can learn to sound more relaxed, more assertive, and more confident. One good technique is to record your voice on tape. "As you play it back, be alert for voice tones that sound apologetic, tentative, meek, or imploring," recommends Norma Carr-Ruffino, a management and communication consultant.

In his book *You Are the Message: Secrets of the Master Communicators*, media consultant Roger Ailes suggests a voice-improvement exercise he calls "tape and ape." Get a cassette tape of a famous actor or actress reading a classic. Record yourself reading the same selection and compare your performance. "Your goal isn't to become a performer," says Ailes. "But when you hear good speech and attempt to emulate it, you will improve your voice."

As Christoper Lasch states in his book *The Culture of Narcissism:* "Nothing succeeds like the appearance of success." So take advantage of those crucial first four minutes. Look your best, move with confidence, speak with conviction—and the job you want can be yours.

You take it from here ...

Responding

1. Find Main Points   According to the article, it takes only four minutes to make a lasting impression, positive or negative, at a job interview. As a class, identify and discuss the three main points this article stresses as important in making a positive impression.

2. Understand Audience and Purpose   With a partner, scan the article and find examples of the author's use of the following techniques:

   • statistics
   • quotations from experts and employment consultants
   • stories from personal experience

   Suggest reasons why the author has used each of these techniques.

3. Note Sentence Types   This article uses strong imperative sentences (short commands) to indicate key tips for success in an interview. One example is in paragraph 12, which begins "Forget about personal style." List at least five other imperative sentences that appear in the article. Suggest why the author put these commands at the beginning of paragraphs.

4. Focus on Writing Style   This article is written as a self-help guide and uses a conversational style, addressing the reader as "you" and using everyday informal language. Rewrite the following colloquial expressions in a more formal style.

   • "she landed an interview" (paragraph 2)
   • "if you play your cards right" (paragraph 4)
   • "it's what's inside that counts" (paragraph 7)
   • "keep a poker face" (paragraph 17)

Extending

5. Make a Checklist   As a class, compile a list of the "Top 10 Tips for a Successful Job Interview" based upon the information provided in this article. Format your list as a checklist.

6. Conduct Mock Interviews   In small groups, review the "Top 10 Tips" checklist from Activity 5. Take turns playing the roles of interviewer and interviewee, with the rest of the group using the checklist to assess the performance of each job applicant. Discuss the results of the role-playing based upon the checklist, remembering to emphasize the strengths as well as the weaknesses of the interviewees.

> ### SELF-ASSESSMENT
> - Did you feel more comfortable being the interviewer or the interviewee?
> - Did you offer constructive and fair criticism of other group members?
> - How was role-playing an interview different from thinking or reading about one?

7. Change Point of View   The success of an interview depends not only on the interviewee but also on the interviewer. Write a short article outlining three or four tips that can be used by an interviewer, explaining the importance of each one. Start each paragraph with a short imperative sentence.

The Far Side

Cartoon by Gary Larson

"OK, Mr. Hook. Seems you're trying to decide between a career in pirating or massage therapy. Well, maybe we can help you narrow it down."

You take it from here ...

Responding

1. Identify the Issue   In your own words, write the main message suggested in this cartoon.

2. Analyze Humour   With a partner, discuss what elements contribute to the humour of this cartoon. Do the picture and caption play an equal role, or is one more important than the other?

3. Write a Caption   Write an alternative caption for this cartoon that suggests an entirely different message but is still associated with the world of work. Share your caption with the rest of the class.

4. Look at Stereotypes   A *stereotype* is a fixed idea that is shared by many, but is usually closed-minded and often untrue. Critics might argue that this particular image reinforces stereotypes. What is one argument these critics could make? List several other work-related stereotypes that some people might hold.

Extending

5. Create a Dialogue   Write a dialogue between parents who want their teenage son or daughter to follow a particular career path and the son or daughter who wants to enter a very different field of work.

6. Prepare a Brochure   Think of a job you would like to do or a service you can offer, then create a one-page brochure advertising your skills and talents to potential clients or employers. Share your completed brochure with a small group of students for feedback and comments.

> **TIP**
> - Consider using word-processing or page-layout software to create your brochure.

PEER ASSESSMENT

- Was the information in the brochure neat and attractively presented?
- Was the text carefully proofread, with no errors in spelling or punctuation?
- Was the content convincing?

7. Assess a Job Skills Survey   Arrange with your teacher or a guidance counsellor to complete a computer-based personal job skills inventory, if one is available in your school. Then write a paragraph that states your reaction to the results in terms of how well the suggested career path meshes with your skills, personality, and interests.

Before you read, think about a time when you were angry because you were frustrated.

As you read, paraphrase each stanza in one sentence.

Notes

Alden Nowlan
(1933–1983) was born in Windsor, Nova Scotia. A well-known poet and journalist, he wrote 24 books and 3 plays in 27 years. He won the Governor General's Award for Poetry in 1967 and was Writer-in-Residence at the University of New Brunswick from 1968 to 1983.

Warren Pryor

Poem by Alden Nowlan

When every pencil meant a sacrifice
his parents boarded him at school in town,
slaving to free him from the stony fields,
the meagre acreage that bore them down.

They blushed with pride when, at his graduation,
they watched him picking up the slender scroll,
his passport from the years of brutal toil
and lonely patience in a barren hole.

When he went in the Bank their cups ran over.
They marvelled how he wore a milk-white shirt
work days and jeans on Sundays. He was saved
from their thistle-strewn farm and its red dirt.

And he said nothing. Hard and serious
like a young bear inside his teller's cage,
his axe-hewn hands upon the paper bills
aching with empty strength and throttled rage.

You take it from here ...

Responding

1. Discover the Story   In a few sentences write a summary of the story that is told in this poem.

2. Find Poetic Devices   This poem uses numerous poetic devices such as *metaphor, simile,* and rhyme. Find at least one example of each.

3. Review Tone   *Tone* is defined as the attitude of the poet or the speaker in the poem toward the subject of the poem. In a sentence or two, describe the tone of this poem, and then compare ideas with a partner.

4. Reflect on a Concept   How would Warren Pryor's parents define success? Have they been successful parents? How would Warren define success? What emotional conflict might he have with his parents? Do you feel sympathy for him or not? Share your ideas in a small group.

TIP

- If you need to review the definitions of these terms, look them up in the glossary at the back of the book.

Extending

5. Explore an Issue   This poem addresses the issue of happiness and fulfillment in one's work. Write a paragraph that explores your attitude toward this statement: "It's better to love your work and be poor, than to hate your work and be rich."

6. Identify a Connection   Many people can understand the frustration that Warren Pryor feels in coping with the pressures of others' expectations. Find song lyrics that deal with this theme, and create a comparison chart showing the similarities and differences with Nowlan's poem.

	Warren Pryor	Song Title
Source of frustration		
Reaction to frustration		

7. Develop Interview Questions   Imagine that you are a local news reporter preparing a profile on Warren Pryor. Develop a series of questions that you would ask his parents, and questions that you would ask Warren himself. Exchange your questions with a partner, and answer your partner's questions according to how you think the parents and Warren would answer them.

He never said much, and for a while we didn't say much to him.

The Hidden Songs of a Secret Soul

by Bob Greene

ESSAY

Notes

Bob Greene is a syndicated columnist with the *Chicago Tribune*. He has written several books, including a collection of reminiscences of his teen years titled *Be True to Your School: A Diary of 1964*.

Lenny was the loneliest of dreamers. No one knew; we wouldn't have known, either, except for the fact that the afternoons got long, and the only way to make it through was to talk. After a time we even talked to Lenny.

He worked in the shipping room of a bottling plant. It manufactured soda pop. Lenny was a thin, slight man in his middle forties with a stammer and a sad face. We worked at long tables. Lenny was the only full-timer at our table; the rest of us were in school, and we came in whatever afternoons we could spare and picked up pocket money for the weekends. For us, the job was a dreary way to kill time. For Lenny, it was his sustenance.

The other full-timers in the room liked to kid Lenny. Most of them were in their twenties, and they passed the day with talk of women and late-night intrigue. Lenny had no wife or family, and he never spoke of a woman.

So when the full-timers became bored with their own talk, they would call over to our table and rag Lenny some. They would ask him about his romances, and when he would become embarrassed and turn away and try not to answer, they would not let up until they became bored with bothering him. They didn't mean anything by it.

He never said much, and for a while we didn't say much to him. We would come in after classes, nod hello to him, and start loading boxes. Lenny had spent most of his life being invisible; we sensed that without really thinking about it. He just seemed happy that we didn't rag him like the others did.

One afternoon, though, he started to talk. He didn't slow up what he was doing, but as he worked he began to ask us about the classes we took in school, the courses we were studying. He asked if any of us were studying English as a major; he wanted to know if any of us were studying the great poets.

None of us thought much about the questions at first; I know I didn't. But after that, a couple of times every week, he would ask the same things. It was always about the poets. On the way back home in the evenings, we would talk about it, and wonder what he meant. One night we determined that we would find out.

So the next day, at break time, we asked Lenny to sit down for coffee with us. We had never had coffee with Lenny before; usually he would disappear on his break. One of us asked him about the poets.

"I just wondered," Lenny said. But we pressed.

He avoided it, and so we dropped it and finished our cups. Just before we were due back at our table, Lenny said, "Sometimes I write poems."

We went back to work and tried to make him tell us more. It was so unlikely, the idea of Lenny who seldom had the nerve to speak, and had trouble when he did, spending time committing his thoughts to paper. When we attempted to question him further, he became uncomfortable and flushed.

"Don't talk so loud," he pleaded. "The others will hear."

We asked him that day if he would let us see his poems, and he said no. We kept it up, though; we wanted to see. Finally he said that he would like to let us see them, but that he was afraid that if he brought them in, the others would find out and make fun of him.

We told him we would go with him to see the poems. He said he would think about it, and we did not let him forget. One day he said that we could come home with him if we wished.

After work we rode the el. He lived in one room. There were not enough places for us to sit. He brought out a large scrapbook. The poems were inside.

They were written all in longhand, with a fountain pen. Even before we started to read them, they looked elegant. Lenny's hand moved with strokes full of flourish and style, confident and strong while Lenny was timid and quiet. And when we did begin to read, the poems were beautiful. The verses were long, and rich with imagery and detail. They told of love, and of spiritual triumphs, and of life in faraway places. They were music. We must have sat and read for an hour, saying nothing. When we finished and looked up, there was Lenny, in his rented room, staring away from us.

"Please never say anything to the others," he said.

We tried to tell him how good the poems were, how he should be proud of what he had done, and not ashamed to let anyone know, but he cut us off.

"Please," he said. "I have to work there."

We went home, and the next day Lenny let us know, without a word, that we were not to talk about the poems again. For a few months we continued to work, and Lenny continued to take the joking from the other full-timers. Then school ended for the summer, and we left the job, and Lenny. We never went back.

The reason I am thinking about this is that I saw him the other day. There was no mistake; it was he. It was on a crowded street, and there was Lenny. I motioned to him, and called his name, and started walking toward him. He saw me; I know he did. He turned around very quickly and walked away, and I knew that I was not supposed to follow.

You take it from here ...

Responding

TIP

• Don't worry about exact dictionary-type definitions. Use the context (words and ideas around the underlined word) to guess at a meaning.

1. **Use Clues to Meaning** Set up a chart similar to the one below. Without using a dictionary, try to arrive at a meaning for the underlined word in each expression as it is used in the essay.

Quotations from the selection	My interpretations
"it was his <u>sustenance</u>" (paragraph 2)	
"late-night <u>intrigue</u>" (paragraph 3)	
"and <u>rag</u> Lenny some" (paragraph 3)	
"most of his life being <u>invisible</u>" (paragraph 4)	
"we rode the <u>el</u>" (paragraph 14)	
"They were <u>music</u>" (paragraph 15)	

2. **Examine Atmosphere** In your notebook, list several conflicts in this essay that help to develop an atmosphere of tension and anxiety.

3. **Focus on the Narrator** What are the narrator's feelings toward Lenny at the beginning of the story? After the narrator discovers that Lenny writes poems? Upon reading Lenny's poems? When the narrator sees Lenny at the end of the selection? Do you think the narrator was offended by Lenny's reaction? Why or why not? Share your ideas in a class discussion.

4. **Speculate about the Ending** Suggest a reason why Lenny ignored the narrator at the end of the essay. Is this an effective ending? Explain your opinion briefly in a paragraph.

Extending

5. **Write an Anecdote** Write a short account of your own unexpected discovery of a special talent in someone you thought you knew very well.

6. **Discuss a Quotation** One of the main issues explored in this story is peer pressure in the workplace. Early in the story, when commenting on the jokes and kidding of Lenny's co-workers, the narrator states "They didn't mean anything by it." Taking this quotation as a starting point, discuss the negative effects of peer pressure in the workplace.

TIP

• Use specific information from the story to suggest an idea for the poem.

7. **Create a Poem** Create the sort of poem that you think Lenny might have written in his scrapbook.

Notes

Shu Ting is the pen-name of Gong Peiyu, who was born in Fujian, China. She was forced to leave high school because of her father's political views and ended up working in a cement factory and a textile mill. While there, she started writing poems with powerful, delicate lyrics that have gained her an international reputation.

Assembly Line

Poem by Shu Ting

In time's assembly line
Night presses against night.
We come off the factory night-shift
In line as we march towards home.
Over our heads in a row
The assembly line of stars
Stretches across the sky.
Beside us, little trees
Stand numb in assembly lines.

The stars must be exhausted
After thousands of years
Of journeys which never change.
The little trees are all sick,
Choked on smog and monotony,
Stripped of their color and shape.
It's not hard to feel for them;
We share the same tempo and rhythm.

Yes, I'm numb to my own existence
As if, like the trees and stars
—perhaps just out of habit
—perhaps just out of sorrow,
I'm unable to show concern
For my own manufactured fate.

You take it from here ...

Responding

1. Find Details   The poet mentions several other assembly lines besides the one at the factory. Identify at least two of these.

2. Make Connections   Nature and the outdoors are often used to symbolize freedom and an escape from the workplace. Is this how they are being used here? Write a paragraph describing the feelings this poet associates with nature.

3. Understand Personification   *Personification* is a technique that gives human qualities to inanimate objects or nonhuman creatures. With a partner, find several examples of personification in this poem.

4. Explore Theme   In a sentence, state the theme of this poem.

Extending

5. Share Advice   Using the ideas expressed by the poet, write a letter to a "Dear Abby" newspaper columnist. Sign the letter with a descriptive name such as "Sick of the Job." Then write a response offering helpful advice to the letter-writer. Share your letters by reading them aloud in class.

6. Research a Career   In small groups, make a list of jobs that usually involve assembly-line work. Use the Internet, library, and other sources (including personal interviews) to find out more about what it is like to work on an assembly line. Present your findings to the class. In a class discussion, compare your findings to the brainstorming you did during the "Before you read" activity.

> **PEER ASSESSMENT**
> - Which presentation was most informative and why?
> - What additional information did you learn from other groups?

She scrambles under the truck with a wrench and half an hour later emerges covered with oil.

For Laurie, Truck Driving Paved Her Road to Freedom

by Danielle Bochove

PROFILE

Fifteen gears, coffee and cigarettes, classical music, and a tank full of diesel—Laurie Dwinnell has everything she wants in life.

Four years ago the 27-year-old had already worked as a real estate assistant, a labourer, and a journalist when she decided to try driving a rig—a family calling.

"It's something I always wanted to do. My father was a trucker and I remember he used to be gone for long periods of time and come back with oranges and grapefruits," she says, wheeling her 32-metre vehicle expertly out of the parking lot of Western Bulk Transport.

And her mother drove a gravel truck for a year, she adds.

Dwinnell breaks every stereotype associated with her profession. In a tough, traditionally male job, she's only 5'3" and 102 lbs, with thick red hair and freckles. Yet she's found a natural balance, neither playing up her femininity nor denying it. Her hair is cropped short, her baggy jeans, a lumberjack shirt, and steel-toed boots are strictly practical. A touch of mascara and lipstick are the only concessions to her sex.

Laurie Dwinnell behind the wheel of her 32-metre truck

She drives a 21 000-kilogram vehicle with 2 tanks, 7 axles, and 30 wheels, called a Super B. It's used for hauling dangerous goods, in her case highly poisonous, flammable, molten sulphur. Every 30 hours, year round, she fills up the tanks in Fort McMurray and hauls the sulphur south to Redwater where Esso uses it to make fertilizer and sulphuric acid.

It's a hard run: a 15-hour shift followed by 15 hours off, which means starting work at a different time each day.

Laurie adjusting the brakes

But she says, "I like the freedom to choose to work at three A.M. I hate nine to five."

It's not hard to stay awake, she adds, because she has to stop to check the tires every two hours and take breaks every six. She also keeps a thermos of coffee handy.

Once out of the city, the highway is straight and unchanging. Grain elevators slide by like giant cardboard dollhouses. Rippling fields of wheat and lush canola gleam in the mid-morning sun.

A flashing sign on the roadside tells trucks to pull over to be weighed. Redwater RCMP are doing safety inspections. They find 3 of her 16 brake pads are slightly misaligned.

She scrambles under the truck with a wrench and half an hour later emerges covered with oil. But back on the road, her easygoing manner doesn't waver; she's glad for the RCMP interference.

"My brakes could be faulty and maybe that mechanic would catch something I wouldn't have," she says. "And if I'm overweight that endangers you, as a motorist."

Dwinnell says the hardest part of becoming a driver is coming to terms with the responsibility.

"Knowing that you've got sixty-two five (62 500 kilograms) on there and if someone cuts in front of you, and you can't do anything, you're going to run right over them."

What isn't tough, she insists, is being a woman, although there are still only a handful of female truckers across the country. She gets startled looks from people on the road, but among her co-workers her sex has never been a problem.

The key, she says, is to "just be yourself. I'm not saying try to be a lady or anything but be yourself. Don't try to be a man because men are tougher than us. They are. But if you can do your job, that's all that matters."

She says the reason so few women drive trucks is not that men try to hold them back, but that women underestimate themselves.

"Every woman I know is shocked and surprised when they find out I'm a driver. I went to my 10-year high-school reunion and they were all happy and excited—but they're not doing it."

At 3:30 P.M., it's time for lunch. The work can be tough, she admits between bites of a roast beef sandwich at the Marianna Lake Lodge Cafe, but there are ways of making the job easier. By keeping equipment well greased, or using a snipe (a kind of crowbar) she compensates for her size.

"You can work around anything if you use your brain. You don't need muscle. It might take a little longer but you don't hurt yourself."

Back on the highway, the fields are gold under the late-afternoon sun and it's a smooth ride into Fort McMurray and Syncrude. By 7:45 P.M. the tanks are full and she's back on the road, heading south.

Driving with a full load is much tougher; the truck labours up even small hills.

It's getting dark and the sun is a sinking glow on the horizon.

Your eyes play tricks when dusk is turning to night, Laurie says. Trees look like animals; you have to stay alert.

She talks a bit about trucker stereotypes— the unwashed driver drinking beer and playing pool in a smoke-filled stop.

"It just doesn't exist. And even when it did exist it wasn't stupid truckers, it was stupid men. It was just easier to call them all truckers," she says angrily.

"They're looking scruffy for a reason. They've been out all day hauling a load."

She also says it's a myth that truckers are lonely people. Most are nature lovers; they drive because they love the scenery. Because of their gruelling schedules and the dangers of the job, they make every second count.

She pulls up in the Marianna parking lot, grabbing her coffee cup. By the time Dwinnell is back on the road, it's completely dark.

Now, more than ever, one has the sense that the forest is threatening to swallow up the road.

Rounding a corner, an oncoming truck resembles a charging monster. The two mechanical dragons snort and flash their high beams through the gathering mist.

When she finally pulls into Redwater, it's 2:30 A.M. and freezing cold. She weighs in, hooks up the 20-kilogram hose, and begins draining the load, one tank at a time.

When she gets to the second tank, the air valve—which has to be opened when the tank drains to prevent it from collapsing—is jammed. She grabs a hammer, climbs on top of the truck, and starts pounding. In the winter, when it's often –30°, she has to use a steam hose just to keep the sulphur running.

Still, the weather, the hours, and the risks are all part of the attraction of trucking. Truckers live for the moment.

"Every day is precious. And our days are longer. We sleep less, we see more in a day."

It's 4:30 A.M. when she finally hands the keys over to her partner. He'll do the same run, be back in 15 hours, and then she'll do it all over again.

You take it from here ...

Responding

1. Discuss Attitude   In a class discussion, consider the following questions:

   - What parts of Laurie's job give her satisfaction?
   - Where does she show concern and responsibility for doing her job well?
   - What are some of the challenges she faces on the job? How does she overcome these challenges?
   - How does Laurie's job fit with her personality?

2. Look at Method of Organization   This profile uses a common journalistic structure that is sometimes known as the "Day in the Life" approach. Using the times and details provided by the author, write out a logsheet of Laurie's 15-hour day.

> **TIP**
>
> - Set up the logsheet with the time in the left-hand margin. Be sure to use a colon to separate the hours and minutes, and indicate morning or evening with "P.M." or "A.M." (e.g., 7:45 P.M.).

3. Search for Imagery   With a partner, find at least three examples of images that create vivid pictures in the mind of the reader. Analyze how the writer has conveyed these images so clearly (e.g., through word choice, and close observation of details).

Extending

4. Express an Opinion   Write a short opinion piece agreeing or disagreeing with the following statement: "Society could not function without stereotypes." Then share your views in a class discussion.

5. Write an Article   Think of other examples of women breaking ground by taking on traditionally "male" jobs. Search the library and Internet for stories that are similar to Laurie's, and write a magazine article focusing on a particular individual or occupation.

It's just not something the North American male usually grows up to be.

The World of the Stay-at-Home Dad

by Andrew Olscher

ESSAY

Notes

Besides being a stay-at-home Dad, Andrew Olscher also describes himself as "a visual and martial artist, writer, musician, and actor." He has a degree in music, and his art has been exhibited internationally. Many examples of his photographs, sculptures, paintings, and cartoons can be found on the Internet.

Mr. Mom: the title of a 1983 comedy film about a husband who exchanges roles with his wife to become a homemaker

veracity: truthfulness

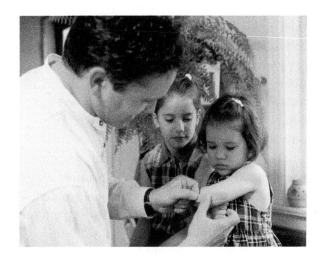

It doesn't seem so long ago that I took my first solo walk behind the baby stroller—the diaper bag slung over the handlebar, packed with enough diapers and wipes to last the better part of two days.

The baby, resembling an oversized bowling pin wrapped neatly in an overabundance of blankets, snoozed comfortably in the fresh late-summer air.

Despite all the talking I had done in the preceding few months about caring little about what others thought of my decision to be a

"stay-at-home" dad, I still gave in to my self-consciousness, the "maleness" that persuaded me to give a little extra weight and strength to my stride as I purposefully toured the neighbourhood.

The warm afternoon passed more than five years ago and with it some of the unsettling feelings that come with taking on a role traditionally reserved for women.

But as much as I would like to think that crossing over into the realm of stay-at-home parenting was a giant step for mankind—yes, I

did mean *man*kind—I have learned that both men and women have a long way to go when it comes to role reversals and sexist attitudes.

Myriad studies and magazine and newspaper articles have been churned out on women in the male-dominated workplace. But what about men in what used to be a female-only domain?

There's nothing like a dose of stay-at-home parenting to make you realize that women are as quick to stereotype men as men are women.

Take the article in *The Toronto Star* some time ago, "No Takers for 'Mr. Mom's' Baby-Sitting Service," about Peter Wright from Cambridge, Ontario, who advertised daycare spaces in his home. His wife said, "No woman would entrust the daily care of her children to a man." She was right. He got virtually no response.

The underlying message is that men don't know how to care for children, or perhaps this man has some more devious motive for advertising. Either assumption is unfair. Add to that the male reporter's reference to "Mr. Mom" and in the minds of many the perception of the stay-at-home dad might round out to be just a little weird.

It is not that the term "Mr. Mom" is terribly offensive in itself. I've only ever heard it used in a lighthearted manner. It's just that after being called that a number of times by both men and women, I have felt a distinct inclination to check whether I have been secretly neutered. Why is it so hard to accept that men who stay at home with their children as the primary caregiver are just that—men.

But whether it be "Mr. Mom," or another term like "baby-sitter" (which also has begun to grate as it conjures up an image falling far short of someone assuming all the responsibilities associated with stay-at-home parenting), the fact remains that it takes a certain amount of time to become accepted as a stay-at-home dad and all the position entails. It's just not something the North American male usually grows up to be. Cooking, cleaning, and taking care of the children is not supposed to be our forte.

But in all fairness, the rewards of being a stay-at-home dad—establishing that special bond with your children, watching them take their first steps, hearing them say those first words, and seeing them grow into unique individuals—far outweigh the negative side of being the object of sexist attitudes.

Being the object of sexual stereotyping can have its advantages. At times it has left me feeling rather special. It has raised my level of self-esteem as I assumed my own position in the male-versus-female arena of misperception.

Once convinced of the veracity of my stay-at-home status, most women tend to treat me with a fair amount of respect. (Having reasonably well-behaved children who eat abnormal amounts of broccoli and bringing homemade lasagne and cream puffs to potluck lunches at my local family resource centre seem to have gone a long way.)

Slipping the bonds of the male stereotype and having become a kindred spirit in a tough profession that offers no pension, no sick leave, no overtime, and in many cases little respect has entitled me to some special privileges. Many traditional male/female barriers have been eliminated. I've been able to gain an insight into what traditionally have been women's and mothers' problems—feelings of isolation and loneliness, occasionally frustration with both your children and spouse, a lack of respect from the government in its refusal to even consider us part of the "official" workforce, to name but a few.

Often, I've gained insight out of necessity and sometimes because women have learned to trust me and have confided in me. I've begun to see things through their eyes and gained a better understanding of what makes all of us tick.

Sadly, though, it has become quite apparent that becoming a stay-at-home dad was by no means a giant step for mankind—or for womankind either. At most I have managed to make a small change in the way some women perceive men. I think it will be a long time before a man like Mr. Wright will have any luck advertising daycare in his home.

Barriers between men and women as a result of sexual stereotyping will probably take more than several generations of stay-at-home dads to bring down. It is just too bad it has to be that way when a good dose of trust, respect, and understanding would quite likely accomplish the same thing.

You take it from here ...

Responding

1. Find the Main Idea   Select the sentence from the essay that you think best states its main idea or thesis. Write out the sentence and explain why it is a good summary of the focus of the essay.

2. Understand the Importance of Details   List three details that make the author's story believable. Why is the fact that the author seems to know what he is writing about important for the point he is making? Share your ideas in a class discussion.

3. Reflect on Audience and Purpose   With a partner, suggest potential audiences for this selection and explain your reasons. What do you think is the author's purpose in writing this essay?

4. Evaluate Experiences   Review the selection and make a list of ways in which the author has been personally enriched by the experience of being a stay-at-home dad.

The World of the Stay-at-Home Dad

Extending

5. Write a Short Position Statement   As a class, discuss what the author means when he says that stay-at-home parents, whether male or female, feel there is "a lack of respect from the government in its refusal to even consider us part of the 'official' workforce." Then, write a short position paper expressing your opinion about whether stay-at-home parents should be paid for the work they do. Support your opinion with reasons.

6. Study Media Images   In a small group, brainstorm a list of movies and TV shows that feature a male caring for small children. Then, working individually, choose one to view and analyze. Notice how the TV/movie character is portrayed—Realistically? Stereotypically? Both? How do the experiences of the male protagonist compare with the ones Andrew Olscher describes? Present your analysis in the form of a brief written report.

7. Switch Point of View   Imagine how people might react to the author's spouse when they discover that she is the main wage-earner while her husband has taken on full-time childcare duties. What feelings might she have, and what problems and benefits might she encounter as a result of her family's decision? Using "The World of the Stay-at-Home Dad" as a model, write an essay that tells the story from her point of view.

She discovered a knack for sword swallowing.

Weird, Odd, and Unusual Jobs and the People Who Love Them

by Charlene Rooke

INTERNET ARTICLE

Notes

Charlene Rooke is an Alberta author who has published books and edited the alumni magazine for the University of Alberta. Her writing has also appeared in *Realm*, the *Financial Post*, and various Calgary magazines.

elicit: draw out

entrepreneur: person who manages a business, aiming to make a profit

tai chi: Chinese martial art using a series of stances and slow moves to achieve well-being and a meditative state

When quizzed on what they want to be when they grow up, children often cite fantastic and unusual careers that involve working with exotic animals or travelling to outer space. Few actually grow up to do such work. But there are some for whom those out-of-the-ordinary dreams do materialize into weird, odd, and unusual jobs—jobs that not only make good party conversation, but which also become the kind of careers where the rewards transcend the raised eyebrows and quizzical looks they get when explaining what they do for a living.

Take Rion White, for example. As a kid growing up in Moose Jaw, Saskatchewan, his primary fascination was with animals. As a teenager, White's interest in the outdoors and hunting led him to become a North American champion deer hunter. Then he began to take an interest in taxidermy, the art of preparing, stuffing, and mounting animal skins. Last year, at age 21, White became the youngest-ever world champion taxidermist at a competition in Illinois. His award-winning moose head featured a pedestal-style mount and a 14-inch-long, lifelike open mouth. "To win, you have to do something out of the ordinary. It's very competitive," says White, who has also worked on full-body mounts of bears, moose, and even an elephant. "Taxidermy demonstrates respect by not discarding the dead animal."

These days, White is more likely to shoot animals with a camera than with a gun, to capture how they move. He also sculpts, paints, and airbrushes—arts that White learned from master craftsmen in Iowa. White is also an entrepreneur. He mentors students at Orion Taxidermy, his four-year-old business that turns out an average of one deer head a day for local and visiting American hunters. "This is my life work, for sure."

Highrise window washer James Orford also started his out-of-the ordinary career at a young age. At 12, he was working for his father's window-cleaning business, but these days you'll find him as high as 340 feet above ground improving the view for tenants of Vancouver's apartments and commercial highrises. Dirt, pollution, salt water, bugs, and, uh, deposits left by high-flying birds are what Orford faces daily. In the line of duty, he may also inadvertently observe building residents in all their manifestations. "You see a lot of weird stuff, bizarre things," Orford laughs.

It's enough to make you fall out of your bosun's chair—that's the contraption, suspended by two cables, that anchors Orford while he works. "Basically, it's a plywood board a bit wider than your butt," he says, with a smile. Such a free-spirited—and free-swinging—job not only gives Orford career satisfaction, but also offers a terrific, ever-changing view of the city. Sure, he says, there are some shifty moments (like 50 km/hour winds that can buffet you against the side of a building with dangerous force), but nothing fazes Orford, who says, "I've been doing this a long time."

There's something to be said for longevity in a dangerous job. Take 35-year-old Megan Evans of Calgary, who, for the last eight years, has been one of only a handful of female sword swallowers in the world. Her unusual job came along when a friend inherited a sideshow museum. Evans, an art college graduate who is a successful visual artist, quips, "Fire eating left a bad taste in my mouth." She discovered a knack for sword swallowing, which today is a lucrative sideline that takes her everywhere from private parties to a recent appearance on the *Maury Povich* show in New York.

Evans's well-conditioned gag reflex makes her a favourite of gastroenterologists, who can poke all manner of implements down her throat (they're no competition for her usual scissors, bayonets, and swords). Despite the dangers, Evans says her job is relaxing: "You have to do tai chi and yoga moves before swallowing the swords; it's a therapeutic thing, almost self-hypnosis."

If an unfortunate sword-swallowing accident lands you in the hospital, you might run into Dov Mickelson, an Edmonton actor who is occasionally hired to play a patient in medical school testing scenarios. In the spectrum of Mickelson's acting career, the gig falls somewhere between doing Shakespeare and the time the stocky, red-haired actor impersonated Elvis and toured a supermarket chain. "You're presenting the medical students with as real a situation as possible. I guess it's what Method acting would really be like," he says.

Several days of training go into a single day of work, during which Mickelson plays a patient for several medical students. "There's a lot on the line for the students. It's very challenging.

It's just you and them, one on one." A physician observes and grades the student—but not the actor. There's no applause or audience feedback, but the work has a different kind of intensity and reward, Mickelson says. It has also had a side effect: "When I go to a doctor, I'm so clear in how I describe my symptoms. It's made me a better patient," he laughs.

While Mickelson focuses on understanding the symptoms of a medical patient, Kristin Tillquist is busy deciphering her true calling, which sounds suspiciously like a dog barking. Three years ago, the 29-year-old Vancouver lawyer became Canada's only pet lawyer. No, she's not placing Fido on the stand, but litigating and negotiating the complex world of contracts, torts, and laws relating to animal bites, purebred breeders, and landlord–tenant disputes surrounding pets.

Tillquist heard about successful American dog lawyers and realized that pet law would fill a niche in the Canadian legal community. "It's not creating a new area, but consolidating this area of the law," explains Tillquist, who says pet law cases were previously scattered among lawyers with various levels of expertise in the area. Her love of animals had something to do with her choice but, she says, "As any lawyer will tell you, if you are emotionally or personally involved, you won't do as good a job." She sits on the Animal Welfare Committee of the Vancouver Regional Branch of the SPCA and says, "I am very much an advocate for animals in my personal life."

For Lisa Rochford, personal life and work are intimately intertwined. The 33-year-old is away from her London, Ontario, home for as much as six months of the year. But her plight certainly doesn't elicit much sympathy, considering her full-time job with Carlar Hospitality Consultants involves staying in luxury hotels around the world and evaluating their service, performance, and facilities. "One of the most important aspects of the job is the ability to notice details," says Rochford, who has a background in hospitality and public relations. "From the moment you enter the hotel to the moment you leave, you're working," she adds, explaining that 18-hour days are the norm. It may sound glamorous, but Rochford says you have to love meeting new people, spending a lot of time alone and, of course, travelling. "It's an incredible opportunity to see the world."

To be of service to humanity is the life goal of Unity Schooley. The 27-year-old recently moved from Nelson, British Columbia, to Vancouver to pursue his goal of bringing joy to kids of all ages with his artistic balloon creations. "Adults are little kids, too," he says. "They need balloons more than kids do. It's good therapy."

Schooley was sitting on a park bench one day, dreaming of a career where customers would come to him; he looked across the park and there was a balloon man, surrounded by fans. After months of practice, Schooley has become a top balloon artist and a regular fixture at Granville Island Market in his rainbow-coloured apron. Schooley can create a life-size, jiggly-eyed Elmo out of a handful of 260s (the trade name for the long, skinny animal balloons) in a few minutes of well-practised puffs, twists, and ties. His work requires good memory, a sense of artistic balance and symmetry, and the endurance to perform all day. "Kids can be pretty demanding," he says.

Perhaps it's an unusual career, but the looks on the faces of the kids in the crowd make it worthwhile. Plus, admits Schooley, who changed his first name to Unity on his last birthday, "I guess I'm a little unusual myself." In that statement, he sums up what all these people know: If you love your job and it suits you, that's the most unique combination of all.

You take it from here ...

Responding

1. Categorize Information   Make a chart summarizing key information about each of the individuals profiled in this article. Use only details specifically stated in the article.

Name	Job	Special skills	Benefits	Drawbacks
Rion White	Taxidermist	hunting sculpting painting airbrushing	• works with animals • often works outdoors	• none stated

2. Make Comparisons   A *comparison* looks at similarities among people, things, or ideas. Even though the individuals and jobs presented in this article are very different, they have several things in common. With a partner, identify these similarities.

3. Achieve Consensus through Discussion   According to the article, for each of these jobs, "the rewards transcend the raised eyebrows and quizzical looks." Write down what you think this statement means, and then share your ideas in a small group. Attempt to arrive at a consensus (common agreement).

Extending

4. Imagine a Dream Job   If you could have any job in the world, what would it be? In your journal, describe your dream job in detail. Include your answers to the following questions:

- What are some probable benefits and drawbacks of the job?
- What would the challenges of the job be?
- Is it a high-risk or a low-risk job?
- Would you work alone or with others?
- What would others say about the way you perform your job?
- Would your job be important to society?

5. Debate an Issue   Have a class debate on the following resolution: "Job satisfaction is more important than job security and steady pay."

SELF-ASSESSMENT
- Did you listen respectfully to others whose opinions differ from your own?
- Did you effectively explain and defend your own ideas?

6. Conduct an Interview   Develop a series of questions that you could use to conduct a short interview with someone you know (e.g., a friend, relative, employer, teacher) about how he or she came to choose a particular career. Use your notes to write a profile of the person you interviewed.

Notes

James Keelaghan is a Calgary-based folk singer and songwriter who studied history at the University of Calgary. Commenting on his education, Keelaghan has said, "I did learn how to spot a good story." He plays more than 300 concerts a year and reads to relax while on the road.

This song, from Keelaghan's 1995 album *A Recent Future*, is based on an actual historical event—the 1949 Mann Gulch fire in Montana that overran 16 firefighters, killing 13 of them. R. Wagner ("Wag") Dodge was the crew foreman, one of three who survived the tragedy only to die of cancer five years later. There is an excellent summary of the event at the following Web address: www.lib.duke. edu/forest/Publications/ 13thfire.html.

Cold Missouri Waters

Lyrics by James Keelaghan

My name is Dodge, but then you know that
It's written on the chart there at the foot end of the bed
They think I'm blind, I can't read it
I've read it every word
And every word it says is death
So, Confession
Is that the reason that you came
Get it off my chest before I check out of the game
Since you mention it well there's thirteen things I'll name
Thirteen crosses high above the cold Missouri waters

August 'Forty-Nine, north Montana
The hottest day on record and the forest tinder dry
Lightning strikes in the mountains
I was crew chief at the jump base
I prepared the boys to fly
Pick the drop zone
C-47 comes in low
Feel the tap upon your leg that tells you go
See the circle of the fire down below
Fifteen of us dropped above the cold Missouri waters

Gauged the fire, I'd seen bigger
So I ordered them to sidehill, we'd fight it from below
We'd have our backs to the river
We'd have it licked by morning,
Even if we took it slow
But the fire crowned, jumped the valley just ahead
There was no way down headed for the ridge instead
Too big to fight it we'd have to fight that slope instead
Flames one step behind above the cold Missouri waters

Sky had turned red, smoke was boiling
Two hundred yards to safety, death was fifty yards behind
I don't know why I just thought it
I struck a match to waist high grass
Running out of time
Tried to tell them, step into this fire I set
We can't make it, this is the only chance you'll get
But they cursed me ran for the rocks above instead
I lay face down and prayed above the cold Missouri waters

And when I arose, like the phoenix
In that world reduced to ashes there were none but two survived
I stayed that night and one day after
Carried bodies to the river
Wondered how I stayed alive
Thirteen stations of the cross to mark their fall
I've had my say, I'll confess to nothing more
I'll join them now, because they left me long before
Thirteen crosses high above the cold Missouri waters
Thirteen crosses high above the cold Missouri shore

You take it from here ...

Responding

1. Answer *W5* Questions   Answer the following questions in point form:

   - Who is Dodge?
   - What happened at the fire?
   - Where did the event described in the song take place?
   - When did the event take place?
   - Why is Dodge telling his story?

2. Interpret Details   Write a paragraph describing in your own words how Dodge managed to save himself.

3. Make Deductions   Dodge is talking to someone visiting him in hospital. He addresses his visitor as "you," not by name. He suggests that his visitor has come to hear a confession. In a class discussion, consider who the visitor might be. What feelings does Dodge seem to have? Why might this be?

4. Assess Context   Would you react differently to this song if you were unaware that it is based on a true story? Does it have more impact because the events described actually took place? Share your ideas with a partner.

Extending

5. Write a Newspaper Article   Using the details in your response to Activity 1 and any other information you can obtain, write a report of the Mann Gulch fire as it might have appeared in a local newspaper the following day.

6. Focus on Genre   As a class, listen to a recording of "Cold Missouri Waters." Then, with a partner, find lyrics (and, if possible, a recording) of another folk song that tells the story of a well-known event. Share the song with the class and compare it to "Cold Missouri Waters."

> **TIP**
>
> - For more details about the story, visit the Web site identified in the Notes section. You can find additional information on the Internet and in the library.

Before you read, as a class, discuss the following question: Should parents or teachers be supportive of your choice of career, even if they don't agree with it?

As you read, make a list of questions you need to ask yourself when making decisions about your own career.

Tamara found herself working successfully in a job that she did not really like.

When Choosing Your Path, Follow Your Heart

by Elizabeth Newton

NEWSPAPER ARTICLE

It's every parent's nightmare. "Mum, Dad, I want to go into the arts."

High-school graduates who want to do something artistic as a career are among the most frequent parent referrals to career counselling.

"Are you sure?"

"What about the penury, the rejection, the total lack of stability?"

Some of the most unhappy working adults, on the other hand, are those who have long wanted to do something more creative with their careers but now feel it is too late to change.

The creative urge is uncommonly strong, yet it is tough to take that first step into a design or applied-arts career. Most people don't. It feels too impractical, too competitive, too risky.

Paul Larocque grew up "personally passionate" about the arts.

"The arts have had a huge impact on me," he says. "Growing up, they were always so important to me. At one time I dreamed about an arts career in my life, but I realized that it wasn't a reality for me."

Larocque chose to pursue event marketing instead.

Those who show strong academic potential can feel pressured to avoid more artistic careers. Tamara Adam was an honour-roll student.

"I knew I had a more creative bent," she says, "but I felt like the only acceptable options for me were doctor or lawyer." She excelled in university but felt "terrified" as she neared graduation.

"I had no idea what to do after." She fell into a job as a trading assistant in commodities and stocks. She actually enjoyed the work at first—it was busy, cutthroat, demanding, challenging. "Then I realized that as much as it

design-ravenous markets like San Francisco and Seattle.

What if you have serious international aspirations?

Make-Up, Art, Cosmetics approached Vancouver-based Tamara Adam to work as their creative trainer across North America.

Adam was promoted to training manager for the United Kingdom, doing the London collections, opening stores, and talking to the press.

As regional manager for the southwestern United States, she now oversees creative, training, and media events for M.A.C.'s biggest market.

All of this creative success and opportunity can make it sound easy, which of course it is not. Most of these jobs require additional schooling in design or management.

There is competition, risk, and the bracing reality of having your art judged against the cold bottom line.

Salaries, though increasing in "hot" markets like the Web, can reach a peak quicker than in traditional industries.

Some people, then, decide to stay in their day jobs and pursue the arts in their spare time.

Ross Penhall is a tremendously successful Vancouver artist with the Buschlen Mowatt Gallery. There is a waiting list for his paintings, but he still keeps his job as a firefighter.

Some people look for creative volunteer work. Others take their corporate skills into a more artistic environment.

Larocque was working in event marketing in Toronto. Wanting to move to Vancouver, he flew out and discussed his corporate skills with various contacts.

Larocque describes a meeting with Catherine Van Alstine, a partner at the executive search firm Ray & Berndston/Tanton Mitchell

was kind of exciting, predicting the markets was nothing I ever aspired to."

Tamara found herself working successfully in a job that she did not really like. With each day, though, she became more entrenched in the world of stocks. She knew she wanted to do something more artistic, but how, what, and at what cost?

Tamara Adam quit her trading job and found a photographer who needed help with shoots and make-up.

"I discovered I had a natural knack for painting faces," she says. Soon she was doing high-profile work for fashion magazines, advertising, music videos, and commercials. She, like others, discovered a growing job market for artistic employees.

Our growing "dot-conomy" has created a demand for more content designers, animators, multimedia artists.

Interior designers and artisans find a more eager, moneyed clientele. The Internet has made it easier for freelancers to dabble in

Inc. in Vancouver, who said, "I've heard everything that you can do, now what do you want to do?"

"I took the risk of sounding flighty and told her what I really want to do is take everything I have learned and apply it in an arts organization," he said.

Larocque was soon on the way to his new job as director of marketing and special events at Arts Umbrella, a vibrant facility bringing art and dance classes to over 30 000 children each year.

"Now when I work," he says, "I can hear the music coming out of the dance studio, smell paints from the arts studio, and be pleasantly interrupted in the middle of the day because someone's testing out new choreography."

You take it from here ...

Responding

1. Summarize Ideas   Summarize the main idea of this article in one to three sentences.

2. Find Arguments   With a partner, identify the reasons why many parents and teachers are reluctant to encourage young people to pursue careers in the arts, and why many people themselves choose not to follow their creative urges, opting instead to stay in jobs they don't really like. Do you share their concerns? Why or why not?

3. Appreciate Tone   Write your responses to the following questions: What is the author's attitude toward those who pursue artistic careers? How can you tell? In what ways are the individuals profiled in this article successful?

4. Note Distinctions   Write a paragraph explaining what Catherine Van Alstine meant by her question to Paul Larocque: "I've heard everything that you can do, now what do you want to do?"

Extending

5. Think Beyond the Title   The advice in the title of this selection, "When Choosing Your Path, Follow Your Heart," can refer to much more than choosing a career path. List some other aspects of life to which this title might apply. Choose one of these, and express the new message in a form of your choice (e.g., a poem, short story, poster, "how-to" brochure, or article).

6. Compose Diary Entries   Imagine that you are a person who is artistic and creative, but you have a job where you have little or no opportunity to express your artistic side. Write a series of diary entries (at least three) about your experience at work and your thoughts about it.

7. Develop a Questionnaire   The criteria students use when making decisions about the work they will do after graduation may vary. With a partner, develop a list of 8 to 12 questions to survey students on this subject. Give your questionnaire to another student pair, and respond to theirs. When you have completed the questionnaires, discuss your responses.

PEER ASSESSMENT

- Was the questionnaire you responded to relevant and well thought-out?
- Did you learn anything from your peers' responses to your questionnaire?

Before you read, as a class, consider the differences between blue-collar and white-collar jobs.

As you read, pay attention to words and phrases that indicate how the author feels about himself, and notice how these feelings change.

"No person ever stood lower in my estimation for having a patch in their clothes."

The Dignity of Work
by Charles Finn

ESSAY

Notes

Charles Finn lives in Argenta, British Columbia.

classism: discrimination against people from a different social class

Henry David Thoreau: famous nineteenth-century American writer who lived a simple, frugal, life

We work in factories, on farms, in blazing sun, and on the sides of the roads, in forests, in ditches. You see us in shipyards, apartment buildings, under your cars. Ask us our names: We're Alex, Rob, Peter, and Hank. We're Sally, Susan, Deborah, and Pam.

What do we do? We bring home a pay cheque, fibreglass in our lungs, and have a few beers. We're what people call working stiffs. We feel that way. We have strong backs, set minds, dirt under our nails. We look you straight in the eye. It's no joke, we say. We have bills to pay.

The other day I was standing in a drugstore looking through a rack of greeting cards. My greasy overalls and thick fingers confirmed I belonged to the dented pickup outside. Turning the carousel, my eyes fell on a black-and-white photo of a well-dressed man and a woman standing on the corner of a busy city street. They were holding a cardboard sign that read, "Will work for latte."

The card got an audible chuckle out of me, more of a snicker really, but my amusement was quickly followed by a very real sadness. It seemed to me the card was exposing a general callousness toward the plight of the poor, and I felt a slight embarrassment because of my filthy clothes.

Still holding the card, I looked around at the other casual but well-dressed customers. I'm not poor, I wanted to tell them, just trying to get by. Then I thought of how many times I'd been to urban centres and walked past the homeless, putting a few coins in their cups but avoiding their eyes. Such uneasiness, I believe, is an indicator of an increasingly harmful society; the accumulated buildup of guilt, silent, yet a subtle crippler of soul.

There was also an undercurrent of classism the card hinted at. Although fictitious, I could hardly imagine this couple accepting a minimum-wage job as high-school janitor or letting themselves sink to the status of a construction labourer like me. It was Thoreau who said, "No person ever stood lower in my estimation for having a patch in their clothes."

The knees of my pants were testimonies to what Henry David would probably have viewed as frugality. These days it's called hard luck, and it goes along with the attitude that to work with your hands implies you don't have the wherewithal to work with your head. The assumption is if you sit at a computer you're more useful than if you mix cement for a living.

To her credit, my mother has always supported me no matter what occupation I've tried, even as a banger of nails, but there are friends who continually ask me when I'm going to get a real job. I'd like to ask them how real is the mechanic that fixes their car when it breaks down, or the nurse who empties bedpans for a living? A doctor is a vital part of any community. So, too, the man who comes every week to haul away garbage.

Still in the store, I realized it's not the odd greeting card, or the media as a whole teaching this classism, it's adults. Too often we're not proud of ourselves or the jobs that we do.

We think people with degrees and white-collar jobs are the only ones worthy to hold their heads in the air. Don't become a farmer, we say to our children. There's no money in that. With this subtle form of bigotry, our children are growing up believing the lower classes are lower beings. We're teaching them a person's worth is gauged by economic, not moral, success.

I didn't buy that card. I went home and reheated some chili. In the shower I scrubbed the tar from my hands and looked down at my feet. Chips of sawdust were being washed out of my hair and sliding past my toes. Each one represented a skill I'd learned and a few pennies earned. Looking in the mirror I was proud of my working-class tan and before going to bed, I fixed my lunch for the next day and set the alarm.

Then for the hell of it, or maybe in defiance, I made a large decaf latte and read for an hour in bed. I told my partner I'd had a good day.

You take it from here ...

Responding

1. Trace Ideas   In your notebook, copy the chart below. Reread the essay, and in one column, list the "put-downs" blue-collar workers receive, and in the other column list the reasons for the author's strong self-esteem.

Put-downs	*Author's reasons for strong self-esteem*

2. Discuss Meanings
   a) With a partner, decide what the following expressions mean as they are used in the essay:
      - "We look you straight in the eye."
      - "the card was exposing a general callousness toward the plight of the poor"
      - "our children are growing up believing the lower classes are lower beings"
      - "We're teaching them a person's worth is gauged by economic, not moral, success."
      - "I told my partner I'd had a good day."

   b) The author holds strong opinions about contemporary society's attitudes to different types of work. What message did you get from reading the essay? Has the article changed your way of thinking? Discuss your views with your partner.

3. Think about Humour   As a class, discuss why the author found the card that said "Will work for latte" humorous at first. What prompted his feelings to change?

Extending

4. Create a Collage   Take a large selection of newspapers and magazines and search for images of blue-collar workers. Prepare a collage of the images and write a paragraph that explains how they support or reject the main ideas expressed in "The Dignity of Work."

5. Debate an Issue   As a class, debate the following topic: A person's income reflects his or her value to society.

Reflecting on the Unit

Responding

1. Recall Key Ideas   Which ideas about the world of work struck you as important or interesting in studying this unit? List five key ideas from this unit that you found particularly useful. Share them in a class discussion, explaining your choices.

2. Find Personal Connections   While this unit deals with the world of work, many of the lessons in it can be applied to other areas—for example, home and family life, social life, education, and personal development. In your journal, list the five key ideas you identified in Activity 1. For each, write a paragraph describing how you might apply it to another area of your life. For example, *Key idea*: You can be different and still be a success. *Applied to another area*: Although friends think it's odd, I still want to learn how to [_____].

Extending

3. Offer Advice   A friend is struggling with the decision of what type of work to pursue after graduation next year. Her parents want her to do one thing, her teachers are encouraging her to do something else, and the place where she worked last summer has offered her a full-time job, with a possibility for promotion within the next year. She doesn't know any more what she really wants to do. Compose an e-mail offering some support and suggestions, using some of the ideas presented in this unit.

4. Research a Life   As a class, brainstorm a list of prominent Canadians. Choose one and research the following question: What challenges did this person meet in order to achieve career success? Include a brief description of the person's family and educational background and other factors that helped or hindered his or her progress. Present your research in an oral report.

> **SELF-ASSESSMENT**
>
> The main focus of this unit is preparing for and understanding the intricacies of the world of work. Identify
> - the most valuable piece of information you learned
> - the most confusing aspect of this unit
>
> Write your response in the form of a letter to your teacher.

Leisure, some degree of it, is
necessary to the health of every
[hu]man's spirit.
— *Harriet Martineau*

If you want to be happy, be.
— *Leo Tolstoy*

[True happiness] is not
obtained through self-
gratification, but through
fidelity to a worthy purpose.
— *Helen Keller*

Leisure, Dreams, and Happiness

Although work is important in determining

one's future, leisure is necessary for achieving balance in life.

As English writer Harriet Martineau's words suggest, leisure

is not only necessary, but vital to a person's well-being.

According to Russian novelist Leo Tolstoy, happiness

requires an act of personal will and a focus on the here-and-

now. Instead of "becoming" or "doing" all the time, we should

leave room in our days and lives to simply "be."

American writer and promoter of social causes Helen

Keller reminds us of the connection between happiness and

helping others.

As you read this unit,
think about the following:

1) How do you spend your
leisure time?

2) What options for
leisure activities are
open to you?

3) What are some ways in
which people can
obtain lasting
satisfaction, fulfillment,
and happiness in life?

4) What is your dream?
What do you really want
to do and accomplish in
your own life?

Before you read, as a class, discuss the reasons why people play sports.

As you read, work actively to picture in your mind the physical movements of the players described in the poem.

Slam, Dunk, & Hook

Poem by Yusef Komunyakaa

Notes

Yusef Komunyakaa
(1947–) is a Pulitzer
Prize-winning Black
American poet who is
also a decorated veteran
of the Vietnam War. He
teaches at Princeton
University and was
elected Chancellor of the
Academy of Poets. His
work is characterized by
short lines, ordinary
spoken language, and
jazz-like rhythms.

Fast breaks. Lay ups. With Mercury's
Insignia on our sneakers,
We outmaneuvered the footwork
Of bad angels. Nothing but a hot
Swish of strings like silk
Ten feet out. In the roundhouse
Labyrinth our bodies
Created, we could almost
Last forever, poised in midair
Like storybook sea monsters.
A high note hung there
A long second. Off
The rim. We'd corkscrew
Up & dunk balls that exploded
The skullcap of hope & good
Intention. Bug-eyed, lanky,
All hands & feet … sprung rhythm.
We were metaphysical when girls
Cheered on the sidelines.
Tangled up in a falling,
Muscles were a bright motor
Double-flashing to the metal hoop
Nailed to our oak.
When Sonny Boy's mama died
He played nonstop all day, so hard
Our backboard splintered.
Glistening with sweat, we jibed
& rolled the ball off our
Fingertips. Trouble
Was there slapping a blackjack

Against an open palm.
Dribble, drive to the inside, feint,
& glide like a sparrowhawk.
Lay ups. Fast breaks.
We had moves we didn't know
We had. Our bodies spun
On swivels of bone & faith,
Through a lyric slipknot
Of joy, & we knew we were
Beautiful & dangerous.

You take it from here ...

Responding

1. Clarify Meaning   Working in small groups, discuss and demonstrate the physical movements of the players. Explain each one of the specialized basketball manoeuvres, such as a "break" and a "lay up." Ask other members of the class to help you clarify any specific moves your group may not understand.

2. Analyze Style   This poem uses figurative language. Choose two *metaphors* (direct comparisons between unlike objects) that you think are particularly effective. Write a brief explanation of the meanings of these metaphors and why you think they are especially powerful.

3. Explore Motivation   With a partner, consider why these boys play basketball. How do they feel when they are on the court? Is the poem about them playing basketball in general or about one specific day when they played basketball? Is this poem only about basketball? Be sure to point to specific lines and phrases in explaining your response.

4. Express Your Views   On the surface, this poem is about the experience of a group of boys. As a class, discuss whether or not "Slam, Dunk, & Hook" is only meaningful for male readers.

TIP

- Refer in detail to specific lines in the poem.

Extending

5. Create a Soundtrack   This poem relies heavily on visual imagery, but there are also many appeals to the sense of hearing. In small groups, make a list of the sounds referred to directly in the poem or implied by the actions described. Create an audiotape made up of sound effects

and brief passages of music that help to capture the overall mood of the poem. Prepare an oral reading along with the soundtrack, and present it to another group of students.

> **Peer Assessment**
> - Did the group choose effective sound effects and music for their soundtrack?
> - Did the tape enhance the appeal of the poem when played along with the reading?

6. Research the Author   Search the Internet to find out more about Yusef Komunyakaa. Prepare a brief oral report either on his life or on the themes of his poetry. Provide a list of addresses for the Web sites you consult.

7. Compare Two Poems   Find and read another poem written by Komunyakaa and write an essay comparing it to "Slam, Dunk, & Hook." Discuss in particular any similarities you detect in style. Do you believe that the poem you chose would have been a better example of Komunyakaa's work to include in this anthology? Comment.

"You can't think negative."

Runyan's Vision? To Inspire the Best in Others

by TOM BARRETT

PROFILE

Notes

For more information on Marla Runyan, read her book *No Finish Line: My Life as I See It*, or visit her Web site at www.marlarunyan.com.

Marla Runyan's transformation from a highly competitive heptathlete to a world-class distance runner is one of the most amazing stories in sports.

She had to completely change her body type and carve off 25 pounds of hard muscle to make the unprecedented switch. In a matter of months she went from being a weight-lifting, shot-putting, sprinting, power athlete with a muscular upper body to a thin, streamlined endurance runner.

So it's not surprising that the 32-year-old American hasn't let the fact she's legally blind stop her either.

Runyan has been confounding the doubters and thrusting aside limitations since she was diagnosed with Stargardt's disease, a degenerative condition of the retina, as a nine-year-old girl.

She kept playing soccer until she couldn't see the ball. She took up track and became a top high jumper and hurdler despite having 20-300 vision in one eye and 20-400 in the other. She is the very definition of what it means to be a winner, wherever she finishes in the race.

"You've got to focus on what you can do and do it as well as possible," she says. "Remind yourself every day of all you have to be grateful for. You can't think negative."

Luckily, Runyan's parents shared her attitude.

"They never set any kind of limitations on me," she says. "They said, 'If you want to do that, try.' As a family we were really good problem solvers. That was really a blessing. Sometimes I think the reaction of parents to a disability is more limiting than the disability itself."

She believes it's become trendy to be a victim in today's society—to sit on the couch and feel sorry for yourself—but that's not her way. In fact, Runyan considers herself very fortunate despite her disability. She enjoys running and competing and is thrilled that she can inspire other people to overcome adversity at the same time.

NEL

Runyan's Vision? To Inspire the Best in Others **111**

"It's a pretty awesome position to be in. To be able to do what I love and to have a positive effect on others—that's a great bonus."

After she made the women's final in the 1500 metres at the Sydney Olympics and ended up finishing in eighth place, she received a tremendous outpouring of affection and support from around the globe.

"I got literally hundreds and hundreds of e-mails," she says. "One child wrote, 'I'm legally blind, but after watching you, my mom says I can ride my skateboard.' Another wrote that she had just been diagnosed with Stargardts and said, 'Thank you for letting me know I'm not alone.'"

Many of the e-mails were written in foreign languages.

"In the whole scheme of things it's more important than the race itself," Runyan says. "If you're put on this earth and you can make a change in someone's life by setting a good example, that's fantastic."

RUNYAN NOT INTIMIDATED EASILY

Of course she would rather make her mark as a great distance runner than as the only legally blind competitor.

She knows her condition doesn't make her slower, but it does create strategic problems. It's difficult for her to slip in and out of the pack, changing positions, when she isn't leading a race.

She can see the track beneath her and uses her undamaged peripheral vision when possible.

But she still can't recognize the faces of her competitors.

Runyan has achieved remarkable success in school and as an athlete since she was a young

Marla Runyan

child growing up in California. After graduating she did not get an athletic scholarship but became a star member of the track team at San Diego State, where she discovered the heptathlon.

She was good enough to make the U.S. Olympic trials in 1996. After setting a national heptathlon record in the 800 metres, she decided to make the switch to middle-distance running.

Her body rebelled somewhat against the long miles of training and she suffered a frustrating series of injuries that cost her two years and drove her to the brink of quitting. She doesn't give up easily, however.

In 1999, she edged Canadian Leah Pells to win the 1500 metres at the Pan-Am Games and made it to the finals of the world championships in Seville, Spain. Then came the Olympics.

She moved up to the 5000 this year, shattering the American indoor record and then finishing first at the U.S. nationals in June to qualify for the Edmonton World Championships.

Runyan is up against Romanian superstar Gabriela Szabo and a number of top competitors, but she doesn't intimidate easily.

Editor's Note

At the 2001 World Championships in Edmonton, Runyan finished ninth of 23 runners in heat one of round one of the Women's 5000 metres. Although she didn't qualify for the final, her time of 15:24:30 would have put her in twelfth place of the final, again ahead of several other sighted contenders.

You take it from here ...

Responding

1. **Rethink Limitations** Share with a partner the list you made before reading, identifying obstacles to a goal. Review your partner's list, and consider what Marla Runyan might suggest if you were to ask her for advice on surmounting those obstacles. Discuss these possibilities with your partner.

2. **Discuss the Structure** Working in groups, discuss the structure of this profile. Be prepared to defend your opinions by making specific references to the text.
   a) Where do you think the introduction to this profile ends? Is this an effective introduction? Could it be improved in any way?
   b) Where do you believe the conclusion to this profile begins? Is this an effective conclusion? Could it be improved in any way?

3. **Express Your Views** Marla Runyan says that it has "become trendy to be a victim in today's society." What does she mean by this comment? Why do you think she would say this? In your opinion, is it a fair observation? Share your views with a partner.

Extending

4. **Ask Questions** The role of a news reporter is to ask questions. Working in small groups, review the information contained in this profile of Marla Runyan, and come up with three to five additional questions you would like to have answered. Then do some research to find the answers, and share your questions and findings with the class.

5. **Make an Inspirational Speech** Like Helen Keller, Terry Fox, and Rick Hansen, Marla Runyan has overcome what, to many, would seem like impossible odds. Research the story of another individual who has achieved success in the face of disability. Work to find an unusual story, one that your classmates might not have heard. Make an inspirational speech based on the achievements of this individual.

6. **Write an Essay of Definition** Write a brief essay on Stargardt's disease, its nature, cause, and treatment.

> **TIP**
> - Consider consulting the following sources during your research:
>   – library materials (books, magazines, journals)
>   – the Internet
>   – Marla Runyan's own Web site (which includes her e-mail address)

> **TIPS**
> - Consult library books and the Internet to research this disease.
> - Use a dictionary to help you define words you do not understand.
> - Prepare a brief outline before writing your essay.
> - Attach a list of sources to your final paper.

Before you read, as a class, list as many Canadian singers as you can. Is there anything about the performers or their songs that identifies them as particularly "Canadian"?

As you read, imagine what kind of music would best suit the words.

Notes

Stompin' Tom Connors, a beloved Canadian troubadour, was born in Saint John, New Brunswick, and was adopted by a family in Skinner's Pond, Prince Edward Island. Between the ages of 15 and 28, while hitchhiking across Canada, he started writing catchy tunes such as "Sudbury Saturday Night" and "Bud the Spud." In 1969, he launched his recording career, later returning all six Juno Awards he won because of what he felt was the Americanization of the Canadian music industry. Very much his own person, Connors nevertheless accepted the Order of Canada, and he still tours.

The Hockey Song

Lyrics by Stompin' Tom Connors

Hello out there, we're on the air, it's hockey night tonight
Tension grows, the whistle blows, and the puck goes down the ice
The goalie jumps and the players bump and the fans all go insane
Someone roars, "Bobby scores!" at the good old hockey game

Oh, the good old hockey game is the best game you can name
And the best game you can name is the good old hockey game

Second period …

Where players dash, with skates aflash, the home
      team trails behind
But they grab the puck and go bursting
      up, and they're down across the line
They storm the crease like bumblebees,
      they travel like a burning flame
We see them slide the puck inside, it's a
      one-one hockey game

Oh, the good old hockey game is the
      best game you can name
And the best game you can name is the
      good old hockey game

Third period …

Last game of the playoffs, too

Oh, take me where hockey players face off down the rink
And the Stanley Cup is all filled up for the champs who win
      the drink

Now the final flick of a hockey stick, and one gigantic scream
The puck is in! The home team wins the good old hockey game

Oh, the good old hockey game is the best game you can name
And the best game you can name is the good old hockey game

You take it from here ...

Responding

1. **Create a Glossary**   Pretend that you know nothing about either Canada or the game of hockey. Working with a partner, create a glossary that lists and defines all the terms in Stompin' Tom Connors's lyrics that you think would need to be explained. Compare your list with those of other members of the class. Defend any differences between your list and theirs.

2. **Focus on Repetition**   Examine the rhyme scheme of these lyrics carefully, and list all examples of repetition of words or phrases. Discuss with your classmates the overall importance of repetition in these lyrics. Does the repetition detract from or add to the impact of Stompin' Tom Connors's sentiments?

3. **Explore Similes**   Stompin' Tom Connors uses two *similes* (comparisons using "like" or "as") in the third line of the second stanza: "They storm the crease like bumblebees" and "they travel like a burning flame." How appropriate are these similes? Invent your own similes to describe the same actions, and share them in a class discussion. Which ones do you think describe the actions most effectively?

Extending

4. **Compare Two Works**   It could be argued that "Casey at the Bat" is the American equivalent of "The Hockey Song." Read Ernest Lawrence Thayer's celebrated poem about baseball and compare it to Stompin' Tom Connors's song about hockey. Write an essay explaining similarities in subject matter and style of the two poems.

5. **Compose Song Lyrics**   Most would agree that hockey is quintessentially a Canadian sport. Brainstorm with your classmates other activities or things that seem truly Canadian. Work together to compose song lyrics on one of these activities in Stompin' Tom Connors's style.

> **TIP**
> - To gain a better appreciation of Stompin' Tom's style, listen to a recording of "The Hockey Song" and some of his other songs.

Before you read, as a class, discuss what it means to be a sports fan.

As you read, make note of your own reactions to the cartoon. Did you smile? Why? What do you believe is the main message of this cartoon?

Herman

Cartoon by Jim Unger

Notes

Jim Unger (1940–) was born in London, England. He came to Canada and began his cartooning career at the *Mississauga Times.* He later moved to Ottawa, where he began creating his famous *Herman* cartoons. He retired in 1992 after producing over 6000 cartoons in 18 years. Unger's original intended name for *Herman* was *Attila the Bum.* In 1990, *Herman* was selected as the first newspaper comic syndicated in communist East Germany after the Berlin Wall came down.

"Are they playing overtime? You must be absolutely exhausted."

You take it from here ...

Responding

1. **Decode Meaning**   Cartoonists usually depend on only a few critical details to get their message across. Working in a group, decide what the reader/viewer needs to understand in order to appreciate the humour of this cartoon.

2. **Consider the Links between Image and Text**   Divide the class into two groups. Those in the first group should cover the picture with a piece of paper and pay attention only to the words. If you hadn't seen the original cartoon, what sort of image would you expect these words to be associated with? Those in the second group should cover the words and consider only the image. If you hadn't read the original caption, what lines could you suggest to suit the picture? As a class, share what you have learned about the link between image and text.

3. **Explain Techniques**   Referring to this cartoon, write an explanation of the differences between the three related techniques of *irony*, *sarcasm*, and *satire*.

> **TIPS**
>
> • Check the glossary at the back of this book or a dictionary for definitions of *irony*, *sarcasm*, and *satire*.
> • Be sure to use specific details from the cartoon to make your points clearly.

Extending

4. **Compare Visuals**   Recreate the scene in Unger's cartoon using photographs of similar objects and characters cut from magazines. Write a one-page analysis describing how your more detailed visual differs in impact from Unger's line drawing.

5. **Create a Collage**   For the next two or three weeks, read the daily comics in the newspaper, looking for common themes about human beings. Then create a collage of cartoons that deal with one particular human characteristic. Write a brief explanation as to why these cartoons belong together.

> **TIP**
>
> • When you clip the cartoon, mark it clearly with the date and source so that you can acknowledge sources at the end of your written commentary.

Just Once

The Moose wanted to carry the ball.

Short Story by Thomas J. Dygard

Notes

Thomas Dygard began writing about sports for the *Arkansas Gazette* in Little Rock when he was in high school. He later covered sports for the Associated Press (AP) and then became chief of a number of AP bureaus in the United States and in Tokyo. Between 1977 and his retirement from the AP in 1993, he found time to write more than a dozen sports novels, including *Running Scared, Halfback Tough, Quarterback Walk-On, The Rebounder,* and *Infield Hit.*

Everybody liked the Moose. To his father and mother he was Bryan—as in Bryan Jefferson Crawford—but to everyone at Bedford City High he was the Moose. He was large and strong, as you might imagine from his nickname, and he was pretty fast on his feet—sort of nimble, you might say—considering his size. He didn't have a pretty face but he had a quick and easy smile—"sweet," some of the teachers called it; "nice," others said.

But on the football field, the Moose was neither sweet nor nice. He was just strong and fast and a little bit devastating as the left tackle of the Bedford City Bears. When the Moose blocked somebody, he stayed blocked. When the Moose was called on to open a hole in the line for one of the Bears' runners, the hole more often than not resembled an open garage door.

Now in his senior season, the Moose had twice been named to the all-conference team and was considered a cinch for all-state. He spent a lot of his spare time, when he wasn't in a classroom or on the football field, reading letters from colleges eager to have the Moose pursue higher education—and football—at their institution.

But the Moose had a hang-up.

He didn't go public with his hang-up until the sixth game of the season. But, looking back, most of his teammates agreed that probably the Moose had been nurturing the hang-up secretly for two years or more.

The Moose wanted to carry the ball.

For sure, the Moose was not the first interior lineman in the history of football, or even the history of Bedford City High, who banged heads up front and wore bruises like badges of honour—and dreamed of racing down the field with the ball to the end zone while everybody in the bleachers screamed his name.

But most linemen, it seems, are able to stifle the urge. The idea may pop into their minds from time to time, but in their hearts they know they can't run fast enough, they know they can't do that fancy dancing to elude tacklers, they know they aren't trained to read blocks. They know that their strengths and talents are best utilized in the line. Football is, after all, a team sport, and everyone plays the position where he most helps the team. And so these linemen, or most of them, go back to banging heads without saying the first word about the dream that flickered through their minds.

Not so with the Moose.

That sixth game, when the Moose's hang-up first came into public view, had ended with the Moose truly in all his glory as the Bears' left tackle. Yes, glory—but uncheered and sort of anonymous. The Bears were trailing 21–17 and had the ball on Mitchell High's five-yard line, fourth down, with time running out. The rule in such a situation is simple—the best back carries the ball behind the best blocker—and it is a rule seldom violated by those in control of their faculties. The Bears, of course, followed the rule. That meant Jerry Dixon running behind the Moose's blocking. With the snap of the ball, the Moose knocked down one lineman, bumped another one aside, and charged forward to flatten an approaching linebacker. Jerry did a little jig behind the Moose and then ran into the end zone, virtually untouched, to win the game.

After circling in the end zone a moment while the cheers echoed through the night, Jerry did run across and hug the Moose, that's true. Jerry knew who had made the touchdown possible.

But it wasn't the Moose's name that everybody was shouting. The fans in the bleachers were cheering Jerry Dixon.

It was probably at that precise moment that the Moose decided to go public.

In the dressing room, Coach Buford Williams was making his rounds among the cheering players and came to a halt in front of the Moose. "It was your great blocking that did it," he said.

"I want to carry the ball," the Moose said.

Coach Williams was already turning away and taking a step toward the next player due an accolade when his brain registered the fact that the Moose had said something strange. He was expecting the Moose to say, "Aw, gee, thanks, Coach." That was what the Moose always said when

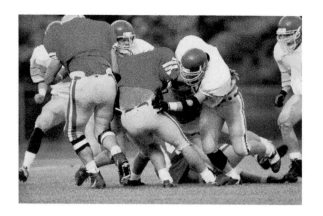

the coach issued a compliment. But the Moose had said something else. The coach turned back to the Moose, a look of disbelief on his face. "What did you say?"

"I want to carry the ball."

Coach Williams was good at quick recoveries, as any high-school football coach had better be. He gave a tolerant smile and a little nod and said, "You keep right on blocking, son."

This time Coach Williams made good on his turn and moved away from the Moose.

The following week's practice and the next Friday's game passed without further incident. After all, the game was a road game over at Cartwright High, 35 miles away. The Moose wanted to carry the ball in front of the Bedford City fans.

Then the Moose went to work.

He caught up with the coach on the way to the practice field on Wednesday. "Remember," he said, leaning forward and down a little to get his face in the coach's face, "I said I want to carry the ball."

Coach Williams must have been thinking about something else because it took him a minute to look up into the Moose's face, and even then he didn't say anything.

"I meant it," the Moose said.

"Meant what?"

"I want to run the ball."

"Oh," Coach Williams said. Yes, he remembered. "Son, you're a great left tackle, a great blocker. Let's leave it that way."

The Moose let the remaining days of the practice week and then the game on Friday night against Edgewood High pass while he reviewed strategies. The review led him to Dan Blevins, the Bears' quarterback. If the signal-caller would join in, maybe Coach Williams would listen.

"Yeah, I heard," Dan said. "But, look, what about Joe Wright at guard, Bill Slocum at right tackle, even Herbie Watson at centre. They might all want to carry the ball. What are we going to do—take turns? It doesn't work that way."

So much for Dan Blevins.

The Moose found that most of the players in the backfield agreed with Dan. They couldn't see any reason why the Moose should carry the ball, especially in place of themselves. Even Jerry Dixon, who owed a lot of his glory to the Moose's blocking, gaped in disbelief at the Moose's idea. The Moose, however, got some support from his fellow linemen. Maybe they had dreams of their own, and saw value in a precedent.

As the days went by, the word spread—not just on the practice field and in the corridors of Bedford City High, but all around town. The players by now were openly taking sides. Some thought it a jolly good idea that the Moose carry the ball. Others, like Dan Blevins, held to the purist line—a left tackle plays left tackle, a ballcarrier carries the ball, and that's it.

Around town, the vote wasn't even close. Everyone wanted the Moose to carry the ball.

"Look, son," Coach Williams said to the Moose on the practice field the Thursday before the Benton Heights game, "this has gone far enough. Fun is fun. A joke is a joke. But let's drop it."

"Just once," the Moose pleaded.

Coach Williams looked at the Moose and didn't answer.

The Moose didn't know what that meant.

The Benton Heights Tigers were duck soup for the Bears, as everyone knew they would be. The Bears scored in their first three possessions and led 28–0 at the half. The hapless Tigers had yet to cross the fifty-yard line under their own steam.

All of the Bears, of course, were enjoying the way the game was going, as were the Bedford City fans jamming the bleachers.

Coach Williams looked irritated when the crowd on a couple of occasions broke into a chant: "Give the Moose the ball! Give the Moose the ball!"

On the field, the Moose did not know whether to grin at hearing his name shouted by the crowd or to frown because the sound of his name was irritating the coach. Was the crowd going to talk Coach Williams into putting the Moose in the backfield? Probably not; Coach Williams didn't bow to that kind of pressure. Was the coach going to refuse to give the ball to the Moose just to show the crowd—and the Moose and the rest of the players—who was boss? The Moose feared so.

In his time on the sideline, when the defensive unit was on the field, the Moose, of course, said nothing to Coach Williams. He knew better than to break the coach's concentration during a game—even a runaway victory—with a comment on any subject at all, much less his desire to carry the ball. As a matter of fact, the Moose was careful to stay out of the coach's line of vision, especially when the crowd was chanting "Give the Moose the ball!"

By the end of the third quarter the Bears were leading 42–0.

Coach Williams had been feeding substitutes into the game since halftime, but the Bears kept marching on. And now, in the opening minutes of the fourth quarter, the Moose and his teammates were standing on the Tigers' five-yard line, about to pile on another touchdown.

The Moose saw his substitute, Larry Hinden, getting a slap on the behind and then running onto the field. The Moose turned to leave.

Then he heard Larry tell the referee, "Hinden for Holbrook."

Holbrook? Chad Holbrook, the fullback?

Chad gave the coach a funny look and jogged off the field.

Larry joined the huddle and said, "Coach says the Moose at fullback and give him the ball."

Dan Blevins said, "Really?"

"Really."

The Moose was giving his grin—"sweet," some of the teachers called it; "nice," others said.

"I want to do an end run," the Moose said.

Dan looked at the sky a moment, then said, "What does it matter?"

The quarterback took the snap from centre, moved back and to his right while turning, and extended the ball to the Moose.

The Moose took the ball and cradled it in his right hand. So far, so good. He hadn't fumbled. Probably both Coach Williams and Dan were surprised.

He ran a couple of steps and looked out in front and said aloud, "Whoa!"

Where had all those tacklers come from?

The whole world seemed to be peopled with players in red jerseys—the red of the Benton Heights Tigers. They were all looking straight at the Moose and advancing toward him. They looked very determined, and not friendly at all. And there were so many of them. The Moose had faced tough guys in the line, but usually one at a time, or maybe two. But this—five or six. And all of them heading for him.

The Moose screeched to a halt, whirled, and ran the other way.

Dan Blevins blocked somebody in a red jersey breaking through the middle of the line, and the Moose wanted to stop running and thank him. But he kept going.

His reverse had caught the Tigers' defenders going the wrong way, and the field in front of the Moose looked open. But his blockers were going the wrong way, too. Maybe that was why the field looked so open. What did it matter, though, with the field clear in front of him? This was going to be a cakewalk; the Moose was going to score a touchdown.

Then, again—"Whoa!"

Players with red jerseys were beginning to fill the empty space—a lot of them. And they were all running toward the Moose. They were kind of low, with their arms spread, as if they wanted to hit him hard and then grab him.

A picture of Jerry Dixon dancing his little jig and wriggling between tacklers flashed through the Moose's mind. How did Jerry do that? Well, no time to ponder that one right now.

The Moose lowered his shoulder and thundered ahead, into the cloud of red jerseys. Something hit his left thigh. It hurt. Then something pounded his hip, then his shoulder. They both hurt. Somebody was hanging on to him and was a terrible drag. How could he run with somebody hanging on to him? He knew he was going down, but maybe he was across the goal line. He hit the ground hard, with somebody coming down on top of him, right on the small of his back.

The Moose couldn't move. They had him pinned. Wasn't the referee supposed to get these guys off?

Finally the load was gone and the Moose, still holding the ball, got to his knees and one hand, then stood.

He heard the screaming of the crowd, and he saw the scoreboard blinking.

He had scored.

His teammates were slapping him on the shoulder pads and laughing and shouting.

The Moose grinned, but he had a strange and distant look in his eyes.

He jogged to the sideline, the roars of the crowd still ringing in his ears.

"Okay, son?" Coach Williams asked.

The Moose was puffing. He took a couple of deep breaths. He relived for a moment the first sight of a half dozen players in red jerseys, all with one target—him. He saw again the menacing horde of red jerseys that had risen up just when he'd thought he had clear sailing to the goal. They all zeroed in on him, the Moose, alone.

The Moose glanced at the coach, took another deep breath, and said, "Never again."

You take it from here ...

Responding

1. Chart the Play   Working in a small group, reread the play-by-play description of Moose's touchdown manoeuvres. Chart the action using circles, arrows, and *X*s to show the movements. When you have finished, discuss whether the reader needs to know about football in order to fully appreciate the humour and outcome of this story.

2. Consider Narrative Voice   The narrator of this story has a definite personality that comes through strongly in the opening pages. Reread the first dozen paragraphs carefully. With a partner, discuss the tone of the narration. What is the speaker's attitude to the Moose? to the situation? to football in general? Compare your reactions to those of other students.

3. Interpret Theme   This selection is as much about team sports as it is about a particular incident in one young player's life. Write a paragraph explaining the message of this story, and how this message can be applied to life in general. Be sure to use specific details and examples in developing your paragraph.

4. Consider What's in a Name   Thomas Dygard introduces his hero with the words, "To his father and mother he was Bryan—as in Bryan Jefferson Crawford—but to everyone at Bedford City High he was the Moose." Are you, your siblings, or friends known differently to people at home and at school? Write a response commenting on how the use of different names (and nicknames) reflects different aspects of an individual's personality.

Extending

5. Compose a News Story   Write a report of the Moose's feat that could have appeared in either Bedford City's local newspaper or the Bedford City High newsletter. Exchange drafts with a partner for proofreading and feedback before you write your final version.

> **PEER ASSESSMENT**
>
> - What is your overall impression of the article?
> - How well does it follow the guidelines for news-story writing?
> - What are its strongest points (e.g., good description, concise writing)?
> - Do you have any suggestions for the final version?

6. Read a Book   Find and read a sports novel written by Thomas Dygard or another author of your choice. Prepare an oral book report, pointing out similarities and differences you may have noted between the novel and this short story. Would you recommend that others read the novel you selected?

Notes

Vickie Sears is a Cherokee writer who lives in Seattle, Washington, where she works as a feminist–therapist.

Pow Wow

Poem by Vickie Sears

There are cool breezes
    in
        warm spring sunslants
            tapping
    the dancers bells
      and
        freeflowing feathers
          rhythmically dipping
with
    weaving bodies.
There are spirit songs
    beating the
      drums.
        heyya heyya heyya
          rises from the throats of
circled
    groundsitting singers.
        dancers
          feel their circle
around
    drumsinging.
There are children
    everywhere
      running
        laughing
  wandering freely
    to explore
      because that is how we grow.

There are eyes that speak
    most of all you need
      to understand
        and
          teasing
from behind blackorb grins
    to keep you
      humbly human
        giving
smiles at your own foolishness.
There are afternoon and evening fires
of fry bread
    beans
       meat
        and beer.
everyone has a plate
    yet
       takes from others.
       children sodapop pass
without asking
    if
       they should share.
        things are good.
people recognize themselves
    as
       ONE
        of the earth circle.
    sing
I am the universe
    as made by the
      Great Spirit.
       ga lv la di   ga dv gi a   a qua dnv do
       (heaven   hear my   heart)
    am a living circle
    as
       the drums tell it.

                        am sun
            as the drums shine it.
                am sky
                        as the drums fly it.
                        and
            I dance it
                sure
                        softly
                            strongly
            prayerfully
                circle
                        on
                            circle
    spirit-healing circles.
            for that time
                our culture
            needs
                no explanation.
                        no missionary speaks of
                            heathen faith.
            efforts to
                make us
                        assimilate
                        are
                worthy only of a joke.
                        for the length of drumming
                            all is
            whole
                as it should be.
                        everyone is
                            full
    circle on circle
            dancing
                the song
                    of
                        living.

You take it from here ...

Responding

1. **Focus on Diction**   Vickie Sears is known for her colourful imagery and diction. This poem is filled with neologisms: new words she has created to express her sense impressions. Working in groups, discuss the effectiveness of such compounds as "sunslants," "groundsitting," "drumsinging," and "blackorb." Create similar words that would suit other parts of Sears's poem.

2. **Explain the Message**   Sears is a committed activist who has strong opinions about the raising of children and the treatment of First Nations people by early missionaries. Review the lines in this poem that express her feelings on these topics. Explain her comments in a brief paragraph. Debate with other members of the class whether the poem would be more or less effective without these lines.

3. **Perform the Poem**   "Pow Wow" is a dramatic poem that lends itself to choral reading. Work with four or five classmates to divide the lines into different roles. Rehearse and then perform the poem for the rest of the class, using your voice to evoke the freedom and joy of Sears's experience.

> **TIP**
> - Consider using sound effects in addition to the words of the poem.

Extending

4. **Research First Nations Literature**   Find other poems that capture a First Nations experience. Prepare an oral presentation of one of these poems, analyzing similarities and differences between it and "Pow Wow."

5. **Compose a Poem**   Write your own poem that captures a particularly happy and triumphant moment in your life. Work to include specific details that will allow your reader to experience the moment as you did.

On the Right Track

She said there was this terrific guy who ate there.

Short Story by Dorothy Chisholm

Notes

Dorothy Chisholm lives and works in Toronto. This story was shortlisted for the 1990 Kingston Regional Literary Awards.

auteur: French word for "author," referring to famous maverick film directors such as Orson Welles, who exercised great control over their films, independent of the Hollywood system.

Grade 13: in Ontario, an additional year of high school geared to university-bound students. Discontinued as of 2003.

I hate trendy, you know what I mean? That's why when Kim said let's go to Yorkville for lunch one day, my first impulse was to say no. Besides, I didn't have any money. I was trying to save for a trip to Florida so I usually ate at the Burger Barn. Kim would say I ate too much junk food. She was into yogurt and salads.

Anyway, Kim says never mind about the money, I'll lend you some until payday. When I pointed out that it would take two subway tokens to get to Yorkville and back, Kim says never mind the subway, walking is good for you.

I asked Kim what was so great about this cafe in Yorkville and she said there was this terrific guy who ate there. She'd seen him a few times when she went there with Sara. Sara was a girl in our office who quit to have a baby right after I arrived. I sort of replaced her, although she had a lot more responsibility than they'd given me. Anyway, Kim had decided that she had to figure out a way to meet this guy.

Kim was about the only friend I had in the office then. I'd only been there a month and most of the other people in the office were pretty old. Kim had some funny ideas but I liked her. She was really good looking. Golden blond hair and skin that took a great tan. She wore a lot of white, which really showed off her tan and also her terrific figure.

Her name wasn't really Kim. It was Joyce, but she didn't like it and had got everybody to call her Kim. I have to admit it suited her better than Joyce did. Anyway, she talked me into going to Yorkville for lunch and to eat a lot. Order a small salad, she says, because you can fill up on the French bread they put on the table before you even order.

The cafe was one of those small restaurants with a lot of white and chrome and plants all over the place. And everyone is drinking white wine or Perrier water.

Kim asks the waiter if they have any special dishes for dieters. She flashes him this big smile and he says maybe you'd like to try a small salad. So she says she'll have a very small green salad and some Earl Grey tea. I order the same thing.

Well Kim hardly ate anything. She just kept looking around while I ate a whole basket of French bread. I was still hungry when we left and the terrific guy hadn't shown up. Never mind, Kim says, patience is its own reward.

I don't know about patience. I think it was more like determination with Kim. We went back about a week later and, this time, he was there. I had to admit I thought he was pretty good-looking. He was dressed kind of preppy, sort of like the ads in *GQ*. That's *Gentlemen's Quarterly*, which I don't read, but Kim never missed an issue. He was wearing a navy jacket, white shirt, striped tie, Rosedale written all over him.

Not exactly a hunk, but better than okay, I told Kim. She looked at me as if I was sort of ignorant and said that understatement was the essence of good taste or something like that.

Anyway, after she'd finished her salad, Kim said she was going to the washroom and I couldn't believe what she did next. Just as she passes his table, she drops her purse. Talk about corny. But, just the way she did it, for a minute I thought it was an accident. He must have thought so too, because he bends over and picks up the purse. Kim flashes him this great smile and it seems to work because his eyes follow her all the way to the washroom. On the way back she stops and says, haven't I seen you in the Manulife Centre? He says yes, I work in there and Kim says well, bye-bye and gives him a little wave.

I couldn't get over her nerve and I also couldn't figure out how she knew the building he worked in. I asked her on the way back to our office, and she says just a lucky guess. I would have found out eventually anyway, she says.

I wondered why she went to all that trouble. She had lots of offers from guys to go out with them. But she turned most of them down because, she said, she knew what she wanted, which was to meet the right type of person. And if you don't get off on the right track, you'll always regret it, she said.

Kim and I started to go to the beach on the weekends to work on our tans and watch the wind surfers. One day I saw this guy I was in grade 10 with. Donny. He's pretty good-looking, nice too, and he tells me he's had a hard time finding a job. But he's working, he says, at the Sears warehouse. We talked for a while and he said he'd give me a call sometime.

Meanwhile, Kim was eyeing this guy in a Ralph Lauren polo shirt and shorts. He was playing frisbee and he had great muscles. On the way home, Kim tells me he has too many muscles. Too much muscle is gross, she says, and probably means he's developed his body instead of his brain.

I told Kim I thought Donny was nice but she says, warehouse, talk about downward mobility. She didn't say it to be mean. She talked like that because she read a lot of magazines. For example, she read *Toronto Life* from cover to cover and she also read *Glamour* and *Cosmo*.

I used to hang out sometimes at this pub near where I lived. I'd go there with Carol, a girl I knew in high school. Kim didn't go to pubs. They're full of jocks, she said. Girls are just another sport to them. She didn't ever go to singles bars, either. Meat markets, she said, they're for losers.

Kim liked to go to expensive boutiques to try on clothes. The first time she asked me to go I told her I couldn't afford to buy anything but she says, don't worry, we're not going to buy anything. We'll just see what we like and then go down to Spadina and get the same thing, only cheaper.

Meanwhile, we kept going to the cafe in Yorkville and sometimes we saw the guy from the Manulife Centre whose name turned out to be Rob. We talked a bit more each time and eventually he and Kim got around to her phone number. But she told him she was just in the process of moving and when she was settled in she'd give him a call.

Which was more or less true because Kim had been trying to talk me into sharing an apartment. She said she was sick of riding the subway all the way from North York and I had to admit it was a long way for me from Etobicoke.

I told Kim I really couldn't afford an apartment but she said we could buy stuff at the Sally Ann and now that she'd finally met Rob we could cut out the lunches in Yorkville. I figured I could put my trip to Florida on hold for a while so I said okay, and Kim found this place in the Annex. It was pretty run down but Kim said when we painted it and put up posters and got some rattan furniture and stuff, it would be great.

My mum said she'd miss me but she understood that I was at an age to be on my own and if I needed anything to just let her know and if it didn't work out she'd always be glad to see me back home.

I don't think Kim had a terrific relationship with her family. I know that when I'd phone and ask for Kim, her mother would always say, just a minute and I'll get Joyce or no, Joyce isn't here. Anyway, Kim's mother told her if she ran out of money, not to bother running back home.

Kim's brother knew a guy who ran a gas station, so he brought his truck around to help us move. My mother gave us some dishes and pots and pans and we took our mattresses but not our beds. Kim said futons were what everybody was using now. Which was okay with me because I figured if this didn't work it would be easier to move.

It was kind of neat having the apartment. Neither of us could cook very well, so we ate a lot of yogurt and frozen stuff and we got some great posters. Kim started to go out with Rob, which was exciting for her. Rob liked to go to concerts and art galleries and to the ROM. Stuff for the mind, Kim said, but we're going to have fun, too. Rob's friend has a boat and we'll go sailing on the lake. When winter comes we'll buy skis, she said, and go to Blue Mountain.

One night when Rob came to take Kim out, she was still in the bedroom putting on her makeup and he starts telling me how much he

admires Kim. It must be tough, he says, for her to be in the city on her own, with no family or anything.

Well, this was news to me because, as far as I knew, her family was alive and well in North York. But I didn't say anything.

Another time, Rob asked me if I wanted to go along with them to a concert at Ontario Place. I really wanted to go but I didn't want to horn in on Kim so I said no thanks, I have to wash my hair. I have to admit that sometimes I got pretty lonely in the apartment and if it wasn't for Donny calling a couple of times, it would have been really boring. But there was also a library right around the corner and I started to take books out and I was doing a lot of reading.

One day at the end of the summer Donny asked me to go to the Ex with him, so I asked Kim if she and Rob would like to go with us. Kim says no, the Ex isn't really Rob's style. I felt kind of sorry for her because she used to like the Ex, but I got the feeling that she didn't think Donny had much class. I have to admit he dressed kind of funny. Like, he wasn't much into fashion and he didn't have one of those neat-o haircuts like the guys in GQ. He just liked to be comfortable, which was okay with me.

So Donny and I went to the Ex by ourselves and we had a great time going on all the rides and stuff. He also won me this big stuffed bear by knocking over bottles with baseballs. It cost him almost $20 but it was fun riding the street-car home with this huge animal on my lap and everybody saying boy are you lucky. I was kind of glad Kim and Rob weren't with us.

When we got home I invited Donny in for a Coke and Kim and Rob were already there. Kim didn't look too happy and I got the idea they'd had a fight. They'd gone to this movie and Kim tells me and Donny how boring it was. Rob says he thought it was great. The director, he says, was saying something really important. Kim rolls her eyes and says she still thinks it was dumb. I hadn't seen the movie but the way Rob was describing it, I thought it sounded interesting. But I didn't say anything. Rob said he studied this director in a film course at university. He's an auteur, Rob says. I didn't know what an *auteur* was then but I made a note in my head and looked it up the next time I went to the library.

Things were getting kind of heavy so I was glad when Donny told a really funny story about a guy at the Sears warehouse who fell asleep on one of the sofas and a couple of other guys loaded him on a truck. Rob laughed a lot but Kim didn't seem to think it was funny. She'd been kind of ignoring Donny anyway, maybe because he was wearing this funny-looking baseball cap he got at the Ex. Rob was wearing a really nice green polo shirt—the kind with the little alligator on it— and white chinos.

Anyway, Rob and Donny seemed to get along fine. Donny told Rob he was thinking of going back to school and Rob said that was really wise, that he should get his grade 13. You need all the education you can get, Rob said. He, himself, was quitting his job at the Manulife Centre and going back for his MBA—to a college in the States.

I looked at Kim and she had a really annoyed look on her face. But Rob didn't notice because he was busy talking to Donny, who was asking him how come he's going for the MBA. Rob says it was his father's idea. If you want to get anywhere in marketing, Rob says, you definitely need an MBA. It will probably take him a year, he says.

I was sort of worried about Kim. She'd always acted so cool about everything. Now, all of a sudden she says, well I don't want to change the subject or anything but why don't we order in a pizza? Which was really weird, because Kim never ate pizza. She said it was fattening and bad for your skin, too.

So we get this giant pizza, all dressed, which lightened things up and we all pigged out on it, even Kim.

Rob went away about a week later and he said he'd write to her, but Kim didn't seem to care much by that time. Well, all this happened last spring and summer and it just shows that you never know how things will turn out.

We had to give up the apartment because the rent went up and by the time we paid it we didn't have enough money to go anywhere. To tell

the truth, I didn't mind giving it up. Cooking was a hassle and carrying a big sack of laundry to the coin wash every Saturday was a real drag. My mum was glad to have me back home, but I never found out how Kim's family reacted. She quit her job in the fall and I kind of lost track of her.

Well, last week I was going to visit my girl friend Carol who's living in North York now and I ran into Kim on the street. She's pushing this really cute baby in a carriage. She still looks great although she's put on some weight. It turns out she's married. To her brother's friend. The one who runs the gas station. And when I say, it's really great to see you again, Kim, she says, by the way, I'm Joyce now. Larry likes it better.

Then she asks me how I'm doing and I tell her fine. I've had a raise since she left and I've been given a lot more responsibility, even more than Sara had. They tell me I could have a nice career there. And now that I'm living at home again, I've saved almost enough money for a trip to Europe next year.

Then she says, how's your social life? I tell her I'm going out with Donny a bit and he's got a better job now. Next fall, he's going back to school to take his grade 13. But it's not serious with Donny and me, I say, because I've got plans of my own.

I didn't tell her that I've been going out with Rob quite a bit, too. Even though he's got his MBA and everything we really have quite a lot in common. But I didn't think it was such a good idea to tell Kim, I mean Joyce, about Rob.

Anyway, she flashes me her great smile and says she's very happy for me and that it sounds like I'm really on the right track.

You take it from here ...

Responding

1. Focus on the Narrator   At the beginning of the story, the speaker hopes to save enough money to travel to Florida. By the end, she has almost saved enough for a holiday in Europe. This is only one of several changes that take place in the speaker's situation, experience, and ambitions. Working with other members of the class, identify and trace these developments as they occur in the story. What do you think caused these changes?

2. **Improvise a Conversation**   A pivotal moment in the story comes in the scene when Kim is annoyed and orders a pizza. Working with a partner, improvise a conversation between Kim and the narrator that helps to reveal and explain Kim's state of mind.

3. **Analyze Values**   "On the Right Track" is a deliberately crafted story that explores many different values. As a class, create a values chart similar to the following. Each time you record an individual's values, also make note of the specific details or comments in the story that reveal these to you.

	Values	Evidence
The narrator	– hates "trendy" – likes travel	– stated in first sentence – saving for a trip to Florida, then Europe
Kim		
Rob		
Donny		

Extending

4. **Paraphrase Dialogue**   This story is told in the first person, but the narrator provides a clear sense of the other characters when she paraphrases conversations they have had. Try this technique yourself. Tape-record a four-minute conversation you have with a friend, and then transcribe it word for word. Examine the transcript, and select the essential elements. Use these to write a first-person account of the conversation, telling a third person what was said.

5. **Write a Short Story**   Choose one of the main characters in this story, and write your own story describing a key event in the character's life that took place some time after the four went off in separate directions. Use clues from the last five paragraphs of "On the Right Track" to get you started.

"I had no idea it was going to turn into this."

Field of Dreams a Real-Life Gem

by WAYNE COFFEY

NEWSPAPER ARTICLE

Notes

Field of Dreams (1989) is a popular American movie based on Canadian W.P. Kinsella's book, *Shoeless Joe*. It tells the story of a farmer, Ray (Kevin Costner), who is inspired to turn a cornfield into a baseball field for the disgraced Chicago Black Sox, who "threw" the 1919 World Series. The fantasy movie is about how people should be given a second chance to fulfill their dreams and desires.

Shoeless Joe Jackson: One of the best baseball players ever, Jackson got his nickname when he played in his stocking feet because his new shoes pinched. Jackson was banned for life from playing baseball after the 1919 series, despite evidence that he didn't cheat: he had the series' only home run, the highest batting average, a record dozen hits, and no fielding errors.

"Oh, people will come, Ray. People will most definitely come."

> – *From the movie* Field of Dreams
> *Dyersville, Iowa*

Clifford Shields is a bearded 66-year-old retiree from Elmore, Ohio, who used to work in the automobile business and whom everybody calls Chick. He and his wife, Veronica, packed up their Taurus wagon recently and drove 400 miles

Field of Dreams, 1989

to the west, arriving in the northeast corner of Iowa just as the sun was disappearing behind the rich, rolling farmland.

When he got into Dyersville (pop. 3800), Shields followed Highway 136 over the railroad tracks and made a right turn at a pig farm. He passed a one-lane bridge and three miles of corn. He made another right on to Lansing Road and just over the crest of a small hill, beyond Al and Rita Ameskamps' farm, Chick Shields looked off to his left and there it was, the green jewel he came to see, carved out of the cornfields.

A perfect summer evening. This was Chick Shields' sixth trip to the Field of Dreams, and as he gazed out at it, he couldn't really explain why.

"You're drawn here," he said. "It's a special place. I guess it goes back to when you were a kid."

It has been a long, hot summer of baseball discontent, of slapped faces and flipped fingers and plummeting attendance.

What's wrong with baseball? So goes the weary refrain. It has been heard virtually everywhere, but not here at Don Lansing's farm, where the game's romance runs deep, where visitors are coming in record numbers from all corners of the country and beyond, six years after *Field of Dreams* arrived in theatres everywhere. "I had no idea it was going to turn into this," said Al Ameskamp, who owns the land that covers left and centre field. (The rest of the field, the farmhouse and surrounding yard are owned by Lansing.)

"I figured, 'We made a movie one year and it'll be back to farming the next year.'"

Ameskamp actually turned left and centre fields back into corn in 1989, the year after filming. Only when he saw the stream of visitors, and the disheartened look on their faces, did he plow under the corn and restore the outfield.

Field of Dreams is a movie about redemption and reconciliation, about an Iowa farmer named Ray Kinsella who heard voices in his cornfield and heeded them.

"If you build it, he will come," the first voice said. Ray Kinsella wound up with a ball field where his corn used to be, with Shoeless Joe Jackson and the other 1919 Black Sox walking out from the stalks to play there.

And finally, with his own father as a young man standing before him, the two of them playing a game of catch together, spectral father and real-life son, connected in a way they never had before.

The film has much more to do with spirituality than baseball, but the field is its artistic centre, and it is clear it is tugging people in powerful ways. An estimated 55 000 people

Ghost players walking out from the stalks to play

will visit this year, more than ever before. On a summer weekend, the number of visitors easily surpasses 1000. Recently, a team from the former Yugoslavia showed up; it was playing a tournament in Wisconsin and when somebody found out how close the team was to Dyersville, it made the trip. In the log book behind the backstop are entries from Utah, Pennsylvania and scores of other states. A father and son from Corpus Christi, Tex., stopped by several weeks ago, planning to stay for an hour or two.

They didn't leave until close to sundown.

The unexpected deluge has spawned a second hotel in town, and a couple of new restaurants. Unlike many small farming communities, the local economy is flourishing. All of this has occurred with scarcely a trace of promotion. There is an active chamber of commerce in Dyersville (with a John Deere tractor out front), and a billboard about the field in Dubuque, 25 miles to the west. That is about it.

Why do people visit? Some come simply out of curiosity, wanting to see a famous movie location. Others come in search of some redemption or reconciliation, hoping life can imitate art. Jacque Rahe, executive director of the chamber, tells of two brothers who hadn't spoken to each other for 30 years.

They met at the field by chance, and wound up making up.

Whatever brings them, many visitors find themselves taken by the serene spectacle of a diamond cut into corn, and by the feel-good ambience of the place. If *Field of Dreams* was the ultimate warm-and-fuzzy experience, the field itself is no less so.

People have been married and have gotten engaged on it. Others have come to sprinkle the ashes of loved ones.

The Carolina Mudcats, a Double-A team in Zebulon, North Carolina, believed enough in the field's positive vibes that they paid Don Lansing to fly down with a bucket of Field of Dreams dirt.

At any time of day, you will see entire families disappear into the outfield corn, just like the ghosts of the Black Sox in the film. Randy and Luann Dibb of Holmen, Wisconsin, and their three children—Alison, 9, Scott, 8, and Martha, 2—did precisely that.

They took pictures in front of the eight-foot stalks, and threw the ball around right field. Over in centre were Dale and Andrea Richards of Pittsburgh, along with their son, Matt, 21. Matt Richards, in a wheelchair, rolled right into the corn until he was out of sight. He wheeled back out with a big smile on his face.

"This place is fantastic," Matt said.

The field is the site of probably the longest continuous pickup game in America. From mid-morning until early evening, people old and young take turns at bat, pitching, fielding. Fathers throw off the mound to sons and daughters. Kids race around the bases. Others shag flies.

"Complete strangers are out there playing as if they've known each other all their life," Al Ameskamp said.

"You want to play a little ball? Want to pitch? Just get in there and go. There's no problem."

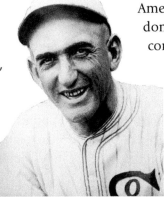

Shoeless Joe Jackson, 1919

Tim Crescenti, an independent filmmaker, did a documentary that aired on ESPN about people who have made pilgrimages to the field. He called it *Dreamfield*. He has been to Dyersville seven times now.

After socking a couple of balls into the crops, Crescenti said, "You just have the most peaceful, tranquil feeling when you're out here. Maybe it's the corn, I don't know."

A huge part of the appeal is that the field has not been junked up in the least. A couple of road signs help you get there, but there is no neon tackiness, no cardboard cutouts of Kevin Costner. There is also no admission charge. Don Lansing and the Ameskamps simply have small donation boxes, asking for contributions to help with upkeep.

"People are real good (about donations)," Lansing said. They also seem to treat the place with near-reverence. There is virtually no litter to pick up, even after a busy Saturday. The sole barrier on the ground is a thin yellow rope that separates the field from Lansing's white farmhouse, which sits on a small rise maybe 50 yards away, also unchanged from the silver screen, right down to the porch swing.

This is not to say the Field is wholly removed from commerce. There are two souvenir stands (though even those are unobtrusive), with more keepsakes available at the chamber of commerce. At the chamber alone, gross sales exceeded $100 000 last year. Add Lansing's souvenir place behind home plate, and the Ameskamps', and the total likely reaches $250 000. Another $250 000 or so is kicked into the local economy from visitors' food, lodging, etc.

Most folks in town are quite bemused by the whole thing. Don Lansing's farm being reborn as a baseball mecca. The bemusement seems to increase as the years go by. "I don't know how much longer the Field of Dreams will last as a tourist attraction," said Rosemary Dreger, who runs the Colonial Inn on Highway 136. "But it isn't slowing down." A day after they arrived at sunset, Chick and Veronica Shields came back to the field again. A short time later, Dan and Gloria Salinas pulled in, along with their aunt and uncle, Sandy and Mel Pearson. The Salinases were in the process of moving to California from Waukegan, Illinois. They had been to the field three weeks earlier. They wanted to see it again before leaving the Midwest.

Dan and Uncle Mel went out and pitched and hit some.

Dan threw batting practice to a guy from New York. It was a warm morning, the sky an almost make-believe blue. A stiff wind rustled the corn. A father and two sons walked into the stalks in left-centre.

A blond-haired girl of about seven hit a grounder to short and was heading for first. Soon an entire uniformed team of California teenagers was arriving. Everywhere you looked, people were playing ball on the Field of Dreams.

"You come over the hill and it's almost like it takes your breath away," Gloria Salinas said.

She said it gave her goosebumps. She couldn't really explain it. What's wrong with baseball? In Dyersville, Iowa, the question goes unasked, because the answer is absolutely nothing.

You take it from here ...

Responding

1. **Consider the Title**   Respond to the following in two or three paragraphs: Why is this article called "Field of Dreams"? What kinds of dreams does the field fulfill?

2. **Write a Personal Response**   The Dyersville field demonstrates the enormous power of movies. Think of a movie that made a strong impression on you. Write your impressions in several paragraphs, describing the elements of the movie that made it memorable and explaining how it changed your own outlook or actions.

Extending

3. **Dramatize an Anecdote**   Coffey reports special moments in the lives of people who have visited the field. Choose one of these scenes to present in the form of a dramatic script, making up details about the characters, and writing dialogue. Read your scripted scenes aloud in small groups.

4. **Research a Sports Team**   Coffey refers to "Shoeless Joe Jackson and the other 1919 Black Sox." Research this group of baseball players and write a short report explaining what makes them important. How were they themselves connected to a "field of dreams"?

Before you read, discuss with the rest of the class the number of different meanings there are for the word "dream."

As you read, ask yourself what kind of dream Langston Hughes is referring to in his poem.

Dreams

Poem by Langston Hughes

Hold fast to dreams
For if dreams die
Life is a broken-winged bird
That cannot fly.

Hold fast to dreams
For when dreams go
Life is a barren field
Frozen with snow.

Notes

Langston Hughes (1902–1967) is an important Black American poet who became famous during the Harlem Renaissance of Black culture in the 1920s. Hughes wrote proudly and sometimes with protest about Black experience.

You take it from here ...

Responding

1. Focus on Illustration   Look at the illustration accompanying the poem and write a paragraph explaining how the image relates to the text. Suggest another image that might have been chosen instead, and explain how it reflects the content of the poem.

2. Examine Poetic Form   This poem is very well known in North America. As a class, examine its construction. What patterns do the stanzas follow in rhyme? rhythm? sentence structure? figurative language? Why do you think these lines are so popular and memorable?

3. Write Another Stanza   Write a third stanza for this poem to imitate Langston Hughes's poetic style, structure, and theme. Share your stanzas in small groups. Read Hughes's poem aloud several times, each time accompanied by a different third stanza. Which of your classmates' stanzas works best with Hughes's composition?

4. Consider Context   In the 1920s, Langston Hughes was known as "The Poet Laureate of Harlem." He believed strongly that his poetry had to reflect himself and his pride in his ethnic background. "Dreams" was first published in 1932. As a class, discuss how having an understanding of the author and the period in which he was writing influences your interpretation of the poem. Does it add to your first understanding of the poem, or does it complicate it?

Extending

5. Debate Conflict   Often, the dreams of parents and children clash. For example, Langston Hughes, who began writing poetry in the eighth grade, always dreamed of being a poet. However, his father was afraid that his son would not be able to make a living as a writer and forced him to study engineering at university instead. Hold an informal debate with other members of the class on the clash between the dreams of parents and their children with respect to the children's future. Should the parents' wisdom and experience necessarily prevail over the children's own wishes and ambitions? Can such conflicts be resolved to everyone's satisfaction? Why or why not?

6. Read Another Poem   Search in the library or on the Internet for more poems by Langston Hughes. Choose one that appeals to you and practise reading it aloud. Then, read or recite the poem to the class. Be prepared to talk about what this poem means to you.

Why Don't You Carve Other Animals?

The picture is now full of life.

Short Story by Yvonne Vera

Notes

Yvonne Vera (1964–), was born in Bulawayo, Zimbabwe, and is one of Africa's major writers. She now lives in Toronto, where she completed a doctorate at York University.

Victoria Falls: spectacular waterfall in Africa. It is the world's largest sheet of falling water.

He sits outside the gates of the Africans-Only hospital, making models out of wood. The finished products are on old newspapers on the ground around him. A painter sits to his right, his finished work leaning against the hospital fence behind them. In the dense township, cars screech, crowds flow by, voices rise, and ambulances speed into the emergency unit of the hospital, their flashing orange light giving fair warning to oncoming traffic. Through the elephants he carves, and also the giraffes, with oddly slanting necks, the sculptor brings the jungle to the city. His animals walk on the printed newspaper sheets, but he mourns that they have no life in them. Sometimes in a fit of anger he collects his animals and throws them frenziedly into his cardboard box, desiring not to see their lifeless forms against the chaotic movement of traffic which flows through the hospital gates.

"Do you want that crocodile? It's a good crocodile. Do you want it?" A mother coaxes a little boy who has been crying after his hospital visit. A white bandage is wrapped tight around his right arm. The boy holds his arm with his other hand, aware of the mother's attention, which makes him draw attention to his temporary deformity. She kneels beside him and looks into his eyes, pleading.

"He had an injection. You know how the children fear the needle," the mother informs the man. She buys the crocodile, and hands it to the boy. The man watches one of his animals go, carried between the little boy's tiny fingers. His animals have no life in them, and the man is tempted to put them back in the box. He wonders if the child will ever see a moving crocodile, surrounded as he is by the barren city, where the only rivers are the tarred roads.

A man in a white coat stands looking at the elephants, and at the man who continues carving. He picks a red elephant, whose tusk is carved along its body, so that it cannot raise it. A red elephant? The stranger is perplexed, and amused, and decides to buy the elephant, though it is poorly carved and cannot lift its tusk. He will place it beside the window in his office, where it can look out at the patients in line. Why are there no eyes carved on the elephant? Perhaps the paint has covered them up.

The carver suddenly curses.

"What's wrong?" the painter asks.

"Look at the neck of this giraffe."

The painter looks at the giraffe, and the two men explode into uneasy laughter. It is not easy to laugh when one sits so close to the sick.

The carver wonders if he has not carved some image of himself, or of some afflicted person who stopped and looked at his breathless animals. He looks at the cardboard box beside him and decides to place it in the shade, away from view.

"Why don't you carve other animals? Like lions and chimpanzees?" the painter asks. "You are always carving giraffes and your only crocodile has been bought!" The painter has had some influence on the work of the carver, lending him the paints to colour his animals. The red elephant was his idea.

Victoria Falls

"The elephant has ruled the forest for a long time, he is older than the forest, but the giraffe extends his neck and struts above the trees, as though the forest belonged to him. He eats the topmost leaves, while the elephant spends the day rolling in the mud. Do you not find it interesting? This struggle between the elephant and the giraffe, to eat the topmost leaves in the forest?" The ambulances whiz past, into the emergency unit of the Africans-Only hospital.

The painter thinks briefly, while he puts the final touches on an image of the Victoria Falls which he paints from a memory gathered from newspapers and magazines. He has never seen the Falls. The water must be blue, to give emotion to the picture, he thinks. He has been told that when the water is shown on a map, it has to be blue, and that indeed when there is a lot of it, as in the sea, the water looks like the sky. So he is generous in his depiction, and shocking blue waves cascade unnaturally over the rocky precipice.

"The giraffe walks proudly, majestically, because of the beautiful tapestry that he carries on his back. That is what the struggle is about. Otherwise, they are equals. The elephant has his long tusk to reach the leaves and the giraffe has his long neck."

He inserts two lovers at the corner of the picture, their arms around each other as they stare their love into the blue water. He wants to make the water sing to them. So he paints a bird at the top of the painting, hovering over the falls, its beak open in song. He wishes he had painted a dove, instead of this black bird which looks like a crow.

The carver borrows some paint and puts yellow and black spots on the giraffe with the short neck. He has long accepted that he cannot carve perfect animals, but will not throw them away. Maybe someone, walking out of the Africans-Only hospital, will seek some cheer in his piece. But when he has finished applying the dots, the paint runs down the sides of the animal, and it looks a little like a zebra.

"Why do you never carve a dog or a cat? Something that city people have seen. Even a rat would be good, there are lots of rats in the township!" There is much laughter. The painter realizes that a lot of spray from the falls must be reaching the lovers, so he paints off their heads with a red umbrella. He notices suddenly that something is missing in the picture, so he extends the lovers' free hands, and gives them some yellow ice cream. The picture is now full of life.

"What is the point of carving a dog? Why do you not paint dogs and cats and mice?" The carver has never seen the elephant or the giraffe that he carves so ardently. He picks up a piece of unformed wood.

Will it be a giraffe or an elephant? His carving is also his dreaming.

You take it from here ...

Responding

1. Describe the Setting   In a class discussion, describe the setting of the story. Where and when does it take place? What are the details in the story that reveal this to you? Is this a pleasant setting? What leads you to your conclusion?

2. Focus on Character   Working in small groups, discuss the painter and carver.

   - What are they like as people?
   - What might they look like?
   - What is their relationship?
   - How are they different from each other?
   - What do they share in common?

Once you have analyzed the characters, report your conclusions to the rest of the class. Then, as a class, consider why the author chose not to give names to the painter and carver.

3. Draw the Picture   Sketch or recreate the image of Victoria Falls produced by the painter. Indicate whether you think his painting is a good one. What basis do you use for making this judgement? How do we know whether any piece of art is good?

4. Interpret Symbols   The carver describes the struggle and rivalry of the giraffe and elephant. As a class, consider whether this struggle is symbolic of anything else in the story. Could it represent a struggle in the larger world outside the story?

Extending

5. Take a Different Point of View   Reread the section in which the little boy's mother buys him the crocodile. Rewrite the incident from the point of view of either the boy or his mother.

6. Debate the Value of Art   What is the purpose of art? Who benefits most from it—the creator or those who view it? Should art be taught in schools? Should public money be spent on it? Using the situation in "Why Don't You Carve Other Animals" as your starting point, hold an informal debate on the value of art for both the artist and the viewer.

Before you read, share with the rest of the class what you think about when you hear the word "Everest."

As you read, note the many dangers described by the author.

Triumph on Mount Everest

Death was everywhere.

Memoir by Stacy Allison

Notes

Stacy Allison was the first American woman to reach the top of Mount Everest. Allison lives with her family in Portland, Oregon, and runs a construction business.

cornice: overhanging snow or ice on a mountain ridge

crampon: spiky plate fastened to climber footwear to prevent slipping

firmament: sky

I could see it now, off in the distance. That last glint of white against a powder blue morning sky. Two hundred yards away. A slow uphill walk in the thin air, perhaps 15 minutes. Each step a physical strain against the altitude, the desolate air, the sudden bursts of high-velocity wind. But there it was, almost close enough to touch. A few more steps, and I would.

But first, the ridge. It slopes up from the left at about 35 degrees, then peaks to the right as a series of cornices—ridges of overhanging ice and snow, poised above a sheer 8000-foot drop. A stress fracture in the snow, crawling up the ridge a few feet to the left of the dropoff, marked the fault line. I kept to the left of the crack in the snow, trying to avoid riding a broken cornice down into Tibet, but still keeping a buffer between my path and where the slope turned steep and fell away on the left.

The worst was behind me, but I was so high now, so exposed. A sudden gust of wind, I thought, could lift me right out of my boots and sail me all the way back to base camp. Or one of these icy overhangs could snap. Or I could catch a crampon on my pants and tumble down the other side of the ridge. Death was everywhere. I forced it down and drilled myself onward. I went as fast as I could, one foot down, then the other. Walking with my ice axe, chunking the tip into the snow. Keeping an eye on the stress fracture, on the bottomless slope to my left. Glancing up, seeing the end of the ridge in the distance. The end of the ridge, and the end of the world. I could make it. As long as I kept moving, I was going to make it.

Pasang was on the ridge now, following my steps about 70 yards behind me. In the distance I could see the Koreans, small specks of colour sitting in the snow. They were on the summit. I was so close. But I couldn't think about it yet, not with these cornices, the drop-off, the stress fracture swerving between. I had to follow that line, and keep moving. I was still digging for breath, feeling the thunder in my chest, still keeping tabs on my numb toes. And still climbing.

The air looked like crystal. The sky was so blue, the sun gleaming yellow and powerful. Even in the cold the rays felt palpable, as if they carried a physical weight. I could see everything. Up above, a few wispy clouds skimmed by the sun, riding the highest winds in the firmament. Behind me, I could look down into Nepal. All but a few of the tallest peaks were covered by thick, billowing clouds. The sky was clearer above the brown plains of Tibet, spread out ahead of me. I could see the plains, rolling away, and closer in I could see the Rongbuk Glacier, where I'd been standing exactly a year earlier.

Mount Everest

Now I was 75 feet away. Walking carefully, minding the crack in the ridge and the tip of my ice axe, my crampons squeaking in and out of the snow. *One foot in front of the other.* Fifty feet. Closer to the Koreans now, close enough to see them snapping pictures of each other. So close, but I wouldn't let myself feel it yet. Not until I was there. Something was swelling inside me, but I pushed it down. I had to keep moving, stay focused on the crack, the steps, reaching out with my ice axe, pulling in another two feet. Taking another step, then another, and reaching out again. Walking faster, feeling the adrenaline starting to flow, surging through my veins and running hot into my fingers and even my dulled toes.

Twenty-five feet. It was unbelievable. Now I knew I was going to make it. I could see the Koreans talking on their walkie-talkie. Just beyond where they stood, I could see blue sky.

Ten feet. This was it. I checked my watch—just past 10:30. September 29, 1988. The Koreans were watching me now, the leader reaching out to shake my hand. "Good, very good!" he called, and beneath my oxygen mask I smiled. But I barely heard him, and kept going, those last few feet to where it ended. It was so strange. After everything, I was walking onto the summit of Mount Everest. It was right there, I could see it clearly just ahead of me. The last few steps, just a little higher, and then there was nothing. The end of the ridge, and then nothing but that clear, empty air.

I stopped climbing.

There was nowhere else to climb.

I was standing on the top of the world.

I felt it now, everything I'd kept bottled up as I came up the ridge. It billowed up from my core, a blinding wave of emotion. I could finally let it all go, the months of controlling my thoughts, of channelling all my energy toward this one purpose. Behind my glasses my eyes blurred. I was wide open now, and I was aware of everything. The wind in my hair, the sweat on my back, the blood washing through my wrists and ankles. I made it. For myself, for Steve and Jim, for everyone. I was standing on the top, looking

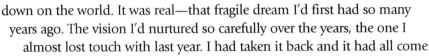

down on the world. It was real—that fragile dream I'd first had so many years ago. The vision I'd nurtured so carefully over the years, the one I almost lost touch with last year. I had taken it back and it had all come true. I was strong enough. I was good enough and lucky enough … and I had come out the other end. After everything, I finally had.

Pasang was still 10 minutes away. So it was just me. A small patch of snow, a lot of sky, and me. The cloud of emotion thinned, then vanished. My eyes were dry again. I took little steps and turned around on the snowy crest of the summit, this way to look over Nepal, then that way to see into Tibet. Behind me the Koreans hung together in a tight circle, laughing and chattering to their base camp on the walkie-talkie. Now I felt strange. *I was on top of the world, but I was alone.* This wasn't how I wanted it to happen. During all those years of wishing, dreaming about it, working for it, I never once imagined I'd be alone when I got to the summit. I wanted to hug someone, to make this dream explode into life by seeing it reflected in someone else's eyes. But I was on top of Mount Everest by myself.

Then Pasang came up. He pumped his ice axe in the air, hooting and yipping with everything he had left in his lungs. The Koreans looked up from their radio and greeted him, slapping his back, pumping his hand. The sight popped the lid off my emotions again, and I walked over to him, reaching out to Pasang and wrapping him in a bear hug. "We did it," I said, my eyes going hot and cloudy again. "We really did it."

The Koreans were putting their packs on now, taking their first steps down the ridge. Then they were gone. Pasang and I had a minute or two to stand alone on the summit, then it was time to get to work.

Back home, we'd engaged donors by promising to entwine their own names with the summit. Now that we were really on top of Everest, we had to provide the payoff. Opening my backpack, I dug in for the Honour Roll, the small roll of microfilm listing the names of all the people who had donated money to our expedition. I scraped a shallow pit in the snow, laid the roll of film inside, and covered it over. But our corporate sponsors expected a more tangible kind of testament. I gave Pasang the camera, then reached into my pack for the corporate banners.

There were 25 of them wrapped in a stuff sack, some as small as a handkerchief, a few as large as a tablecloth. I planted my pink flamingo in the snow, then sat down and unrolled the first banner. Pasang snapped a few photos, and then we moved on to the next one, then the next. The task soon grew tedious. My smile started to hurt, and I began to get cold. To make things even more difficult, the wind was blowing up again. The gusts kept blowing my parka hood off my head. That made me worry about holding up the larger banners—what if one blew out of my fingers?

After a while, I pulled off my oxygen mask and took a stab at breathing the thin, cold air of the jet stream. My body felt it immediately, but my head stayed clear. It seemed livable, and it made me think of Jim and Steve. I wished they had come up with me.

During the half-hour it took to shoot the corporate photos, Pasang and I were all business. Once we were done, however, we had a few minutes to ourselves. We snapped a few pictures of each other, and I shot a series of panoramas. Then I reached into my pocket for my own artifacts. Climbing the mountain gave me something to take away. It felt only appropriate to leave a small part of me behind. I had a little piece of turquoise a Tibetan yak herder had given me in 1987. He'd lived in the shadow of the mountain for his entire life, but never dreamed of climbing it, so I promised to take something of his to the top. I had a baggie of blessed rice I took from our altar at base camp the day we set out for the summit. I had a prayer scarf, a snapshot of me with David, and, finally, a Susan B. Anthony silver dollar.

I looked at my watch. It was getting late now, after 11:00. We didn't have that much time, but I still felt I had to ground myself. I thought about the mountain's spirit. The Mother Goddess of the Earth. I thanked her for being kind enough to let me climb her. I prayed she'd let me get down in one piece, too. I looked at my watch again, and saw I'd already been on top for close to 45 minutes. I caught Pasang's eye and gestured down. He looked surprised.

"Now?"

"Soon. In a minute," I said.

We stood together, looking out over the world beneath us. I wanted to remember everything. The cold, dry air between my lips, the wind pushing against my back, the way the silvery wisps of cloud jetted across the sky. I needed to remember it, to keep the image deep inside the vaults in my memory bank. This was the top of Everest. The dream of a lifetime. I looked around. There had to be something for me to latch onto. A perfect image I could remember that would objectify why I'd come, for now and forever. But nothing came into focus. It was hard to believe, after so many years, but the summit of Everest was just snow and ice. A mountain summit, pretty much like any other mountain summit. I was contemplating this when Pasang looked over at me and said: "We spend two months getting to the mountain, carrying things up the mountain, climbing the mountain. We work like dogs, then spend so little time on top, and now we go back down. What's the meaning?"

I shook my head. How do you define ambition? People do strange things—stand on their heads, play computer games, write 100 000 prayers to Buddha. You find your talent, and see how far it will take you. You do what makes you feel the most alive.

You take it from here ...

Responding

1. Examine Style   The first paragraph contains a series of sentence fragments. Rewrite it to make the sentences grammatically correct. Compare your version with Stacy Allison's and decide which version is more effective, giving reasons for your response.

2. Consider Motivation   "Death was everywhere," says Stacy Allison early in her memoir. Working in groups, list each of the dangers she confronted on her climb up the ridge. What reason(s) does she give for taking such risks?

3. Discuss Symbolism   Stacy Allison left a number of objects at the summit of Everest. Discuss each of these items with the rest of the class. Suggest why she might have chosen these particular mementos.

Extending

4. Write a Poem   Poetry is a condensed language in that poets use as few words as possible to tell their readers about an experience. Use Stacy Allison's memoir as the basis for a poem about reaching the top of Mount Everest. Borrow her words if you wish, but work to capture her emotions and the entire experience at the top of the world in as few well-chosen words as possible.

TIP

- The Web site at www.everestnews. com/everest1.htm is a good starting point for information on Everest "firsts."

5. Consider Gender   Do you think that Stacy Allison's gender makes her accomplishment more remarkable than it would have been for a man? Explain your opinion in your journal. Then, research other Everest milestones, such as the first successful climb, the first summit by a woman, the first summit by a climber with a disability, and so on.

    Use this information in a short personal essay on the possibilities of breaking through obstacles or stereotypes to achieve important goals in life.

6. Debate Commercialism   Stacy Allison spent half of her time at the top of the world posing for photographs as she held up various corporate logos. This was required as payment for sponsorship of the expedition. Discuss with the class your reaction to this situation. Is there too much emphasis today on companies and logos? Or do these companies deserve the visual recognition for their contributions?

Out of This World

Starting our spacewalk, I was the first one at the door.

Memoir by Chris Hadfield

Notes

Chris Hadfield (1959–), a colonel in the Canadian Armed Forces, grew up on a corn farm in Milton, Ontario. His work with out-of-control F/A-18 planes did not go unnoticed by NASA, and he was chosen by the space agency to be an astronaut in 1992. Hadfield was the first Canadian to walk in space. He now works as a CapCom (the voice of Mission Control, talking to astronauts in space). According to one record, he has logged 480 hours in space.

Entering the vacuum of space for the first time is a form of rebirth. You push your head out of the space shuttle's air lock, and it's like coming out of a womb into the world. After years of training and simulation, suddenly you are there. You're outside, and the vista is just overwhelming. I am absolutely slapped in the face with an incredibly vivid view of the International Space Station and the world below from horizon to horizon. It's as stunning a juxtaposition as you can imagine.

I had some tasks in the vicinity of the air lock that I had to do right away. I wanted to focus on those, sort of like how a sprinter concentrates on those first four or five paces before he can start thinking about the rest of the run. I knew I was going to be outside for seven hours or so. But I just couldn't help myself. The view is so breathtaking and beautiful that you feel you're insulting it not to stop and take it in.

It takes about 90 minutes to suit up for a spacewalk. But it takes years of preparation to get to that point—about four years in my case. I had been on a NASA shuttle mission in November 1995, but still I had to go through advanced training for the 11-day flight aboard the shuttle *Endeavour* at the end of April. The No. 1 objective was to bring to life the giant robotic Canadarm2 on the International Space Station. The arm [built by MD Robotics of Brampton, Ontario] will act as a crane that will help with the construction and functioning of the station. The main goal of our mission was unloading and installing the arm, which even when folded is as big as a truck. In fact, it's too big to fit in the back of the shuttle, so they had to fold it in half and then fold it in half again. It was bolted to a huge cradle-shaped pallet. The plan was to pick up the cradle with the shuttle's smaller robotic arm—the original Canadarm—lift it over the shuttle and install that entire cradle on the space station. Then we were to plug in connecting cables and bring the arm to life on the side of the space station. When it was finally in place, Canadarm2 was to pass the

Hadfield, right, and fellow astronaut John Phillips head off to the shuttle's launchpad.

cradle to Canadarm, which was to put it back in the shuttle's cargo bay.

First we had to get into space. To climb aboard a shuttle on the launchpad, which is already pointed toward the sky, you have to crawl in on hands and knees, and worm your way into your seat and get strapped in by a technician and another astronaut who is supporting the launch. Then it's a couple of hours that you're basically sitting on your back with your feet and knees up in the air until the time that you can launch. Sitting there I just had a keen desire to get on with it and make it happen. It's like trying to lift up the shuttle with my emotion, just straight will of thought. For 46 months I had been readying myself and training specifically for this flight, and we had almost 2000 people, Canadian friends and guests, down at the Cape Canaveral launch site in Florida. You're not fearful. You're not particularly nervous. It's like an exam you know all the answers to, and you're just waiting for the bell to go. That was the feeling in my chest.

The most dangerous part of the flight is the first 8.5 minutes. The launch is extremely violent when the engines light. You are on the end of a 67-m whiplash. There's enough raw power to lift an apartment building off the ground, and you're sitting in the middle of that. There's this heavy, violent shaking like being caught in the jaws of some enormous dog and being rattled and pushed until you get through the atmosphere, which takes about 90 seconds. We get up to three times earth's normal gravity through our chests.

It's smoother after two minutes, when you really start to accelerate because you don't have the drag of the air anymore. You feel the big changes in acceleration. You get lighter and lighter, and the acceleration gets heavier and heavier. Eventually we have to bring the throttles back to decrease the thrust out of the engines; otherwise the speed can rip the fuel tank off the shuttle. We go from sitting on the launchpad to being weightless in orbit in 8.5 minutes. It's an amazing transition.

It takes a while to adjust once you are up there. You are falling toward the earth perpetually, but you are going fast enough sideways that the horizon falls away from you at the same rate you are falling. In this environment your eyes tell you that you are sitting in a room, but your inner ear tells you that you are falling. That causes a lot of dizziness. Everything inside your body is floating instead of sitting where gravity normally puts it. Your body feels the symptoms—not being able to balance properly, having an upset stomach—and concludes you've poisoned yourself. So it typically makes you want to throw up as a defense mechanism. We call it space-adaptation sickness and, like motion sickness or seasickness, it responds to medication. After a day or two, you adapt.

The morning of the first spacewalk was our fourth day in space [April 22]. Getting dressed starts with placing biomedical sensors against your chest, just as if you are preparing to get an electrocardiogram. This enables the doctors on the ground to monitor your condition. Next you put on what is essentially a diaper because you're going to be inside this pressurized suit for about nine hours. Then you put on long underwear and above that a liquid-cooling garment, which is made up of small plastic tubes all over your body, except your head and your hands. Next is the suit, which weighs about 70 kg to 80 kg. It's extremely cumbersome to move in, primarily because it's big. You're wearing your entire life-support system on your back, so it's very massive and bulky. Also, it's pressurized, so if you relax your arms stick out. And your field of view is somewhat limited. If you turn your head, you face your ear cup because the helmet doesn't turn with you. So you can't see what's behind you or what's above you. You have to turn your whole body to see. It takes a lot of training to move with any sort of grace.

Starting our spacewalk, I was the first one out the door, followed by Dr. Scott Parazynski. One thing you notice out there is the silence. The internal spacesuit fans are almost whisper quiet. It's peaceful. Then there's the blackness. Space is just black until you get into the shadow of the earth. But the earth is crystal clear. You can see the atmosphere—a thin multicoloured veil on the rim of the horizon—and entire weather systems. You can be working outside and be distracted by Africa going by.

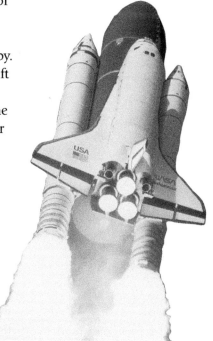

We always have one tether on us, so if we lose our grip and start to drift off into space we can reel ourselves in like a fish on a long line. We also wear a jet pack on our backs—the equivalent of a parachute—so if that line breaks, you can fire little thruster jets and fly yourself back to the station or the shuttle like Buck Rogers. Even tethered, you're basically a one-person spaceship, absolutely separate and isolated from everything else on earth. You're moving at about 8 km per second or about 28 000 km/h, orbiting the earth every 92 minutes. In that environment, a tiny particle of space dust—say, a fleck of paint or something smaller than your baby fingernail—could puncture your spacesuit. Still, the suit is pretty well protected. It is 16 layers thick and includes rubbery bladders and layers made of Kevlar-type material. In case it does spring a leak, we carry an extremely high-pressure oxygen tank around the kidneys, so you have enough spare oxygen to feed the leak for a while—long enough, you hope, to drag yourself back to the air lock to plug into the shuttle's oxygen system and keep yourself from bursting like a balloon. But in all the American, Soviet and Russian spacewalks, nobody has ever been hurt or even suffered the bends.

Thousands of Canadians came out to watch the *Endeavour's* seven-man crew go up into orbit

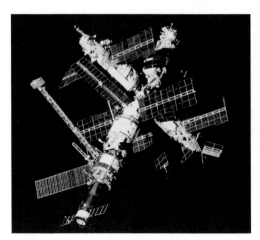

The International Space Station—with its new addition curled beneath—keeps moving inexorably at 8 km per second as the shuttle pulls away.

You're going around the world quickly enough that the angle of the sun is constantly changing, like the shadow of a tree rapidly going from one side of a field to another. The lighting affects everything and changes from minute to minute. Just the space station itself, which is such a huge collection of cylinders and angular parts and wires and plumbing, is an ever-changing kaleidoscope of colours and shadows. And the huge solar panels, which are gold in the daytime, turn blood red as the sun rises and sets, which happens about 16 times a day. You go through a transition from the brilliant-white, blinding sun into absolute pitch darkness of the sunset period in about 15 seconds. The station is 15 stories tall. Being next to it is like standing on the balcony of an enormous building and looking straight down. And it is moving relentlessly around the world. It is as though you're hanging off the bow of a huge ship that is unstoppably moving through the water.

There were a couple of times during the spacewalks when I wasn't doing anything critical while it was dark, and I shut off the lights on my suit so I could really look at the world in the darkness. Once we were in the southern hemisphere, and I saw the Southern Lights, or Aurora Australis, which were quite active. I could see green, shifting lights beaming as if straight out of the earth for thousands of kilometres off to one side. It was like the earth was a lightbulb covered in black that had little holes in it, and these beams of light were coming up out of the planet. Then of course there are the stars, which don't even twinkle because there's no atmosphere in the way. And the Milky Way is a solid band of white.

The second spacewalk, two days later, was probably more impressive and exciting for me because you miss things, of course, the first time you do them. But we had things that weren't going right on the second walk, and I was racing around the outside of the space station for seven and a half hours going from task to task. We were disconnecting the robotic arm's power from the temporary lash-up on its launch cradle and then reattaching it through a whole new set of wires. For a while it didn't power up properly, and there was no obvious explanation. After testing lots of connections, we finally found the problem.

I was pleasantly surprised at how comfortable and natural it felt to be working on the outside of a spaceship for the first time. Our training in the virtual-reality lab in Houston and in the underwater pool, this enormous swimming pool where we built the space station over and over again, was excellent preparation. Ours was the most complex robotic flight ever carried out in space. We had both Canadian-built arms operating simultaneously from the two spacecraft, a very complicated thing to do.

Being the first Canadian to walk in space was a big symbolic event with psychological impact. The overwhelming emotions were pleasure and relief after our success and pride in what we had done. I've had some interesting experiences as a fighter pilot and a test pilot. And since I flew to Russia's Mir in 1995, I've now docked with two space stations. But I would unequivocally say walking in space was the most incredible experience.

You take it from here ...

Responding

1. **Discuss Authorial Voice**   With one or two other students, read between the lines and decide what sort of person you believe Chris Hadfield to be. Would you like to meet him in person? Point to specific details in his writing that lead you to your conclusion.

2. **Analyze Imagery**   This account contains some powerful imagery, in particular, details that appeal to the senses of sight, hearing, and touch as well as the sensations of motion and bodily reactions. Working in small groups, chart the imagery in this selection, grouping the images according to the senses they appeal to.

3. **Organize Information**   Much of the information in this selection is expressed in numerical terms (e.g., 11-day flight, 46-month training). Extract as many of these numerical facts as you can, and use them to create a Mission Fact Sheet.

Extending

4. **Research a Career**   It's a long way from a corn farm in Ontario to outer space, but that's the journey Chris Hadfield took. Use library or Internet sources to find information on the qualifications an individual needs in order to become an astronaut, or to work in another unusual career. Present your findings in the form of your choice (e.g., report, Want Ad, job fair recruitment poster, résumé).

5. **Hold a Debate**   Canada has contributed considerably to the space program in the past decade. Naturally, this involves spending money. Research the costs and benefits of Canadian participation in the space program. Then hold a formal debate on the motion: "Be it resolved that Canada should continue to participate in the American space program."

"I want something good to come from the bad things that have happened to me."

Four Who Make a Difference

by JENNIFER BURKE CRUMP

PROFILES

With their multicoloured hair shaved close to their heads or shaped into towering mohawks, the group of 28 street kids and patients from Ottawa's Children's Hospital of Eastern Ontario mental-health ward attracted a lot of attention at the prestigious Camp Fortune skiing facility in the Gatineau Hills.

In the middle of the group stood Isabelle Rivard, their teacher and mentor. She looked just like one of the kids, and in fact, she was. Barely 17, her lips, tongue, and an eyebrow pierced, this former drug user was the sole reason a group of troubled young people were discovering snowboarding that day in January 1997.

As her eyes scanned the group, her confident, calm voice alternately encouraged and cautioned. "Take your time, don't try too much yet," she warned the more eager members. "You are going to have to do this yourself; I can't do it for you," she bluntly told others who seemed more timid.

The FreeRide Snowboarding Project takes groups of street kids to Camp Fortune every Monday for six weeks. For kids who have lived with depression, self-mutilation, suicidal behaviours, and other mental-health problems, snowboarding has proved to be a healthy way to cope with emotional trauma. "It gives them something to look forward to and work toward," says Sarah Brandon, a coordinator for Youth Net/Réseau Ado, a mental-health and early-intervention program affiliated with Ottawa's Children's Hospital that works with communities in both Ontario and Quebec.

No one understands this better than Isabelle. As a teen, she progressed from marijuana to hard drugs. She'd party all night and return to her home in Touraine, Quebec, to sleep the day away. She was constantly at war with her parents, who struggled to help her as the drugs drew her into a deadly spiral of depression. When it became unbearable, she would mutilate herself, scarring her arms in a vain attempt to ease her emotional pain.

After nothing else seemed to work, Isabelle's parents took her to the Children's Hospital, which had facilities for clinically depressed youths. Isabelle arrived defiant, apathetic and adrift. While the hospital provided a safe haven, it seemed more like a prison to her. An avid snowboarder, she craved the physical excitement and mental escape the sport gave her, though from her hospital window she couldn't even see the ski hills, much less reach them.

Then fate stepped in. In conversation one day, Youth Net's Brandon discovered Isabelle's passion for snowboarding and engineered a day on the slopes for the two of them. Isabelle's transformation amazed Brandon.

Believing others could feel the way she did on the slopes, Isabelle created the FreeRide Snowboarding Project and approached Youth Net for support. The Youth Net team, which includes a mix of youths, facilitators, and clinicians, made her a deal: Isabelle could organize the program as long as she shunned drugs and didn't try to hurt herself.

To raise funds, she asked Ottawa shop owners to donate raffle prizes, for which she sold tickets. She found snowboarding volunteers from a local high school and from Camp Fortune to help her teach the street kids and patients. Next she approached Peter Sudermann, Camp Fortune's owner, who agreed to give the kids passes and boards at ridiculously low rates.

Founded in 1997, the FreeRide Snowboarding Project received a Pan-Commonwealth Youth Service Award in November 2000. And Isabelle? "Snowboarding put me back on my feet," she says. Today she is a happy, self-confident young woman balancing full- and part-time jobs while living in Whistler, British Columbia, a stone's throw from the ski hills—where she snowboards daily.

Good Medicine—Isabelle Rivard knew that snowboarding could get troubled kids back on their feet.

At 16, Lance Relland was a promising dancer with the Royal Winnipeg Ballet School. But in July 1996, shortly before he turned 17, the auburn-haired, brown-eyed Edmontonian was informed he had a rare, deadly form of acute lymphoblastic leukemia—and four to seven months to live.

Lance had no intention of giving in to illness any more than he had given in to other challenges he'd faced in his young life—whether it was coming to terms with his Métis heritage or mastering classical ballet.

Still, doctors were vague about Lance's type of leukemia and its treatment. "I need to find out everything I can about this disease. I need to know what can be done," Lance told his mother.

While searching for information on the Internet, he found references to a monoclonal antibody against leukemia cells that had been discovered by researchers at the University of Minnesota. This antibody treatment seemed to be working for people with his type of leukemia. It was available only in the United States, however, and the provincial government would not pay for it.

Undaunted, Lance's family and friends started a foundation in September 1996 and raised more than $100 000 to cover the costs of his treatment at the Fairview-University Medical Centre in Minneapolis. Lance received the monoclonal antibody there and in October had a bone-marrow transplant from his brother. Four and a half years later, Lance remains cancer-free.

During his stay in hospital and while recovering as an outpatient, Lance spent hours talking to other cancer patients. Many, he found out, lacked basic knowledge about their illness and had no idea how to locate needed information. He also met kids whose parents and doctors had been unable to find matching bone-marrow donors. *I want something good to come from the bad things that have happened to me,* he decided as he flew home to Alberta.

On his return, Lance persuaded the foundation set up in his name to keep going and to make patient education its focus. The result: The Lance Relland Medical Foundation now provides to cancer and other patients in Edmonton access to Internet documents as well as a $200 000 medical library provided by an anonymous donor. It also helps fund patients seeking medical treatment not covered by the Alberta government.

But for Lance, this still wasn't enough. During his research, he had discovered that the aboriginal population had only 1-percent representation on Canadian and U.S. bone-marrow lists. Ideal donors are found first within a patient's family, then his or her ethnic group. So in 1998 Lance set up the Aboriginal Bone Marrow Registries, which accept donors from any ethnic group in North America but focus on recruiting Indian, Métis, and Inuit people.

Lance has since travelled to reserves and high schools across Alberta to convince people to join the registries and to push for a healthy lifestyle. "One illegal drug injection or exposure to HIV or Hepatitis C will prevent you from donating," he tells his audience, "and someday, someone in your family might need you." Lance's aboriginal registries now list over 800 donors.

In 1999 Lance began his studies in medicine at the University of California, Riverside, and he continues to support the foundation and registries he started.

❧

Haliburton, Ontario, teenager Amy Brandon had known Russell Snoddon since they were both in kindergarten, where Amy's mother, a special-education assistant, would come in to help the young Down syndrome boy. By the time Amy and Russell reached high school, the boy was a frequent visitor to the Brandon household. "Let's play cops and robbers," Russell would plead, and Amy, playing the bad guy, would let Russell arrest her, over and over.

In 1998 Amy heard about a new program at Haliburton Highlands Secondary School called Lunch Buddies—a program that paired high-school students with special-education students in an attempt to integrate them into high-school life. Before the program, the special-ed students would often hang around in a separate room and watch movies at lunchtime. Many students tended to avoid them. *They just don't know how to interact with them,* Amy realized.

Inspired by her experience with Russell, Amy volunteered with Lunch Buddies, and after one year she took it over. She went from class to class explaining the program and urging her fellow students to join. She held meetings to give other volunteers a chance to ask questions and raise concerns. "What am I supposed to do when she won't stop hugging me?" asked one volunteer, clearly concerned about the invasion of her personal space but worried about hurting her buddy's feelings. Amy remembered Russell's affection. "Just tell her calmly and gently that you don't like it," Amy replied. "She'll understand."

With Amy's guidance, Lunch Buddies grew from 10 volunteers to over 40. Suddenly, there was a new attitude of acceptance and tolerance in the school. The special-ed kids became more confident and mixed freely with the other students.

An acquaintance of Amy's thought J. Douglas Hodgson Elementary, right next to the high school, could use a similar program. So when the teachers at Hodgson gave Amy the go-ahead, she approached her Lunch Buddies volunteers. "Does anyone want to help?" Ten students offered their assistance.

Lunch hour soon became a completely different experience for the special-education kids at Hodgson. There were high-school students in the playground helping to organize games, while Amy scheduled pizza parties and days when volunteers helped the children bake cookies and make crafts. During one hectic cookie-baking session, Andrew, a cute, mischievous boy with Down syndrome, solemnly looked up at Amy and gave a tug on her clothing. Amy bent down to his level and he kissed her cheek, whispering softly, "Thank you."

The impact of the Lunch Buddies program on the community as a whole was nothing short of amazing, says Cheryl Anderson, executive director of the Haliburton County Association for Community Living. The special-education kids are having a great time interacting with people who aren't adults. The high-school students know they are making a difference. And a new generation of young volunteers is being created.

Lunch Buddies—Amy Brandon, with Russell Snoddon and Lisa Burk

～

When Joe Hooper of Victoria was 13, he would probably have been labelled an at-risk youth. His 16-year-old sister had run away from home when he was 10, his family was facing financial difficulty, and his parents' marriage was breaking up. The red-haired, freckle-faced youth had moved from school to school as his parents tried to deal with their problems. At each new school, Joe tried to fit in or get the attention of his peers—most often by doing what he calls "really stupid things": lighting stink bombs and experimenting with alcohol and drugs.

Then, in grade 12, a teacher took Joe and his classmates to listen to a group of Holocaust survivors. That day in April 1994, something one of them said struck a chord in Joe.

Dr. Peter Gary, a Hungarian émigré, had lost most of his family during World War II. "In 1941 my mother and I were taken to the forest and the Nazis machine-gunned us. My mother saved me by throwing herself on me. I was 17." Gary spent the next three and a half years in concentration camps before he was finally liberated, emaciated and dying of typhus. "Do you think I'm angry?" he asked his rapt audience. "I'm not. You must go through life with your hand held out in friendship, not anger."

Here was a man who had been through hell but wasn't angry and held no grudge, thought Joe in wonder. Then he reflected on his own anger—at his past, his family—and his selfish behaviour, his attempts to get attention. *Everything is not about me,* he realized.

Inspired, he thought of ways he could reach out to others, just as this man had. He began making phone calls. He landed first at a day camp for intellectually handicapped children. Then he volunteered at an English-as-a-second-language centre, where he helped newly arrived immigrants settle in. Then later, during his second year at the University of Victoria, he took a part-time job with the

Saanich recreation services department and its youth activity centre.

When other staff members would lose patience and want to kick one of the kids out of the centre, Joe would think, *What can I do to keep him here?* Kenny,* an unemployed 18-year-old alcoholic and habitual thief, was someone the centre had banned when its staff could no longer cope with his drunken behaviour. Joe learned that Kenny was interested in weight lifting and got him a pass to a local gym, where the two would meet and talk.

Persuaded by Joe to enter a rehab program for his drinking, Kenny was ultimately accepted back at the centre and went on to find a full-time job.

Having mentored Kenny and others, Joe would often hang out at the skateboard park adjacent to the youth activity centre and a local convenience store, talking to teenagers who gathered there. He began to notice one young man who hung around but was never part of any group. Max,* Joe discovered, was a poor aboriginal boy, a loner with no self-confidence who was frequently ridiculed.

One day Max met Joe cycling around on his mountain bike. Joe offered to let him try it. "I never learned to ride a bike," the boy replied with some embarrassment. Joe was stunned—the kid was 17!

Over the next few months, Joe and his friend Greg taught the boy to ride, then found him a secondhand mountain bike. At the Hartland Mountain Biking Park outside Victoria, they put the new biker to the test, and Max proved to be a natural. "Today Max is a sponsored mountain-bike racer in national competitions," Joe says with pride.

Backed by the Saanich police, who donated the bikes, and employees of a local cycle shop,

who volunteered to repair them and provide training, Joe went on to raise funds to transport kids from the youth activity centre to the mountains.

The program he initiated last year, called Wheels in Motion, became an outstanding success, with many young people learning better social skills and developing self-confidence. And although Joe now lives in Ottawa, his program is still running.

Young volunteers like Isabelle, Lance, Amy, and Joe are growing in number. Statistics Canada reports that between 1987 and 1997, youth volunteer rates nearly doubled at a time when the rates for most other age groups remained relatively stable. "Despite what some mainstream media would have you believe, there is a strong social conscience among youths," says Steve Carroll, a program manager at Volunteer Canada.

Many still volunteer through existing, traditional organizations like the United Way, the Canadian Cancer Society and the Heart and Stroke Foundation. But a growing number of teens are striking out on their own, creating solutions for their communities' problems in ways that are both innovative and highly successful.

Leslie Evans, executive director of the Youth Volunteer Corps of Canada, says the best ideas often come from the kids themselves, whether it's a fashion show for seniors in St. John's, Newfoundland, or a blanket drive for the homeless in Nanaimo, British Columbia. Across Canada young people are organizing soup kitchens or toy drives, tutoring children, raking lawns for seniors, cleaning up parks. And our communities are the better for it.

* Names have been changed for privacy.

You take it from here ...

Responding

1. **Review Order** Working in a small group, complete a summary chart for each of the four individuals profiled. Then discuss why Jennifer Burke Crump might have chosen to arrange the profiles in this order. In particular, why did she begin with Isabelle Rivard and end with Joe Hooper? If you believe that a different order would have been better, try reading the article aloud as you think it should have been arranged.

Profile	Age and Situation	Volunteer Activity	Motivation and Reward
Isabelle Rivard			
Lance Relland			

2. **Discuss Theme** This article is made up of a series of anecdotes. Anecdotes typically illustrate a point or illuminate an idea, and are generally intended to involve readers and hold their attention. With a partner, identify two or three anecdotes pertaining to each of the four characters. What point or idea does each one illustrate? Did certain anecdotes hold your attention more than the others? Explain.

3. **Select a Winner** Imagine being asked to choose just one of these four individuals to be winner of the Youth Volunteer Award. Debate with your classmates who should be given the award. Then hold a vote to select the winner.

> **TIPS**
> - Establish objective criteria for selecting a winner.
> - Choose a moderator, who should make sure that everyone has a chance to speak.
> - Make your final vote a secret ballot.

Extending

4. **Create a Poster** This article describes many ways of making a difference in other people's lives. Decide which one of these volunteer activities you would like to promote. Then create an inspirational poster urging people to become involved.

5. **Write Profiles** Working in a small group, pick a theme for creating profiles of people in your own school and community. Choose any theme that interests you (e.g., "top sports figures," "the best dancers," "super shopkeepers," "the friendliest neighbours"). Each member of your group should write one profile. Then gather the profiles, organize them, write a general conclusion, and publish them as a single article.

Before you read, tell a partner what you observed when you first looked out the window this morning.

As you read, make a note of any words or phrases you think are especially descriptive.

Coyote's Morning Cry

In the stillness the coyotes' songs rang like tenor bells across a mile of muted, fragile grass.

Notes

Sharon Butala (1940–) was born in Nipawin, Saskatchewan. She is the author of several novels and short-story collections. Her nonfiction works include *The Perfection of the Morning*, which was nominated for a Governor General's Literary Award in 1994, and *Coyote's Morning Cry.* Her first novel, *Country of the Heart*, was nominated for the Books in Canada First Novel Award.

Memoir by Sharon Butala

This morning when I pulled up the blind in our bedroom and began to turn away, I was stopped by what I saw. I stood and stared at the view of the hills across the river from the house. It wasn't fully light yet, perfectly still, no wind at all, and the sky was rough-surfaced, low, and a deep purple. But below it, all the fields and hills of grass were frosted to a pale, silvery cream. Frost had even muted the harsher angles of the hills, and transformed this barren landscape from its usual early-morning hyper-real, almost frightening, clarity, giving it the quality of a distant, half-remembered, lovely dream.

In the kitchen, Peter stood looking out the window. "Listen to the coyotes," he said. It was a summons that for some reason I couldn't ignore. I went to the front door, opened it and stepped out onto the frost-covered deck, where the dozen barn cats, deserting the heat-lamp warmth of their winter bed, had gathered to wait for their breakfast.

In the stillness, the coyotes' songs rang like tenor bells across a mile of muted, fragile grass. The chorus came from the edge of the hills to the north and from the east, and was answered from somewhere in the grassy field by the stackyard, the one that used to be home to burrowing owls. A single voice it was that replied from there, a soloist with a voice stronger, richer, and yet more pure of tone than the others, and they were silenced for a moment, I thought surely by its beauty. The solo ending on a clear, soaring note, the others responded in a motley chorus, their former exuberance calmed, I chose to think, by reverence. I listened till I was too cold to stand outside any longer, then, silenced and grateful, I went back inside to begin my morning's work. It didn't even occur to me to wonder what their song meant.

You take it from here ...

Responding

1. Draw a Plan   Locate each of the physical elements on the property that are noted by Butala. Then draw a plan that shows the relationship of these elements to each other. Label your drawing clearly. When it is finished, compare your drawing with a partner's. How similar are they?

2. Debate Meaning   With two or three other students, discuss what Butala means by the final line of this selection. Do you have any suggestions as to why the coyotes were howling? Refer to clues in the passage that lead you to this conclusion.

3. Discuss Tone   Write a one-paragraph response to each of the following:
   a) What was the impact of the morning scene on Butala?
   b) What was the impact of the coyotes' howling on Butala?

TIP
• Don't settle for an instant answer. Comb the description carefully for words that hint at Butala's feelings and mood.

Extending

4. Write a Poem   The descriptions of the landscape in the first section and the howls of the coyotes in the second are almost poetic. Selecting some of Sharon Butala's own words as a starting point, choose one of these sections and rewrite it as a brief poem.

5. Research Symbols   The coyote is a powerful symbol in First Nations' mythology. Research the symbolism behind this creature or another North American animal. Make a brief oral report to the class on your findings.

6. Write a Descriptive Passage   Butala's description of the landscape is just over 100 words in length. Recalling the image you saw when you first looked out the window this morning, write your own descriptive passage of about 100 words, choosing each word carefully to capture the details of the scene as fully as possible.

Reflecting on the Unit

Responding

1. **Present Orally**   There are four poems/lyrics in this unit: "Slam, Dunk, & Hook," "The Hockey Song," "Pow Wow," and "Dreams." Which one had a personal connection to you in terms of your own experiences? In a two-minute speech, explain why that particular selection stood out above the rest.

2. **Categorize Information**   The theme of this unit is "Leisure, Dreams, and Happiness." Review the selections and identify the category or categories to which each one belongs, and then show the information in a Venn diagram. Compare diagrams with one or two other students. Did you agree on your placements? Do you share the same understanding of the different meanings of these words and how they interrelate?

Extending

3. **Compile an Encyclopedia**   With a partner, research online, in newspapers, magazines, and other sources a list of 10 extraordinary accomplishments and the ordinary people who accomplished them. Research the details of two of these remarkable feats and answer the following questions: What were the circumstances behind the accomplishment? (For example, was it planned? Was it spontaneous?) Who or what was involved in the situation? Summarize your findings for each in a one-page illustrated report. Collect these reports to make a class encyclopedia of inspiring achievers.

4. **Reflect on Leisure Time**   "Leisure" is different for everyone, but its importance in helping us lead well-rounded lives is the same. As you revisit selections studied in this unit, think about those to which you could relate. Then, write a personal essay expressing your views on the importance of leisure time and the kinds of things you like to do, or would like to do, with yours.

> **SELF-ASSESSMENT**
>
> The main focus of this unit is the importance of our leisure time, pursuing our dreams, and our overall happiness. Identify
> - the most valuable and inspirational thing you learned
> - any obstacles that you now realize you need address
>
> Write your response as a personal journal entry.

Technology evolves so much
faster than wisdom.
– *Jennifer Stone*

Other than life experience,
nothing left a deeper imprint on
my formative self [than media].
– *Letty Cottin Pogrebin*

You can tell the ideals of a
nation by its advertisements.
– *Norman Douglas*

Media and Technology

We live in a technology-centred world, constantly responding to new innovations and media images.

The quotation by journalist Jennifer Stone suggests that there may be a time lag between the introduction of new technologies and our adjustment to them; it may take time for us to understand how they affect us.

Columnist Letty Cottin Pogrebin suggests that media, such as movies and television, affect us significantly and change our values and the way we see ourselves, others, and the world.

As you look at the advertisements in this unit, think about British writer Norman Douglas's words and the influence of advertising on Canadians' ideals and personal values.

As you read the selections and examine the visuals in this unit, think about the following:

1) How do media, technology, and advertising affect our values and quality of life?

2) What are some of the issues and concerns raised about our "brave new world"?

3) What are some of the benefits brought about by media and technology?

Dilbert

Cartoon by Scott Adams

Notes

Scott Adams's popular cartoon strip, *Dilbert*, focuses on the trials of working in a typical high-tech office. The strip began in 1989 and now appears in more than 2000 newspapers in 61 countries.

Scott Adams

You take it from here ...

Responding

1. Share Your Response   In a small group, recount your own experiences with automated voice-messaging systems, and indicate whether or not you sympathize with Dilbert. What advice might you offer people who are in a similar situation to help them avoid becoming frustrated and angry?

2. Comment on Details   Write one or two paragraphs commenting on specific details that contribute to the cartoon's humour. Consider the topic, text, and drawing style, as well as the physical features and attitude of the character. Share your response with a partner.

3. Consider Effect of Medium on Message   Working in a small group, state the message of this cartoon in one sentence. Consider how the same point might be made in a different form (e.g., an essay, a radio documentary, a video). How would this affect the message? Using this selection as an example, discuss what makes cartoons effective in communicating messages to diverse audiences.

4. List Related Frustrations   With a partner, brainstorm a list of everyday frustrations related to modern technology (e.g., computer crashes, accidentally setting the VCR to tape the wrong show, or being put on hold by a friend who has call-waiting). Share your list in a class discussion.

Extending

5. Write a Letter of Complaint   As Dilbert, write a formal letter of complaint to the company you were trying to call, expressing your frustration about their automated answering system. Your letter can be either serious or humorous, but express your point in language appropriate to a business letter, and use a standard business-letter format.

> **SELF-ASSESSMENT**
> * Did you find it easy or difficult to express your frustration while remaining polite? Explain.

6. Express Yourself   Select one of the technology-related frustrations from the list you made in Activity 4 to explore further. Choose a form of representation (e.g., a cartoon, a comedy monologue or skit, a collage, a poem), and present your work to the class.

Should we ban them?

Cellphones

by Rex Murphy

TV EDITORIAL

The National, January 19, 2001

Notes

CBC journalist Rex Murphy was born and raised in St. John's, Newfoundland. An award-winning reporter, he has contributed pieces for many CBC programs including *The National, Cross-Country Checkup, Morningside, Midday,* and *Sunday Report*. He divides his time among Toronto, Montreal, and St. John's.

dexterity: skill in using part of the body or mind

gravitate: be attracted to, move toward

obnoxious: disgusting

pundit: someone who is an expert; an authority

subsidiary: subordinate branch

There may be more obnoxious agencies of human misery and torment than the cellphone. But they are few: Being mistaken for a wheat field by a cloud of locusts. Being buried alive with a loop of the soundtrack from *Titanic*. Attending a constitutional conference; being mistaken for a pundit. Interviews from film festivals.

In Toronto, which is the vanguard of so much of what we recognize as true human enlightenment on this planet, there is a movement to have the use of cellphones in cars banned by law.

I'm not so sure that this is altogether such a healthy idea. The wonderful dexterity and nimbleness of Toronto pedestrians is one of the glories of the globe. Watching a group at any crosswalk in this city is like being in your own *National Geographic* special. Cheetahs are sluggish, gazelles are clumsy, in comparison with the Toronto pedestrian staring down a Porsche, a yuppie, and her portable handheld.

Every person who crosses a street in this city knows that the BMW bearing down on them is really a mobile telephone booth with a licence to kill. Everyone knows that if it's a choice between keeping one eye on the road and one out for pedestrians, or hitting the speed dial to negotiate the finer points of the divorce settlement at 80 miles an hour, the cellphone is going to win every time.

It's helpful to think of the great highways leading into this city, the 401 and the Don Valley, as essentially a giant switchboard on radial tires, travelling at 140 km per hour; and of the people behind the wheel on these highways as so preoccupied absorbing information from their stockbrokers, or their nannies, as to have no time at all to acknowledge the information that they've just cut off an 18-wheeler transport truck, and are about to vacuum up some poor Ford Taurus under the bonnet of their chattering SUV. Reach out and touch someone is such a vivid little slogan.

The windshield in any car with a cellphone could just as well be made of lead as glass, for its only purpose is to maintain the privacy of the call, not to clarify the direction of the car. And now that cellphones also have Internet capacity, to the wonderful ability to talk and drive at the same time we may add the pleasure of authorship; composing witty e-mails while whizzing through the red light and nailing the bike courier is such a higher function of the human brain, which, as all will acknowledge, is simply wasted merely keeping track of the traffic and people in front of you.

Some people say cellphones are as bad as alcohol. I think this is a slander on booze. Alcohol is something which, when added to the human mind, makes it lazy, and careless, and stupid. Cellphones in cars gravitate to those minds that are that way already.

Should we ban them? I think Mothers Against Drunk Driving should open a subsidiary. I may give them a call.

For *The National*, I'm Rex Murphy.

You take it from here ...

Responding

1. Link Exaggeration and Humour   Find at least two examples of exaggeration, and, in one or two paragraphs, explain how each example adds humour to the editorial.

2. Examine Diction   The author's attitude to his topic is reinforced by the words and images he uses. Review the editorial and jot down words and phrases that are particularly effective in expressing the author's feelings about cellphone use. Compare lists with one or two other students.

3. **Compose a Voice-Mail Message** The CBC invites listeners and viewers to respond to its programs by voice mail. If you were to phone Rex Murphy's voice mail with a response to his opinion on cellphones and driving, what would you say? First, write out your message, and then present it orally to the class.

Extending

4. **Debate the Issue** Form two sides in your class to debate the resolution: The use of cellphones in cars should be banned by law.

5. **Draft a Policy** Pretend that you are the principal of a school and you need to address the issue of students using cellphones at school. You do not want to allow the use of cellphones in the classroom or in the halls, but you acknowledge that students may need to have a cellphone to contact family members or others for various reasons. With a partner, develop a policy statement or set of rules that takes both sides of the issue into account.

No special effect can make us feel the way it felt to see the World Trade Center collapse on live TV.

Not Like the Movies: Hollywood and Tragedy

by Fred Topel

WEB PAGE ARTICLE

Notes

Fred Topel is an entertainment writer, writing online for the *Daily Radar* and for newspapers such as *The Palisadian Post* and *Entertainment Today*. He has a special interest in action/adventure movies, his favourite genre. This article was posted on an action-adventure movie Web site (http://actionadventure.about.com) on September 15, 2001.

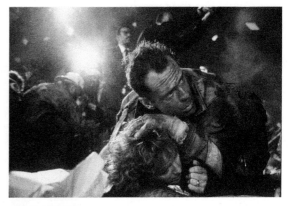

Die Hard, 1988

I was asked to think of an article to address Tuesday's [the September 11, 2001] tragedy, and I thought the most silly and insensitive thing I've heard in all of this tragedy is newscasters suggesting it is like something out of a movie. The attacks on the World Trade Center and Pentagon are not like something out of a movie. I've seen plenty of movies about terrorists, and even the best, most realistic ones are nothing like what I've seen on the news.

The Siege may be one of the most realistic films about terrorism. A scene where a bus loaded with passengers explodes is sudden and shocking, like it must really be. However, the film also shows Denzel Washington storming into a hostage situation to take out the bad guys. Though the film deals with the effects of terrorism on race relations, it ends with a Hollywood convenience, letting the hero find and defeat the villains. Things do not resolve so simply in real life.

Arlington Road dealt with terrorism on a personal level, with Jeff Bridges suspecting his neighbour, Tim Robbins, of terrorist plans. The bombing at the end is realistic, and the terrorists have the upper hand in the finale. Perhaps that is close to what happened, but in the film it was used to resolve the character relationships. It's unsettling and effective, but everything related back to Jeff Bridges, not the people who were hurt.

Perhaps the most famous movie about terrorists is *Die Hard*. Those terrorists turn out to be thieves with no political agenda. *Die Hard 2* and *Die Hard With a Vengeance* have real terrorists, but again these are Hollywood action movies. We don't get attached to the people who get hurt (except one scene with a plane in *Die Hard 2*, but otherwise we don't know the bombing victims) and everything wraps up neatly in the end.

The Tom Clancy movies deal with terrorists and realistic government operations, but *Patriot Games* has the terrorists go on a private revenge mission, *Clear and Present Danger* sends Harrison Ford into action mode to rescue our boys, and *Hunt for Red October* has the Russian turn into a good guy.

New York, 2001

Toy Soldiers had teenagers fighting the terrorists who took over their school. It had some interesting insights about the negotiation process and was a great movie about youth empowerment, but a fantasy.

The Rock, one of my favourite movies of all time, had terrorists [who are] considerate of children and harm none of their hostages. They only kill the Navy SEALS because of a chaotic, uncontrollable situation. Surely the real terrorists were not as considerate as Ed Harris in *The Rock*.

There is nothing wrong with these movies. These are great movies. But what happened in New York is not like a movie. Real people were hurt. No special effect can make us feel the way it felt to see the World Trade Center collapse on live TV.

Maybe I'm reading too much into the comments. Perhaps the people at CNN just meant that the explosion looked like a movie effect. Except with a movie, you'd see the shot from three different angles and hear Dolby Digital effects all around you. In real life, you see a ball of fire and people die. As a movie connoisseur, maybe I'm oversensitive, or maybe it's the stress of experiencing the worst part of history I've ever lived through, but it seems some media entities are trying too hard to relate events to Hollywood.

In other news, some movies are being delayed in their release, notably *Big Trouble* (which involves a spoof of airport terrorism) and *Collateral Damage* (Arnold going after terrorists who killed his family). The ending of *Men in Black 2* will be changed because it originally took place at the World Trade Center.

Other films that take place in New York are actually going to be digitally altered to remove the World Trade Center. I personally think that is overreacting. We'd all understand that those movies were shot in New York before the tragedy, and going to the trouble of digitally altering the skyline seems like they're trying too hard to seem sensitive. But maybe they're just as unsure of how to handle things as I am.

My best wishes to anyone who has lost someone in the attacks or flights.

You take it from here ...

Responding

1. Determine the Motivation for Writing   As a class, identify what comments from the media prompted the author to write this article. Discuss whether you made similar comments when the incident took place, or if you heard others who did. Do you agree with Fred Topel that such comments were "silly and insensitive"? Why or why not?

2. Summarize the Author's Key Points   Create a two-column chart. In the left column, list each of the action-adventure movies referred to in the first half of the article. In the right column, indicate why the author thinks each movie fails to portray an actual terrorist attack.

Action-Adventure movie	Problem with movie
The Siege	while the movie appears realistic, the ending resolves the problems of the hostage situation and the race relations issues too easily

3. Consider Style   With a partner, choose one word to describe Fred Topel's writing style. Note at least three instances where he addresses his readers directly in this article. Explain how he does so, and describe the effect this technique has upon the reader.

Extending

4. Justify a Point of View   The author thinks that Hollywood moviemakers overreacted by digitally altering images to remove the World Trade Center. As a movie executive, write a press release that explains why your company has decided to digitally edit images following the terrorist attacks.

5. Respond to Poll Results   A readers' poll taken shortly after Fred Topel posted this article asked, "Are the terrorist attacks in New York and Washington, DC like something from a movie?" In response, 85 percent indicated, "Yes, there are some similarities." Write one or two paragraphs explaining why you think so many people responded this way. Conclude by expressing your own opinion.

The Far Side

Cartoon by Gary Larson

Notes

Gary Larson (1950–), was born in Tacoma, Washington. He loved to draw when he was young, but loved science more. (The scientific world later honoured Larson by naming a louse and a butterfly after him!) The award-winning Larson cartooned for 14 years, retiring in 1995 to live in Seattle.

THE FAR SIDE® BY GARY LARSON

© 1991 FarWorks, Inc. All Rights Reserved/Dist. by Creators Syndicate

"Don't worry, Jimmy—they're just actors ... and that's not real ketchup."

You take it from here ...

Responding

1. **Find Story Elements in the Cartoon**   Write your responses to the following questions about the "story" of the cartoon:

   - What is the setting?
   - Who are the characters?
   - What is the "plot"?
   - What theme is suggested?

2. **Consider the Caption**   With a partner, consider the importance of the caption in this cartoon. Suggest one or two alternatives. Do the new captions work as well? Did you choose the same angle? Compare captions with another pair of students.

3. **Compare Cartoons**   In a small group, compare and contrast this selection with one of the other cartoons in this unit. In your discussion, consider such things as

   - theme and subject matter
   - characters
   - overall "look" and style
   - details that contribute to humour

Extending

4. **Research a Cartoonist**   Research Gary Larson or another well-known cartoonist, and prepare a brief oral report for the class. Include how the cartoonist's personal background and interests are reflected in his or her work, and any recurring themes and issues the cartoonist addresses.

TIP

- Illustrate your points with samples of the cartoonist's work.

5. **Research an Issue**   Conduct preliminary research on the effects of media violence on young children. Investigate whether small children can tell the difference between real violence and the "pretend" violence shown in movies and on TV. Can exposure to TV and movie violence desensitize children to real violence, making them more accepting of it, and more likely to behave aggressively themselves? Present your findings in an essay.

> **SELF-ASSESSMENT**
> - Have you made your points clearly and concisely?
> - Did you include a list of all the sources you consulted?

Finding Forrester

by Sebastien Pharand

ONLINE MOVIE REVIEW

Notes

Sebastien Pharand is a film student and writer living in Toronto and Ottawa. He has contributed several reviews to Moviefan Online (www.moviefanonline.com). This review was posted on January 7, 2001.

This holiday season has been pretty bad for movies, exactly like the rest of the year. There were not many movies to go crazy about this year, but I can finally add another one to the list. *Finding Forrester* is one of the most evenly composed and touching films of the year. This is one of the best films I've seen that deals with the art of writing. This is an important film that left me baffled. Who knew that Gus Van Sant was such a sensible director?

Jamal Wallace (Robert Brown) is a sixteen-year-old boy who [has] lived most of his life in the Bronx. He goes to high school there, he lives there, and he plays basketball there. Early on, we are told about a neighbourhood legend; just beside the basketball court, where Jamal usually plays, lives an old man who hasn't gone outside in decades. He lives cooped up in his apartment every day of the year, never stepping outside, not even to go grocery shopping. Jamal is fascinated

by this man and soon enough, he is dared by his friends to break into the house and bring something back to them.

Jamal is caught in the act and scurries from the apartment in a hurry. But on his way out, he drops his backpack in the apartment. It is in this backpack that Jamal, who also happens to be a brilliant boy, keeps all the notebooks in which he writes his stories and his thoughts. A few days later, when Jamal gets his backpack back,

he opens his notebooks to find that every page has been read by the old man and that he has left comments on every page; comments like "where are you taking me?" "great passage," "elaborate," and so on.

Soon enough Jamal befriends the old man. The man in question is William Forrester (Sean Connery), an old man who, at one time, found success with a novel he wrote. But his novel, *Avalon Landing*, was the only thing he ever wrote. Forrester still lives on the money this book brings him. He is afraid to leave his apartment and he is a little compulsive in his behaviour.

Slowly, Forrester will teach Jamal how to reach his full potential. He will show him that he has a gift for the written word and that this gift should not go to waste. And Jamal will teach the old man how to live again by trying to ease his fear of public places. And during all of this, Jamal is accepted at a private school, where he will play basketball and where he will follow a more intellectual education. But everything will come crumbling down when one of the school's teachers thinks that Jamal has been reproducing material that is not his own.

This is a very intelligent film about the power of believing in ourselves. Gus Van Sant, who also did another masterpiece called *Good Will Hunting*, created one of the most touching films of the year. Sant doesn't stay focused solely on the father-son relationship between Jamal and Forrester; he mixes everything with some gritty urban images and basketball. Some people might think that the whole thing looks too much like *Good Will Hunting*, but it isn't. It can be seen as a close cousin, but *Finding Forrester* is an original piece that stands on its own. The film has the power to show us what a real writer does and how a real writer writes.

As the film progresses, the relationship between Jamal and Forrester becomes much more dramatic. They aren't simply teacher and student, but they become father and son. Forrester does not have a family and Jamal lost his father when he was much younger. So both of them will fill the other's gap in order to give each other faith in life once more.

This film is simply amazing. It doesn't fall into all the typical clichés that we associate with this type of film. Instead, it stays far away from conventionalities to become a very important and yet a very original work. Sant knows exactly what he wants to show and how he wants to show it, and his confidence as a director is the first thing you notice while watching this film. He gives us many close-ups of fingers typing on the typewriter, he gives us many close-ups of characters' eyes, and he gives us many long shots of the two main characters typing away, creating their own personal masterpieces.

Of course, it helps that Forrester is such a strange and compulsive character. Connery looks at ease in this role. At times, you almost believe that Connery has been Forrester for all those years. And add to this a brilliant performance by the young Robert Brown and by the talented Anna Paquin and you get a film that hits a touchdown on every level.

Finding Forrester is a lot more than a simple ode to the craft of writing. The film is so well done, and so well-acted, that I found myself lost in its story. When the film was over, I looked at my watch and I couldn't believe that two and a half hours had passed. This is the type of film that makes you lose all notions of time. *Finding Forrester* is, simply put, this year's best drama.

BOTTOM LINE:

A film starring Sean Connery as a compulsive writer who befriends a brilliant young man, and the whole thing directed by Gus Van Sant? Could it be any good? Well, it is. It's a lot more than just good. You have to recognize the skill of everyone that was involved with the creation of this picture while watching the film. It takes a lot to create a film that is so evenly balanced. *Finding Forrester* will remain embedded in my mind for a long time. Give the film a shot and I'm sure it'll have the same effect on you.

You take it from here ...

Responding

1. Read between the Lines   With a partner, share the impressions you have of the author based on the tone and word choice in the review. Why might this reviewer particularly like this movie?

2. Identify Themes   Reread the review and make a list of the movie's themes as described by the reviewer. Compare your list with a partner's.

3. Understand Form   As a class, look at several examples of newspaper movie reviews, and create a list of their main features. Use the list to evaluate this selection: Does it cover all of the features you listed? If you were asked to edit this review for publication in a newspaper, what changes would you suggest?

4. Write a Personal Response   Based on the information presented in this movie review, would you choose to see *Finding Forrester*? Explain your response in a paragraph.

Extending

5. Summarize a Plot   A key element in any movie review is the plot summary, which gives a brief overview of the movie's content without giving away the whole story. Choose a movie you have seen and write a one- to two-page summary of the plot, being careful not to reveal too much. Exchange your work with a partner for feedback.

> ### PEER ASSESSMENT
> - Was the summary clear and well-organized?
> - Was it informative without being too specific?
> - Would it help you decide whether or not to see the movie?

6. View the Movie   View *Finding Forrester*, and then write your own review, using the list of features created in Activity 3 as a guide. Share your review with a small group. What do the group's reviews have in common? How are they different? Do they express a wide range of opinions? Do they emphasize different aspects of the movie (e.g., plot, conflict, cast, direction) equally?

Before you read, in a class discussion, share what you know about the 1941 military attack on Pearl Harbor.

As you read, decide what movie genre you would expect *Pearl Harbor* to be.

Pearl Harbor

Movie Poster

You take it from here ...

Responding

1. Discuss First Impressions   In a paragraph, describe your first impressions of this poster. What mood does it set? What feelings does it evoke in the viewer? Consider how colour and choice of images contribute to this effect.

2. Analyze Visual Information   With a partner, list the various images shown on this poster. Beside each item listed, suggest what it reveals about the subject and story line of the movie.

3. Brainstorm Captions   Working in a small group, come up with four brief and compelling captions or slogans that could be added to this poster. Try to come up with captions that would capture viewers' attention and interest.

Extending

4. Analyze Another Poster   Find an example of a poster for a movie you have seen. In a brief oral presentation, describe how the poster communicates essential details of the movie. Suggest why certain images were selected over other possibilities, looking at what elements of the story they reveal, and how. To what audience is this poster meant to appeal?

TIP

• Examples of posters can be found on the Internet, at the library, movie promotional magazines (at theatres), and at video stores.

5. Research a Career   Posters such as the ones in this unit are created by graphic artists. Learn about the career of a graphic artist, using the following questions to guide your research:

• What does a graphic artist do?
• What education and training is required?
• Which learning institutions offer courses in graphic arts?
• What is the average income for a beginning graphic artist? For an experienced one?
• What are some related employment opportunities?

Present your findings in the form of your choice (e.g., an illustrated article or report, a short video or radio documentary, or an interview).

Before you read, as a class, discuss what information—in the form of words and pictures—is typically included in a movie poster. What is the main purpose of a movie poster?

As you read, jot down the information the poster reveals—directly and indirectly—about the movie.

A.I.

Movie Poster

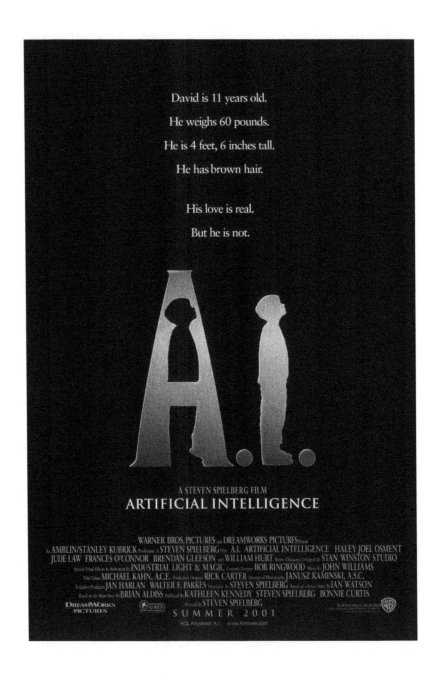

You take it from here ...

Responding

1. Discuss Content   Share with a partner the notes you took while viewing the poster. What does the poster reveal about the movie? What does it leave out? What questions does it raise? In your opinion, is this an effective poster that would prompt people to go and see the movie? Explain.

2. Consider Design   In one or two paragraphs, describe the design and overall look of this poster and your own response to it. In what way do you think the design of the poster might reflect the content of the movie?

> **TIP**
>
> • To get an idea of the content of *A.I.*, review Brian Aldiss's short story *Supertoys Last All Summer Long* (see Unit 1), on which the movie is based.

3. Compare and Contrast Posters   Working in a small group, compare and contrast this poster with the previous selection, the *Pearl Harbor* movie poster. Choose five criteria (e.g., use of colour, artwork, words) and discuss them in relation to each poster. Then, identify which poster you find more appealing, giving reasons for your opinion.

Extending

4. Plan a Poster   Recalling the class discussion on the main purpose and content of movie posters, draft an original poster for a movie you have seen. Combine text and an appropriate image (or combination of images) that you feel will arouse viewers' curiosity and entice them to see the movie. Present your work to a small group.

5. Consider Business Aspects   Movie posters not only attract audiences to movies, they also generate revenue themselves when they are sold to fans. As a class, discuss other ways in which movies generate revenue. What types of "spin-off" products have been associated with past movies? How have other industries cooperated with the movie industry in promoting their products?

Before you read, discuss as a class what you know about the 1970 Apollo 13 mission.

As you read, think of one or two words to describe your emotional reaction to the image and words.

Apollo 13

Movie Poster

You take it from here ...

Responding

1. Describe Reaction   Share with two or three other students the words you chose to describe your emotional reaction to the poster. Did more than one student choose the same words? Did most students have the same overall impression?

2. Focus on Words   This poster contains five words of dialogue from the movie: "Houston, we have a problem." These words were made famous in 1970, when Apollo astronaut James Lovell reported to the command centre in Houston that there had been an explosion on the spacecraft. In a paragraph, suggest why these five words were chosen for inclusion on the poster. Do you think the poster would be less effective without them?

3. Discuss Probable Reactions   The Apollo 13 crisis affected not only the astronauts stranded in outer space, but also

   • the astronauts' families
   • workers at Mission Control
   • manufacturers who supplied parts for the spacecraft
   • the general public—in the United States and around the world—who watched the crisis unfold on television

   As a class, discuss how each of these groups must have felt from the moment they heard, "Houston, we have a problem."

Extending

4. View the Movie   View the movie *Apollo 13* and write a short speech on one of the following themes:

   • the importance of strong leadership
   • keeping a cool head during a crisis
   • the power of teamwork

   Describe how this quality contributed to the resolution of the crisis in the movie.

5. Write a Monologue   Working with a partner, brainstorm a list of high-risk occupations (e.g., astronaut, test pilot, firefighter, military personnel). Choose one of these, and write two monologues, one from the perspective of someone who has chosen this occupation, and another from the perspective of someone close to that person (e.g., spouse, child, best friend). Consider why an individual would choose to work in this profession.

Sony Clié

Print Ad

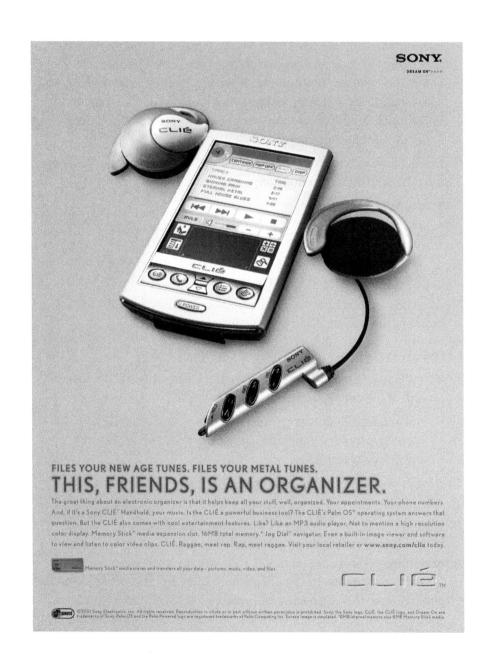

You take it from here ...

Responding

1. Assess Information   With a partner, list all the facts the picture and written text reveal about the product. To what extent would this information help you decide whether to buy this product? Identify any additional information you would need, and where you might find it.

2. Analyze Writing Style   Reread the ad copy (written text) and choose one or two words that describe the writing style. List at least three specific techniques the copywriter used to achieve this style, then share your list with two or three other students.

3. Consider Target Audience and Placement   Write your responses to the following questions, and then share your ideas in a class discussion:
   a) What types of people would likely be interested in this product?
   b) What types of people do you think would find this ad appealing? (Cite specific details from the ad to support your response.)
   c) Where might you place this ad to reach the audience? Suggest two magazines that might run it, and explain your choices.

Extending

4. Comment on Technique   As a class, discuss the various techniques advertisers use to promote products and services, such as the use of testimonials, humour, or a bandwagon appeal ("everyone else has one!"). Do some techniques appeal to you more than others? Analyze the techniques and overall approach taken by this ad: what does it say directly about the product? What does it imply (say indirectly)? Consider how this product might be advertised using different techniques.

5. Design an Ad   Using one of the advertising techniques discussed in Activity 4, design a new ad to sell this product. Write new copy, and sketch the layout of the ad. Present your design to the class.

Forest Stewardship Council

Print Ad

YOU DON'T HAVE TO BE A SPECIAL AGENT TO PROTECT OUR FORESTS

Everyone can help. Ask for the **FOREST STEWARDSHIP COUNCIL** label when you buy wooden furniture, flooring, lumber and other forest products. The nonprofit **FSC LABEL** is your assurance that forests are managed well. That's why environmental, social and Indigenous groups support the FSC. For more information visit www.fsccanada.org or call toll free 1-877-571-1133.

FSC
Forest Stewardship Council
Global Leaders in Responsible Forestry

Pierce Brosnan photo donated by Nigel Parry, CPI

You take it from here ...

Responding

1. Examine Purpose   What is the purpose of this ad? What does the advertiser hope the viewer will do as a result of seeing the ad? Respond in a paragraph.

2. Discuss Target Audience   Working in a small group, list several characteristics to describe the probable target audience for this ad. Include details such as age, education, occupation, gender, and interests. On what did you base your suggestions? The choice of celebrity? The organization sponsoring the ad? Share your ideas in a class discussion.

3. Focus on Endorsement   *Endorsement* is an advertising technique in which a famous person recommends a product or service, or supports an organization or cause. Does the idea that Pierce Brosnan supports the FSC make you want to learn more about the organization? Would you find the ad more appealing, or convincing, if a different celebrity or individual were featured instead? Explain your views to a partner.

Extending

4. Analyze Advertising   Working in a small group, find and analyze up to three other print ads that feature a celebrity to promote a product or organization. In your analysis consider the following:

   - What is being advertised or promoted?
   - What is the likely target audience for this ad? Is there a clear relationship between the choice of celebrity and the likely target audience?
   - What is the relationship between what is being promoted and the individual endorsing it? Is it an obvious, direct relationship (e.g., a mayor promoting tourism to his or her city, or an athlete endorsing athletic equipment), or is it more symbolic?
   - To what extent does the fact that this celebrity is lending his or her support to the ad campaign affect your response to the ad? Does it make the claims more convincing? Does it make the ad more appealing? Explain.

5. Design a Different Ad   Borrowing techniques used in this selection, design a new ad. Choose a celebrity (it could be someone from the past or present, and a real or fictional character) and an organization or cause that he or she will endorse. Write the text for the ad, and sketch the artwork and placement of text on the page. Present your design to the class.

Before you read, as a class, share what you know about Anna Kournikova and tennis.

As you read, decide how the sequence of events listed at the bottom relates to the model. How does the wording tie in the product with Anna Kournikova and her sport?

Lycos

Print Ad

You take it from here ...

Responding

1. **Examine Word Play**   As a class, reread the text at the bottom of the poster, paying no attention to the visuals and the product information. What would you assume is being described? Discuss how this description relates, first, to Anna Kournikova, and second, to the service being advertised.

2. **Explore Design**   Write a one-word description of the overall look and feel of this ad. Follow this with two or three paragraphs analyzing how this has been accomplished. In your analysis, consider

   - use of light and dark to highlight certain elements on the page.
   - choice of colour
   - the model's pose
   - angle of the shot
   - choice of fonts and type sizes
   - relative prominence of image, text, and brand logo on the page

> **TIP**
>
> - To appreciate the effect of each technique, consider how the impact of the ad would change if different choices had been made.

Extending

3. **Define Target Audiences**   Imagine that this ad is one of a series that the advertiser has planned to reach various target audiences. List three specific audiences this advertiser might reasonably target. Include details of age, education, occupation, gender, and interests. Then, list two magazines in which you might place an ad to reach each target audience, noting reasons for your choice. What changes, if any, would you make to the ad in order to appeal to the audience? Share and compare your ideas in a small group discussion.

4. **Focus on a Technique**   Make a collage poster of print ads illustrating a specific advertising technique (e.g., use of humour, celebrity endorsement, testimonial). Present it to the class, pointing out how the technique is used, who it is trying to persuade in each case (the target audience), and your assessment of its effectiveness.

Yonge Street, Willowdale, #4, 1995

Photograph by Robin Collyer

Notes

Robin Collyer (1949–), a well-known Toronto sculptor and photographer, was born in London, England. This photograph was included in a calendar by Adbusters, a Vancouver-based consumer activist organization aimed at citizens interested in "combating marketing pollutants in the mental environment."

You take it from here ...

Responding

1. Identify Advertising Graphics   As a class, share the list of products you recognized in the image. For each one, specify the features of each sign that helped you identify the product even without seeing the name.

2. State an Opinion   Brand names and logos often appear prominently on personal clothing such as baseball caps, sweatshirts, and so on. Often these items cost more than those without the brand names. What makes people willing to pay more in order to display a well-known logo? Do you think companies should pay the wearers, instead, as "human billboards" who advertise their products? Discuss your views in a small group.

3. Explain Satire   This photograph was included in an *Adbusters'* calendar. *Adbusters* criticizes the advertising industry and consumerism through the use of *satire*. Write a paragraph explaining the use of satire in this picture.

TIP
- Review the definition of *satire* in the glossary.

Extending

4. Create a Parody   With a partner, look at past issues of *Adbusters* magazine or visit the Adbusters Web site at www.adbusters.org and find examples of spoof ads they have created. Then choose an advertisement and imitate its style in a humorous way to create your own parody.

5. Role-Play a Town Council Meeting   A controversy has developed in your community. At a town council meeting, a group of residents has proposed that, although current storefront signage is acceptable, all other advertising signs and billboards should be banned within 10 m of any city street. Members of the business community are outraged by the plan. Town council members are as yet undecided. As a class, role-play a town council meeting to resolve the issue.

TIP
- Start by listing some arguments for and against the proposal.

6. Explore a Theme   Explore the theme of "advertising as visual pollution" using the form of your choice (e.g., poem, collage, short story). Present your work to the class.

People around you buying lots of stuff? Ask them why.

Buy Nothing Day Provokes Pause for Thought

by Liane Faulder

NEWSPAPER COLUMN

I've been skulking, guiltily, to the curb these past few Thursday nights.

Under cover of darkness, the collar of my green terry cloth robe pulled up around my face, I've been taking load after load of stuff that used to be in my basement out to the sidewalk to be picked up by the garbage crew.

I'm in the process of moving, and the mounds of stuff I have collected since my last move, not to mention my mother's castoffs, given to her by her mother, who didn't want them either, make me feel slightly sick.

I've made donations to a charitable garage sale and run still-serviceable snowsuits and hats over to the Bissell Centre Thrift Shop. Daily, I heave green garbage bags full of old clothes to the bin at Value Village. Friends with younger children are the recipients of a tea set, never used, a children's stamp kit, and undershirts long outgrown.

And still it keeps coming.

Broken chairs not worth fixing. Boxes of old *National Geographic* magazines. An enormous, heavy cardboard tube I thought I'd have a use for but don't. And shamefully, a down-filled sleeping bag that developed a huge and unsightly burn when put in the dryer and was never, ever going to get fixed.

Which brings me to Michael Kalmanovitch. The indefatigable owner of Earth's General Store on Whyte Avenue could be seen this week straddling his bicycle on the median at 109th Street, near the High Level bridge, during rush hour. He was holding out a giant sign.

"Buy Nothing Day—November 28" read the sign. If only I'd listened to the cries of ecologists like Michael way back when I was buying the things I'm now throwing out. What then?

It's a question worth pondering, if only one day a year.

Now in its fifth year, Buy Nothing Day is a chance to go for 24 hours without making a consumer purchase, just to see how it feels.

"It's a symbolic act," says Scott Harris, 24, one of the organizers of Friday's events. "To go 24 hours in our culture without buying anything is an event."

The goal, long-term, is not to stop people from buying altogether, but rather to encourage conscious, thoughtful consumption.

"It's an opportunity to step back and ask simple questions. Do I need it? Where does the product come from and was it made under conditions I agree with? What's going to happen to this when I'm done with it? These questions don't get asked on a conscious level," says Harris.

Timed to coincide with the Christmas buying frenzy, Buy Nothing Day turns traditional sales hooks upside down. Organizers have planned some alternative carolling at local malls where they will also be giving away 100 percent off coupons as incentive to not buy.

Gift boxes full of empty promises will be passed out, along with packages of adventure, happiness, and love, things we're promised daily through television ads for cosmetics and four-by-fours.

Buy Nothing Day is a clever approach which is growing in popularity. When it started, the event was confined to people in a handful of Canadian centres who read *Adbusters* magazine. Today, a Web site connects anti-shoppers from New Zealand to England.

Though it's like trying to stop a forest fire with a bucket of sand, Buy Nothing Day appeals to me.

Statistics on the greedy consumption of the Western world only serve to make me feel guilty. Buy Nothing Day makes me think. Do I want this thing that pulls me inexorably to the checkout counter? Or do I need it? What's the difference?

Here's another thing good about Buy Nothing Day. A great wave of helplessness sweeps the country as people are overwhelmed

by issues perceived beyond their control—from global warming to the widening gap between rich and poor.

Buy Nothing Day is a tiny reminder that small efforts are meaningful. There are plenty of things individuals can control, including just how much of the consumer culture they want to be part of.

People around you buying lots of stuff? Ask them why.

Feel panic-stricken by Christmas? Concentrate on people you want gathered around the tree rather than gifts under it.

"There's nothing wrong with consumption," says Harris. "People need things and always will. But does this much consumption actually increase anyone's well-being? I don't think there would be a huge impact on the labour market if we were all not buying Slinkies."

You take it from here ...

Responding

1. **State an Opinion** In one or two paragraphs, state whether or not you support Buy Nothing Day. Explain your opinion with reference to at least three ideas from this column.

2. **Understand the Context** With a partner, list the ways in which supporters of Buy Nothing Day challenge consumerism. Discuss why the author is attracted to the ideas associated with this event.

3. **Consider Writing Style** Liane Faulder writes informally, addressing the reader in a conversational manner. Find two sentences that exemplify this style, and then rewrite them more formally. Compare the impact of the two styles on the reader.

4. **Write a Letter** In a letter to the editor, respond to the question posed in the last paragraph: "But does this much consumption actually increase anyone's well-being?"

> **SELF-ASSESSMENT**
> - Did you state the question and your response clearly at the start of your letter?
> - Did you provide reasons to support your opinion?
> - Did you proofread your work to ensure correct spelling and punctuation?

> **TIPS**
> - Consider using a page layout program to create your final copy.
> - Use graphics and a variety of fonts to enhance the impact of your brochure.

Extending

5. **Create a Brochure** Use the information in this column and in other sources to create a brochure that will explain the concept of Buy Nothing Day to others and persuade them to participate.

6. **Try the Concept** As a class, designate your own Buy Nothing Day and try to avoid buying anything for 24 hours. Individually, write a journal entry commenting on the experience, and share it in a follow-up discussion with the class.

Before you read, decide whether you think watching TV can be harmful to small children. Explain your views in a class discussion.

As you read, think about how the title relates to the poem.

Television's Child

Poem by Glen Kirkland

Notes

Glen Kirkland, born in McLennan, Alberta, is a long-time Edmonton teacher, consultant, poet, playwright, and textbook editor. He has said, "A poem that works brings into relief the colours, shapes, and textures of our humanity. It not only speaks to us, but speaks for us."

The moment he slipped
from the womb,
his parents plugged
his umbilical cord
into a living room outlet
and sat him in a corner,
where his eyes
grew large with cathode glow,
his mind throbbed with shifting colours,
and his ears
echoed with voices
speaking always to
someone else.

He was fed
and clothed,
it's true,
but no one ever spoke to him
and expected a response.
His parents told him things like,
"Go to bed,"
"Eat your vegetables,"
and "Turn that down,"
and he always did.

His mom and dad thought him
good-natured, obedient,
and quiet.
They didn't worry,
for in their hectic days,
they needed their child to be
the way he was.

When the boy was 6
and still spoke no more
than a few words,
his parents decided
to unplug his cord
and see if their boy
would talk to them
and seek out friends.
From the first minute of silence,
the boy missed television;
for he was empty of language
and colours and movement.
The world around him
lay passive,
awaiting his touch.

His parents stood by watching
as he blinked
and tried to find within himself
some understanding of
pattern, forward movement,
possibilities.
Nothing was there
that made sense, however.
His mind was a scrapbook
of images that did not connect,
his present was simply
where he was now, and
his future was
empty of possibilities.

"Oh, plug him in again!"
cried his mother.
"I can't stand to see him
look so alone."
And so, he glowed again
with cathode eyes
and stray thoughts of selfhood
went running back

into a forest of
shifting colours,
wondrous sounds, and
profound numbness.

You take it from here ...

Responding

1. Consider the Title   As a class, discuss how the title relates to the poem. Consider what the title suggests about the parents of the young boy.

2. Use Comprehension Skills   Write your responses to the following questions:
   a) How did the parents communicate with their son?
   b) Why did the parents leave the child in front of the TV for such long periods?
   c) What effects does the television have on the child's intellectual and social development?
   d) What happened to the boy after he was "unplugged"?
   e) Why did the mother insist the child be "reconnected" to the television?

3. Identify Literary Devices   With a partner, review the definitions of *metaphor*, *alliteration*, and *assonance* in the glossary or a dictionary. Then, find examples of each of these in the poem.

Extending

4. Create a Cartoon   As a class, discuss the theme of this poem, and express it in a single sentence. Then, working individually, create a cartoon that expresses the same theme in a humorous, thought-provoking way. Share your work with the class or in small groups.

5. Write a Sequel   Write a short story describing the young boy from "Television's Child" many years later as an adolescent or adult.

> **TIPS**
>
> In your sequel, consider revealing
> - how the character has changed and how he has stayed the same
> - what he has discovered about life and reality
> - how well he communicates with others
> - his attitude toward TV (for himself, and if he is a parent, for his children)

Before you read, as a class, discuss your views on the importance of monitoring children's television viewing.

As you read, think about the message of the cartoon.

Calvin and Hobbes

Cartoon by Bill Watterson

Notes

Bill Watterson (1958–) was born in Washington, DC. His comic strip *Calvin and Hobbes* was first syndicated in 1985 and was carried in more than 2400 newspapers around the world. Watterson won the Reuben Award for Outstanding Cartoonist of the Year by the National Cartoonists Society in 1986 and 1988. Watterson no longer produces the daily strip; the last one appeared in December 1995.

You take it from here ...

Responding

1. Discuss Message   As a class, discuss the point(s) the cartoon makes about children's exposure to violence on television.

2. Comment on Humour   In a paragraph, explain why the cartoon is funny. Refer to both the visuals (e.g., facial expression and body language) and the dialogue.

3. Consider Sources of TV Violence   In small groups, discuss whether you think the statement that "by the age of six, most children have seen a million murders on television" is realistic. Brainstorm different genres of television programming that might show scenes of violence (e.g., news reports, cartoons). How many of these sources do you think children are exposed to? Do you think young children are affected by this exposure? Explain.

Extending

4. Create a Parenting Poster   Design a poster offering tips to parents on how to limit and guide a young child's television viewing (e.g., "Five Things Kids Can Do Instead of Watching TV," "Five Ways to Use TV Responsibly").

5. Role-Play a Live TV Discussion Show   As a class, role-play a TV talk show with a live studio audience made up of parents, teachers, and child specialists. Today's show addresses the question: "Does seeing violence on TV cause violent behaviour in children?" Choose a TV host and two panellists, each supporting a different side of the argument, to respond to audience questions and comments. Audience members should be prepared to respond to the host when called upon to present their views on the issue and on the comments made up to that point.

6. Research Television Ratings   Research how industry codes and government regulations influence children's television viewing. Do you think parents/guardians generally pay attention to the ratings? Explain.

The producers thought the story wasn't "Native enough" for their purposes.

What Colour Is a Rose?

by Drew Hayden Taylor

ESSAY

Notes

Drew Hayden Taylor, an Ojibway from Curved Lake Reserve, writes for stage and screen. He is also known for the satirical articles from his witty collections of essays such as *Funny, You Don't Look Like One: Observations of a Blue-Eyed Ojibway* (1998).

ad nauseam: repeatedly to the point of sickness

synonymous: the same as, similar to, or associated with

W.P. Kinsella: William Patrick Kinsella (1932–) was born in Edmonton and went on to write a book about the famous baseball player Shoeless Joe Jackson, which became the source of the movie *Field of Dreams*. His stories about Natives, such as those in *Born Indian* and *The Moccasin Telegraph*, have prompted accusations of expropriation and stereotyping from Native critics.

As a Native writer there are always three questions I get asked, *ad nauseam*, whenever I give a lecture or a reading for a non-Native audience. Question one: "What do you feel about cultural appropriation?" My answer: "About the same as I feel about land appropriation." Question two: "When you write your plays or stories, do you write for a specifically Native audience or a White audience?" My answer: "I'm usually alone in my room when I write, except for my dying cactus. So I guess that means I write for my dying cactus." The final, and in my opinion, most annoying question I often get asked is: "Are you a writer that happens to be Native, or a Native that happens to be a writer?"

I was not aware there had to be a difference. I was always under the impression that the two could be, and often were, synonymous. But evidently I am in error. Over the past few years of working as a professional writer, I have slowly begun to understand the rules of participation in the television and prose industry in terms of this difference. It seems there is a double standard. Surprise, surprise.

It is not uncommon, though deemed politically incorrect, for White writers to write satires about Native people quite freely, particularly on television. Notice many of the

"people of pallor" script credits on such shows as *North of Sixty* (which, granted, does have one talented Native writer), *Northern Exposure* (I guess I'll have to move to the North since it seems that's where all the Native people live), and movies like *Where the Spirit Lives* or *Dance Me Outside*. All these shows have strong, identifiable Native characters created by non-Natives.

However, should a Native writer want to explore the untrodden world outside the Aboriginal literary ghetto, immediately the fences appear, and opportunities dry up. Evidently, the Powers That Be out there in the big cruel world have very specific ideas of what a Native writer can and can't do. Only recently, a friend of mine submitted a story to a new CBC anthology series in development, about Native people, called *The Four Directions*.

His story outline was soon returned with an explanation that the producers thought the story wasn't "Native enough" for their purposes. I myself submitted a story to the producers, and during our first story meeting, I received a stirring and heartfelt lecture about how they, the producers, were determined to present the Native voice as authentically and accurately as possible, and how committed they were to allowing us Native-types the chance to tell our

stories our way. I was then asked if I could cut the first eight pages of my twenty-seven page script. Oddly enough, they seemed puzzled by my sudden burst of laughter.

I once wrote an episode of *Street Legal* and accidentally caught a glimpse of a memo from the producer to a story editor asking him to rewrite the dialogue of my Native Elder to "make him more Indian." I guess as a Native person, I don't know how real "Indians" talk. Bummer. These are just a few examples of the battle Native writers often face.

I hereby pose a question to these people who judge our stories. I personally would like to know by what set of qualifications these people examine Native stories. Is there an Aboriginal suitability quotient posted somewhere? If there is, I would love the opportunity to learn more about how I should write as a Native person.

For a story to be "Native enough," must there be a birch bark or buckskin quota? Perhaps there are supposed to be vast roaming herds of moose running past the screen. Oh geez, I guess I'm not Native enough. I momentarily forgot, moose don't herd, they just hang out with flying squirrels that have their own cartoon show.

Or maybe I's got be good writer like dem Indians whats W.P. Kinsella writes about. It no sound like any Indian I ever hears, but what the hell, I maybe win bunch of awards. On second thought, you never mind. I get headache trying write like this.

So what's a writer to do? Damned if he does, damned if he doesn't. And what if I want to write stories about non-Native people? It's possible, but will I be given a chance? I'm sure I could do it. I've learned enough about how White people really live from watching all those episodes of *Married With Children* and *Baywatch*.

This all brings us back to the original question. Am I a writer who happens to be Native, or a Native that happens to be a writer? Do I have a choice? I think that the next time I get asked that, I'll ask the equally deep and important question: "Is a zebra black with white stripes, or white with black stripes?"

Just watch. They'll make that into a racial question.

You take it from here …

Responding

1. Appreciate Tone   In a small group, reread the introductory paragraph and discuss what we learn about the author's attitude to his topic from his responses to each of the three questions. What additional indications of his attitude did you note in the essay? Suggest an adjective that describes the author's tone.

2. Find Supporting Evidence   With a partner, consider what the author means when he says, "It seems there is a double standard" for Native writers. What evidence does he use to support this position?

3. Understand an Analogy   An *analogy* compares one thing with something else in order to explain a point. The author compares the question of whether he is mainly a "writer who happens to be a Native" or "a Native that happens to be a writer" with the question of whether a zebra is black with white stripes or white with black stripes. In a paragraph, explain this analogy and state whether you think it effectively illustrates the author's dilemma.

4. Interpret the Title   With a partner, consider the title of this essay. How does it relate to the author's main point or thesis? Share your thoughts in a class discussion.

Extending

5. Write a Satirical Essay   Satire is used to criticize the current state of affairs in a society in order to promote social change. Satire is often humorous, but it usually has a sharp edge of criticism. Using this essay as a model, write a short satirical essay on an issue that is important to you.

6. Create a Collage   The article claims that non-Native individuals are determining the voice and portrayal of Native peoples in the media. As a class, consider what other groups might be similarly affected (e.g., youth, women, certain cultural groups), and discuss how specific groups are stereotyped in the media. Then, work with one or two other students to create a collage representing "two voices" of a particular group. For one "voice," use media images that show a stereotyped view of the group, for the other, find images created by the group members themselves. Present your collage to the class.

Zits

Cartoon by Jerry Scott and Jim Borgman

Notes

Zits, the popular comic strip about the life and times of 15-year-old Jeremy Duncan, began in 1997 and runs in over 1000 newspapers worldwide. It has been voted the Best Comic Strip twice by the National Cartoonists Society.

Jerry Scott, writer and co-creator of *Zits,* began his career by taking over the *Nancy* strip. He then co-created *Baby Blues* (which is based on his experiences with his second daughter) before going on to do *Zits.*

Jim Borgman, Pulitzer Prize-winning cartoonist, was raised in blue-collar neighbourhoods of Cincinnati. He was hired by the *Cincinnati Enquirer* one week after graduation to start work cartooning.

Jim Borgman and Jerry Scott

You take it from here ...

Responding

1. Identify the Message With a partner, discuss the stereotypes presented in this cartoon. Is this portrayal accurate, in your experience?

2. Examine Effect Read aloud the boxed text at the bottom of the last frame ("The ve-e-e-e-r-r-ry beginning ..."). With a partner, discuss what effect is achieved by the "stretched" spelling and the addition of the ellipsis dots ("...") at the end. How would the effect be different if it were written in the standard form ("The very beginning.")?

3. Write about a Personal Experience In your journal, describe a time when you helped a friend or family member learn to use a new technology (e.g., how to surf the Internet or use a computer program, or how to use a new cellphone or DVD player). How did you approach the task—were you mainly patient or impatient? Did you take a humorous or serious approach? Did you learn anything new in the process of teaching?

Extending

4. Promote Your Abilities Imagine that you are applying for a part-time job teaching basic computer skills to children or adults. Draft a résumé highlighting your related experience, computer skills, and personal qualities that would enable you to do the job well. When you have finished, exchange drafts with a partner for proofreading and feedback.

TIP

- Be selective when listing your skills. For example, knowledge of the Internet or word processing would be more relevant on a résumé than knowledge of computer games.

PEER ASSESSMENT

- Was the information on the résumé relevant and neatly presented and free of errors in spelling and punctuation?
- What suggestions did you offer to improve clarity or content?

5. Conduct a Survey As a class, develop a set of questions to discover what types of technologies were available to earlier generations of high-school students. Include questions pertaining to leisure and entertainment, work and education, domestic life, and communications. Then form four groups to conduct the surveys, and report on your findings.

TIPS

- Each group member should interview one or two adults.
- Try to include respondents for each of the past five decades (1950s–1990s).

Technological change has done something our ancestors would never have believed: made experts of the young.

Turning the Generations Upside Down

by Ellen Goodman

NEWSPAPER COLUMN

Notes

Ellen Goodman (1941–) is a columnist for *The Boston Globe*. Her work appears in over 400 newspapers. She won a Pulitzer Prize for Distinguished Commentary in 1980.

avocation: hobby

obsolete: out of date; no longer used

peripheral: not that important

shoe last: fitting for a shoe to help keep its shape

vocation: career; life's work

It is evening when my mother, whose life is booby-trapped by technology, calls. She is having an electronic breakdown. The television set, which once merely and manually went on and off, now requires a series of instructions before it will obey.

There are numbers to be entered on two remote controls that are not remotely within her control at this moment. Something has gone awry.

To avoid an emergency house call, I talk her through the system step by step. The scene is not unlike the old war movie in which a ship-to-shore appendectomy is performed by telephone. Eventually, the patient is saved.

I hang up the phone flush with my own prowess, more than a bit intolerant of my elder's difficulty coping with the television. The word I use is "phobic." The feeling I have is superior.

But my smugness doesn't last long. Within days I am confronted by my own younger generation. They cannot understand why I am not up to speed—their speed—on the equipment we share. Why do I hesitate to program the VCR? Why have we never logged on the new computer program? It's really, we are told, fun. The feeling that I have is of incompetence.

What I am describing is nothing unique to my family. There is a three-generational model of technological life in America. Seventysomething meets fortysomething meets twentysomething.

The model has become the central sitcom of modern times. All across America, 10-year-olds are called from their bedrooms to work the video camera; 12-year-olds are wrenched from their homework to program the VCR; 14-year-olds come home from dates to fix the glitch in the computer.

We find it amusing, take it for granted, and rarely think about the vast revolution that has turned the generations upside down. Technological change has done something our ancestors would have never believed: made experts of the young.

In part, this is the story of America itself. When immigrants came to this country, they left behind not only the language but the cultural knowledge that made them surefooted guides through the old, traditional world. In America, their children became interpreters of new words and ways.

Now each generation emigrates to a new technological country. Elders learn this technology as a second language, haltingly, imperfectly. Children grow up bilingual.

The pace of change seems to make experience obsolete. It's one of the things about being a parent now. Fewer of us have a skill to teach our children. Fewer children apprentice themselves to us as adults. There are times when we lose confidence that what we have to teach has any meaning.

A man becomes a printer and his grandchildren lay out newspaper pages on computers. A woman learns the intricacies of preserving food and her children buy a refrigerator.

One generation has a storehouse of home remedies and the next generation takes penicillin. For every man who teaches his child to fish there is another who tries to learn Nintendo from that same child.

The things that elders still show the young—how to hit a ball, plant a tree, tell a story—have become peripheral to their daily economic survival. They are the stuff of avocation rather

than vocation. Indeed, parents and children spend their time together before, after, around work. We have become each other's extra-curricular activity.

In all of this, the one subject that the elders are entrusted with as if it had some permanence is "family life." We are told to teach our children "values." But we all forget that values were once learned while watching, while working, beside the older generation.

Values came in the conversation over a shoe last or the hem of a skirt. Respect came from the knowledge of the older generation and the acknowledgement of the young.

The wonder is that technology hasn't severed the cord between generations, but just frayed it. The wonder is that the older generation still is expert in the subject that never becomes obsolete: life.

Skill comes quickly, but wisdom comes, if at all, slowly. Technology favours the young, but the soft information about our human kind, our own behaviour, needs aging. In the end, it's not a bad exchange for a little problem with the VCR.

You take it from here ...

Responding

1. **Explore the Introduction**   What specific incident caused the author to think about the impact of technology on different generations in today's society? Identify two words or expressions that suggest how the author's mother might have felt about technology at the time of the incident.

2. **Consider Irony**   In a paragraph, describe how the author felt after assisting her mother. Identify what caused this feeling to change. What is ironic about the situation?

TIP

- See the glossary at the back of this book to review the definitions of these terms.

3. **Identify Literary Techniques**   With a partner, review the selection and find examples of the following literary techniques:

Literary technique	Example from the article
personification	
pun	
simile	
metaphor	
rhetorical question	
parallel structure	

4. **Connect Title and Thesis**   Write a paragraph explaining how the title of this column is connected to its thesis (main idea). Share your ideas with another student.

Extending

TIP

- Include sound effects and stage directions as necessary.

5. **Script a Scene**   Divide the class into four groups. With your group, script a scenario that illustrates the author's comment that there is a "three-generational model of technological life." Rehearse your scene and present it to the class in the form of a video, radio program, or live performance.

> **GROUP ASSESSMENT**
> - How did your group decide on the form and content of the scenario?
> - Did group members readily agree on roles and responsibilities?

6. **Offer a Different Perspective**   Near the end of the column, the author states, "The wonder is that technology hasn't severed the cord between generations, but just frayed it." Draft a letter to the editor presenting a different view, that "Far from severing, or even fraying, the cord between generations, technology has brought them closer together."

TIP

• A relevant article on this topic is "Logged On to the Guy Next Door" in Unit 1.

7. **Write Instructions**   Imagine that you are employed as a technical writer and you have been assigned to work on an instruction manual for a common technological device such as a portable CD player. Your task is to write the step-by-step instructions for performing a specific function, such as playing a CD. Ask a partner to review your instructions and to suggest ways to improve them. If possible, have your partner test the instructions by following them exactly as written.

PEER ASSESSMENT

As you review your partner's instructions, consider the following:
• Were the instructions clear and to the point?
• Did the instructions follow the correct sequence?
• What suggestions did you offer?

Before you read, think about the steps you usually take when searching for information on the Internet.

As you read, list three items of information that you did not know about searching the Web.

First of all think up a series of words that relate to your topic.

Be Specific When Searching the Web

by ANdy WAlkeR

TECHNOLOGY COLUMN

Notes

Andy Walker is a syndicated journalist and managing editor/CEO of a Toronto-based company, Cyberwalker Media Inc. Since 1989, he has written about technology issues for over 50 newspapers in North America, including the *Toronto Sun, The Toronto Star, Vancouver Province,* and *Edmonton Journal.*

Question: I got onto the Internet last year and have figured out Yahoo and sites like that. But when I get results from them it's not always exactly what I want. Is there some mysterious secret I don't know about? – P.I.

Answer: There are many secrets that lie within those search engine pages, but they are not immediately obvious. Here are a few advanced techniques.

Search engines work by comparing the words that you type in their query boxes to a massive library of indexed Web pages. They use software to study Web pages and rank them according to topics and keywords. Some engines, like Yahoo, also use humans to categorize pages.

Simply typing one or two words into the search box and clicking on the search button is not enough.

Think of walking into a library and telling the librarian that you're looking for information on "pets." Chances are that the librarian will ask you to be more specific. If she found every book containing the word "pets" for you, the pile would be very high. Essentially, that's what happens when your search is too vague on a search engine. It looks for every Web page it can find in its index with that word in it and lists hundreds and hundreds of results, which can be disheartening to a novice searcher.

Engines rank sites based on several criteria: The word frequency on the page. Where the word is located in the page (the closer to the top, the better). Whether or not the owner of the page has specified the word as a keyword in special hidden tags. The engines also look at whether or not the words are in headlines or titles, as well as image descriptions.

So to be an effective Internet researcher, you need to find ways to tell the search engine specifically what you want. First of all think up a series of words that relate to your topic.

If it is "pets," perhaps you're thinking about getting one. The search phrase "choose a pet" would be a better choice.

If you use a phrase, put quotation marks around the words. The search engine will look for that exact phrase in its library of links. Always check the second page of the search results. There is usually a link or button at the bottom of the first results page. Often, you'll find what you're looking for two or three pages into the search results.

If you were interested in information about dogs as pets and you know which breed you want, you should use that information in your keywords. In my house, we have a Keeshund called Dreyfus. (He looks like a small long-haired husky that rolled in the ashes.) If I wanted more information on his breed, I might use the search terms "dog+keeshund." Ignore the quotes in this case, but note the plus sign (+). That search phrase would mean: find all Web pages perhaps with the word "dog" in them, but definitely with the word "keeshund." If I used "dog–keeshund" (note the minus sign), I would be telling the engine to find Web pages about dogs, but to exclude any pages that included the word "keeshund."

You can also use brackets to help specify your searches. The search criteria "dog AND (keeshund OR poodle)" will find all pages that have the words "dog" and "keeshund" and the pages that have the words "dog" and "poodle."

The words AND, OR, NOT, and NEAR are called Boolean operators and can be used on most search engines. The search syntax "dogs AND cats" means find pages with both words.

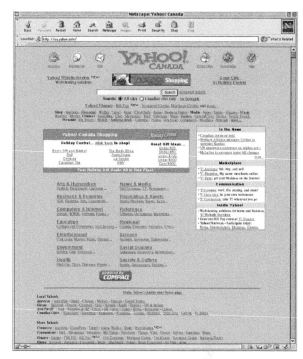

Yahoo.com offers many tips on how to get better search results.

The search syntax "dogs OR cats" finds pages about either. The NOT operator is used in conjunction with AND. So "dogs AND NOT cats" would find all pages with the word "dogs" that exclude the word "cats."

If you use the "NEAR" operator, you can find pages where your keywords are within 10 words of each other on the page. The asterisk operator (*) can be used to find matches on words that are similar. The search term "world*" would result in pages that include words like "worlds," "worldwide," "worldly," as well as the actual word "world."

You can mix and match all these techniques to do fairly elaborate searches. Not all search engines support all these advanced features. Most do, though.

If a site has index categories, as Yahoo does, it's often better to search by category.

Canada.com is another site that has special links to advice on how to search the Web as efficiently as possible.

Yahoo has human editors who categorize Web pages by topics. Instead of typing search terms, click down through the categories, which are often several levels deep, to find great sites related to your topic. This is a good technique to use if you're just browsing or are unsure what specific area you are interested in.

I quite like the natural language search engines. AskJeeves.com is quite useful. On this site, you type in your question, as you'd pose it to another human being. "Jeeves" will respond with results that include what other search engines find as well as related sites rated by AskJeeves.com staff. It will also suggest related search terms.

Finally, it's worth looking for links or buttons on the search engines that refer to advanced searches. These Web pages often list advanced search techniques as well as tips on how to specifically search the search engine site you are currently working on.

Below are some Web addresses of advanced search tip pages on four of the popular Canadian search engines.

- Yahoo Canada
  http://ca.search.yahoo.com/search/ca/syntax?

- AltaVista Canada
  www.altavistacanada.com/en/help/adv_help.html

- Canada.com
  www.canada.com/search/web/help_search.asp

You take it from here ...

Responding

1. Identify Audience and Purpose   Who is the target audience for this column? What is the author's purpose? Share your ideas with a partner, and justify them with specific references to the selection.

2. Examine Style   With a partner, describe the author's writing style and discuss how it contributes to the purpose of the column. What techniques does the author use to explain his points clearly?

3. Find Facts   Write your responses to the following questions:

- How do search engines work?
- What problem is caused by using a search word that is too vague or general?
- Which five criteria do search engines use to rank sites?
- What purpose do brackets serve in a search?
- When should quotation marks be used in a search?
- What point does the author make by using the example of his dog Dreyfus?
- What are the special features of the Yahoo and AskJeeves search engines?

4. Organize Information   In a chart, list the four words known as Boolean operators, and explain the function of each one.

Boolean operator	Function of the Boolean operator
AND	

Extending

5. Conduct an Advanced Search   Use some of the techniques identified in the selection to find the following information:

- the names of the individual members of your favourite band
- the names of the individual members of any popular 1970s band
- the TV show that won the Emmy for outstanding comedy in 1992
- the team that won Olympic gold for hockey in 1988

Take notes on your search, identifying the search engine, keywords, symbols, and Boolean operators you use in each attempt. Note the most useful Web sites you find, as well as any problems you encounter and how you attempted to solve them. Use your notes to prepare a short report on the process.

6. Draft an E-Mail Question   Compose an e-mail that you might send to a newspaper columnist who specializes in answering computer-related questions. Share your question with the rest of the class and see if someone in the class has the answer. Was any theme evident among the questions in the class?

Reflecting on the Unit

Responding

1. Debate a Quotation   In the words of journalist Jennifer Stone, "Technology evolves so much faster than wisdom." Working in a small group, discuss what this quotation means. Decide whether you agree or disagree, and give reasons to support your views.

2. Consider Pros and Cons   With a partner, review the selections in this unit and consider the effects of media, technology, and advertising on our values and quality of life. In a three-column chart headed "Media," "Technology," and "Advertising," list some positive and negative ways in which our lives and values are affected by each of these.

3. Reflect on Consumerism   A quotation at the beginning of this unit states: "You can tell the ideals of a nation by its advertisements." As a class, choose two current Canadian TV advertisements and discuss what they reveal about "the ideals" of Canada.

Extending

4. Write an Editorial   As a class, arrive at a definition of "media literacy." Then, based on specific ideas presented in this unit, write an editorial arguing that media literacy is as important to today's students as the traditional literacy skills of reading and writing have always been.

5. Examine the Power of Media   Consider how mass media influence our opinions on particular subjects. In a short essay, describe a time when your own opinions or actions were influenced by the media. For example,

   - You formed a new opinion based on a news report
   - You bought something, or did something, because of an advertisement
   - You understood a serious issue after seeing a cartoon about it

> **SELF-ASSESSMENT**
>
> The main focus of this unit has been on how media and technology affect our lives. Identify
> - the most thought-provoking information you read
> - subjects about which you would like more information
>
> Write your response in your journal and share it in a group discussion.

In youth we learn; in age we understand.
— *Marie Ebner-Eschenbach*

We do not know the true value of our moments until they have undergone the test of memory.
— *Georges Duhamel*

What families have in common the world around is that they are the place where people learn who they are and how to be that way.
— *Jean Illsley Clarke*

MEMORABLE MOMENTS and INFLUENCES

This unit focuses on the formative years of a person's life, from childhood through to young adulthood.

Baroness Marie Ebner-Eschenbach sees youth as a time of learning experiences that help us, eventually, to understand who we are, where we are from, and why we are the way we are.

Writer Georges Duhamel points out that we often do not know at the time of an early experience how influential it will be in our lives. Only later do we discover its true value and meaning.

Jean Illsley Clarke, a family psychology consultant, tells us that family often plays a key role in defining us and establishing our identities.

As you read this unit, reflect on your own past and family. Consider the following questions:

1) How are we creatures of a specific time, place, and culture?

2) What is truly valuable about family ties and family influences?

3) How do the experiences of childhood and youth "mark" us for life?

4) How do others in our lives help shape who we are?

My Old Newcastle

Now the town is three times as large, and fast-food franchises and malls dot the roadside.

Memoir by David Adams Richards

Notes

David Adams Richards (1950–) is a novelist and poet from Newcastle, New Brunswick. His first book of poems, *Small Heroics* (1972), launched his career. His compassionate novels include *The Coming of Winter*, *Hope in the Desperate Hour*, and *Nights Below Station Street*. He won the Governor General's Award for fiction in 1988. He currently lives in Toronto.

derelict: hobo

redundancy: repetition; repeated pattern

Rhodes scholar: winner of the prestigious Rhodes scholarship for study at Oxford University

tommy-cod: small saltwater fish

In Newcastle, N.B., which I call home, we all played on the ice floes in the spring, spearing tommy-cod with stolen forks tied to sticks. More than one of us almost met our end slipping off the ice.

All night the trains rumbled or shunted their loads off to Halifax or Montreal, and men moved and worked. To this day I find the sound of trains more comforting than lonesome. It was somehow thrilling to know of people up and about in those hours, and wondrous events taking place. Always somehow with the faint, worn smell of gas and steel.

The Miramichi is a great working river.

There was always the presence of working men and women, from the mines or mills or woods; the more than constant sounds of machinery; and the ore covered in tarps at the side of the wharf.

But as children, sitting in our snowsuits and hats and heavy boots on Saturday afternoons, we all saw movies that had almost nothing to do with us. That never mentioned us as a country or a place. That never seemed to know what our fathers and mothers did—that we went to wars or had a flag or even a great passion for life.

As far as the movies were concerned, we were in a lost, dark country, it seemed. And perhaps this is one reason I write. Leaving the theatre on a January afternoon, the smell of worn seats and heat and chip bags gave way to a muted cold and scent of snow no movie ever showed us. And night came against the tin roofs of the sheds behind our white houses, as the long spires of our churches rose over the town.

Our river was frozen so blue then that the trucks could travel from one town to the other across the ice, and bonfires were lit by kids skating; sparks rose upon the shore under the stars as mothers called children home at 9 o'clock.

All winter long the sky was tinted blue on the horizon, the schools we sat in too warm; privileged boys and girls sat beside those who lived in hunger and constant worry. One went on to be a Rhodes scholar, another was a derelict at 17 and dead at 20. To this day I could not tell you which held more promise.

Spring came with the smell of mud and grass burning in the fields above us. Road hockey gave way to cricket and then baseball. The sun warmed, the ice shifted, and the river was free. Salmon and sea trout moved up a dozen of our tributaries to spawn.

In the summer the ships came in, from all ports to ours, to carry ore and paper away. Sailors smoked black tobacco cigarettes, staring down at us from their decks; blackflies spoiled in the fields beyond town, and the sky was large all evening. Cars filled with children too excited to sleep passed along our great avenues lined with overhanging trees. All down to the store to get ice cream in the dark.

Adolescent blueberry crops and sunken barns dotted the fields near the bay, where the air had the taste of salt and tar, and small spruce trees seemed constantly filled with wind; where, by August, the water shimmered and even the small white lobster boats smelled of autumn, as did the ripples that moved them.

In the autumn the leaves were red, of course, and the earth, by Thanksgiving, became hard as a dull turnip. Ice formed in the ditches and shallow streams. The fields became yellow and stiff. The sounds of rifle shots from men hunting deer echoed faintly away, while women walked in kerchiefs and coats to 7 o'clock mass, and the air felt heavy and leaden. Winter coming on again.

Now the town is three times as large, and fast-food franchises and malls dot the roadside where there were once fields and lumberyards. There is a new process at the mill, and much of the wood is clear-cut so that huge acres lie empty and desolate, a redundancy of broken and muted earth. The river is opened all winter by an ice-breaker, so no trucks travel across the ice, and the trains, of course, are gone. For the most part the station is empty, the tracks fiercely alone in the winter sun.

The theatre is gone now, too. And those thousands of movies showing us, as children filled with happy laughter someplace in Canada, what we were not, are gone as well. They have given way to videos and satellite dishes and a community that is growing slowly farther and farther away from its centre. Neither bad nor good, I suppose—but away from what it was.

You take it from here ...

Responding

1. **Analyze the Title**   Consider the tone of the title for this selection. Why is it "My Old Newcastle" and not "My Newcastle," "Old Newcastle," or simply "Newcastle"? What does the wording suggest about the author's feelings toward the changes in the town? Share your ideas with one or two other students.

2. **Discuss Purpose**   Locate the sentence, "And perhaps this is one reason I write." As a class, discuss what the author means by this statement.

3. **Discuss the Value of Movies**   The author states that, when he was a child, "we all saw movies that had almost nothing to do with us." As a class or in a small group, discuss whether this is typical of your own experience. Do you think it is important for children to see movies that reflect their own world, showing places and situations with which they can identify? Explain.

Extending

4. **Write a Memoir**   David Adams Richards writes about changes that have occurred in his hometown from the time he was a young boy. Write your own memoir about changes you have observed in your community since you were a small child.

5. **Create a Travel Brochure**   Check encyclopedias, government Web sites, and other sources to find out more about the Miramichi River area of New Brunswick. Create a tourist pamphlet that highlights the area's attractions for visitors.

6. **Represent a Scene**   The author's writing style appeals to the senses, making it easy for the reader to imagine in detail each scene and season he describes. Choose one descriptive paragraph and represent it visually in the form of your choice (e.g., a collage, sketch, folk art picture, or a cover for a CD or anthology titled "My Old Newcastle"). Present your work to a small group.

TIPS

- Begin by brainstorming a list of details you remember from the past.
- Select the details that seem to be most different from the present.
- Consider how you feel about these changes: are they good, bad, or indifferent?
- Use Richards's memoir as a model for organizing your ideas.

TIPS

- Use maps, photographs, and/or illustrations to enhance your text.
- Consider using a page-layout program to create the final version.

The Still-Boiling Water

"When I was finally pulled out of the pot, pieces of my skin remained on its sides."

Memoir by Chrystia Chomiak

Notes

Chrystia Chomiak (1948–) was born in a displaced persons' camp in Germany and later settled in Edmonton, Alberta. She studied art history and Slavic studies in Toronto. Chomiak has been an activist, researcher, editor, and art curator.

baba: "grandmother" in Ukrainian

borsch: beet soup

émigré: someone who has left his or her native country, often for political reasons

By the time I arrived, they were already sitting around the kitchen table, drinking wine and laughing. The long dining room table had been set for 24, and the house was full with the sweet smell of beets cooking with wild mushrooms, bay leaves, fresh dill, peppercorns, and just the right touch of tomatoes and carrots as the Christmas borsch slowly simmered on the stove. The kitchen counters were covered with cookie sheets holding tiny pockets of transparently thin pastry filled with a mixture of wild mushrooms and onion, ready to be boiled. They had finished their preparations for Christmas and had started their stories. Each one of my six aunts talks louder than the other, and they all laugh at the same time. Their first stories are always about their boyfriends and husbands, old and new, and who's coming with whom that year. Then they go back to the small two-bedroom house that they grew up in, and the stories become quieter and the laughter slowly stops. And that's when this story is told.

"When I was three years old," my aunt Maria starts, "I fell into a large canning pot of still-boiling water, which my mother had left on the kitchen floor. When I was finally pulled out of the pot, pieces of my skin remained on its sides. After this accident, I stopped speaking for three-and-a-half months—for my entire stay at the hospital."

My baba interrupts. She is always the first to tell the story. This is her story. She begins by talking about her suffering, about her poverty in Canada, about the constant numbing work of raising six daughters. Then she talks about the accident and how she could not stop crying, how she almost lost her daughter Maria. She turns to me, looks me squarely in the eyes, and says, can you imagine losing your own child, watching her die?

She recounts the day's events—preparing the fruit for canning, preparing the jars for canning, preparing the shelves for more jars. She spends considerable time describing the size of her canning pot, the weight of the jars, that she had no one to help her, that while she canned she also looked after her six children. She adds that she had to can in order to have food for the long, cold Edmonton winters, and that it was very hard for her to provide for her children.

She says that she was tired that day, that all morning Maria and Natalia had repeatedly called her and that she had told them not to bother her anymore. She repeats this point a couple of times and tells me how she had to run up and down the stairs, from the basement to the kitchen, each time they called her. She adds there was a newborn in the house, sleeping in the upstairs bedroom.

Then she says that when she heard her children calling her—still yet another time—that that time she decided not to run upstairs but to finish her work instead. She adds that when she finally went upstairs it was she who plunged her hands into the still-boiling water and pulled Maria out. It was she who wrapped Maria in blankets, carried her to the cab, and went to the hospital with her. After a pause she describes—with some amazement—that during the whole ordeal, Maria did not cry, and that instead Maria tried to comfort her and kept asking her to stop crying. "Maria did not cry," my baba repeats and they are all silent, waiting.

Then she describes the scene at the hospital: how the doctors placed them on adjoining beds, how they instantly connected them—by tube—one arm to the other—one life to the other—no questions—how they lay there alone, she in her house dress stained with peach and plum juices from the morning's canning—giving blood—giving life—again.

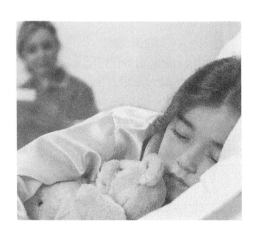

She describes the visits—the daily visits for three-and-a-half months—to the hospital. Daily, walking the seven blocks to the bus stop—every afternoon—taking the bus to the General Hospital, staying just a short time—"I had children at home—little children," she says—and then returning. From the house to the hospital, from the hospital to the house, every day. She adds that Maria stopped talking after the accident, and that she feared that Maria would be mute for the rest of her life.

Then she describes the afternoon, at the hospital, when Maria finally spoke. It was when she came to the hospital with an old friend, an émigré doctor, Maria's godfather, just days before Maria was to go home. He gave Maria a ring, she says, and it was then that Maria finally spoke for the first time in three-and-a-half months: "And where is my bracelet?" At that point my baba finishes her story, sits back, shakes her head from all the remembering, and smiles.

Then it is Natalia's turn. She begins her story by crying. She begins by saying that it was not her fault that Maria fell into the pot. That it could have been her. That Maria had done the same things to her. Then Natalia stops.

At that point, Maria asks her, "What happened? What were we playing?"

"Tug-of-war."

"And what did you do?"

"I let go of my end and you fell into the pot. You were standing too close. You had done the same to me," she adds. "You had let go of the rope before and I had fallen. It was your turn to fall. You started it."

Then in great detail, Natalia recounts how she tried to pull Maria out of the pot, but that the water was too hot. She describes how Maria was stuck to the pot and that the pot was too high for her to reach into. She repeats how she ran up and down the stairs, several times, up and down, all the time afraid to leave Maria alone, all the time calling her mother for help. Natalia recounts how she could not explain to her mother what had happened, as she ran up and down the stairs, until finally her mother understood. Then Natalia adds that it was she who went next door and asked Mrs. Parks for help, and it was she who called the cab that took Maria and my baba to the hospital.

Natalia describes how she stood by the front window of their house waiting, all afternoon, not moving, waiting for her mother and Maria to return. She describes how she told her father what had happened, when he finally came home from work. She adds that all during that time she did not move from her spot, in front of the window, until her mother finally returned, late that night.

Then Natalia talks about the long months that Maria was gone and how she had been told that Maria could no longer speak. She says that she could not understand what this really meant, but that deep down, all the time that Maria was gone, she felt guilty. Then Natalia adds that when Maria finally returned from the hospital, she wore a new cream-coloured satin dress, with smocking on the front, and that she gave Maria a new doll, but that Maria said nothing to her.

Only when the others have told their stories does Maria tell hers. She starts by describing the day. She talks about its warmth and that she wore a sundress. She talks about the jars of canned fruit that her mother had

prepared, how they glistened when they were set on the table. She adds that her mother told her to stay away from the pot, that it was too heavy to lift onto the table.

She talks about the fun Natalia and she had that morning, how they laughed and played and how delighted they were in their disobedience as they called their mother, all morning, just for fun. Then she adds that she does not actually remember falling into the pot, but that she does remember calling out for help. She describes the commotion, the panic around her, but repeats that she felt no pain. She adds that she tried to comfort her mother during their drive to the hospital.

Then she recounts arriving at the hospital and how she expected everyone to be dressed in white, but that they were all in green. She says that the only things that she remembers from the first weeks in the hospital is her mother's blood flowing into her in the emergency room, how warm it felt, and then the repeated elevator rides—going up and down and up and down, and rolling along the corridors while lying on a bed. She describes how the doctors examined her and looked at her skin and talked about cutting skin from one place and attaching it to another. She always adds that they talked to each other as if she were not there.

When she was feeling better, Maria says that she was placed in the infant ward—infants who cried all day—and how angry she became because she was not an infant. She was three years old. She describes the constant noise of the bottles, being brought in and out, day and night, and the revolting smell of the diapers all around her and that she could not sleep there. She adds how long and hot the afternoons were in the hospital and how lonely she felt, alone in that ward and how she cried, silently, every afternoon until she fell asleep.

Maria tells us that at first she pleaded with the nurses to move her, but that they did not or would not understand her. "They shouted at me to be quiet." She states that she also asked her mother, again and again, to move her to another place—away from the infants—but that her mother did nothing about it. My baba says that Maria is making this part up.

Maria recounts the afternoon when she became hysterical with desperation and how the nurse came and yelled at her, but that she still was not understood. Maria says that it was that afternoon, after the nurse left, that she finally knew that no one could hear her and that was when she decided not to speak any more.

She tells us about the next visit of her parents and how startled they were when she did not answer them and how they called on Dr. Michalchan, the only Ukrainian-speaking doctor at the hospital, to examine her, but that she would not answer him. "I remember all of them speaking to me, all of them, but I just didn't answer."

Lastly, she repeats the story of her godfather's visit and adds that he spoke directly to her and promised her a gold ring and a gold bracelet when he returned. Maria recounts her godfather's return, and that just as he had promised he gave her a gold ring and how happy she was. She says that she waited until he was about to leave before she asked: "And where is the bracelet that you promised me?" She adds how excited they both became when she spoke and how her mother laughed her deep throaty laugh and how beautiful she looked.

Finally she describes the day she went home, how she rubbed the new dress her mother had brought her against her cheek—smooth, creamy satin. She describes how beautiful it felt, and how proud she was, riding home in it. Then Maria adds that when she came home, Natalia pushed a doll into her hands and that all her sisters stared at her as if she was from another planet.

You take it from here ...

Responding

1. Recreate the Introduction   In setting the scene in the first paragraph, the author reveals several details about the family and their cultural background. Replace details of the setting, food, and holiday festival with concrete images drawn from your own family experiences.

2. Consider Unanswered Questions   With a partner, discuss the extent to which the memoir answered all the questions that arose as you read it. Did you anticipate reading about certain details that, in the end, were not included? List these, and suggest why they may not have been dealt with in detail. Share your list and your responses in a class discussion.

3. Discuss Story-Telling Rituals   Maria starts the story, but is interrupted because her mother is always the first to tell her side. Consider why the story might always be told in the same order. Think about any ceremonies or rituals in your own family that are carried out according to a set order of participants. Why do you think this is so? Share your responses in a small group.

4. Introduce Another Point of View   Work with a partner to write a new section of the story, as told by one of the sisters who was not directly involved in the incident. Include some details about the sister (e.g., her name, her age at the time) and relate her thoughts about what happened and about the reactions of her mother, Natalia, and Maria.

Extending

5. Write Your Own Family Story   It is not uncommon for families to have stories that are repeated when they gather together. Write your version of a dramatic incident in which you were involved with another family member. Share your version with the family member you feel closest to (not necessarily the one who was directly involved in the story). Does your version differ in any way from the other person's memory of the event? Write a journal entry describing how similar or different the memories were.

6. Investigate Domestic History   In a society where supermarkets, nursery schools, and family cars are commonplace, the world of this story can seem remote. Ask your parents, guardians, or older relatives about what domestic tasks their grandparents—or if possible, their grandparents' parents—had to perform as part of daily life. See how many generations back you can go, and note how times have changed our way of life. Share your stories orally with the rest of the class.

Notes

Michael Crummey (1965–) was born and raised in Newfoundland, and now lives in Kingston, Ontario. A highly regarded poet, he won the Bronwen Wallace Award for poetry in 1994. His debut novel, *River Thieves*, was nominated for the 2001 Giller Prize.

spoor: the track or trail of a wild animal

Lilacs

Poem by Michael Crummey

The well is contaminated and we have to
drag a bucket of water up from the brook;
we pull handfuls of lilacs from the trees
outside the open windows and set them
in glasses through the house to mask the smell
of rooms shut up with themselves for years

There are old saucers of poison placed
on countertops and mantlepieces, spoor in the pantry
and Dad tells me how he'd chase mice through
the house with a stick when he was a boy
although it was considered bad luck for the fishing
and his father forbid killing them
during the season; in Labrador, he says
you could follow the paths they'd beaten
through the long grass in the dark
but no one raised a hand to them all summer

There are still two beds in the room
where my father was born in nineteen-thirty
and we roll out our sleeping bags there,
then walk to the corner store for food and beer;
later I watch his face in the pale light
of the coleman lantern
try to connect him to what I know of that time
dust bowl photographs, soup kitchens
stories of vagrants at back doors offering
to chop wood for a meal

but I know I have it hopelessly wrong—
he wanted nothing more for me
than that I should grow up a stranger to all this
that his be one of the lives I have not lived

After the lights are put out
there is a silence broken only by the sounds
we make as we shift in our beds and
the occasional scuffle of mice in the hallway;
the age of the house gives a musty
undertone to the sweet smell of the lilacs
and it seems stronger in the darkness
so that I imagine I am breathing in what's left
of the world my father knew
while the part of him that has never
managed to leave here is asleep across the room

You take it from here ...

Responding

1. Think about Title   As a class, discuss the significance of lilacs in this poem. Why do you think the poet chose "Lilacs" as the title? Would another title be as appropriate? Explain.

2. Discuss Motivation   With two or three other students, try to imagine the circumstances that led to this visit to the father's childhood home. Compare ideas with another group.

3. Establish Context   In the third stanza, the speaker mentions "that time." To what time is he referring? What evidence in the poem supports your conclusion? Share your ideas in a class discussion.

4. Consider Emphasis   Review the poem with a partner, paying particular attention to the context surrounding the references to mice. Discuss what these references represent or reveal about the father's childhood life and circumstances.

Extending

5. Investigate Symbolism   Some plants and flowers hold special significance for people. Lilacs, for example, are often associated with spring. For that reason, they have come to symbolize qualities such as first love, virginity, and youth. Do some research on the symbolism of five other flowers. According to your research, what messages have been associated with each one? Present your results in the form of an oral account or as a poster or a pamphlet.

6. Analyze Superstitions   The idea that chasing mice was bad luck for fishing is a classic superstition. In small groups, brainstorm as many superstitions as you can. Select five, and research their origins: where and when did they first appear? What experience or beliefs are they based on? Share your findings with the class, and discuss your own opinions on these superstitions: do you believe them? Why or why not?

We knew we were the luckiest kids in the world.

A Son's Eulogy for His Father

by JUSTIN TRUDEAU

SPEECH

Notes

Pierre Elliott Trudeau (1919–2000) was born in Montreal and was Prime Minister of Canada from 1968 to 1979, and 1980 to 1984. He is perhaps best remembered for the Official Languages Act (1969), the Charter of Rights and Freedoms, and the Constitution Act (1982), which gave Canada its independence from Great Britain.

Justin Trudeau is the eldest son of Pierre Elliott Trudeau and Margaret Sinclair.

Complete text of the eulogy given by Justin Trudeau at his father's funeral in Montreal.

Friends, Romans, countrymen …

I was about six years old when I went on my first official trip. I was going with my father and my grandpa Sinclair to the North Pole.

It was a very glamorous destination. But the best thing about it is that I was going to be spending lots of time with my dad because in Ottawa he just worked so hard.

One day, we were in Alert, Canada's northernmost point, a scientific military

Justin Trudeau delivers a eulogy for his late father during the state funeral at the Notre-Dame Basilica in Montreal on October 3, 2000.

installation that seemed to consist entirely of low shed-like buildings and warehouses.

Let's be honest. I was six. There were no brothers around to play with and I was getting a little bored because dad still somehow had a lot of work to do.

I remember a frozen, windswept Arctic afternoon when I was bundled up into a Jeep and hustled out on a special top-secret mission. I figured I was finally going to be let in on the reason for this high-security Arctic base.

I was exactly right.

We drove slowly through and past the buildings, all of them very grey and windy. We rounded a corner and came upon a red one. We stopped. I got out of the Jeep and started to crunch across towards the front door. I was told, no, to the window.

So I clambered over the snowbank, was boosted up to the window, rubbed my sleeve against the frosty glass to see inside and as my eyes adjusted to the gloom, I saw a figure, hunched over one of many worktables that seemed very cluttered. He was wearing a red suit with that furry white trim.

And that's when I understood just how powerful and wonderful my father was.

Pierre Elliott Trudeau. The very words convey so many things to so many people. Statesman, intellectual, professor, adversary, outdoorsman, lawyer, journalist, author, prime minister.

But more than anything, to me, he was dad. And what a dad. He loved us with the passion and the devotion that encompassed his life. He taught us to believe in ourselves, to stand up for ourselves, to know ourselves, and to accept responsibility for ourselves.

We knew we were the luckiest kids in the world. And we had done nothing to actually deserve it.

It was instead something that we would have to spend the rest of our lives to work very hard to live up to.

He gave us a lot of tools. We were taught to take nothing for granted. He doted on us but didn't indulge.

Trudeau and his sons, Sacha, Justin, and Michel, attend Canada Day celebrations on Parliament Hill, 1983.

Many people say he didn't suffer fools gladly, but I'll have you know he had infinite patience with us.

He encouraged us to push ourselves, to test limits, to challenge anyone and anything.

There were certain basic principles that could never be compromised.

As I guess it is for most kids in grade 3, it was always a real treat to visit my dad at work.

As on previous visits, this particular occasion included a lunch at the parliamentary restaurant, which always seemed to be terribly important and full of serious people that I didn't recognize.

But at eight, I was becoming politically aware. And I recognized one whom I knew to be one of my father's chief rivals.

Thinking of pleasing my father, I told a joke about him—a generic, silly little grade school thing.

My father looked at me sternly with that look I would learn to know so well, and said: "Justin, never attack the individual. We can be in total disagreement with someone without denigrating them as a consequence."

Saying that, he stood up and took me by the hand and brought me over to introduce me to this man.

He was a nice man who was eating there with his daughter, a nice-looking blond girl a little younger than I was.

He spoke to me in a friendly manner for a bit and it was at that point that I understood that having opinions that are different from those of another does not preclude one being deserving of respect as an individual.

This simple tolerance and (recognition of) the real and profound dimensions of each human being, regardless of beliefs, origins, or values—that's what he expected of his children and that's what he expected of our country.

He demanded this with love, love of his sons, love of his country, and it's for this that we so love the letters, the flowers, the dignity of the crowds, and we say to him, farewell.

All that to thank him for having loved us so much.

Trudeau's famous pirouette

My father's fundamental belief never came from a textbook.

It stemmed from his deep love for and faith in all Canadians, and over the past few days, with every card, every rose, every tear, every wave, and every pirouette, you returned his love.

It means the world to Sacha and me. Thank you.

We have gathered from coast to coast to coast, from one ocean to another, united in our grief, to say goodbye.

But this is not the end.

He left politics in '84. But he came back for Meech. He came back for Charlottetown. He came back to remind us of who we are and what we're all capable of.

But he won't be coming back anymore. It's all up to us, all of us, now.

The woods are lovely, dark and deep. He has kept his promises and earned his sleep.

I love you, papa.

You take it from here ...

Responding

1. Identify Allusions   There are several references in this eulogy to elements Justin Trudeau was confident his audience would recognize. These include *allusions* (brief references) to literature as well as to famous aspects of Pierre Elliott Trudeau's life and personality. Working in a small group, list as many of these allusions as you can. Which of these allusions do you understand right away? Which require clarification? Share your list in a class discussion.

2. Consider Audience   Justin Trudeau had the difficult task of standing up before the entire country to talk about his private relationship with his father. Which parts of the speech seem most personal and which parts seem to be directed more to the Canadian public? How do you know? Record your response in your notebook.

3. Debate Humour   The mourners broke into laughter when Justin delivered the line, "And that's when I understood just how powerful and wonderful my father was." As a class, identify what made the mourners laugh, and debate whether humour belongs in a eulogy.

4. Hear the Eulogy   The words on the page are compelling, but Justin Trudeau's delivery of the speech gave them even more power and emphasis. As a class, listen to an audio recording of the eulogy and, afterwards, compare the impact of the two versions. Consider the effect of the pacing of the delivery (slowing down and pausing at appropriate moments) and variations of tone of voice (e.g., moving from matter of fact to dramatic, or from quiet to forceful).

Extending

5. Recall a Lesson Learned   Justin Trudeau recalls being taught many lessons by his father. Recall a time when you benefited from the experience of someone older and wiser than yourself. Write a personal essay about what you learned and how you have applied that lesson in your own life.

6. Share an Anecdote   Think of a moment in your own childhood when you suddenly realized something significant about one of your parents or another adult who has been influential in your life. Craft this moment into an *anecdote,* choosing your words and sentences carefully to highlight the drama of the moment. Share your anecdote with a small group.

PEER ASSESSMENT

As you listen to each anecdote, consider the following:
- Is the point clear and concise? Is the message memorable?
- Does it effectively convey the speaker's thoughts and feelings at the time?
- Is the speaker relating it in a way that is engaging, keeping the audience attentive?

Before you read, as a class, share your own stories about the day you learned to ride a bicycle.

As you read, pay attention to the sentence structure of the poem.

To a Daughter Leaving Home

Poem by Linda Pastan

Notes

Linda Pastan (1932–), an award-winning poet, was born in New York. She was poet laureate of Maryland from 1991 to January 1995. Her poems have appeared in such periodicals as *The Atlantic Monthly* and *The New Yorker*, and she has published many volumes of poetry.

When I taught you
at eight to ride
a bicycle, loping along
beside you
as you wobbled away
on two round wheels,
my own mouth rounding
to surprise when you pulled
ahead down the curved
path of the park,
I kept waiting
for the thud
of your crash as I
sprinted to catch up,
while you grew
smaller, more breakable
with distance,
pumping, pumping
for your life, screaming
with laughter,
the hair flapping
behind you like a
handkerchief waving
goodbye.

You take it from here ...

Responding

1. Discuss the Title   In your notebook, explain the relationship between the event implied in the title and the event described in this poem.

2. Focus on Tone   What is the speaker's reaction to seeing her daughter learn to ride a bicycle? What words suggest this emotional response? In your opinion, is this response natural? Or is it surprising? Share your opinion with a partner.

3. Experiment with Form   Technically, this poem is a single long sentence broken up into 24 short lines. In a small group, discuss why you think the poet chose to break up the sentence as she did. Individually, try rewriting the poem in a different way: perhaps as a straight prose paragraph, or with different line breaks, or even in a different shape such as a bicycle. Compare your version with the original, and discuss the impact of changing the way the poem is presented.

4. Imagine Another Point of View   Although this event is told from the mother's point of view, we learn a lot about the daughter's reactions. Retell the story, this time from the daughter's point of view. Write the account either as another poem, as a journal entry, or through the script of a conversation between the daughter and a friend. As you write, keep in mind the daughter's age when she tells the story.

5. Write a Personal Response   Think of an occasion when you felt as exhilarated as the little girl in the poem. Describe the experience in a journal response.

Extending

6. Read Poetry   Find more examples of Linda Pastan's work. Select a poem that appeals to you, and bring it to class to share with a small group of students. When all of the poems have been presented, identify any similarities in style and subject matter between them and "To a Daughter Leaving Home."

7. Write about Leaving Home   Write a poem or short story about a daughter or son leaving home to attend college or begin a job.

Garson

"You are my best buddy."

Memoir by Wayson Choy

Notes

Whenever Garson and I played together as boyhood friends, even the most callous adults would be distracted by his bright-eyed charm. His genuinely shy smile would melt grown-up hearts. Though undersized, even for an eight-year-old, Garson mirrored his older brothers' tough-guy stance that made young women swoon. Men, like friendly giants, bent down to lift him up, up … *up* … tossing him giggling onto their shoulders. While he flinched, doting women knelt down to pinch his cheeks. Everyone wanted to hug or pick up Garson. Dawdling beside him, I was the ugly duckling waiting to be noticed.

I wanted to crush him.

Almost two years older than Garson, I was half-a-head taller, his unofficial big brother, and I hungered for the physical affection showered so lavishly on my smaller pal. Being a Chinatown son, I was expected to have outgrown my need for physical affection, and any feeble attempts on my part to get the same kind of attention that Garson abundantly attracted—like stupidly raising both my arms in expectation of being lifted up—were met with disdain. I was absurdly too tall for picking up, too bony for hugging. I had just turned ten and hated to look like a stranded fool, so I soon quit trying. My arms stayed stiffly by my side. Jealousy clung to me like cobwebs.

Besides, whenever we were compared as boys, Garson always won out. He was smarter, slim like his sisters, athletic like his older brothers Gar and Spike. He had bright intelligent eyes and a vocabulary equal to mine.

Grown-ups said to me, if they noticed me at all, "Sonny, you watch out for Garson. You take care of your little brother."

If they really knew Garson, the agile one, the smarter one, as Mother had pointed out a few times to Father, people would be saying instead, "Garson, you take care of Sonny."

Mother never said she would have actually preferred Garson for her own son, but I could guess what she sometimes thought.

Even my mother betrayed me.

Garson, decent even then, never really took advantage of his drawing powers; he himself hardly noticed them. He said to me, "You are my best buddy." I agreed. Whenever someone picked on him, I stood up for him. Once I tried to defend both of us from Stan Yee and his two older brothers. The three boys shoved and punched me, and, laughing, tossed me into the bushes for my puny efforts at self-defence. Garson ran away.

"You should be as smart," Mother said, removing my torn shirt and ignoring my tears.

After that episode, we smaller kids kept watch on each other, screaming *"Run! Run!"* if we spotted any one of "them." I would bang on our front door; Mother would quickly let me in; and Winky would dart out, race down the steps, barking wildly, and chase them away.

In the hierarchy of children, we picked-on kids did our share of picking on others. There was an older boy—he looked to be 12 or 13— who sometimes wandered down our street. He softly sang to himself and spoke in a funny-sounding, snorting way. One of his suspenders always slipped off his shoulder, and the other was safety-pinned to his shirt. If one of us pulled at the tail of his shirt, he spun about, dancing like a clown St. Vitus, his legs wobbly, his arms waving. We were drawn to him, as we were drawn to the sideshow tents at the Pacific National Exhibition.

Giggling with our collective power, we threw sticks and kicked dirt at this gentle, dream-like figure who visited our street, but who never understood how ordinary boys thought. We distorted our faces to mock his own, and he always smiled, gap-toothed, to think we were his playmates. At first, I ran away from the sight of him. Then I stood to watch him go by. Most times, we would merely mimic his motions and let him go on his way. Sometimes Mr. Kelly or Mrs. Mah would yell at us to leave him alone.

One day, one of the older boys threw a rock at him, missed, and pushed him down onto the cobbled road. Something like bloodlust infected the pack of older boys that surrounded the fallen outlander.

"C'mon and have some fun," one of the older boys shouted at us kids standing on the sidewalk, watching. First one, then, two, then all five of us darted into the road. In the screaming mêlée, most of my childish kicks missed their mark; arms flailing, my blows fell upon the backs of other boys. We didn't stop until a honking car horn warned us away. Everybody scattered, shrieking like hyenas.

When I got home later that afternoon, Mother was on the telephone in our hallway.

"He's just walked in," she said in Toisanese to whoever was on the phone. She held the receiver away from herself and began to look me over.

"Did you do anything bad today, Sonny?"

"No," I said. I hadn't stolen anything or broken any windows. Winky jumped up and down on me, licking my face.

Mother continued to look me over carefully.

"That skinny white boy that's funny-looking," she said. "The *sung-khin* boy—you know the one I mean?"

I nodded my head, expecting to be knuckled on my head for taking part in beating him up.

"Don't touch him again," Mother said, her voice trembling. "Don't go near him. You don't want to be crazy, too, do you?"

"No," I said, and walked away.

The poor boy never showed up on our street again, nor did he show up anywhere else. The neighbours told Mother his family had him put away in a place with tall cement walls and a locked iron gate, far from boys like me.

In dreams he came back to visit me. Against his jerky, gentle ways, his questioning face, I have never had an answer.

You take it from here ...

Responding

1. Discuss Attitude Sonny says of Garson that he "wanted to crush him." Yet Garson was also his "best buddy." With a partner, discuss Sonny's complex attitude toward Garson. Why were they friends?

2. Write a Diary Entry Return to each of the comments Sonny makes about his mother. This time, try to put yourself into the mother's shoes, and imagine what she was thinking about her son in each case. Write a diary entry expressing her thoughts and concerns.

3. Read between the Lines   Wayson Choy ends this excerpt with the statement, "I have never had an answer." What is the question to which Choy seeks an answer? What are his feelings, now that he is older, about his behaviour as a child? Discuss your responses in a small group.

Extending

4. Write a Personal Response   Recall a time when you felt jealous of your best friend or someone else close to you. Write a personal response describing the situation and explaining how you now feel about your own reactions.

5. Write an Editorial   Interview several students in your school about any incidents of bullying they might have witnessed or heard about. Include questions such as

   - What causes bullying? (e.g., The bullies themselves? Victims who "bring it on themselves"? General intolerance in society?)
   - What can be done to prevent bullying? What is being done?

   Write an editorial on the topic in which you take an appropriate stand, from suggesting ways to stop bullying to praising the school community for its successful handling of the problem.

Before you read, as a class, share stories about moving when you were younger.

As you read, consider how you would feel in the narrator's place.

Home Sweet Home

A totally empty feeling filled my insides.

Memoir by Jennifer Aubrey Burhart

Notes

Jennifer Aubrey Burhart wrote this memoir when she was a high-school senior. After high school, she went on to study math education and psychology at university.

It was December 22nd. The blustery wind swept the countless snowflakes across my front yard. My dad was shovelling the driveway. His nose was red. With every breath he took, a white puff escaped into the air. Before you could blink, it disappeared into the cold, crisp air.

Inside, my mother was packing the last of the boxes. As I entered the front door, the thought that after today I would never enter that door again burned a hole in my stomach. I picked up my dog and sat cross-legged with him on my lap on the cold, wooden floor. I had no choice but to sit there; there was no furniture in my house. I sat in a daze, just thinking. In my mind, there was just no reason for my parents to make me, a once-happy twelve-year-old, move. I had two best friends right across the street. I did well in school and always kept my room clean. Plus, this was "my house." By no means did I want a couple of strangers living here. These recurring thoughts danced around in my mind. I had so many questions, but no answers.

Out the front window I could see the orange top of a truck pull in the driveway, and I knew it was the final moving van. Instantly, three men came barrelling in the back door like World War III was starting. The stale smell of nicotine encircled their bodies. I coughed silently, so as not to be noticed, for my eyes started to fill with tears. I watched helplessly as the men, my mother, and my dad loaded the truck. My dog even seemed to wince as he stared out the window. I wondered if he were sad, too, or if he just longed to play outside in the snow.

The slam of the truck's doors plugged my eardrums.

My mom came in and turned off the overhead light. She zipped up my jacket for me, seeing how immobile my limbs were. A totally empty feeling filled my insides.

My mom was very solemn and spoke not a word. I imagined, for my sake, she felt remorse. I was in a semi-conscious state. For the first time in my life, I wondered what "home" would be to me tomorrow. Mom then put our dog in my arms and followed me out the back door. The sound of the bolted lock triggered more tears.

I climbed in the back seat of our red station wagon, shivering. My face stung from windburn, and my salty tears didn't help. Dad climbed in with Mom and backed down the driveway. I glanced once more at our dainty white house with black trim. I swear the big pine tree my grandfather planted in front of my bedroom window long ago was waving to me, underneath its snow-covered branches.

You take it from here ...

Responding

1. **Write Advice**   Do you feel sorry for the narrator? Why or why not? Write a letter, either to the girl or to her parents, expressing your reactions to the situation and offering advice.

2. **Analyze Style**   The narrator is recalling an event that took place when she was 12 years old. As a class, identify elements that effectively recapture the emotion and expression of the 12-year-old girl. Are there any elements in the writing that reflect the more mature writer, as she looks back on this event? Explain.

3. **Write a Personal Response**   What would be *your* reaction if you went home today and were told that you would be moving? How would this compare to the feelings you would have if you were younger? Write your response in your journal.

Extending

4. **Write a Script**   Choose any of the adults mentioned—mother, father, or movers—and imagine how they were feeling about the girl. Write a script in which two or more of these adults discuss the child's reactions. Working with other students, perform your scripts for the rest of the class.

5. **Conduct Internet Research**   Check the Web sites of major moving companies and other sources that offer advice on helping children to cope with the stress of changing homes. Compile the advice into an illustrated pamphlet or an article for a parents' magazine.

Before you read, explain to a partner your image of the traditional family farm. What does it look like? How is it organized? Who lives there?

As you read, take your time, reading and rereading the poem until the scene gradually becomes clear.

Notes

Leona Gom (1946–) was born in Peace River, Alberta, and has taught at the University of Alberta and the University of British Columbia. She edited *event* literary magazine for nearly 10 years and has published several novels and books of poetry.

Moved

Poem by Leona Gom

The earth begins, already,
to reclaim what once was trees;
rotting logs collapse,
roofs are bending
in a slow ballet,
and everywhere
the green grass fires
lick at lumber.
    Already sold, these acres
will be ploughed next year,
remains of buildings
burned or buried,
and a field of grain,
hungry for the newly-broken soil,
will rise from the forgotten
bones of barns.
    Around the yard
the farm machines,
strangely still this fall,
grow from rubber, tired stems.
Their metal blossoms,
huge and red and rusty,
await their own harvest—
auction.
    And we three—born here,
who grew here,
who climbed the trees
        ran down the river-banks,
        swam in the dugout,
        hid in the hayloft,
        rode horses as rein-free as we—

grown weary of wonder now,
cling to our separate cities,
refusing to repay this farm
for what it was
and what we are.

You take it from here ...

Responding

1. Paraphrase the Poem   The poem is divided into four stanzas. For each one, write one or two sentences to explain its main idea.

2. Analyze Metaphors   Much of the power of this poem comes from its figurative language. Working in a small group, list as many *metaphors* as you can detect. For each one, identify the image and what it is compared to.

3. Discuss Tone   Identify the three people described in the poem. How are they related to this scene? What is their attitude to it? List three or four adjectives to describe the narrator's feelings. In a class discussion, explain why you have chosen these particular words.

4. Write an Introduction   This poem describes a rural Canadian experience. If you were to send it to a pen pal in a distant country, what background information would he or she need in order to understand it? Share your ideas in a class discussion. Then, write the letter to accompany the poem, explaining its background to your pen pal.

Extending

5. Present a Poem   Leona Gom has published several books of poetry. Find other poems she has written that deal with a similar setting or have a similar style. Choose one to present to the class. In your presentation, explain why you chose this poem, and identify its similarities with "Moved."

6. Write a Personal Essay   Think of something that you have discarded or left behind, only to realize afterwards the importance it had in your life. It could be something as simple as an old toy or piece of clothing, or it could be a house or community you used to live in. Write a one- or two-page essay identifying what was discarded or left behind, and why, and what you now realize it meant to you.

Before you read, debate whether there is such a thing as a "generation gap."

As you read, try to get a sense of the writer's personality and what is important to her.

Between Ourselves: Letters between Mothers and Daughters

My dearest mother, I cannot be protected by you.

Letter by Unknown Author

Notes

This letter is an excerpt from the book *Between Ourselves: Letters Between Mothers and Daughters, 1750–1982* (1983) edited by Karen Payne.

ambivalence: mixed feelings; being in two states of mind

June 1981

Dear Mummy:

This last trip to India with you has brought home to me a few hard facts—facts that I wanted to avoid seeing for some time. As you well know, you and I have had a few arguments and several days of tensions during the trip. As I approach my seventeenth year I suddenly ask myself where do I belong. I know this is the usual teen-age identity crisis, etc., etc. You came to this country when you were slightly older than I am and married my father and admired the American lifestyle and tried to be an American as much as you could. I am born of you who are Indian and my father who is American. Of course, I am American. Except for a few trips to India I have little to do with India outwardly. But, I feel how much you would like me to become Indian sometimes. I cannot explain it with examples. But I feel it in my bones. The India that you never quite shook off your system comes back to you now and you want to see your daughter live it, at least partly.

Yes, mummy, I know I am wrapped up in many superficial things, things my friends and peers indulge in and I can understand your need to protect me. But, I am part of them and in order for me to be accepted by my friends sometimes I do things which do not always please me either. I need their approval and I want to be like them sometimes. But, your good intentions to teach me those good Indian things then clash. Although I dislike the superficiality of my friends, I cannot move back to your lifestyle just because it is better (for you) or more ancient or deep. Let me live the life I am surrounded by and reject and suffer as I wish and as many of my friends are going through …

While I understand your point, I must admit sometimes I really do not know how to communicate to you what I really feel. Words seem to fail on both sides. That's why I am writing this letter. Perhaps it will be a bit easier. Dad does not seem to be the problem in this regard. When I argue with him or reject something he wants me to do, I do not feel such ambivalence as I do when the same thing happens with you. Isn't it strange! Perhaps, I am a bit Indian under my skin after all. Although, every time I visit India, after the first two weeks of love and food, I begin to weary of all the slow sloth and all the rest. I ache to come back to my superficial friends with whom I do not always need to use even language. It's the communication that I feel is at stake between you and me and between India and me. Mummy, you did not have to grow up in America; you grew up in India and could keep a lot of nostalgia and good memories when you decided to reject India. When you criticize me, you never think that we were born in two different worlds and that makes a big difference between us even though I am your flesh and blood as you often point out, rightly.

My dearest mother, I cannot be protected by you. Forgive me if I remind you of something you related to me many times. You could not be protected by my grandparents (your parents) when you decided to embrace this culture along with my father. Nor can you protect me despite the fact that we are not separated by physical distance. Perhaps, we are separated by something else and I suspect, that is India.

I have never written a letter like this before in my short life. I feel good about writing this and I would like to hear what you have to say. Ma, perhaps, you and I still can be friends in this way that you and your mother could not be. Let's try. I love you.

Yours,

Rita

You take it from here ...

Responding

1. Analyze Conflict   Working with a partner, list the sources of friction between Rita and her mother. What, specifically, do they seem to argue about? For each issue, decide if it is a result of Rita's double cultural background, or if it is simply the result of a generation gap. Share your responses in a class discussion.

2. Offer Advice   What kind of person does Rita seem to be? What are her ambitions? How does she treat her parents? Write a letter to Rita offering her your encouragement and advice.

3. Write a Monologue   Imagine how Rita's mother would respond to this letter. Write a monologue in which she talks to her husband or a close friend, describing the letter and her reaction to it.

4. Assess Character's Choice   With a partner, discuss why you think Rita chose to write her thoughts rather than confront her mother with them directly. What do you think she gained by doing this? Do you believe she lost anything? Share your thoughts with another student pair.

Extending

5. Draft a Personal Letter   Think of someone to whom you would like to say something that is difficult. The subject may be negative or positive, but it should be something you feel awkward putting into words. Try writing out your feelings in a letter. (It is not necessary to send your letter, just undergo the process of expressing your ideas on paper.)

> **SELF-ASSESSMENT**
> - How easy or difficult was it to express yourself?
> - Did the writing process help you clarify your feelings?
> - How did you feel once you expressed those feelings?

6. Discuss Canadian Identity   It is often said that there is no such thing as a purely Canadian cultural background: our citizens claim ancestry from a multitude of nations. But, if you had to define it, what do you think it would mean to be "Canadian"? As a class, develop a list of those things that you believe define Canadian culture.

Before you read, write
a personal response
explaining how you would
feel about leaving home
for a long period of time.

As you read, imagine
yourself in the position of
the narrator.

Notes

Glen Kirkland's best-known
poem, "Departure," was
originally called "Leaving
Home," but he changed it
because the title had
been overused by other
writers. Kirkland actually
wrote the poem about
20 years after leaving
home in response to a
question that he asked
himself: "What was a
memorable emotional
event from my past?" He
points out that the boy
wants to leave regardless
of the reference to leaving
a reproduction of himself
behind. He says, "The
shorter lines reflect the
awkward emotions of the
moment."

Departure

Poem by Glen Kirkland

leaving home
I stand with my dead
grandmother's suitcases in hand
coat slung carelessly over my shoulder
the car loaded down with
all my possessions
packed in boxes tied doubly
with string
(like a refugee from some
old movie)

my father coughs
shakes my hand
and offers me a last-minute
yellow screwdriver with
interchangeable heads

my mother kisses me
and says
as long as I have a sense of
humour
I will
survive

in the doorway now
I smile awkwardly and mutter
goodbye

my mother asks
again
have you
got
everything

yes
I say
I've got it
all

and
frightened suddenly
I want to paint my name
in huge red letters
on the ceilings and walls
of every room
carve my initials in
the coffee table
and leave a life-sized reproduction of myself
asleep upstairs

TIPS

- Develop a rough script, adding to the words in the poem.
- Discuss what all three characters would be thinking as each line was said.
- Block the scene, working out where and how each actor will move.
- Rehearse the lines until you can perform them naturally.

You take it from here ...

Responding

1. Establish the Situation   Discuss with a partner the scene portrayed in this poem. What is the setting? Why is the speaker leaving? Work together to write a summary paragraph to explain the situation and the emotions underlying the poem. Compare your ideas in a class discussion.

2. Dramatize the Scene   Work with two other students to bring this scene to life. As you rehearse, identify the parts of the poem you found most challenging to act out. Why was this so?

3. Analyze Form   Transcribe this poem, writing it out as a prose paragraph without any of the line breaks used by the poet. Examine the two versions side by side. What is lost by presenting the poem in this fashion? What has the poet gained with each of the breaks? Write a brief analysis explaining the importance of these breaks. In your commentary, explain at least two breaks that you feel are particularly effective.

Extending

4. Write a Similar Poem   Imagining how the parents in this poem are feeling about the speaker's departure, write a poem from the perspective of either the mother or the father.

5. Write a Narrative   The speaker's boxes and suitcase are clearly full. Imagine what they might contain. Then write a narrative passage in which the speaker or one of the parents checks the contents one last time. Consider what the character is feeling as he or she sees each of the items and thinks of the associations of each one (e.g., a stuffed toy, a favourite piece of clothing, a letter of acceptance to a job or college). Read your passage to a small group. As a group, choose the best one and have the author read it to the class. After the readings, hold a class discussion comparing the different approaches taken.

PEER ASSESSMENT

For each narrative, consider the following:
- Are the emotions and thoughts expressed consistent with your opinion of the character?
- Is the writing interesting and entertaining? Is the approach taken especially creative? Explain.

6. Predict and Script a Reaction   What do you think the parents will do once their son has left? Write the script for a discussion the parents might have at dinner that night as they think about their son and the empty bedroom.

Long, Long after School

*"She was beautiful,"
he added softly. "She
was a real lady."*

Short Story by Ernest Buckler

Notes

Ernest Buckler (1908–1984) is a much-beloved Canadian short-story writer and novelist. Born in Dalhousie West, Nova Scotia, he spent most of his life on his family's farm in Annapolis Royal. This story comes from his classic collection, *The Rebellion of Young David and Other Stories* (1975).

Paul Jones: dance in which partners are exchanged according to a pattern

I ran into Wes Holman the very day I was collecting for Miss Tretheway's flowers. But it never came into my head to ask him for a contribution.

Miss Tretheway had taught grade 3 in our town for exactly 50 years. She had died the night before in her sleep. As chairman of the school board I had thought it would be fitting if all the grade 3 alumni who were still around made up enough money to get a really handsome "piece." She had no relatives. If I'd given it an instant's consideration I'd have known that Wes himself must have been in grade 3 some time or other; but I didn't.

Wes was just coming through the cemetery gate as I was going in. Wes "looks after" the cemetery, and I sometimes take a shortcut through it on my way to work. I should say that Wes is our local "character." His tiny house up behind the ballpark is furnished with almost nothing but books, and he can quote anyone from Seneca to Henry James. But that's his job: caretaker-about-town.

When I spoke to him about Miss Tretheway, a curious change came into his face. You couldn't say that he turned pale, but his stillness was quite different from the conventional one on such occasions. I had expected him to come out with some quote or other, but he didn't say a word.

He didn't go to her funeral. But he sent her flowers of his own. Or brought them, rather. The following day, when I took the shortcut again, I surprised him on his knees placing them.

His little bunch of flowers was the most incongruous thing you could imagine. It was a corsage. A corsage of simple flowers, such as a young boy sends his girl for her first formal dance. And more incongruous than its presence in the circumstance of death was its connection with Miss Thretheway herself. I'm quite sure that Miss Thretheway never once had a beau send her flowers, that she'd never been to a dance in her whole life.

I suppose it would never have occurred to me to question anyone but Wes about his motive for doing a thing like that. But I asked Wes about it with no thought of rudeness whatever. Wes's privacy seemed to be everyone's property. There was probably a little self-conscious democracy in the gesture when we talked to him at all.

"She was so beautiful," he answered me, as if no other explanation was needed.

That was plainly ridiculous. That Miss Tretheway was a fine person for having spent a lifetime in small, unheralded services could not be disputed—but obviously she hadn't *ever* been beautiful. Her sturdy plainness was never transfigured, not even for an instant, by the echo of anything winsomer which had faded. Her eyes had never been very blue, her skin very pink, or her hair very brown. She wasn't very anything. Her heart might have been headlong (I think now that it was), but there was always that curious precision and economy in her face which lacks altogether the grain of helter-skelter necessary to any kind of charm. In short, even when she'd been a girl, she'd been the sort of girl whose slightest eagerness, more than if she were ugly or old, a young man automatically shies away from.

"But, Wes," I said, half-joking, "she wasn't beautiful. What made you say that?"

His story went something like this. He told it with a kind of dogged, confessional earnestness. I guess he'd come to figure that whenever we asked him a personal question he might as well satisfy our curiosity completely, first as last.

"Perhaps you remember how the kids used to tease me at school," he said. (I didn't. I guess those things stick in your mind according to which end of the teasing you happen to be on.) "If the boys would be telling some joke with words in it to giggle over, they'd look at me and say, 'Shhhh…. Wes is blushing.' Or if we were all climbing up the ladder to the big beam in Hogan's stable, they'd say 'Look at Wes. He's so scared he's turning pale.' Do you remember the night you steered your sled into mine, going down Parker hill?"

"No," I said. "Did I do it on purpose?"

"I don't know," Wes said. "Maybe you didn't. I thought you did."

Maybe I did. I don't remember.

"I was taking Mrs. Banks's wash home on my sled, and you were coasting down the hill. The basket upset and all the things fell out on the snow. Don't you remember … Miss Tretheway came along and you all ran. She helped me pick up the stuff and shake the snow off it. She went with me right to Mrs. Banks's door and told her what had happened. I could never have made Mrs. Banks believe *I* didn't upset the stuff myself."

"I'm sorry," I said. I probably *had* done it on purpose.

"That's all right," he said. "I didn't mind the boys so much. It was the girls. You can't hit a girl. There just wasn't anything I could do about the girls. One day Miss Tretheway was showing us a new game in the schoolyard. I don't remember exactly how it went, but that one where we all made a big circle and someone stood in the centre. I put my hand out to close up the ring with the biggest Banks girl, but she wouldn't take it. She said, 'Your hands are dirty.' Miss Tretheway made us both hold out our hands. She said, 'Why, Marilyn, Wes's hands are much cleaner than yours. Maybe Wes doesn't like to get *his* hands dirty, did you ever think

about that?' She took Marilyn's place herself. Her hand felt safe and warm, I remember … and I guess that's the first day I thought she was beautiful."

"I see," I said.

I did, and yet I didn't. The Wes I remembered would hate anything with the suggestion of teacher's pet about it. The only Wes I could seem to remember was the Wes of adolescence: the tough guy with the chip on his shoulder.

He was coming to that. But he stuck in an odd parenthesis first.

"Did you ever notice Miss Thretheway," he said, "when … well, when the other teachers would be talking in the hall about the dances they'd been to over the weekend? Or when she'd be telling some kid a story after school and the kid would run off right in the middle of a sentence when she saw her mother coming to pick her up?"

"No," I said. "Why? What about it?"

"Oh, nothing, I guess." He drew a deep breath. "Anyway, I decided I'd be stronger and I'd study harder than anyone. And I was, wasn't I? I did. Do you remember the year they voted me the best all-round student in High School?" (I didn't. It must have been after I'd graduated.) "I guess I just can't remember how happy I was about that. I guess I was so happy I could believe anything. That must have been why I let the boys coax me into going to the closing dance." He smiled. "I thought since they'd voted for me … but you can't legislate against a girl's glance."

Those were his exact words. Maybe he'd read them somewhere. Maybe they were his own. I don't know. But it was the kind of remark which had built up his quaint reputation as the town philosopher.

"I didn't want to go out on the dance floor," he said. "I'd never danced a foxtrot or anything. The girls all had on their evening dresses, and somehow they looked different altogether. They looked as if they wouldn't recognize *themselves* in their day clothes. Anyway, the boys grabbed hold of me and made me get into a Paul Jones. I was next to Toby Wenford in the big ring. Jane Evans was right opposite me when the music stopped, but she danced with Toby instead—and the girl next *to* Jane just glanced at me and then went and sat down. I guess it was a pretty foolish thing to do, but I went down in the basement and drove my fist through a window."

"Is that the scar?" I said. I couldn't think of anything else to say.

"Oh, it was a lot worse than that," he said. He pulled up his sleeve and traced the faint sickle of the scar way up his arm. "You can hardly see it now. But I almost bled to death right there. I guess I might have, if it hadn't been for Miss Thretheway."

"Oh?" I said. "How's that?"

"You see, they didn't have any plasma around in bottles then," he said, "and in those days no one felt too comfortable about having his blood siphoned off. I guess no one felt like taking any chances for me, anyway. Mother said I could have hers, but hers wasn't right. Mine's that odd type—three, isn't it? Miss Tretheway's was three, too … and that's funny, because only 7 percent of people have it. She gave me a whole quart, just as soon as she found out that hers would match."

"I see," I said. So that was it. And yet I had a feeling that that *wasn't* it—not quite.

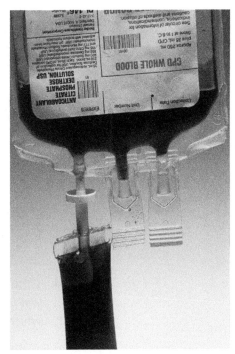

"She used to come see me every day," he said. "She used to bring me books. Did you know that books … well, that for anyone like me that's the only way you can …?" He hesitated, and I knew that that wasn't quite it either.

Not until he spoke again, when he spoke so differently, was I sure that only now was he coming to the real thing.

"Do you know what Miss Tretheway said when I thanked her for the transfusion?" he said. "She made a joke of it. She said: 'I didn't know whether an old maid's blood would be any good to a fine young specimen like you, Wes, or not.' The thing I always remember, I knew that was the first time she'd ever called herself an old maid to anyone, and really felt like laughing. And I remember what *I* said. I said: 'Miss Tretheway, you're making me blush.' And do you know, that was the very first time I'd ever been able to say *that*, and laugh, myself."

There was quite a long silence.

"She was beautiful," he added softly. "She was a real lady."

The cemetery is right next to the river. I looked down the river where the cold December water lapped at the jagged ice thrown up on the banks, and I thought about a boy the colour of whose skin was such that he could never blush, and I thought about a girl who had never been asked to a dance. I thought about the corsage. My curiosity was quite satisfied. But somehow I myself had never felt less beautiful, or less of a gentleman.

You take it from here ...

Responding

1. Isolate the Time Frame   Several remarks, activities, and observations in the story suggest that it is set in an earlier time. Working with a partner, review the story and identify clues to when the story occurred. According to your evidence, when do you believe the story took place?

2. Role-Play the Characters   Work in groups of four to portray the main characters in the story. Each person in the group should take one of the following points of view:

   - the narrator describing Wes *after* he had told his story
   - Wes describing the narrator
   - Miss Tretheway describing Wes
   - the narrator describing himself *before* he heard Wes's story

   > **PEER ASSESSMENT**
   > - Which presentation was most convincing?
   > - Were details from the story used effectively in presenting each of the characters?

3. Consider Lessons   This story contains many lessons about life and values. Identify three of these lessons, expressing each in a single sentence. Share these with a small group of students.

Extending

4. Write a Speech   Imagine that, following her retirement, Miss Tretheway was invited to speak to a graduating class of teachers. Write a speech in which she shares her memories and offers advice to the new teachers.

5. Compose a Letter   Think of an adult or teacher who made a special difference in your life when you were younger. Compose a letter to this individual explaining how much his or her actions meant to you.

6. Test Memory   The narrator had completely forgotten his part in an important incident in Wes's life. Memory plays tricks on us all. Think of something very important, perhaps even hurtful, that happened to you when you were much younger. Ask someone else who was involved at the time to relate his or her memory of the event. Do your memories match? Report to the class on your findings.

The Last Lullaby

"Don't tell me! You're getting married!"

Short Story by Marie Moser

Notes

Marie Moser, an eighth-generation French-Canadian author, was born and educated in Edmonton. Her first novel, *Counterpoint* (1986), dealt with the history of French-Canadian settlement in Alberta. Moser has raised four children and has taught them traditional French songs and Christmas rituals.

"I don't think this was such a good idea, coming here," she says. Paul and Lisette are sitting in his car stopped at the curb in front of the Heritage Villa for Senior Citizens.

"You want me to meet the relatives, don't you?" he says. He takes her left hand and adjusts her blue sapphire engagement ring.

"Of course I do. It's just ... well, she's an old-fashioned French-Canadian lady, set in her ways."

"What did you say to call her? Ma tent ..."

"Ma *tante* Elodie. It means 'aunt,' even though she's really my great-aunt."

He jumps out of the car and hurries to her side to open the door. "After you, *mademoiselle*."

She holds onto his arm as they enter the bright lobby. Ferns cascade from macramé hangings in every corner.

"Her suite is over here," she says as she leads him away from the lobby. A lively piano tune and a chorus of voices fill the hallway with sound. The music stops for a moment and then the same line of the song is played again.

"That sounds like one of ma tante Elodie's songs. She still plays the piano. I think she turned 91 on her last birthday. When I was small, she'd sit me down beside her at the piano and teach me French songs."

"You never told me that."

"It's not that important."

The door of the suite is open. Paul and Lisette stand outside the door looking at the circle of four women around the piano. They are wearing identical black tams and vests over white shirts. Three of the women hold up their music sheets while the fourth, frailer than the others, stands in her walker and looks over at another's music.

The woman sitting at the piano is noticeable for the pure white of her hair, pulled tightly to the top of her head in a pearl-coloured bun. The song ends with three loud chords. The pianist turns around to talk to the quartet and notices Paul and Lisette at the door. For a moment she does not recognize Lisette, then she smiles.

"We'll take a rest now, girls, and meet at half-past four for another rehearsal," she says. "I have an important visitor now: my great-niece. Come in, Lisette."

The four turn to look at her, smiling. She walks directly to her great-aunt, who is rising slowly from the piano bench, and puts her arms around the small woman.

"Ma petite Lisette …"

"Ma tante Elodie. I brought someone to meet you. This is my fiancé, Paul Malory."

"Don't tell me! You're getting married!" Her dark brown eyes widen behind her glasses as she extends a thin hand to Paul. "I'm so pleased to meet you, young man."

When the last of the quartet has shuffled away out the door, ma tante says to Lisette, *"Mais c'est un très beau garçon!"*

Lisette cringes; she had been hoping she would not speak French. Quickly, she whispers to him, "She says you're very handsome."

"It's all right. I figured it was something like that. I really liked that song you were playing, ma tante."

"Your fiancé does not talk French?" she whispers loudly to Lisette.

"Well, no.…"

"I was simply asking. Welcome, welcome, Paul. Please sit down. I was reviewing a few songs with the quartet. We're having a concert for the villa tonight."

She lowers herself carefully onto a kitchen chair and faces Paul and Lisette on the couch. "And what do you do?" she asks Paul.

"I'm studying to be a civil engineer."

"You're going to work on the railroad?"

"No, ma tante." Lisette looks at Paul who is smiling broadly. "He's going to university so he can design bridges and roads."

"Oh my, isn't that silly of me?" She hides her mouth in a girlish gesture when she laughs.

"Not at all," Paul says. "My grandfather thought the same thing when I told him."

"You are lucky to get a good education. I wanted to study music when I was young but my father, he would not let me go. That's the way it was in those days." She takes a tissue and wipes her forehead. "Such a warm day. Would you like a glass of lemonade? I had some made for the quartet. Lisette, pour us three glasses and I'll get some cookies."

Lisette goes to the kitchen and sees a pink rectangular plate, with a pattern like tattered lace, sitting in the middle of the table. The sun shining on it gives it an iridescent glow. She delicately touches the scalloped edges. "Where did you get this plate? It's so pretty."

"It belonged to my mother—let me see—that would be your great-grandmother, wouldn't it?" She places some cookies on it and carries it out to the living room. Lisette hurries to pour the lemonade and follows her.

"Look, Paul. This is ma tante's mother's plate. Isn't that amazing?"

"Yes, yes it is," he says, peering at it and reaching for a cookie. "Did you come from a big family? Lisette hasn't told me too much about her past."

"She hasn't?" She frowns at Lisette. "But there are so many good stories—" She pauses and then brightens. "Then, I will have to tell you some of our family history."

She wets her lips as she thinks, then begins the story slowly. "My parents came west in September of 1905. We were six in the family. I had four older brothers and a baby sister. I was five years old at the time. My father had been a shopkeeper in a town called St. Scholastique in Quebec, and he left to start a new life on his own land. Too, he had many sons and thought he would have lots of help on the farm. My parents took the colonists' train to Calgary and then got on some kind of cattle train up to Strathcona, just on the other side of Edmonton. They had to hire some wagons to take their belongings up to Morinville where my mother had a cousin with a big house. It was a long journey in those days. I was young but I remember it started to rain and rain, and the roads turned to mud and one of the wagons overturned. Me and my mother and little sister got thrown into a ditch. We were pulled out soaking wet. It was terrible. We were close to my mother's cousin's house, but my little sister got sick from her fall in the water and … she died a few days later. You can imagine how my poor mother felt. About eight months later, your grandmother was born, and then six more children, three boys, and three more girls."

She sips her lemonade and takes a bite from her cookie. She doesn't look at either of them as she appears to search her memory. "I'll show you some pictures."

She pulls out a photo album from the cupboard under the china cabinet and sits between them. The album is arranged chronologically, starting with her own parents' parents, and then the pictures of her family when they first arrived in Morinville. The first pictures are starkly black because everyone is dressed in mourning for the baby who died. Later, there are more joyous pictures of a picnic outside, with a long table set up with food. The last picture is a large one of the family standing in front of the new house, the girls with lace collars on their dresses and the boys in their Sunday suits.

"Look at the size of that family!" Paul says.

"Everyone had large families in those days … and yet there are only two people in that picture left living today."

"See, that's my grandmother there," Lisette says. "The one with the long hair on her shoulders."

"You look a lot like her, did you know that?" Paul says.

"Yes, yes," agrees ma tante. "Same eyes, same nose. I was thinking the other day that, of the one hundred and seventy-three people descended from my parents, there are only four families who have kept our traditions and our language."

"Things change, ma tante. It's not that important any more," Lisette says. She realizes what she has said when they both turn to her. Paul shakes his head slightly.

"Lisette, you too?" Ma tante says it quietly and then with a sigh closes the album and sets it back on the shelf.

"It's true," Lisette says, straightening. "It's not part of my life anymore."

Her great-aunt looks at her and then her gaze drops to her hands on her lap. "It's all right, Lisette. I understand how it is."

The conversation has been dampened and uneasy moments pass.

Finally, ma tante says, "But what am I thinking? I have to give you something for your engagement."

She looks about her suite pensively and her eyes settle on the plate with the one remaining cookie. "I will give you your great-grandmother's plate."

"Oh no, ma tante. I couldn't take that."

But her great-aunt has already removed the cookie. She opens a drawer, finds tissue paper and wraps up the plate. "I have lots of other plates. I told you she never used them. Well, neither did I, until recently." She hands the package to Lisette, pressing her hands around it.

Then it is time to go. While they are standing and exchanging goodbyes, ma tante takes Lisette by the hand and says, "Wait. There's something I want you to hear."

She sits at the piano, her frail hands searching the keys for the right chords. She begins to sing:

* *Fait dodo, bébé à maman*
Fait dodo, tu auras du lolo
Papa est en bas, qui frappe du marteau,
Maman est en haut, qui fait du chocolat
Fait dodo, bébé à maman,
Fait dodo, tu auras du lolo.

Her voice is gentle but strong; the melody and words so familiar that she sings without thinking. "Your mother sang this song to you when you were a baby cradled in her arms. It is the song my mother sang to me and to your grandmother. No one knows where the lullaby comes from; it has always been in our family. I hope you will not forget it."

She stands up again and opens her arms. Lisette bends over to receive a last hug. "Please come and see me again and I'll tell you more stories, Paul. About my own family. Maybe about Lisette next time."

"Goodbye, goodbye...."

They walk down the hallway with the soft notes of the lullaby following them until they are outside.

As he opens the car door, Paul says, "What does that mean: 'fait dodo'?"

"It means go to sleep."

He sits in and rolls down the window before starting the car. "What a big family. Two rows of kids—like a classroom picture."

"Now you know. I told you she was an old-fashioned French-Canadian lady."

"I thought she was very nice. Sharp, too. Isn't it amazing how well she can play that piano?"

"I guess some things you don't forget."

On the drive home Lisette is relieved that it is all over. It doesn't matter what her great-aunt said. She unwraps the plate and looks at it, something her great-grandmother set on her table. Perhaps she too will pass it on to her children.

She sits silently in the middle of the seat, close to Paul, and tries to remember the lullaby. How did it go again? She has forgotten some of the words already.

---

* Go to sleep, mother's little baby
Go to sleep, you will get some water (wah-wah)
Daddy is downstairs, hitting his hammer
Mother is upstairs, making chocolate
Go to sleep, mother's little baby
Go to sleep, you will get some water

She holds the plate close to examine the lace design and she sees that a tiny crack runs the entire length of the plate. She wonders why such an incredible feeling of sadness falls over her.

You take it from here ...

Responding

1. **Create a Family Tree**   Using details from the story, create Lisette's family tree. In a paragraph, explain why you think there is so much emphasis in this story on the size of the family.

2. **Write a Profile**   Imagine that the retirement home in which tante Elodie lives has a monthly newsletter for the residents. Write a profile of tante Elodie that would be suitable for such a publication, giving some of her background but focusing on her present activities and circumstances as well. Illustrate your profile with a drawing or photograph of someone you think might resemble tante Elodie.

3. **Focus on Conflict**   Search the story for clues that reveal Lisette's attitude to her great-aunt and to her family background in general. Write a brief essay explaining Lisette's feelings. In your conclusion, suggest reasons why you think she feels this way.

4. **Discuss the Conclusion**   At the end of the story, Lisette "wonders why such an incredible feeling of sadness falls over her." As a class, discuss why she might feel sad. Do you believe that the story would have been improved if it had ended in a clear statement? Explain.

Extending

5. **Write a Script**   Imagine it is three months later, and it is Paul and Lisette's wedding day. At the reception, tante Elodie has been catching up with many members of their large family who are in attendance. At last she and the bride and groom have a chance to talk. Write a script of the conversation between them.

6. **Gather Lullabies**   Share with members of your class one or two lullabies you remember from your childhood. Working in small groups, find more lullabies from different cultures, and organize them into an anthology. Include illustrations and explanatory notes for the lullabies, and add an introductory section giving an overview of the contents and describing what the lullabies have in common.

TIPS

- Assign spaces for people even if you don't know their names.
- Label these people as "daughter" or "son" as appropriate.

TIPS

- Begin by setting the scene, describing the room, the people, the music, and so on.
- Consider following up on some references in the story. For example, have Lisette's attitudes toward family and tradition changed? Have tante Elodie's?

TIP

- Include a complete list of sources, including Web-page addresses, that you consulted in your research.

Before you read, write a paragraph describing something you experienced long ago that you can still remember in great detail.

As you read, take your time, reading and rereading until the poet's ideas become clear.

Notes

Kuroda Saburo (1919–1980), a Japanese poet born in Kuro City, Hiroshima Prefecture, grew up in Kagoshima City. He served in the Japanese army in the Second World War; after the war, he started a literary magazine and began writing in earnest.

Strangely Fresh

Poem by Kuroda Saburo

it appears quite unexpectedly
from the depth of oblivion
like a lost object
that comes out
from under fallen leaves
piled up by winter winds—

the strangely fresh memory
of a moment of a day long gone by
why is it so?
what does it mean to me?
it is a simple thing
almost too simple a thing—

a deserted white country road in midsummer
which I saw from the train window traveling alone
the tune of someone's bright whistling I heard
on a station platform after an air raid
the faint scent of perfume
of a woman I passed by in the fog-filled valley of a night

You take it from here ...

Responding

1. Explain the Subject   The poem begins with the word "it." As a class, decide what "it" is. What is so noteworthy about "it"?

2. Discuss Contrast   With a partner, discuss how the second stanza of the poem differs in content from stanzas one and three. What role does it play in the poem?

3. Present the Poem   Work in groups of three to memorize the poem (one stanza each) and prepare to present it to the class. Rehearse the reading several times, experimenting with different ways to express the lines, and adding appropriate pauses. When you can move smoothly from one voice to the next, perform the poem for the rest of the class.

> **GROUP ASSESSMENT**
> - How did you decide how to divide the poem?
> - Did you readily agree on how to interpret the poem? If not, how did you resolve your differences?
> - Did you offer and receive help and feedback from group members as you prepared the presentation?

Extending

4. Write a Story   Each of the three memories recorded in the final stanza suggests a short story. Choose one of these memories and write a short story in which the details of the memory are a key part of the storyline.

5. Illustrate a Story   Create an illustration to complement the short story you wrote in Activity 4.

Before you read, jot down any images that come to mind when you read the title, and share them with a partner.

As you read, imagine the landscape in which this poem takes place.

The Spring of Youth

Poem by Ulivfak

Sadly I recall
the early spring of my youth:
the snow melted,
the ice broke,
long before usual.

I stood scenting game
in the hot sun,
muscles taut,
sweat dripping from my face.

Look! Someone's out there
on the slapping lake-water,
slowly dragging reindeer
behind a kayak,
or noisily taking leave
for a dangerous sea-journey.
Could that be me?

As a hunter on land
I was undistinguished.
My arrows seldom reached
the reindeer in the hills.
But from a kayak,
hunting in the wake
of swimming bulls,
I had no match.

Thus I still re-live
the early spring of youth.
Old men seek strength
in the thaw of younger days.

Notes

"Spring of Youth" is one of many songs from Greenland and Canada's north collected and translated into Danish by Knud Rasmussen. These were later translated into English by Tom Lowenstein in the 1970s.

You take it from here ...

Responding

1. Write a Diary Entry   Imagine you are a visitor to the community in which the speaker lives. Write a diary entry about meeting the speaker based on all the information you can glean from the poem.

2. Analyze Imagery   There are many images in this poem that appeal to the senses. Working with a partner, identify the images and organize them into a chart under the headings "sight," "sound," "smell," and "touch." Do some images fit more than one category? Does one type of imagery dominate, or is there a balance in the poem?

Sight	Sound	Smell	Touch
the snow melted			the hot sun
the ice broke			

3. Discuss Tone   The poem opens with the word "sadly." Is sadness the overall tone of the poem? Does the tone change at any point in the course of the poem? What other words could you use to describe the tone? Discuss your ideas in a small group.

4. Identify Theme   What is the central message of this poem? Is it limited to the Inuit culture? Or is it a universal theme? Write several paragraphs expressing your views.

Extending

5. Explore Other Works   The spring season is associated with youth in many works of literature. Working as a class, list as many poems, stories, plays, and songs as you can think of that relate spring and youth. Search anthologies and the Internet to find another poem or song based on this relationship. Then, write a report that explains why you chose that particular piece, your own impressions of the piece, and its similarities to "The Spring of Youth."

6. Conduct an Interview   Interview an older person about his or her life as an adolescent or a young adult and, if possible, about an important event or experience from that time. Then, using your interview notes, present your findings orally to the class.

TIPS

- Before the interview, decide on
  - what you want to know
  - some questions you can ask to obtain that information
- During the interview, be sure to
  - listen attentively
  - ask for clarification as needed

Reflecting on the Unit

Responding

1. Consider Personal Relevance   The selections in this unit have focused on the unit theme, "Memorable Moments and Influences," presenting many aspects of home and family. Choose the selection with which you identified most strongly, and prepare a two-minute speech to explain your choice.

2. Elaborate on a Statement   "Each of us is a creature of a specific time, place, and culture." Elaborate on this statement in a small-group discussion, citing examples from the selections in this unit and from personal experience and observation.

3. Interpret a Visual   Working with a partner, examine the collage in the introduction to this unit. Identify how each image in the collage reflects the unit theme. Suggest two more images that could be added to the collage, giving reasons for your choices.

Extending

4. Respond Creatively   What are some early experiences that have helped shape who you are today? Who have been some of the most influential people in your life? Using a creative form of your choice, such as a collage, poem, memoir, or scrapbook, attempt to capture and present these formative influences.

5. Write a Monologue   Every family has memorable moments that touch the lives of all its members. Of course, each member will recall these moments in a slightly different way. Recall a comical incident in which you were involved that is told by family members time and time again. Write two monologues, one from your point of view and one from that of another family member. Consider the influence, if any, that moment had on your life.

> **SELF-ASSESSMENT**
>
> The main focus of this unit is on memorable moments and influences and how they shape who we are. Identify
> - what you now consider the most powerful influence on developing character
> - what you had trouble understanding or accepting
>
> Write your response in a personal essay.

Nothing is intrinsically valuable;
the value of everything is
attributed to it, assigned to it
from outside the thing itself,
by people.
— John Barth

"What I believe" is a process
rather than a finality.
— Emma Goldman

When you choose anything,
you reject everything else.
— G.K. Chesterton

Values, Beliefs, and Choices

As a graduating student, you may find yourself getting more philosophical—about grade 12 and about life as well. This is a good year to take stock—to think about what you believe and value, and how you will go about making the important choices facing you.

American writer John Barth indicates that value is in the eye of the beholder: what is worthless to one person may well be priceless to another.

American anarchist Emma Goldman reminds us that our values and beliefs can change, just as we do.

Finally, English humorist G.K. Chesterton identifies the value of making choices that take *all* things into consideration.

As you ponder the unit selections, try to answer the following questions:

1) Where do values come from?

2) What are some worthwhile values and beliefs?

3) What causes people to make poor choices?

4) What roles do ethics and morality play in helping us make positive choices and decisions?

Before you read, consider how small details can reveal a great deal about what is important to a person. What are some details that might reveal a great deal about you?

As you read, notice details that reveal something about the character.

Zits

Cartoon by Jerry Scott and Jim Borgman

Notes

Zits, the popular comic strip about the life and times of 15-year-old Jeremy Duncan, began in 1997 and runs in over 1000 newspapers worldwide. It has been voted the Best Comic Strip twice by the National Cartoonists Society.

Jerry Scott, writer and co-creator of *Zits,* began his career by taking over the *Nancy* strip. He then co-created *Baby Blues* (which is based on his experiences with his second daughter) before going on to do *Zits.*

Jim Borgman, Pulitzer Prize-winning cartoonist, was raised in blue-collar neighbourhoods of Cincinnati. He was hired by the *Cincinnati Enquirer* one week after graduation to start work cartooning.

Jim Borgman and Jerry Scott

You take it from here ...

Responding

1. Read the Details   Working with a partner, list the little things that reveal Jeremy's character and feelings. What other details are important in the cartoon? What do they reveal?

2. Consider Dramatic Irony   *Dramatic irony* occurs when what a character says or believes contrasts with what the reader or other characters know to be true. In a small group, describe the dramatic irony in this cartoon, and discuss how it contributes to the humour.

3. Explore Related Ideas   In a class discussion, suggest some other values or choices that create differences of opinion between parents and their children. Have you ever experienced a situation similar to Jeremy's? If so, how did you resolve it? Or did you?

Extending

4. Draft a Cartoon   Try your hand at using dramatic irony for comic effect. Brainstorm various humorous scenarios in which the values of a parent and teenager are at odds, although one of them is unaware of it. Choose one, and draft the dialogue and sketch the visuals for a three-panel cartoon.

5. Focus on Visual Technique   Examine the selection and notice how the various perspectives (e.g., close-up, wide-angle, high, low), facial features, body language, and other details contribute to the meaning and humour of the cartoon. Apply some of these techniques as you finalize the dialogue and visual presentation of the cartoon you drafted in Activity 4. Present your cartoon to the class.

> **PEER ASSESSMENT**
>
> As you view others' cartoons, consider the following:
> - Can you identify the ironic situation?
> - Was the scenario a familiar one, something you could relate to? Was it insightful?
> - Did the cartoonist make good use of details to reflect character and values?

Before you read, recall the best words of wisdom anyone ever gave you.

As you read, notice any pieces of advice that you could, do, or should apply in your own life.

Desiderata

Poem by Max Ehrmann

Go placidly amid the noise and haste
and remember what peace there may be in silence.
As far as possible be on good terms with all persons.
Speak your truth quietly and clearly and listen to others,
even the dull and ignorant; they too have their story.
Avoid loud and aggressive persons; they are vexatious to the spirit.
If you compare yourself with others you may become vain or bitter;
for always there will be greater and lesser persons than yourself.
Enjoy your achievements as well as your plans.
Keep interested in your career; however humble;
it is a real possession in the changing fortunes of time.
Exercise caution in your business affairs,
for the world is full of trickery.
But let this not blind you to what virtue there is.
Many persons strive for high ideals
and everywhere life is full of heroism.
Be yourself.

Notes

Max Ehrmann was an Indiana lawyer and poet. "Desiderata" was written in the early 1900s.

aridity: dullness; lack of life spirit

desiderata: things desired or needed

feign: fake; pretend

perennial: lasting a long time, or recurring again and again

placidly: peacefully

Especially do not feign affection.

Neither be cynical about love,

for in the face of all aridity and disappointment

it is as perennial as the grass.

Take kindly the counsel of the years,

gracefully surrendering the things of youth.

Nurture strength of spirit to shield you in sudden misfortune.

But do not distress yourself with imaginings.

Many fears are born of fatigue and loneliness.

Beyond a wholesome discipline be gentle with yourself.

You are a child of the universe no less than the trees and the stars.

You have a right to be here.

And whether it is clear to you or not,

no doubt the universe is unfolding as it should.

Therefore be at peace with God,

whatever you conceive him to be,

and whatever your labours and aspirations in the noisy confusion of life,

keep peace with your soul.

With all its sham and drudgery and broken dreams

it is still a beautiful world.

Be cheerful. Strive to be happy.

You take it from here ...

Responding

1. Relate to Unit Theme   As a class, discuss how this poem relates to the theme of this unit, "Values, Beliefs, and Choices." In your discussion, consider what the longstanding popularity of this poem reveals about our society's collective values and beliefs.

2. Focus on Style   Working with a partner, reread the poem and pay close attention to the effect achieved by the poet's choice of words and the use of techniques such as *parallel structure* and varied sentence lengths. Paraphrase several lines of the poem into "everyday" language, and consider the difference in impact.

3. Respond Personally   Choose one piece of advice and expand on it in a journal entry, describing how you might apply it in your own life.

Extending

4. **Compare with a Contemporary Piece**   In June 1997, *Chicago Tribune* columnist Mary Schmich wrote a column in the form of a list of advice to graduating students. Shortly afterward, it gained widespread fame as the novelty song "Everybody's Free (to Wear Sunscreen)." As a class, obtain and read Schmich's "sunscreen" column (and/or listen to the recording). Then, working in a small group, analyze the similarities and differences between it and "Desiderata." In your analysis, take note of advice that is offered (a) only in "Sunscreen," (b) only in "Desiderata" and (c) in both.

   Use a three-column chart to organize your notes. Finally, compare the columns, considering how the societal context at the time each was written could account for the differences.

"Sunscreen" (1997)	"Desiderata" (early 1900s)	Both

5. **Write Your Own Desiderata**   Write an article, song, or poem that will stand as a statement of your values and beliefs, and your advice, to the next generations. As you write, edit, and rewrite, show that you are able to manipulate language for effect as the author of "Desiderata" has done. Examine how he has used stylistic techniques such as parallel structure and a variety of sentence lengths, and incorporate some of these techniques into your own work.

Notes

Joan Bond has published poetry in *Dandelion* and *Pottersfield Portfolio*.

Because You Waited

Poem by Joan Bond

Because you waited at the dentist's, reading magazines
while I was checked   x-rayed   cleaned
and given old toys and a new toothbrush

Because you waited in the parked car, doing cross stitch
while I pointed   bent low   swayed high
in pink ballet shoes and a black leotard

Because you waited at the library, flipping pages
while I re-wrote on foolscap the list of books
I had used in my research paper, but
had forgotten to record the exact footnotes

Because you waited in the study, watching midnight movies
while I laughed   blushed   danced
and was given a new kiss and old poetry lines

I now can wait for you as you rock
in your single room with its creme curtains
your face, a tapestry of intricate soft folds
your hair, a bluish cloud of August sky

I now can wait for you as you rise
leaning all your years on the shaky, wooden cane
and curl your bone-thin fingers over my hand
not knowing I need your hands far more
than you need mine

You take it from here ...

Responding

TIP

• "Reading between the lines" means going beyond what is stated in so many words. Find clues in the poem to help you imagine additional details about the characters.

1. **Read Between the Lines** Working with a partner, carefully reread the first four stanzas. What do you learn about the person being addressed? What do you learn about the speaker? Support your insights with details from the poem.

2. **Appreciate Style** Locate where in the poem the time jumps. Write a sentence describing what is expressed before the jump, and another sentence describing what is expressed following it. Has the poet used this jump in time effectively? Creatively? Explain your views in a paragraph.

3. **Explore Poetic Devices** This poem is powerful because it skilfully uses poetic devices to intensify its meaning. In a three-column chart, quote and comment on an example of image word(s), parallel structure, purposeful line breaks, layout, metaphor, and symbol.

Poetic device	Quoted example	What the device adds to the poem
image word(s)		

Extending

4. **Reflect on Values** In a reflective personal essay, discuss the choices that the two characters in this poem make, and identify what values these choices reflect.

5. **Represent the Poem** Find one illustration that you feel represents this poem. Prepare a brief oral presentation explaining your choice and demonstrating how it relates to the poem.

PEER ASSESSMENT

• Did the presenters clearly explain their choices and relate them to the poem?
• Which illustration did you think most effectively reflected the content and values expressed in the poem? Explain.

6. **Write Your Own Tribute** Think about someone who has shown you great kindness over the years, whom you would like to thank. Write a free-verse poem dedicated to that person.

You stick with them what brung you, my daddy always said.

Dogs and Books

by Christie Blatchford

NEWSPAPER COLUMN/PERSONAL ESSAY

Notes

Christie Blatchford graduated from the Ryerson journalism program in 1973 and went on to write columns for the *Toronto Sun* and *National Post*. She is well known for her honest, no-holds-barred writing style.

disparage: run down or criticize

Edna St. Vincent Millay (1892–1950): popular American poet whose work praised life, love, and individual freedom

The Jungle Book: popular children's book of animal stories by Rudyard Kipling (1865–1936)

vengeance: revenge for an injury

At some of the lowest moments of my life, in my times of worst despair, I have depended on two categories of friends to pull me through, and neither has ever let me down. One is books; the other is dogs.

This is not meant to disparage my human friends, some of whom I have relied on heavily, all of whom I love. But, as we all learn sooner or later, people can't always be with you when you need them. Sometimes, they mean to say the right thing, the comforting thing, but they say the wrong one. Other times, they have problems of their own and cannot be strong for you. Even when they are there, to hold your hand and kiss it better, they cannot take away the source of your unhappiness.

Books can. And so can dogs.

Books are the ultimate escape. When my heart has been broken, when I worry about my job or my writing, when I feel let down, betrayed, or unloved, I read a book. As a young woman in search of romance, I read, oddly enough, John D. MacDonald's Travis McGee books. When no one else was there to play the part, Travis was my white knight, a man both rough and tender, who loved both his friends and a woman who was loyal and sexy, fierce and faithful.

When my dad was in hospital and I was frantic he would never, ever get out, I could lose myself only when I read. I read everything, anytime—in the bathroom, on the subway, waiting for a bus, and every night before I fell asleep. And when my father went into hospital for the last time, and when he died, I cried and

cried, and then remembered and remembered. The only thing that could stop the tears and the memories was reading. Much later, when I feared he was slipping away from my memory, I could bring him back, as sharp as daylight, by reading the book of Edna St. Vincent Millay's poetry he'd given me, or Kipling's *The Jungle Book* that he used to read to me as a child, or one of his favourite novels.

Not throughout my life, but for periods of it, the other source of comfort and love was my dog. As a pudgy young girl with all the usual insecurities, I came home from school every day to the wholehearted adoration of Lucky, a big, ham-footed, foolish boxer. As a shy, easily embarrassed (and thus perfectly normal) teenager, it was sweet Mickey who welcomed me. As a reasonably young adult, I looked to wondrous, even-tempered, overtly affectionate Susie. And now, as a fairly well-adjusted, usually happy adult, I have Blux, the big black half-Labrador with paws like hamburger buns and a heart the size of his geographic name.

It is trite to say that dogs love you no matter what; but they do, and there are times when the human being craves undemanding, uncritical, and wholly accepting love. If you're lucky, you get it as a child, from your parents; but as you become an adult you lose the right to remain uncriticized. They may love you anyway, but they are likely to explain that "anyway" at great and painful length. You can ignore a dog, leave him unattended and unwalked for far too long; yet the minute you walk through the door, he will be all over you like a cheap suit. You can be mean to a dog, and he will forgive you; what's more, he will never remember your meanness, let alone extract vengeance. When you want to play, so will he; when you need hugging, he will, too. When you crave quiet, pleasant company, that's just what he'll give you; when nothing and no one can make you laugh, he can reduce you to stupid, teary howling within seconds. When everyone you know is busy or in love or on vacation or booked up, it will be his distinct pleasure to be available.

Dogs are individuals as much as people are, but all dogs that are treated well share some delightful characteristics: loyalty, generosity, and a temperament that is warm and loving. And though it is silly to imbue them with human characteristics or understanding, they are nonetheless bright, inquisitive creatures who can immensely enrich your life. Also, they are worthy of love. Probably, there are some nice people around who happen not to like dogs, but I'll be damned if I can think of any.

I remember a friend whose three-year relationship abruptly ended. Suddenly, he was cut off from everything familiar—the woman he still loved, the house they had worked on together, the bed he knew, the street he was fond of, neighbours he knew, flowers he had planted. When he left, all he took were his clothes and a small knapsack of personal treasures.

He moved into a stark, modern apartment; he had virtually no furniture but cardboard boxes. David and I lived nearby, and I saw him frequently in those days; and many times, when he thought no one would notice, I caught him looking with incredible love and gratitude at a large tan-and-white object on the floor beside him.

His dog was the one familiar, beloved face in his brave new world. He was properly appreciative, and respectful, and enamoured of her for simply being with him. And later, when his life straightened out, as it usually does for good people, and there was a new woman to share things with, he never forgot what his hound had meant to him in the dark days. You stick with them what brung you, my daddy always said. And nine times out of ten, that's a hound.

Now, if only I could find a dog who'd read out loud to me: a jug of wine, a book to read, a dog beside me panting in the sun, tail wagging in slow motion in the heat. Well, that's heaven.

You take it from here ...

Responding

1. Form an Opinion   Do you agree that books and dogs—more than friends—can help ease a person's unhappiness, or do you have other ideas on the subject? What do you usually choose to comfort you during dark moments in your own life? Share your thoughts with a partner.

2. Focus on Diction   How does the writer make her article seem friendly, almost as if she is speaking to you one-on-one? Find three or four examples from the article and, in a class discussion, comment on how each one reflects a personable, approachable personality.

3. Focus on Tone   Although the essay refers to several unhappy events, the author's overall outlook appears to be optimistic. Find at least four quotations that exemplify the positive tone of the essay.

Extending

4. Write a Memoir   Write a memoir in which you reflect on the value of things that take you away from your woes. Perhaps you, too, turn to a dog or a book, or perhaps you have something else—another kind of pet, an engrossing hobby, or a sport. Develop your memoir with concrete examples, and try to achieve a strong, energetic tone in your writing.

5. Prepare an Introduction   Suppose that Christie Blatchford is coming to speak to your class and you have been chosen to give a short speech introducing and welcoming her. The problem is that you know very little about her—the only information you have is in this essay. Fortunately, through her personal stories, her tone, and the way she writes, Ms. Blatchford reveals a good deal about herself. Based on your insights, write a one-minute speech of introduction and welcome. Be prepared to present your speech to the class.

Before you read, ask yourself if you believe in anything that you cannot explain scientifically.

As you read, keep the title of the story in mind, and note any details that relate to it.

Fox Hunt

His mind wandered, and he began to daydream.

Short Story by Lensey Namioka

Notes

Lensey Namioka was born in Beijing and emigrated to the United States. She writes popular books for young adults, including *White Serpent Castle*, *Village of the Vampire Cat*, and *Island of Ogres*. "Fox Hunt" is based on her homeland experience; she has said that she wanted to write about the fox spirit in a new context.

mandarin: official of high rank in the Chinese Empire

PSAT: Preliminary Scholastic Aptitude Test: an American preparatory college exam similar to the departmental and diploma exams in Canada

Andy Liang watched the kids from his school bus walk home with their friends. He could hear them talking together and laughing. He always got off the bus alone and walked home by himself.

But this time it was different. A girl got off the bus just behind him and started walking in the same direction. He wondered why he hadn't seen her before. She was also Asian American, which made it all the more surprising that he hadn't noticed her earlier.

As he tried to get a better look, she went into the neighbourhood convenience store and disappeared behind a shelf of canned soup. He peered into the store, hoping for another glimpse of her. All he saw were some of the kids from the bus getting bags of potato chips and soft drinks.

Andy sighed. He was used to being a loner, and usually it didn't bother him—not much, anyway. But today the loneliness was heavy. He overheard the other kids talking, and he knew they were planning to study together for the PSAT. From the looks of the snacks, they were expecting a long session.

Andy would be practising for the test, too, but he would be doing it by himself. *I'm better off doing it alone, anyway,* he thought. *Studying with somebody else would just slow me down.*

The truth was that none of the others had invited him to study with them. *So all right,* he said to himself, *they think I'm a grind. What's wrong with that? I'll be getting better scores on the PSAT than any of them, even if there's nobody to coach me.*

He finally found the girl standing in front of a case of barbecued chicken. She was staring so hungrily at the chickens that his own mouth began watering, and he would have bought a piece on the spot if he had the money. But with the change in his pocket, he had to be satisfied with a candy bar.

Leaving the store, he reached his street and passed the corner house with the moody German shepherd. As usual, it snapped at him, and he automatically retreated to the far side of the sidewalk. Although the dog was on a chain, Andy didn't like the way it looked at him. Besides, a chain could always break.

Today, the dog not only snapped, it began to bark furiously and strained against its chain. Andy jumped back and bumped against the girl he had seen earlier. Somehow she had appeared behind him without making any noise.

He apologized. "I didn't mean to crash into you. That dog always growls at me, but today he's really barking like crazy."

The girl shivered. "The dog doesn't seem to like me very much, either." Before he had a chance to say anything more, she turned and walked away.

Again Andy sighed. He hadn't even had a chance to find out what her name was or where she lived. Was she Chinese American, as he was? What grade was she in? At least she went on the same school bus, so there was a chance of seeing her again.

But he didn't have much hope that she would be interested in him. Girls didn't go for the quiet, studious type. Last year, one of the girls in his geometry class had asked him to give her some help after school. That went pretty well, and for a while he thought they might have something going. But after she passed the geometry test, she didn't look at him again.

Maybe if he studied less and went in for sports, girls would get interested in him. But then his grades might slip, and his parents would never let him hear the end of it. He had to keep his grades up, study hard, be the dutiful son.

His brother had managed to get a math score of 800 on the PSAT, and now he was at Yale with a full scholarship. Andy had to try and do as well.

More than once he had asked his parents why it was so important to get into a good college. "Lots of people get rich in this country without going to college at all," he told them.

His father would draw himself up stiffly. "The Liangs belonged to the mandarin class in China. I've told you again and again that to become a mandarin, one had to pass the official examinations. Only outstanding scholars passed, and only they had the qualifications to govern the country."

Andy's father always got worked up about the subject. He might be only a minor clerk in America, he said, but he was descended from a family of high-ranking officials in China.

Another thing Andy noticed was that when his father went on at length about the illustrious Liang family, his mother always listened with a faint smile. She seemed to be amused for some reason.

But that didn't stop her from also putting pressure on Andy to study hard. Every night, she would ask him whether he had done his homework, and she double-checked his papers to make sure everything was correct.

Normally Andy didn't mind doing his homework. He liked the satisfaction of a job well done when he finished a hard problem in math. But lately, all the extra work preparing for the exam was beginning to get him down. His mind wandered, and he began to daydream. He had visions of becoming a snake charmer, making a balloon trip over the Andes, or practising kung fu in Shaolin Temple. He saw himself in the English countryside, riding a galloping horse in a fox hunt.

He tried to stop wasting time on these stupid daydreams. Maybe his mind wouldn't wander if he had someone to study with. But nobody wanted to study with him. Nobody wanted to spend time with a nerd.

Next day, the girl got off the bus again with Andy, and this time, instead of going into the convenience store, she began to walk with him. When they reached the yard with the German shepherd, they both automatically backed away from the fence.

Andy and the girl looked at each other and grinned. He was encouraged. "I'm Andy Liang. Are you new in the neighbourhood?"

"We moved here last week," she replied. "My name is Leona Hu. But Leona is a silly name, and my friends call me Lee."

She was inviting him to call her Lee and including him among her friends! Andy could hardly believe his luck. An attractive girl was actually ready to be friends. He was grateful to the German shepherd.

The girl had big almond-shaped eyes. Andy had overheard Americans saying that Chinese had slanty eyes, although his own eyes did not slant. Lee's eyes, on the other hand, definitely slanted upward at the corners.

Her hair had a slightly reddish tint, instead of being blue-black like his own. She wasn't exactly beautiful, but with her hair and her slanting eyes, she looked exotic and fascinating.

When they came to his house, Andy wished he could keep Lee talking with him. But she smiled at him briefly and went on. He had to stop himself from running after her to find out where she lived. He didn't want her to think that he was pestering her.

Was she going to take the PSAT this year? If she was, maybe they could study together!

At dinner that night, his father went on as usual about how important it was to do well on the PSAT. "We immigrants start at the bottom here in America, and the only way we can pull ourselves up is to get a good education. Never forget that you're descended from illustrious ancestors, Andy."

Again, Andy noticed his mother's faint smile. Later, he went into the kitchen where he found her washing the dishes. "Why do you always smile when Father gives me his pep talk about education? Don't you agree with him?"

"Oh, I agree with him about the importance of education," his mother said. "I'm just amused by all that talk about *illustrious ancestors*."

"You mean Father wasn't telling the truth about Liangs being mandarins?" asked Andy. He took up a bunch of chopsticks and began to wipe them dry. Usually, his mother refused his help with the chores. She wanted him to spend all his time on his homework.

But tonight she didn't immediately send him upstairs to his desk. She rinsed a rice bowl and put it in the dish rack. "Well, the Liangs haven't always been mandarins," she said finally. "They used to be quite poor, until one of them achieved success by passing the official examinations and raising the status of the whole Liang family."

"Hey, that's great!" Andy liked the idea of a poor boy making good. It was more interesting than coming from a long line of decadent aristocrats. "Tell me more about this ancestor."

"His name was Fujin Liang," replied his mother. "Or I should say Liang Fujin, since in China, last names come first." Again she smiled faintly. "Very well. You should really be studying, but it's good for you to know about your ancestors."

Liang Fujin lived with his widowed mother in a small thatched cottage and earned money by looking after a neighbour's water buffalo. His mother added to their meagre income by weaving and selling cotton cloth. It was a hard struggle to put rice in their bowls.

But Fujin's mother was ambitious for him. She knew he was smart, and she decided that he should try for the official examinations. In theory, any poor boy could take the examinations, and if he passed, he could raise his family to mandarin status. But rich boys could afford tutors to help them study. For Fujin, even buying a book was a luxury.

He was so eager to learn that he crouched under the window of the nearby school and tried to eavesdrop on the lessons. Whenever he saved enough money to buy books, he would read them while seated on the back of the water buffalo.

Once he was so absorbed that he walked the buffalo into a rice paddy. But he managed to read the precious books until he knew them all by heart.

Through hard work he grew up to be a fine scholar. His mother thought he was finally ready to take the examinations, but he himself wasn't so confident. The other competitors were the sons of rich families, who could afford the very best tutors.

He continued to study late every night, until his head began to nod. So he tied the end of his pigtail to a nail in the ceiling, and whenever his head fell forward, the pigtail jerked him awake.

One night, while he was struggling to stay awake over his book, he heard a soft voice behind him. "A fine, hardworking young man like you deserves to pass the examination."

Fujin whirled around and saw a beautiful girl standing behind him. Somehow she had appeared without making any noise. She had huge, bewitching eyes that slanted sharply. Could he be dreaming?

"Let me help you," continued the girl. "I can act as a tutor and coach you."

"And that was how your ancestor, Liang Fujin, got the coaching he needed to pass the examinations," said Andy's mother.

Andy blinked. "But … but who was this mysterious girl? And how come she was such a great scholar? I thought women didn't get much education in the old days."

His mother laughed. "Nobody in the Liang family would say. But I'll give you a hint: When the girl lifted her skirt to sit down, Fujin caught a flash of something swishing. It looked like a long, bushy tail!"

It took Andy a moment to get it. Then he remembered the Chinese stories his mother used to tell him, stories about the *huli jing*, or fox spirit. The mischievous fox, or *huli*, often appeared in the form of a beautiful girl and played tricks on people. But in some of the stories, the fox fell in love with a handsome young man and did him a great service. She expected a reward for her service, of course, and the reward was marriage.

"So my ancestor passed the examinations because he was coached by a fox?" asked Andy.

"That story is a lie!" cried Andy's father, stomping into the kitchen. "It was made up by malicious neighbours who were jealous of the Liangs!"

Andy's mother shrugged and began to pack the dishes away. His father continued. "Liang Fujin passed the examinations because he was smart and worked hard! Don't you forget it, Andy! So now you can go up to your room and start working!"

His father was right, of course. Fox spirits belonged in fairy tales. He, Andy Liang, would have to study for the PSAT the hard way.

Andy was delighted when Lee told him that she was also planning to take the PSAT. She agreed that it would be a good idea to study together. He was eager to begin that very evening. "How about coming over to my house? I'm sure my parents would love to meet you."

Actually, he wasn't sure how delighted his parents would be. He suspected that they would be glad to see him with a Chinese American girl, but they'd probably think that a girl—any girl—would distract him from his studies.

He was half sorry and half relieved when she said, "I'm going to be busy tonight. Maybe we can go to the public library tomorrow afternoon and get some sample tests and study guides."

That night he had a dream about fox hunting. Only this time, he found himself running on the ground trying to get away from the mounted horsemen and howling dogs. There was somebody running with him—another fox, with reddish hair and a bushy tail. It flashed a look at him with its slanting eyes.

Andy and Lee began studying sample PSAT tests at the library. Working with someone else certainly made studying less of a drudgery. Andy felt relaxed with Lee. He didn't suffer the paralyzing shyness with her that seized him when he was with other girls.

She was really good at finding out what his weaknesses were. English grammar was his worst subject, and Lee fed him the right questions so that the fuzzy points of grammar got cleared up. As the days went by, Andy became confident that he was going to do really well on the PSAT. At this rate, he might get a scholarship to some famous university.

He began to worry that the help was one-sided. *He* was getting first-rate coaching, but what was Lee getting out of this? "You're helping me so much," he told her. "But I don't see how I'm helping you at all."

She smiled at him. "I'll get my reward someday."

Something about her glance looked familiar. Where had he seen it before?

They had an extra-long study session the day before the exam. When they passed the corner house on their way home, the German shepherd went into a frenzy of barking and scrabbled to climb the Cyclone fence. Both the chain and the fence held, fortunately. Lee looked shaken and backed away from the fence.

At Andy's house she recovered her colour. "Well, good luck on the exam tomorrow." She looked at him for a moment with her slanting eyes, and then she was gone.

Again, he thought he remembered that look from somewhere. All during supper, he was tantalized by the memory, which was just out of reach.

That night he dreamed about fox hunting again. It was more vivid than usual, and he could see the scarlet coats of the riders chasing him. The howling of the dogs sounded just like the German shepherd. Again, he was running with another fox. It had huge slanting eyes, bright with mischief.

He woke up, and as he sat in his bed, he finally remembered where he had seen those huge, slanting eyes. They were Lee's eyes.

Next day Andy met Lee at the entrance to the examination hall. He suddenly realized that if he said her name in the Chinese order, it would be Hu Lee, which sounded the same as *huli*, or fox.

She smiled. "So you know?"

Andy found his voice. "Why did you pick me, particularly?"

Her smile widened. "We foxes hunt out our own kind."

That was when Andy knew why the German shepherd always snapped at him. He himself must be part fox. His ancestor, Liang Fujin, had accepted help from the fox spirit after all, and she had collected her reward.

You take it from here ...

Responding

1. Relate Details to Title   As a class, discuss how details relating to the title are woven through the story. How do they hold the key to the story?

2. Look at Foreshadowing   Working with a partner, find several examples of *foreshadowing* (clues to what will come later). For each one, identify the question(s) it raises, and explain how it connects with later events in the story. Present your ideas in a chart.

Example of foreshadowing	Explanation
But this time it was different. A girl got off the bus.... He wondered why he hadn't seen her before.	Question: What is the significance of the girl's sudden arrival? Connection: It ties in with the story his mother tells and his own future.

3. **Identify Parallels** With a partner, look at the parallels between the story-within-a-story and the main story, considering the situation, the characters, and what happens to them. If the parallel continues, what will happen to Andy?

4. **Examine Character** In a written response, examine Andy's values, noting what has influenced these values, and what decisions and choices they lead him to make.

Extending

5. **Write a Myth or Fairy Tale** Write a myth or fairy tale linking an event in or aspect of your own life with an imagined ancestral past. Remember that such stories have a sense of long ago, and they deal with improbable or fantastic events.

> **SELF-ASSESSMENT**
> - What techniques did you use to give the story a mythical, long-ago feel? Did you succeed?
> - Evaluate the experience of imagining an unknown "ancestral past." Was it challenging? Interesting?

6. **Design a Visual** Design a visual to accompany the story you wrote in Activity 5. Try to capture the key images and themes of your story as well as its mythical or fairy-tale quality. Share your visual with the class or a small group, explaining how it relates to your story.

> **TIP**
> - You can create an original drawing or use existing images (e.g., from old magazines, computer illustration programs, or Internet sources)—or use a combination of original and found images.

Before you read, consider the following question: Are yesterday's values necessarily better than today's?

As you read, try to recall an experience in your own life that relates to this poem.

Notes

Jacqueline Oker, of Peterson Crossing, British Columbia, is a member of the Doig River Indian Band. A graduate of the En'owkin International School of Writing, she has gone on to social work studies, and now lives in Penticton.

A Forgotten Yesterday

Poem by Jacqueline Oker

The old woman sits on stretched moose hide
and scrapes hair off with her steel scraper
her grandson made for her
She stops for a moment
Tears thunder down her wrinkled face
She thinks about her people
They were all killed in a forest fire
when she was a young girl
Now alone
the last of her family bloodline
She scrapes the hide she will sell
at the store

She remembers her mother
She used to dry moose meat
pick blueberries
flesh moose hides
and make clothes for the
icy winters
around the tepee that
has since been replaced by
walls
Brown-skin women come to her
and pay her money to flesh
their moose hides
and make their dry meats
They do not know how to

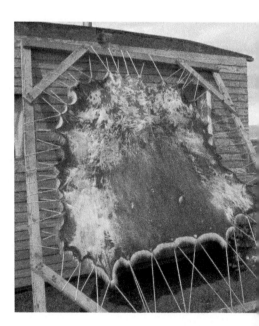

A forgotten yesterday
she has mastered
She knows it
like the creases
in her wrinkled
bent fingers

Who will take my place, she thinks
she gazes to the rolling hills
Young people do not want to know
about a forgotten yesterday
They want to play
video games instead
She scrapes the hide

You take it from here ...

Responding

1. Examine Values   What values does the old woman believe the younger generation will never possess? Do you think her concerns are warranted? Share your views in a small-group discussion.

2. Respond Personally   The woman in the poem wonders, "Who will take my place." If you had the opportunity to talk to her, what would you say? Develop a thoughtful personal response, and present it in the form of a letter to the woman.

3. Examine Theme   Write a two-paragraph discussion on the theme of this poem. In the first paragraph, state the theme and relate it back to the poem. In the second, discuss the truth of this theme—does it apply only to the situation described in the poem, or is the theme universal? Support your ideas, using examples from your own experience if you can.

Extending

4. Conduct an Interview   The woman in this poem is disheartened by the knowledge that traditions she carried on from her mother's generation will likely end with her own. Individually, or in pairs, discuss this idea with an elderly relative or acquaintance. Ask if he or she shares this

concern. Are there certain traditions and ways of doing things from the past that he or she would like your generation to know about and preserve? Summarize your discussion and present it to the class.

SELF-ASSESSMENT
- What did you learn about past traditions from your discussion?
- Were there any you would like to carry on?

5. Write a Position Paper   Write a position paper in which you respond to ideas generated by the poem. As a first step, define the position you want to take and defend, or choose one of the following:

- The poem represents stereotypes rather than distinctive truths about the generations.
- The poem reveals distinctive truths about the generations.
- Yesterday's values were better (or not better) than today's values.

"Buy your daughter a football—and a doll for your son."

Nonsexist Child-Rearing: The New Parent Trap?

by Lisa Wilson Strick

MAGAZINE COLUMN

Notes

androgynous: having characteristics of both sexes

egalitarian: relating to equality

forsythia: yellow-flowered shrub

rhetoric: persuasive language or argument

Utopia: refers to a perfect society found nowhere on earth; based on Sir Thomas More's classic of the same name (1516)

"Boys will be boys," my parents said when my brother sent a fly ball through the dining-room window. The same tolerantly amused expression applied when the neighbour's teenage son got drunk and wrecked the family car.

Comments directed *my* way were different: Don't get your dress dirty, don't raise your voice, don't let that boy *touch* you. The message was clear: Boys were expected to be rough-and-ready troublemakers, while girls were supposed to be pristine and demure.

In the sixties feminists vowed to change all that. The sex-role stereotypes we grew up with had become straightjackets for too many of us. Nonsexist parenting was advanced as the answer. "Get those girls out of ruffles!" modern mothers insisted. "Buy your daughter a football—and a doll for your son. Treat the kids alike and we'll have sexual equality in twenty years."

I bought the rhetoric. When my turn came I made a determined effort to be a nonsexist parent. I dressed my two sons in pink overalls and I built them a dollhouse. My husband helped by making a more visible contribution to the household chores. ("Look at Daddy sewing a button on his shirt! When his thumb stops bleeding, Daddy is going to *iron* the shirt!")

For a while it actually worked. When my sons were two and four they *preferred* the delicate porcelain tea set I'd given them over their more traditional "boy toys."

When my older son was five, however, he suddenly became interested in nothing but guns. (Well, I can't say *nothing* but guns; he also liked spears, swords, and knives.) He was forever popping out of unexpected places pointing a pudgy finger at me and exclaiming, *"Bang! You're dead!"*

"Where could he possibly have learned this?" I asked my husband in a panic. "His friends are all gentle souls, and I've never let him watch anything more violent than *Sesame Street* on television!"

"I don't know," my husband admitted. "But I remember my brother and I enjoyed the same games. Let's just see how it goes."

How it *went* was that my younger boy soon developed aggressive tendencies too. "I want a soldier set!" the tot begged; "I wanna be G.I. Joe!" Meanwhile, big brother spent most of his time cutting down my forsythia and making bows and arrows from the twigs. "Maybe we should just get them the cap gun and the soldier set," my husband suggested. I agreed. The weapons they were making were far more dangerous than anything at the store.

That was the end of the tea set. It has been replaced by an arsenal that includes everything from battery-powered laser pistols to plastic armour. A miniature version of the Allied forces of World War II has taken up residence in the dollhouse.

They don't spend *all* their time slaying dragons and re-enacting the Battle of the Bulge. My sons also like "borrowing" my tools and taking furniture apart. They like racing cars and wrestling. In other words, they like being traditional *boys*—and I haven't been able to do anything about it.

Mothers of little girls I know aren't faring much better. For years one friend has dressed her daughter in jeans, sweat shirts, and sneakers. "I don't want her feeling physically restricted like we did," she explained. "If the kid wants to climb a tree, I want her to feel free to *do* it."

The child has never wanted to climb a tree. What she *wants* is to come to my house and play with the boys' dolls. This little girl does not want to wear pants either. "She wants dresses trimmed with lace," her mom declares. "She wants patent-leather Mary Janes with satin *bows*! Where did I go wrong?"

I'm not sure either of us did go wrong—except in our temporary inability to appreciate the kids for what they are. We found ourselves looking at our healthy, able children and feeling like failures.

Nonsexist parenting is fine as long as it supports a child's individuality—but I think we have come dangerously close to replacing the old myths about masculinity and femininity with a new one. Today's youngsters are supposed to be super-children—androgynous beings who are smart, sensitive, aggressive, and loving all at the same time. To develop such impossibly well-rounded individuals some parents are going to extremes. I know one mother who insisted that her unwilling daughter join a highly competitive Little League team because "girls have to learn to be tough today." Another is sure that allowing her son to play basketball will interfere with the development of his "artistic side." (She arranged ballet lessons instead.)

Perhaps this is progress; in my day artistic boys were called "sissies" and girls couldn't participate in Little League at all. But some of today's children don't seem to have any more choices than we did. They aren't even permitted the faults tolerated in the "bad old days" when boys were *supposed* to be dirty and noisy, and girls were allowed to be squeamish and shy.

Our vision of the perfect nonsexist human being sometimes blinds us to simple facts of nature. Studies have shown that girls and boys really *are* different—in mind as well as in body.

If so, why are we teaching children to distrust their drives to be "girlish" or "boyish"? Instead of paving the way to a new egalitarian world, we could be creating the most sexually confused generation of all time.

I'm not sorry I gave nonsexist parenting a try. My pistol-packing sons *do* like to cook. And thanks to their father's example, they consider setting the table and scrubbing the bathtub their duty. But I've stopped telling them what a male *ought* to be.

I never thought Utopia would mean a world in which everybody thought alike, anyway. I'd prefer a world in which men and women are no longer ashamed of being different—but have learned to respect each other for it. Instead of teaching girls to act like boys and boys to act like girls, let's start teaching self-acceptance and acceptance of others. Then maybe we'll achieve *real* equality: a culture in which masculine and feminine traits are equally valued.

You take it from here ...

Responding

1. Summarize Ideas   Using your own words, summarize in two or three paragraphs what the writer says about traditional child-rearing and nonsexist child-rearing. What are her ideas for the future?

2. Respond to Ideas   With a partner or in a small group, discuss your views on several of the writer's specific ideas. Some examples are

   - "Treat the kids alike and we'll have sexual equality in twenty years."
   - "Today's youngsters are supposed to be super-children—androgynous beings who are smart, sensitive, aggressive, and loving all at the same time."
   - "Studies have shown that girls and boys really *are* different—in mind as well as in body."
   - "Instead of paving the way to a new egalitarian world, we could be creating the most sexually confused generation of all time."

3. Understand Tone   Consider the following, and compare ideas with a partner:
   a) How would you describe the tone of this article? Is it consistent throughout, or are there deliberate variations?
   b) How does the author make her article readable and personal, yet also serious?

Extending

4. Extend the Conclusion   How would you go about teaching children self-acceptance and acceptance of others? Discuss the issue as a class and then, individually, write an extension to the idea of the last paragraph.

5. **Examine Media Views**   Working in a small group, do a media analysis to examine how views of men and women have changed over the years. Choose three movies or TV shows with similar themes (e.g., romantic comedies, dramatic movies or TV series, sitcoms). One of these should be recent (within the past decade); the other two should be from earlier decades. In your analysis, be sure to include

   - the year (movie) or decade (TV show)
   - a description of activities, interests/concerns, and unspoken assumptions about male and female characters
   - some concluding comments on how media portrayals of males and females have (and have not) changed during the time studied, according to your sample

   Summarize your analysis in a chart, and present your findings to the class.

6. Write a Personal Essay   Write a personal essay in which you examine how you were raised. Would you consider your own upbringing "typical" as described in this article? Were many of your games and toys conventionally gender-specific (e.g., dolls for girls, toy trucks for boys), or was the opposite true? Or neither? Use specific examples from your life to develop your ideas.

The Chaser

"So," said Alan, "you really do sell love potions?"

Short Story by John Collier

Notes

John Henry Noyes Collier (1901–1980) was a British author of several novels and short stories. "The Chaser" was published in 1940 and was adapted for television as a *Twilight Zone* episode in 1960.

"Out, damned spot!"—allusion to Shakespeare's Lady Macbeth, whose guilty imagination was trying to remove blood of a murder from her hands

siren: enchanting woman

"Out, brief candle!"—allusion to a line spoken by Macbeth, who became weary of living a life of crime and murder

au revoir: until we meet again

Alan Austen, as nervous as a kitten, went up certain dark and creaky stairs in the neighbourhood of Pell Street, and peered about for a long time on the dim landing before he found the name he wanted written obscurely on one of the doors.

He pushed open this door, as he had been told to do, and found himself in a tiny room, which contained no furniture but a plain kitchen table, rocking chair, and an ordinary chair. On one of the dirty buff-coloured walls were a couple of shelves, containing in all perhaps a dozen bottles and jars.

An old man sat in the rocking chair, reading a newspaper. Alan, without a word, handed him the card he had been given. "Sit down, Mr. Austen," said the old man very politely. "I am glad to make your acquaintance."

"Is it true," asked Alan, "that you have a certain mixture that has—er—quite extraordinary effects?"

"My dear sir," replied the old man, "my stock in trade is not very large—I don't deal in laxatives and teething mixtures—but such as it is, it is varied. I think nothing I sell has effects which could be precisely described as ordinary."

"Well, the fact is—" began Alan.

"Here, for example," interrupted the old man reaching for a bottle from the shelf. "Here is a liquid as colourless as water, almost tasteless, quite imperceptible in coffee, milk, wine, or any other beverage. It is also quite imperceptible to any known method of autopsy."

"Do you mean it is a poison?" cried Alan, very much horrified.

"Call it cleaning fluid if you like," said the old man indifferently. "Lives need cleaning. Call it a spot remover. 'Out, damned spot!' Eh? 'Out, brief candle!'"

"I want nothing of that sort," said Alan.

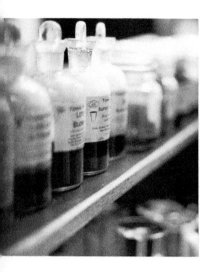

"Probably it is just as well," said the old man. "Do you know the price of this? For one teaspoonful, which is sufficient, I ask five thousand dollars. Never less. Not a penny less."

"I hope all your mixtures are not as expensive," said Alan apprehensively.

"Oh, dear, no," said the old man. "It would be no good charging that sort of price for a love potion, for example. Young people who need a love potion very seldom have five thousand dollars. Otherwise they would not need a love potion."

"I'm glad to hear you say so," said Alan.

"I look at it like this," said the old man. "Please a customer with one article, and he will come back when he needs another. Even if it *is* more costly. He will save up for it, if necessary."

"So," said Alan, "you really do sell love potions?"

"If I did not sell love potions," said the old man, reaching for another bottle, "I should not have mentioned the other matter to you. It is only when one is in a position to oblige that one can afford to be so confidential."

"And these potions," said Alan. "They are not just—just—er—"

"Oh, no," said the old man. "Their effects are permanent, and extend far beyond the mere casual impulse. But they include it. Oh, yes, they include it. Bountifully. Insistently. Everlastingly."

"Dear me!" said Alan, attempting a look of scientific detachment. "How very interesting!"

"But consider the spiritual side," said the old man.

"I do, indeed," said Alan.

"For indifference," said the old man, "they substitute devotion. For scorn, adoration. Give one tiny measure of this to the young lady—its flavour is imperceptible in orange juice, soup, or cocktails—and however gay and giddy she is, she will change altogether. She'll want nothing but solitude, and you."

"I can hardly believe it," said Alan. "She is so fond of parties."

"She will not like them any more," said the old man. "She'll be afraid of the pretty girls you may meet."

"She'll actually be jealous?" cried Alan in a rapture. "Of me?"

"Yes, she will want to be everything to you."

"She is, already. Only she doesn't care about it."

"She will, when she has taken this. She will care intensely. You'll be her sole interest in life."

"Wonderful!" cried Alan.

"She'll want to know all you do," said the old man. "All that has happened to you during the day. Every word of it. She'll want to know what you are thinking about, why you smile suddenly, why you are looking sad."

"That is love!" cried Alan.

"Yes," said the old man. "How carefully she'll look after you! She'll never allow you to be tired, to sit in a draught, to neglect your food. If you are an hour late, she'll be terrified. She'll think you are killed, or that some siren has caught you."

"I can hardly imagine Diana like that!" cried Alan.

"You will not have to use your imagination," said the old man. "And by the way, since there are always sirens, if by any chance you *should*, later on, slip a little, you need not worry. She will forgive you, in the end. She'll be terribly hurt, of course, but she'll forgive you—in the end."

"That will not happen," said Alan fervently.

"Of course not," said the old man. "But, if it does, you need not worry. She'll never divorce you. Oh, no! And, of course, she herself will never give you the least grounds for—not divorce, of course—but even uneasiness."

"And how much," said Alan, "how much is this wonderful mixture?"

"It is not so dear," said the old man, "as the spot remover, as I think we agreed to call it. No. That is five thousand dollars; never a penny less. One has to be older than you are, to indulge in that sort of thing. One has to save up for it."

"But the love potion?" said Alan.

"Oh, that," said that old man, opening the drawer in the kitchen table, and taking out a tiny, rather dirty-looking phial. "That is just a dollar."

"I can't tell you how grateful I am," said Alan, watching him fill it.

"I like to oblige," said the old man. "Then customers come back, later in life, when they are rather better off, and want more expensive things. Here you are. You will find it very effective."

"Thank you again," said Alan. "Goodbye."

"*Au revoir*," said the old man.

You take it from here ...

Responding

1. Find Details That Reveal Character   Find two subtle but very significant details in the first two paragraphs that begin to tell us the kind of man Alan Austen is. How does our understanding of Alan's character evolve from these early details? Is Alan revealed to be a *static character* or a *dynamic character*? Compare your response with another student's.

> **TIP**
> - A *dynamic character* undergoes a significant, lasting change in the story, while a *static character* does not.

2. Look at Characters' Values and Beliefs   In a paragraph, describe the kind of woman Diana will become once she is given the potion. In another paragraph, explain why Alan believes he will be happy with her once she has changed. What appear to be Alan's values and beliefs about relationships? Diana's?

3. Appreciate Allusions   Diana is the Roman name for the Greek goddess Artemis, the patroness of young unmarried women. Diana was the huntress, determined never to marry, and if a man got too close to her she would turn him into a stag and hunt him to death. With a partner, discuss how knowing this reference extends your insight into the story.

4. Understand the Subtext   Working in a small group, consider why the old man begins by referring to the "spot remover," its cost, and the need one might have to save up for it. Why does he refer to it again at the end, before he sells the love potion? What does this sinister subtext to the whole story suggest? (Hint: Translate the old man's final words to Alan, as he departs.)

5. Explain Title   Look up "chaser" in the dictionary, and write a paragraph explaining the play on words in the title.

Extending

6. Produce a Radio Play   Work in a group to present this story as a radio play. Create a script, including parts for a narrator, Alan, and the old man, and inserting instructions for sound effects and music. Rehearse the readings thoroughly, trying to capture appropriate intonation and timing for the dialogue. Then, record your radio play and present it to the class.

> **GROUP ASSESSMENT**
> - How did you choose your roles (e.g., scriptwriter[s], readers, coach[es], technical crew)?
> - Did all group members have a chance to contribute equally?
> - Did any problems or conflicts arise? If so, how did you solve them? If not, how did you prevent them?

7. Examine Ideals   Write a short reflective essay in which you identify the ideals (perfect models) we have in our culture about perfection and love. Consider the role played by the media in shaping these ideals. Then, offer your own, realistic, ideas about perfection and love that can serve as a guide for people in the real, as opposed to the ideal, world.

Before you read, recall some fairy tales you read as a child. What were the conflicts, and who prevailed?

As you read, identify who is in conflict, and predict who will win in the end. Notice whether your ideas change as you read.

The White Knight

"Is evil then triumphant?"

Fairy Tale by Eric Nicol

Notes

Eric Nicol (1919–), a former and long-time columnist for the *Vancouver Sun*, is one of Canada's top humorists. He has won the Leacock Medal for Humour three times, and was appointed to the Order of Canada in 2001.

motley: a colourful suit worn by a clown or jester

Once upon a time there was a knight who lived in a little castle on the edge of the forest of Life. One day this knight looked in the mirror and saw that he was a White Knight.

"Lo!" he cried. "I am a White Knight and therefore represent good. I am the champion of virtue and honour and justice, and I must ride into the forest and slay the Black Knight, who is evil."

So the White Knight mounted his snow-white horse and rode into the forest to find the Black Knight and slay him in single combat.

Many miles he rode the first day, without so much as a glimpse of the Black Knight. The second day he rode even farther, still without sighting the ebony armour of mischief. Day after day he rode, deeper and deeper into the forest of Life, searching thicket and gully and even the tree-tops. The Black Knight was nowhere to be seen.

Yet the White Knight found many signs of the Black Knight's presence. Again and again he passed a village in which the Black Knight had struck—a baker's shop robbed, a horse stolen, an innkeeper's daughter ravished. But always he just missed catching the doer of these deeds.

At last the White Knight had spent all his gold in the cause of his search. He was tired and hungry. Feeling his strength ebbing, he was forced to steal some buns from a bakeshop. His horse went lame, so that he was forced to replace it, silently and by darkness, with another white horse in somebody's stable. And when he stumbled, faint and exhausted, into an inn, the innkeeper's daughter gave him her bed, and because he was the White Knight in shining armour, she gave him her love, and when he was strong enough to leave the inn she cried bitterly because she could not understand that he had to go and find the Black Knight and slay him.

Through many months, under hot sun, over frosty paths, the White Knight pressed on his search, yet all the knights he met in the forest were, like himself, fairly white. They were knights of varying shades of whiteness, depending on how long they, too, had been hunting the Black Knight.

Some were sparkling white. These had just started hunting that day and irritated the White Knight by innocently asking directions to the nearest Black Knight.

Others were tattle-tale grey. And still others were so grubby, horse and rider, that the mirror in their castle would never have recognized them.

Yet the White Knight was shocked the day a knight of gleaming whiteness confronted him suddenly in the forest and with a wild whoop thundered towards him with levelled lance. The White Knight barely had time to draw his sword and, ducking under the deadly steel, plunge it into the attacker's breast.

The White Knight dismounted and kneeled beside his mortally wounded assailant, whose visor had fallen back to reveal blond curls and a youthful face. He heard the words, whispered in anguish: "Is evil then triumphant?" And holding the dead knight in his arms he saw that beside the bright armour of the youth his own, besmirched by the long quest, looked black in the darkness of the forest.

His heart heavy with horror and grief, the White Knight who was white no more buried the boy, then slowly stripped off his own soiled mail, turned his grimy horse free to the forest, and stood naked and alone in the quiet dusk.

Before him lay a path which he slowly took, which led him to his castle on the edge of the forest. He went into the castle and closed the door behind him. He went to the mirror and saw that it no more gave back the White Knight, but only a middle-aged, naked man, a man who had stolen and ravished and killed in pursuit of evil.

Thereafter when he walked abroad from his castle he wore a coat of simple colours, a cheerful motley, and never looked for more than he could see. And his hair grew slowly white, as did his fine, full beard, and the people all around called him the Good White Knight.

You take it from here ...

Responding

1. Examine the Allegory   This fairy tale is an allegory—a story in which the characters and situations are more symbolic than real. Nicol tells us that the knight lives in a forest that is Life, that he is a White Knight and represents good, and that he has a calling to slay the Black Knight, who is evil. However, the story is more complicated than this. Write one or two paragraphs explaining how this is so, then share your response in a small group.

2. Look at Meaning   Work with a partner to examine more closely the struggle of good versus evil in Nicol's tale, and decide how this fairy tale answers the young knight's question, "Is evil then triumphant?"

3. Write and Discuss a Moral   If this fairy tale ended with the line, "And the moral of the story is ...," how would you fill in the blank? Discuss your response with a small group. Were any two responses alike? What does the possibility of different answers suggest about this tale?

4. Relate the Story to Our Society   What behaviour or beliefs of our own society is Nicol criticizing in this modern fairy tale? Discuss your ideas with the class.

Extending

5. Compare Characters   Think about the White Knight and another character, such as Alan in the previous selection, "The Chaser," whose actions are guided by some sort of personal quest. In a reflective essay, analyze each character's personality, motivations, and objective(s). Note what each character fails to understand, and examine any significant moral issues that arise, along with the consequences of their good intentions.

6. Make a Speech   Consider the following statement: "Sometimes good people have to do bad things." Develop this idea into a three-minute speech and present it to the class.

> **SELF-ASSESSMENT**
> - Did you strongly agree or disagree with the statement before you began to write your speech? Or did you have mixed feelings?
> - Did your position change or become more defined as you wrote?

Two Fishermen

"Somebody's got to do my job. There's got to be a hangman."

Short Story by Morley Callaghan

Notes

Morley Callaghan (1903–1990), born in Toronto, was Canada's first internationally recognized short-story writer. He began writing seriously in 1923 and produced 15 novels including *The Loved and the Lost* (1951), which won the Governor General's Award. He was nominated for the Nobel Prize and was made a Companion of the Order of Canada.

hangman: Canada had a hangman until the death penalty was abolished in 1976. (The last hangings occurred in 1962.)

The only reporter on the town paper, the *Examiner*, was Michael Foster, a tall, long-legged, eager young fellow, who wanted to go to the city some day and work on an important newspaper.

The morning he went into Bagley's Hotel, he wasn't at all sure of himself. He went over to the desk and whispered to the proprietor, Ted Bagley, "Did he come here, Mr. Bagley?"

Bagley said slowly, "Two men came here from this morning's train. They're registered." He put his spatulate forefinger on the open book and said, "Two men. One of them's a drummer. This one here, T. Woodley. I know because he was through this way last year and just a minute ago he walked across the road to Molson's hardware store. The other one—here's his name, K. Smith."

"Who's K. Smith?" Michael asked.

"I don't know. A mild, harmless-looking little guy."

"Did he look like the hangman, Mr. Bagley?"

"I couldn't say that, seeing as I never saw one. He was awfully polite and asked where he could get a boat so he could go fishing on the lake this evening, so I said likely down at Smollet's place by the power-house."

"Well, thanks. I guess if he was the hangman, he'd go over to the jail first," Michael said.

He went along the street, past the Baptist church to the old jail with the high brick fence around it. Two tall maple trees, with branches dropping low over the sidewalk, shaded one of the walls from the morning sunlight. Last night, behind those walls, three carpenters, working by lamplight, had nailed the timbers for the scaffold. In the morning, young Thomas Delaney, who had grown up in the town, was being hanged: he had killed old Mathew Rhinehart whom he had caught molesting his wife when she had been berry-picking in the hills behind the town. There had been a struggle and Thomas Delaney had taken a bad beating before he had killed Rhinehart. Last night a crowd had gathered on the sidewalk by the lamp-post, and while moths and smaller insects swarmed around the high blue carbon light, the crowd had thrown sticks and bottles and small stones at the out-of-town workmen in the jail yard. Billy Hilton, the town constable, had stood under the light with his head down, pretending not to notice anything. Thomas Delaney was only three years older than Michael Foster.

Michael went straight to the jail office, where Henry Steadman, the sheriff, a squat, heavy man, was sitting on the desk idly wetting his long moustaches with his tongue. "Hello, Michael, what do you want?" he asked.

"Hello, Mr. Steadman, the *Examiner* would like to know if the hangman arrived yet."

"Why ask me?"

"I thought he'd come here to test the gallows. Won't he?"

"My, you're a smart young fellow, Michael, thinking of that."

"Is he in there now, Mr. Steadman?"

"Don't ask me. I'm saying nothing. Say, Michael, do you think there's going to be trouble? You ought to know. Does anybody seem sore at me? I can't do nothing. You can see that."

"I don't think anybody blames you, Mr. Steadman. Look here, can't I see the hangman? Is his name K. Smith?"

"What does it matter to you, Michael? Be a sport, go on away and don't bother us anymore."

"All right, Mr. Steadman," Michael said very competently, "just leave it to me."

Early that evening, when the sun was setting, Michael Foster walked south of town on the dusty road leading to the power-house and Smollet's fishing pier. He knew that if Mr. K. Smith wanted to get a boat he would go down to the pier. Fine powdered road dust whitened Michael's shoes. Ahead of him he saw the power-plant, square and low, and the smooth lake water. Behind him the sun was hanging over the blue hills beyond the town and shining brilliantly on square patches of farm land. The air around the power-house smelt of steam.

Out on the jutting, tumbledown pier of rock and logs, Michael saw a little fellow without a hat, sitting down with his knees hunched up to his chin, a very small man with little grey baby curls on the back of his neck, who stared steadily far out over the water. In his hand he was holding a stick with a heavy fishing-line twined around it and a gleaming copper spoon bait, the hooks brightened with bits of feathers such as they used in the neighbourhood when trolling for lake trout. Apprehensively Michael walked out over the rocks toward the stranger and called, "Were you thinking of going fishing, mister?" Standing up, the man smiled. He had a large head, tapering down to a small chin, a birdlike neck and a very wistful smile. Puckering his mouth up, he said shyly to Michael, "Did you intend to go fishing?"

"That's what I came down here for. I was going to get a boat back at the boat-house there. How would you like if we went together?"

"I'd like it first rate," the shy little man said eagerly. "We could take turns rowing. Does that appeal to you?"

"Fine. Fine. You wait here and I'll go back to Smollet's place and ask for a row-boat and I'll row around here and get you."

"Thanks. Thanks very much," the mild little man said as he began to untie his line. He seemed very enthusiastic.

When Michael brought the boat around to the end of the old pier and invited the stranger to make himself comfortable so he could handle the line, the stranger protested comically that he ought to be allowed to row.

Pulling strong at the oars, Michael was soon out in the deep water and the little man was letting his line out slowly. In one furtive glance, he had noticed that the man's hair, grey at the temples, was inclined to curl to his ears. The line was out full length. It was twisted around the little man's forefinger, which he let drag in the water. And then Michael looked full at him and smiled because he thought he seemed so meek and quizzical. "He's a nice little guy," Michael assured himself and he said, "I work on the town paper, the *Examiner*."

"Is it a good paper? Do you like the work?"

"Yes, but it's nothing like a first-class city paper and I don't expect to be working on it long. I want to get a reporter's job on a city paper. My name's Michael Foster."

"Mine's Smith. Just call me Smitty."

"I was wondering if you'd been over to the jail yet."

Up to this time the little man had been smiling with the charming ease of a small boy who finds himself free, but now he became furtive and disappointed. Hesitating, he said, "Yes, I was over there first thing this morning."

"Oh, I just knew you'd go there," Michael said. They were a bit afraid of each other. By this time they were far out on the water which had a mill-pond smoothness. The town seemed to get smaller, with white houses in rows and streets forming geometric patterns, just as the blue hills behind the town seemed to get larger at sundown.

Finally Michael said, "Do you know this Thomas Delaney that's dying in the morning?" He knew his voice was slow and resentful.

"No, I don't know anything about him. I never read about them."

"Aren't there any fish at all in this old lake? I'd like to catch some fish," he said rapidly. "I told my wife I'd bring her home some fish." Glancing at Michael, he was appealing, without speaking, that they should do nothing to spoil an evening's fishing.

The little man began to talk eagerly about fishing as he pulled out a small flask from his hip pocket. "Scotch," he said, chuckling with delight. "Here, take a swig," Michael drank from the flask and passed it back. Tilting his head back and saying, "Here's to you, Michael," the little man took a long pull at the flask. "The only time I take a drink," he said still chuckling, "is when I go on a fishing trip by myself. I usually go by myself," he added apologetically as if he wanted the young fellow to see how much he appreciated his company.

They had gone far out on the water but they had caught nothing. It began to get dark. "No fish tonight, I guess, Smitty," Michael said.

"It's a crying shame," Smitty said. "I looked forward to coming up here when I found out the place was on the lake. I wanted to get some fishing in. I promised my wife I'd bring her back some fish. She'd often like to go fishing with me, but of course, she can't because she can't travel around from place to place like I do. Whenever I get a call to go some place, I always look at the map to see if it's by a lake or on a river, then I take my lines and hooks along."

"If you took another job, you and your wife could probably go fishing together," Michael suggested.

"I don't know about that. We sometimes go fishing together anyway." He looked away, waiting for Michael to be repelled and insist that he ought to give up the job. And he wasn't ashamed as he looked down at the water, but he knew that Michael thought he ought to be ashamed. "Somebody's got to do my job. There's got to be a hangman," he said.

"I just meant that if it was such disagreeable work, Smitty."

The little man did not answer for a long time. Michael rowed steadily with sweeping, tireless strokes. Huddled at the end of the boat, Smitty suddenly looked up with a kind of melancholy hopelessness and said mildly, "The job hasn't been so disagreeable."

"Good God, man, you don't mean you like it?"

"Oh, no," he said, to be obliging, as if he knew what Michael expected him to say. "I mean you get used to it, that's all." But he looked down again at the water, knowing he ought to be ashamed of himself.

"Have you got any children?"

"I sure have. Five. The oldest boy is fourteen. It's funny, but they're all a lot bigger and taller than I am. Isn't that funny?"

They started a conversation about fishing rivers that ran into the lake farther north. They felt friendly again. The little man, who had an extraordinary gift for storytelling, made many quaint faces, puckered up his lips, screwed up his eyes and moved around restlessly as if he wanted to get up in the boat and stride around for the sake of more expression. Again he brought out the whiskey flask and Michael stopped rowing. Grinning, they toasted each other and said together, "Happy days." The boat remained motionless on the placid water. Far out, the sun's last rays gleamed on the waterline. And then it got dark and they could only see the town lights. It was time to turn around and pull for the shore. The little man tried to take the oars from Michael, who shook his head resolutely and insisted that he would prefer to have his friend catch a fish on the way back to the shore.

"It's too late now, and we may have scared all the fish away," Smitty laughed happily. "But we're having a grand time, aren't we?"

When they reached the old pier by the power-house, it was full night and they hadn't caught a single fish. As the boat bumped against the rocks Michael said, "You can get out here. I'll take the boat around to Smollet's."

"Won't you be coming my way?"

"Not just now. I'll probably talk with Smollet a while."

The little man got out of the boat and stood on the pier looking down at Michael. "I was thinking dawn would be the best time to catch some fish," he said. "At about five o'clock. I'll have an hour and a half to spare anyway. How would you like that?" He was speaking with so much eagerness that Michael found himself saying, "I could try. But if I'm not here at dawn, you go on without me."

"All right. I'll walk back to the hotel now."

"Good night, Smitty."

"Good night, Michael. We had a fine neighbourly time, didn't we?"

As Michael rowed the boat around to the boat-house, he hoped that Smitty wouldn't realize he didn't want to be seen walking back to town with him. And later, when he was going slowly along the dusty road in the dark and hearing all the crickets chirping in the ditches, he couldn't figure out why he felt so ashamed of himself.

At seven o'clock next morning Thomas Delaney was hanged in the town jail yard. There was hardly a breeze on that leaden grey morning and there were no small white-caps out over the lake. It would have been a fine morning for fishing. Michael went down to the jail, for he thought it his duty as a newspaperman to have all the facts, but he was afraid he might get sick. He hardly spoke to all the men and women who were crowded under the maple trees by the jail wall. Everybody he knew was staring at the wall and muttering angrily. Two of Thomas Delaney's brothers, big, strapping fellows with bearded faces, were there on the sidewalk. Three automobiles were at the front of the jail.

Michael, the town newspaperman, was admitted into the courtyard by old Willie Mathews, one of the guards, who said that two newspapermen from the city were at the gallows on the other side of the building. "I guess you can go around there, too, if you want to," Mathews said, as he sat down slowly on the step. White-faced, and afraid, Michael sat down on the step with Mathews and they waited and said nothing.

At last the old fellow said, "Those people outside there are pretty sore, ain't they?"

"They're pretty sullen, all right. I saw two of Delaney's brothers there."

"I wish they'd go," Mathews said. "I don't want to see anything. I didn't even look at Delaney. I don't want to hear anything. I'm sick." He put his head back against the wall and closed his eyes.

The old fellow and Michael sat close together till a small procession came around the corner from the other side of the yard. First came Mr. Steadman, the sheriff, with his head down as though he were crying, then Dr. Parker, the physician, then two hard-looking young newspapermen from the city, walking with their hats on the backs of their heads, and behind them came the little hangman, erect, stepping out with military precision and carrying himself with a strange cocky dignity. He was dressed in a long black cut-away coat with grey striped trousers, a gates-ajar collar and a narrow red tie, as if he alone felt the formal importance of the occasion. He walked with brusque precision till he saw Michael, who was standing up, staring at him with his mouth open.

The little hangman grinned and as soon as the procession reached the doorstep, he shook hands with Michael. They were all looking at Michael. As though his work were over now, the hangman said eagerly to Michael, "I thought I'd see you here. You didn't get down to the pier at dawn?"

"No. I couldn't make it."

"That was tough, Michael. I looked for you," he said. "But never mind. I've got something for you." As they all went into the jail, Dr. Parker glanced angrily at Michael, then turned his back on him. In the office, where the doctor prepared to sign a certificate, Smitty was bending down over his fishing-basket which was in the corner. Then he pulled out two good-sized salmon-bellied trout, folded in a newspaper, and said, "I was saving these for you, Michael. I got four in an hour's fishing." Then he said, "I'll talk about that later, if you'll wait. We'll be busy here, and I've got to change my clothes."

Michael went out to the street with Dr. Parker and the two city newspapermen. Under his arm he was carrying the fish, folded in the newspaper. Outside, at the jail door, Michael thought that the doctor and the two newspapermen were standing a little apart from him. Then the small crowd, with their clothes all dust-soiled from the road, surged forward, and the doctor said to them, "You might as well go home, boys. It's all over."

"Where's old Steadman?" somebody demanded.

"We'll wait for the hangman," somebody else shouted.

The doctor walked away by himself. For a while Michael stood beside the two city newspapermen, and tried to look as nonchalant as they were looking, but he lost confidence in them when he smelled whiskey. They only talked to each other. Then they mingled with the crowd, and Michael stood alone. At last he could stand there no longer looking at all those people he knew so well, so he, too, moved out and joined the crowd.

When the sheriff came out with the hangman and two of the guards, they got half-way down to one of the automobiles before someone threw an old boot. Steadman ducked into one of the cars, as the boot hit him on the shoulder, and the two guards followed him. The hangman, dismayed, stood alone on the sidewalk. Those in the car must have thought at first that the hangman was with them for the car suddenly shot forward, leaving him alone on the sidewalk. The crowd threw small rocks and sticks, hooting at him as the automobile backed up slowly towards him. One small stone hit him on the head. Blood trickled from the side of his head as he looked around helplessly at all the angry people. He had the same expression on his face, Michael thought, as he had had last night when he had seemed ashamed and had looked down steadily at the water. Only now, he looked around wildly, looking for someone to help him as the crowd kept pelting him. Farther and farther Michael backed into the crowd and all the time he felt dreadfully ashamed as though he were betraying Smitty, who last night had had such a good neighbourly time with him. "It's different now, it's different," he kept thinking, as he held the fish in the newspaper tight under his arm. Smitty started to run toward the automobile, but James Mortimer, a big fisherman, shot out his foot and tripped him and sent him sprawling on his face.

Mortimer, the big fisherman, looking for something to throw, said to Michael, "Sock him, sock him."

Michael shook his head and felt sick.

"What's the matter with you, Michael?"

"Nothing. I got nothing against him."

The big fisherman started pounding his fists up and down in the air. "He just doesn't mean anything to me at all," Michael said quickly. The fisherman, bending down, kicked a small rock loose from the road bed and heaved it at the hangman. Then he said, "What are you holding there, Michael, what's under your arm? Fish. Pitch them at him. Here, give them to me." Still in a fury, he snatched the fish, and threw them one at a time at the little man just as he was getting up from the road. The fish fell in the thick dust in front of him, sending up a little cloud. Smitty seemed to stare at the fish with his mouth hanging open, then he didn't even look at the crowd. That expression on Smitty's face as he saw the fish on the road made Michael hot with shame and he tried to get out of the crowd.

Smitty had his hands over his head, to shield his face as the crowd pelted him, yelling "Sock the little rat. Throw the runt in the lake." The sheriff pulled him into the automobile. The car shot forward in a cloud of dust.

You take it from here ...

Responding

1. Understand the Story   Working with a partner, list the instances of betrayal that occur in the story. Identify which of these you think is the central one.

2. Look at Characters' Beliefs and Choices   Create a three-column chart, listing the main characters in the first column. In the second column, write down what that character believes in, supporting your ideas with evidence from the story. In the third column, indicate how the character upholds or walks away from that belief.

3. Compare Characters   Review the story and extract as many details as you can about the physical appearance and personality of Michael and K. Smith (Smitty). Use adjectives and descriptive phrases (e.g., "eager," "a little fellow without a hat") and events from the story to create a character sketch for each one. Then, in a paragraph, describe how the two characters are similar.

4. Examine the End of the Story   Working with a partner, explain why the mob turns against Smitty at the end of the story. What is Michael's decision regarding the mob's behaviour? What is the irony of this situation?

5. Discuss Heroes   As a class, discuss what makes a character heroic. Is there a hero in this story? If so, who is it? Defend your answer. If you feel there is no hero, explain why.

Extending

6. Discuss Difficult Jobs   With a partner, brainstorm a list of jobs that can be emotionally difficult to perform. Then, individually, select two jobs to consider further. For each one, write a brief description of the responsibilities involved, and suggest some examples of the emotional challenges the job might present. Consider the personal qualities people working in these areas might need to succeed in their work.

7. Present an Editorial Speech   Imagine you are the news editor for a national television network. There has been extensive news coverage of the hanging and related events in the town where "Two Fishermen" is set. Tonight on the evening news you are giving a three-minute editorial commenting on the dramatic events and the issues behind them. Write your thought-provoking and analytical editorial statement, and read it to the class as you would if you were on-air.

What do you do?

A Matter of Ethics

by Douglas Todd

SELF-EVALUATION

Notes

Douglas Todd is the religion and ethics columnist for the *Vancouver Sun*.

One of comedian Steve Martin's favourite university courses was philosophy.

He never remembered the details of fact-based courses like geography. But he says people remember just enough about philosophy "to screw you up for the rest of your life."

For example, all Martin recalls from ethics class was the question: "Is it OK to yell 'Movie!' in a crowded firehouse?"

I can't promise as entertaining an ethics primer as Martin, but maybe this 10-question ethics quiz can be a touch more illuminating.

I've asked a few real philosophers to help cook up a variety of ethical challenges. They're drawn from everyday life, about living and classic scholarly debates. A few of the questions are highly controversial. Others are hypothetical, without clear answers. Still, they force us to confront crucial moral issues.

Start by reading the 10 questions. If you can, discuss them with friends and relatives. Then look at the philosophers' answers and comments below.

Don't cheat by peeking at the answers before you've thought out your moral position. That would be unethical.

Well, not really.

Enjoy yourself.

THE QUESTIONS

1) You and nine others are taken prisoner by an extremist political group. The group says it will set nine prisoners free, including you, if you agree to execute one prisoner. If you don't do as the extremists ask, all of you will be killed. What do you do?

2) The staff at your office take up a collection for the food bank, and you are going to drop it off. A fellow employee who has

recently fallen on very hard times asks you if she could have the money. Do you quietly let her have the cash?

3) You have mixed emotions about panhandlers. Sometimes you feel harassed by them on the street, other times you feel sorry for them. Should you give to these beggars?

4) During the Second World War, a young Frenchman had an ailing mother who was completely dependent upon him. The young man, however, wanted to join the French Resistance to fight the Nazis. What was more important for him?

5) A friend buys a computer program and offers you a free copy. Do you use it?

6) Your family travels to another province to visit relatives and your child misses two days of school. Your child's teacher is a stickler for attendance, and you have to write a letter about the missed days. You fear the teacher will hold it against your child if he finds out she missed time for a trivial reason. Do you write a note saying the child was sick?

7) A famous violinist succumbs to a deadly disease. The only way he can survive is if his organs are permanently attached to your organs (say, your kidneys) for the rest of your life. Are you obliged to hook up?

8) You sit on a board and a confidential matter arises. You are uncertain about what to do and want advice from outside the board. Should you turn to your spouse, with whom you confide most matters?

9) An employee of a charity has stolen some money, but was caught. The money was repaid, the employee left, and security measures were tightened. The press, however, is sniffing around. As an officer of the charity, do you cover up the theft to prevent the public losing confidence in a good cause?

10) CD players are on sale and you want one. But a friend says you should donate the money to a Third-World aid program and save the lives of starving people. What do you do?

THE ANSWERS

1) While justice-loving people would never sacrifice an innocent person's life to save their own hide, UBC philosopher Paul Russell says this well-known case isn't that easy. Russell leans toward the utilitarian idea that the consequences of actions matter—it makes a difference how many people would live as a result of one dying. However, Russell says one of the important things to learn from this horrendous scenario is that certain ethical choices should never be easy, but require struggle over one's principles.

2) Since the money was donated to the food bank, not the employee, Langara College philosophy instructor Dale Beyerstein says it shouldn't go to the colleague who is down on her luck. If the colleague doesn't want a special office collection taken for her, she'll have to go to the food bank herself.

3) Panhandling is a toughie. Every major religion extols the virtue of charity. But the

western work-ethic condemns pennilessness as a lack of industry, says UBC ethicist Louis Marinoff. We all have a perfect right not to give to panhandlers. But Marinoff suggests there is a "philosophical economy" to begging. When you give to a beggar, you are alleviating raw human need. Since the number of panhandlers on Canadian streets is not as high as it is in New York or Mexico City, Marinoff suggests it might be wise to give to a Canadian panhandler to help avoid our society deteriorating to disastrous levels.

4) The famous existentialist philosopher Jean-Paul Sartre posed this question, says Russell. Sartre thought the Frenchman's dilemma about whether to serve his mother or the Resistance illustrated how there is no such thing as objective truth, that all moral decisions are relative. But Russell thinks the man's problem mainly shows why some ethical conundrums are conundrums; they mark the point where two important values come into conflict. Sartre's dutiful son would have to make his decision, Russell says, after carefully looking at the particulars of his situation—weighing his relative usefulness to the Resistance against what he could arrange for his mom.

5) A lot of people do it these days, but Beyerstein says pirating software is not only unethical but illegal. It deprives a software company of its right to a profit. It has the same moral status as photocopying large parts of a book rather than buying your own copy, says Beyerstein. However, if the software is no longer available, he says, the moral situation changes. And, though it's not strictly legal, Beyerstein believes there is nothing wrong with borrowing a program to try it out. If you end up wanting the software, however, you should buy it.

6) The main purpose of a note to the teacher is to satisfy authorities you were aware of your child's absence, says Beyerstein. You would do this by writing a simple note saying: "Mary was away from school Monday and Tuesday. Yours truly, etc." Why lie, she says, when you don't need to?

7) This provocative question connects to the abortion controversy. U.S. philosopher Judith Jarvis Thomson uses this hypothetical case to suggest society doesn't have the right to force mothers to bring fetuses to term (or to force someone to donate bone-marrow). Although Russell believes the analogy has some value, he believes it doesn't take seriously how our responsibilities to one another change depending on the relative intimacy of our relationships.

8) Maintaining confidentiality depends on circumstances, says Beyerstein. If a group's commitment to confidentiality is aimed at preserving the privacy of individuals, you should respect the right to privacy. However, if confidentiality is designed simply to preserve the board's bargaining position (perhaps over how much it's willing to pay to buy a piece of property), Beyerstein says you would not be violating the board's trust if you talked to your spouse and asked him to keep the matter confidential.

9) The public has a right to know how charitable funds are handled, says Beyerstein. You should consult with officers of the charity before giving an interview to the press. But when you do, it's appropriate to emphasize how the theft problem is under control and there was no loss to the charity.

10) Say goodbye to the CD player, writes well-known U.S. philosopher Peter Singer in *Famine, Affluence and Morality*. Singer says

we're all morally required to give up trivial things to provide major advantages for someone else. Our obligation to those in dire need is too strong to leave to the whims of charity, says Singer. Russell, however, says the trick is figuring where to draw the line on our obligation to those who are suffering. We create new problems, Russell says, if we give away so much we no longer feel we have much of a life to live.

You take it from here ...

Responding

1. Discuss the Questions and Answers As a class or in a large group, go through the questions and the answers one at a time. Share your own responses to each issue. Do you agree with your classmates' answers? Do you agree with the philosophers' answers? As the discussion progresses, make notes on changes you would make to any of your original answers.

2. Think about Group Values and Beliefs Which one of the moral issues created the most discussion in Activity 1? As a class, discuss why you think this particular issue raised the most controversy. What does this suggest about your group's interests, values, and beliefs?

> **TIP**
>
> • In case you don't disagree with *any* of the philosophers' answers, choose one and take an opposing stance anyhow, just for the sake of examining a different perspective.

3. Support Your Opinion Choose one of the philosophers' answers with which you disagree, and write a two-paragraph response. In the first paragraph, explain why you disagree, and in the second, write the answer that you would substitute, giving reasons to back up your opinion.

Extending

4. Present Another Ethical Dilemma
   a) Discuss one of the following dilemmas with a small group: how would you respond to these situations?
      • You really need to go into the mall just for a minute, and the only parking space available is reserved for those with disability permits. You happen to be driving a relative's car, which has such a permit in the window. Would you take the space? What if you have a sprained ankle? Think of some other "What if" possibilities that might make you reconsider.
      • Someone in your family needs a certain medicine in order to live. You can't afford to buy it, and there is no other legal way to obtain it immediately. Should you steal it to save his or her life?

b) Imagine a new ethical dilemma that could be added to the self-evaluation. Present your ethical dilemma to the group, then lead the discussion of various responses.

5. Find Other Questionnaires   Working in small groups, find other questionnaires that have been developed to help clarify values or beliefs. Choose one or two that are suitable for class participation and discussion. Distribute them to the class to be completed and returned to your group. For each one you complete, attach a brief evaluation of the questionnaire itself. In your evaluations, consider the following criteria:

- Is it serious or just for fun?
- Is it thought-provoking?
- Are the results it offers insightful?

Finally, gather up the questionnaires your group distributed and, as a group, compile the results and evaluations into a report. Share the results with the class.

"For the first few moments I sat stunned."

Death Watch

by THOMAS FIELDS-MEYER

PROFILE

Notes

Thomas Fields-Meyer is an associate editor of *People* magazine.

It was the fall of 1983, just weeks after the Soviet Union had shot down Korean Air Flight 007, killing all 269 aboard, and Cold War tensions were running high. Stanislav Petrov, then 44 and a Soviet army lieutenant colonel, was in his 10th year as commander of a team monitoring surveillance satellites. Just after midnight on Sept. 24, as Petrov sipped tea 55 miles from Moscow in a bunker at a secret military installation called Serpukhov-15, a warning panel flashed a message: MISSILE ATTACK.

Thus began the hour in which a military pilot's son from the Ukraine saved the world from a nuclear holocaust. Petrov, now 59, retired and living modestly outside Moscow with his unemployed son, kept silent about the incident for years. Only in the past six months have his actions become widely known in the West. "I don't feel I did anything heroic," Petrov says. "I did my duty defending the motherland. That was my job."

No sooner had the missile warning appeared than a siren blared and his computer displayed the word START, signalling that an intercontinental missile from a U.S. base was headed toward the Soviet Union. "For the first few moments I sat stunned," says Petrov, whose role was to evaluate the situation and alert his superiors. "In theory I knew what to do, but I just couldn't think what order I should do it in."

The stakes could not have been higher. Launching a counterattack would surely have led to a devastating nuclear exchange between the superpowers, wiping out millions of people. "I had to use my knowledge and keep a clear head," he says. "But I tell you this: My little hands were trembling! I'm only human."

Listening to reports from his staff over an intercom with one ear and a telephone with the other, he noticed something amiss: Though the computer receiving signals from satellites was warning of a missile, ground-based radar installations were showing no sign of attack. In less than three minutes, he concluded it was a false alarm. "It was partly a gut feeling that no one could really want to start another world war," he says, "and also that they wouldn't start it with a single missile." Then, horrifyingly, the siren sounded anew, and he received alerts of four more missile launches. But Petrov held off from confirming an attack, fearing that to do so would trigger a counterattack. "That would be the end—too terrible to imagine," he says. "I didn't want to be responsible for that."

Finally, noting that almost all the equipment showed no sign of trouble, he concluded that the alarm was false. He phoned a top military chief but found him very drunk. "To put it bluntly," says Petrov, "he obviously didn't take in a word of what I was saying." Within four hours, a military investigative team arrived from Moscow, sealing off the facility and interrogating the staff for three straight days. The investigation found that sunlight reflecting off clouds had thrown off the detection system, but his superiors, embarrassed, never publicly recognized Petrov's critical act of restraint.

Suffering from stress, he left the army a year later, ending a military career of 27 years. As a boy, in Kotovsk, near Odessa, he had longed to become a military pilot like his father. But his mother persuaded him to study radio technology instead, and he joined the army at 18. While posted in the distant Russian Far East province of Kamchatka, he met his wife, Raisa, a cinema projectionist. He joined a satellite-monitoring team in 1972.

"There was no time to think, 'My God, is this the start of a nuclear war? Will I ever see my wife again?'" says Petrov (at home in Fryazina).

After his military service he moved his family (including daughter Yelena, now 32, and son Dmitri, 29) to Fryazina, outside Moscow, where he worked for a satellite-system maker. (Raisa died of a brain disease in 1997.) Though recent publicity about the incident—which U.S. nuclear-security experts confirm very likely happened as he says—has brought fan letters from around the globe, Petrov, now living in relative anonymity in a run-down three-room apartment, shuns the attention. "Well, look at me," he says. "Do I look like a hero?"

You take it from here ...

Responding

1. Discuss Title As a class, consider the title. Did it entice you to read further? Was the story what you thought it would be, based on the title? Explain.

2. **Examine Petrov's Decision and Its Results**   With a partner, review the profile and respond to the following questions:

   - What decision did Petrov make?
   - How much time did he have to think about it?
   - What support did he have?
   - What consequences might he—and his country—have faced if he had been mistaken and there really had been missiles headed his way?
   - What consequences did his decision prevent?
   - Why wasn't Petrov immediately honoured for what he did?

3. **Assess Values**   Make a chart in which you list values you believe Petrov holds, and give evidence to support each one. Share your chart with another student. Discuss how the values you identified contributed to Petrov's "heroic" status among the people who wrote to him after hearing his story.

TIP

- To gain a deeper appreciation of Petrov and his courage, search the Internet or library and read some additional articles about him.

Extending

4. **Write a Letter of Nomination**   Write a persuasive and detailed letter to a national awards committee in which you nominate Stanislav Petrov for an international unsung-hero award.

5. **Write a Scene**   Working in a small group, write a scene for a play based on the life of Stanislav Petrov. You can show the events described in the profile itself, or you might choose to focus on an earlier or later event (real or imagined) in Petrov's life. Perform a reading of your scene for another group or for the class, and invite their comments.

There are no monuments to these people, no moving ceremonies of remembrance.

Lest We Forget Our Capacity to Kill

by STEPHEN HUME

NEWSPAPER COLUMN

Notes

Stephen Hume (1947–) is an award-winning author and journalist, and is currently a senior writer and columnist at the *Vancouver Sun*. From 1981 to 1989 he was editor-in-chief and general manager of the *Edmonton Journal*. In addition to his journalism work, he is the author of several books of poetry, essays, and natural history.

cenotaph: a war memorial. The word stems from the Greek words for "empty tomb," a monument to those who have died and are buried elsewhere.

This time next week [on Remembrance Day] we will be preparing to remember the 114 000 men and women who were killed in the service of their country.

More than 77 000 of them lie scattered in European graves, far from their native Canadian soil. Another 20 000 have no known graves and leave us only lists of names on cenotaphs and the parchment pages of memorial books. Still others lie in Asia, Africa, the Middle East.

A million young men and women between the ages of 18 and 45 served in Canada's armed forces nearly 50 years ago. More than 96 000 of them became casualties.

The enormity of this loss is difficult to imagine. Try to think of the entire present strength of Canada's armed forces. Every private, sergeant, major, general—they would not be enough to fill the graves already filled.

We would need two more armies of similar size to fill the hospital beds with the wounded who survived.

So next weekend we will sweep the early winter snow away from the war memorials, go out into the cold and pay tribute with our wreaths.

The guns will fire their salute and the strains of "The Last Post" will hang on the air while we take a moment of silence to reflect upon the nature and magnitude of the personal sacrifices made on our behalf.

This symbolic affirmation of the substance of those sacrifices by both the living and the dead is only right and proper.

Yet this week, perhaps we should also take a moment to remember the other sacrifice—the millions and millions of innocent bystanders, the grandfathers, the nursing mothers, the little children, the shopkeepers, the peasants, who died as the soldiers died.

The vast majority of these people were not soldiers, they were simply victims.

There are no monuments to these people, no moving ceremonies of remembrance.

Some of them were the "enemy," if you can call a baby too young to crawl an enemy. Some of them were "allies." A lot of them just got in the way.

It's worth remembering these people because the Great War, the war in which almost 200 000 Canadians shed their blood, was considered the war to end war.

Instead it proved only the grisly foreshadowing of the carnage to come.

Since then the toll of war dead has mounted to proportions undreamed of by our grandfathers.

The state wedding of science to warfare, the industrial mechanization of slaughter—this is the terrible legacy from which too many of us avert our eyes for too much of the year.

Since the war to end war, perhaps 150 million human beings have been slain, 10 million of them civilians killed in the years of "peace" since 1960.

It is worth considering all these things when we set out next week to remember those who gave their lives to put an end to war, because the sad truth is that we who go on living have largely made a mockery of those sacrifices.

I do not question the importance of paying sincere tribute to those who laid down their lives on our behalf, but it is indeed an irony to remember them in the context of a world in which the accepted military strategy of defence has become the eradication not of armies, but of whole societies.

Some of us glimpsed the future even in the act of making that sacrifice. Donald Pearce, writing in the journals quoted in Heather Robertson's remarkable anthology *A Terrible Beauty*, had this to say:

"Once I used to get quite a thrill out of seeing a city destroyed and left an ash-heap from end to end. It gave me a vicarious sense of power… But it is not that way any more. All I experience is revulsion every time a fresh city is taken on. I am no longer capable of thinking that the destruction of a city is a wonderful or even a difficult thing, though some seem to think it even a heroic thing.…

"It is all so abysmally foolish, so lunatic. It has not the dramatic elements of mere barbarism about it; it is straight scientific debauchery.

"A destroyed city is a terrible sight. How can anyone record it?—the million smashed things, the absolutely innumerable tiny tragedies, the crushed life works, the jagged homes, army tanks parked in living rooms—who could tell of these things I don't know; they are too numerous to mention, too awful in their meanings. Perhaps everyone should be required to spend a couple of hours examining a single smashed home … be required, in fact, to list the ruined contents of just one home; something would be served, a little sobriety perhaps honoured."

Having mastered the art of smashing cities and murdering millions, we now bring the destruction of continents and the slaughter of billions within the realm of probability.

This is what we should contemplate when we go next week to remember those whom we sent to lay down their lives in the name of peace.

You take it from here ...

Responding

1. Identify Main Points   The author writes about three different levels of remembrance we should contemplate on Remembrance Day. As a class, discuss each of these. Hume introduces a fourth idea at the end. Paraphrase this idea, and discuss whether you think he should have developed it more in this article, stating why or why not.

2. Express Your Opinion   Do you agree that "we have made a mockery" of the sacrifices of those whom we remember on Remembrance Day? Write a personal response in which you examine and extend this idea.

3. Respond to a Quotation   The quotation from Donald Pearce suggests that everyone should be required to examine a "smashed home." With two or three classmates, discuss what he means when he says, "something would be served, a little sobriety perhaps honoured."

Extending

4. Choose a Form   Recalling your discussion in Activity 3, think about the experience and meaning of spending "a couple of hours examining a single smashed home." Choose a form in which to present your own ideas about the impact of such an experience. You might, for example, write a moving poem, create a thought-provoking collage, design a museum display of selected personal effects, or write a stream-of-consciousness narrative on the process.

5. Connect to Recent Events   In a personal essay, relate the ideas expressed in "Lest We Forget" to the events surrounding the September 11, 2001, terrorist attack on the World Trade Center in New York City and the Pentagon in Washington. Include your thoughts on whether, and how, these recent events have affected your own views on Remembrance Day.

Suddenly the things we once took for granted are more precious.

Thankful Just to Be

by Rick McConnell

EDITORIAL

Notes

This editorial appeared on the Thanksgiving weekend following the September 11, 2001, terrorist attacks on the United States.

It feels different this year, more important, somehow.

This year, we will remember the dead as we celebrate the living, we will think about those who lost so much because we have been reminded, in the starkest and most frightening way, just how much there is to lose.

This year, we will be thankful simply to be alive.

It feels different this year because we are different, because we have been changed by what we saw, what we heard and read, what we know and wish we knew, what we no longer believe and what we wish we still believed.

When we light candles on the dinner table this time, will it be possible to not think of burning buildings, will it be possible to not think of a thousand tiny flames flickering in the darkness at vigils held all over the United States?

When we wrap the leftover turkey this time, will it be possible to not think of countless souls huddled in refugee camps near the Afghan border?

Once, long ago, in seemingly simpler times, Canadians held Thanksgiving Day and Armistice Day in the same week. Now, perhaps, we understand how fitting that was.

Things seem different this year because the safe and secure world we once took for granted no longer feels so safe, so secure.

Terrorist attacks in the United States have made us fearful, have made us question ourselves and our country's role in the world. That, in part, was the intention.

But the attacks should also remind us that our strength comes from the ties that bind us, as families, as communities, as a nation. Those ties have not been broken. They will, in fact, be stronger now.

Look up from the page and think of all the people who read only what their governments allow, who have nothing to read, who can't read and have no one to teach them how.

Turn on the tap and be thankful water, hot or cold, comes out. Flick that switch and see the lights shine. Listen for the clock and whir of the furnace coming on. Remember, there are places where such things would seem incredible.

Open a kitchen cupboard, see all the cans and boxes, some you can't remember buying. Remember, there are people who have no money for food, or for the cupboards.

Look at the telephone and think of the husbands and wives, sons and daughters, who made final phone calls from doomed airliners that day. Think of the frantic New Yorkers calling and calling, hoping to hear voices they will never hear again. Think of people who have no telephones, no one to call if they did.

Go outside and smell autumn's sweet breath. Pick up a leaf and be thankful for what nature teaches us about promises to keep. In a place where green turns gold, where new becomes old, we are accustomed to the cycles of life. Some people live in a world that is always brown, where promises are seldom made or kept.

Walk along the street and read the names on campaign signs, study the faces of people willing, eager, to represent you on city council, on the school board. Be thankful you get to choose. Remember, this marvellous machine we call democracy is a relatively recent invention.

Walk by a school and be thankful that we can squabble about what to teach our children and what to spend doing so and how much to pay our teachers. In Afghanistan, girls are forbidden to learn.

It's true we have children among us, small and frail, who go to school hungry. But there are places in the world where children rise with the sun and go, not to school but to work, hungry, places where children starve.

Watch the flag fluttering there. It flew at half-mast, for a while, and the once-bright red may have faded in the sun, but it still stands for freedom and peace, for tolerance. In some places, those things are in short supply.

Be thankful for past struggles and victories great and small, and remember that tyranny and terror are not new.

Walk by a hospital, think of the million-dollar machines, the doctors and nurses working there. We spend billions on health care and talk about our "crisis," hire ex-premiers to conduct two-year, cross-country check-ups. But there are places where people die by the thousands, for want of a few pennies worth of medicine.

Walk past the mall and think of the things you wanted to buy last month, had to buy last month, couldn't live without last month. What were they again? What are the things you really can't live without?

In this land of plenty we are graspers, by nature and by cultural imperative, constantly seeking bigger and better, fancier and faster, prettier, newer. How important this weekend to remember that a hand always reaching for more cannot embrace and protect the things it already holds.

We will, perhaps, slow down a little, now, for a day or two.

We will, perhaps, take time out to prepare traditional meals, talk to distant relatives, gather with family and friends.

We will, perhaps, consider the true meaning at the heart of this holiday, and in that way regain some small measure of control in a world largely beyond our control, a world at times seemingly out of control.

We will, perhaps, remember to be thankful. Just to be.

You take it from here ...

Responding

1. **Focus on Ideas** Choose two or three statements from the selection that you think express its most important ideas, and write your thoughts on each in a short paragraph.

2. **Find Juxtaposed Images** *Juxtaposition* is the placing of contrasting images side by side for dramatic effect. Find three examples in the selection where images or details are juxtaposed, and explain what ideas are emphasized by each set of contrasts. Present your answer in written or chart form.

3. **Look at Deeper Meaning** McConnell points out what we have to give thanks for, but he also criticizes our society. Make notes in point form or create a chart to identify and comment on his specific points of criticism. Then, discuss his points, along with your own views, with a small group of classmates.

4. **Consider Unity and Coherence** Examine how specific words and ideas in this editorial lead to and connect with the last two sentences. In a paragraph, explain what makes the ending of the editorial strong, in terms of both style and meaning.

Extending

5. **Examine Your Own Life** If, for a month, you bought only what you truly need, not the extras you merely want or think you need, what would you eliminate from your life? How would your life change? How would you change? Present your ideas in a class discussion.

6. **Create a Statement of Thanksgiving** Create your own statement of thanksgiving. It can be in the form of a personal essay, a poem, a song, a manifesto, a photo essay, or a collage. Be prepared to present it to the class.

"Why not die," I thought miserably, "and save everyone a lot of trouble."

Christopher Reeve's Decision

by CHRISTOPHER REEVE

AUTOBIOGRAPHY EXCERPT

Notes

Christopher Reeve is a popular American actor-director whose life was changed by a riding accident that resulted in a tragic spinal-cord injury. He is best known to millions of fans as the hero of the *Superman* movies. After his accident, he directed and starred in a successful remake/adaptation of Alfred Hitchcock's *Rear Window*. His autobiography is titled *Still Me*.

On Memorial Day weekend in May 1995, my world changed forever. I was competing in an equestrian event in Virginia when my horse, Buck, decided to put on the brakes just before the third jump.

When he stopped suddenly, momentum carried me over the top of his head. My hands were entangled in the bridle, and I couldn't get an arm free to break my fall. All six feet four inches and 215 pounds of me landed headfirst. Within seconds I was paralyzed from the neck down and fighting for air like a drowning person.

I woke up five days later in the intensive-care unit at the University of Virginia hospital in Charlottesville. Dr. John Jane, head of neurosurgery at the hospital, said I had broken the top two cervical vertebrae and that I was extremely lucky to have survived. He told my wife, Dana, and me that I might never be able to breathe on my own again. But my head was intact, and my brain stem—so close to the site of the injury—appeared unharmed.

Dr. Jane said my skull would have to be reconnected to my spinal column. He wasn't sure if the operation would be successful, or even if I could survive.

Suddenly it dawned on me that I was going to be a huge burden to everybody, that I had ruined my life and everybody else's. *Why not die,* I thought miserably, *and save everyone a lot of trouble?*

As family and friends visited, my spirits were on a roller-coaster ride. I would feel so grateful when someone came a long way to cheer me up. But the time would come when everybody had to leave, and I'd lie there and stare at the wall, stare at the future, stare in disbelief.

When I would finally fall asleep, I'd be whole again, making love to Dana, riding, or acting in a play. Then I'd wake up and realize that I could no longer do any of that; I was just taking up space.

One day Dana came into the room and stood beside me. I could not talk because of the ventilator. But as we made eye contact, I mouthed the words, "Maybe we should let me go."

Dana started crying. "I am only going to say this once," she said. "I will support whatever you want to do because this is your life and your decision. But I want you to know that I'll be with you for the long haul, no matter what."

Then she added the words that saved my life: "You're still you. And I love you."

I can't drift away from this, I began to realize. *I don't want to leave.*

DANA AND ME

A crisis like my accident doesn't change a marriage; it brings out what is truly there. It intensifies but does not transform it. Dana rescued me when I was lying in Virginia with a broken body, but that was really the second time. The first time was the night we met.

It was June 1987, and a long-term relationship of mine had ended. I was determined to be alone and focus on my work. Since childhood I had developed the belief that a few isolated moments of happiness were the best you could hope for in relationships. I didn't want to risk too much because I was certain that disappointment would follow.

Christopher Reeve and his wife, Dana, January 12, 1997

Then one night I went to a cabaret with friends, and Dana Morosini stepped onstage. She wore an off-the-shoulder dress and sang "The Music That Makes Me Dance." I went down hook, line, and sinker.

Afterwards I went backstage and introduced myself. At the time, I was an established film actor. You wouldn't think I'd have a problem with a simple conversation with a woman. But when I offered her a ride to the party we were all going to, she said, "No thanks, I have my own car." All I could say was "Oh." I dragged myself out to my old pickup truck, trying to plan my next move.

Later I tried again. We talked for a solid hour. I have no idea what we talked about. Everything seemed to evaporate around us. I thought to myself, *I don't want to make a mistake and ruin this.*

We started dating in a very old-fashioned way. I got to know Dana's parents, and we developed an easy rapport. And Dana was instantly comfortable with my two children, Matthew and Alexandra. It filled me with joy.

Dana and I were married in April 1992. Three years later came my accident and Dana's words in the hospital room: "You're still you."

I mouthed, "This goes way beyond the marriage vows—'in sickness and in health.'"

She said, "I know." I knew then and there that she was going to be with me forever. We had become a family.

LAUGHTER, CHEERS, AND HOPE

As the operation drew closer, I became more frightened, knowing I had only a fifty-fifty chance of surviving. I lay frozen much of the time, thinking dark thoughts.

My biggest fear had to do with breathing. I couldn't take a single breath on my own, and the ventilator connections didn't always hold. I would lie there at three in the morning in fear of a pop-off, when the hose just comes off the ventilator. After you've missed two breaths, an alarm sounds. You hope someone will come quickly. The feeling of helplessness was hard to take.

One very bleak day the door to my room flew open and in hurried a squat fellow in a surgical gown and glasses, speaking with a Russian accent. He announced he was my proctologist and had to examine me immediately.

My first thought was that they must be giving me way too many drugs. But it was my old friend, comedian Robin Williams. For the first time since the accident, I laughed.

My three-year-old, Will, also gave me hope. One day he was on the floor playing when he suddenly looked up and said, "Mommy, Daddy can't move his arms anymore."

"That's right," Dana said. "Daddy can't move his arms."

"And Daddy can't run around anymore," Will continued.

"That's right; he can't."

Then he paused, screwed up his face in concentration and burst out happily, "But he can still smile."

On June 5, I had my operation. It was a success. My doctor predicted that with time I ought to be able to get off the respirator and breathe on my own.

Three weeks later I moved to the Kessler Institute for Rehabilitation in West Orange, N.J. The worst days there were when Bill Carroll, the respiratory therapist, would test my vital capacity, a measure of how much air I could move on my own. I was failing miserably. To even consider weaning yourself off the ventilator, you need a vital capacity of about 750 cc, but I could hardly move the needle above zero.

Christopher Reeve as Superman, 1977

At about this time I had to decide if I would attend the annual fund-raising dinner of the Creative Coalition, an organization of people in the arts. The dinner was scheduled for October 16 at the Pierre Hotel in New York City. I felt obligated to go, especially because Robin Williams was to be honoured for his charitable work.

Still, I worried about making the trip into Manhattan. It would be the first time I would be in public since my accident in May. Would my muscles go into a spasm as they often did? Would I have a pop-off?

Dana and I talked it over and decided that the psychological advantages of going outweighed the physical risks. We dusted off my tuxedo, and on the afternoon of the 16th, I braced myself for the unknown.

For nearly five months I'd been cruising in a wheelchair at five kilometres an hour. Now I was strapped into the back of a van driving into the city at 90 kilometres an hour. As we hit bumps

Christopher Reeve's Decision **325**

and potholes, my neck froze with tension, and my body was racked with spasms. Once at the hotel, I was quickly transferred to a suite with a hospital bed to rest. The whole experience was more intense than I had anticipated.

At last it was time for me to present Robin with his award. For a split second I wished a genie could make me disappear. As I was pushed onto the stage, though, I looked out to see 700 people on their feet, cheering. The ovation went on for more than five minutes.

From that moment on, the evening was transformed into a celebration of friendship. Later, as we bounced through the Lincoln Tunnel back to New Jersey, I was so excited I hardly noticed the rough ride. Back at Kessler, Dana produced a bottle of chardonnay, and we toasted a milestone in my new life. I'd made it!

MOVING THE DIAL

I made up my mind—I wanted to breathe on my own again.

On November 2, Bill Carroll, two doctors and a physical therapist brought in the breathing equipment, took me off the ventilator and asked me to take ten breaths. Lying on my back, I was gasping, my eyes rolling up in my head. With each attempt I was able to draw in only an average of 50 cc. But at least I had moved the dial.

The next day I told myself over and over that I was going home soon, and imagined my chest as a huge bellows that I could open and close at will. I took the ten breaths, and my average was 450 cc. *Now we're getting somewhere*, I thought.

The following day my average was 560 cc. A cheer broke out. "I've never seen progress like that," Carroll said. "You're going to get off this thing."

After that I practised every day. I went from seven minutes off the ventilator to 12 minutes to 15. Just before I left Kessler, I gave it everything I had and breathed for 30 minutes on my own.

I'm happy that I decided to keep living, and so are those who are close to me. On Thanksgiving, 1995, I went home to spend the day with my family for the first time since the accident. When I saw our home again, I wept as Dana held me. At the dinner table each of us spoke a few words about what we were thankful for.

Will said simply, "Dad."

You take it from here ...

Responding

1. Write a Summary   After the moment that changed his life forever, Christopher Reeve made the choice of whether to die or to live. Write a summary explaining what helped him make his decision, and what has resulted from it.

2. Examine Choices   Talk with a partner and try to appreciate the magnitude of Dana's choice to support her husband no matter what. In your discussion, consider the ways in which the accident changed *her* life forever.

3. Write a Personal Response   Write a journal entry examining how this excerpt from Christopher Reeve's autobiography has affected the way you see your own life. Try to include quotations from the excerpt with your own reflections.

4. Consider Perspective   This piece is presented from a first-person perspective (using "I"). With a partner, discuss how it would be different if it had been told from a third-person perspective, as a biography instead of an autobiography. Would it be as effective? Explain.

Extending

5. Write an Article   One of Christopher Reeve's best-known movie roles was as the title character in *Superman*. Write an article in which you develop the idea that Christopher Reeve is more of a superman today than he was when he played the comic-book hero.

6. Research Medical Advances   Christopher Reeve's courageous decision to go on living has had benefits that extend far beyond his immediate family and social circle. His story has inspired millions, and he has become a powerful advocate for spinal-cord research. Search Internet and library sources for information on what Christopher Reeve has done for this cause. What advances have been made in this area? What remains to be done? Choose an aspect of this topic and develop it into a multimedia presentation to present to the class.

TIP

- The Christopher Reeve Paralysis Foundation Web site at www.paralysis.org/ is a good place to begin your investigation.

Reflecting on the Unit

Responding

1. Prepare and Present an Argument   Consider the following moral dilemma: Walking home from school, you see your friend smoking marijuana. He admits it has become a regular thing, but insists that it's not a problem. You have noticed a change in his behaviour and are becoming concerned. What do you do? Do you tell a teacher? Your parents? His parents? Do nothing at all? Something else (specify)? Choose a course of action and prepare a logical and persuasive argument and present it to a small group.

2. Reflect on a Quotation   At the beginning of this unit is a quotation by Emma Goldman: "What I believe is a process rather than a finality." As a class, discuss the meaning of the quotation. Then, recall something you used to believe, but have changed your mind about within the last few years, due to life experience. Share your recollections with a partner.

Extending

3. Create a Resource Manual   Imagine that you are working for a consulting firm that is preparing a self-help manual designed to assist people in making good decisions. Working in a small group, search library and Internet resources for relevant information (e.g., articles offering advice on making personal choices, books on developing decision-making skills, relevant Web sites, seminars). Compile the most useful information into a binder. Write an introduction explaining the purpose of the manual, and include a summary list of the top 10 tips for making good decisions and choices.

4. Write a Modern Fairy Tale   Read or review Eric Nicol's "The White Knight." Then, choose one of the ethical dilemmas presented in "A Matter of Ethics" and write an allegorical modern fairy tale modelled after Nicol's story.

> **SELF-ASSESSMENT**
>
> The main focus of this unit is on values, beliefs and choices. Identify
> - the most life-enhancing ideas
> - what you disagreed or struggled with
>
> Write your response as a journal entry.

Every individual has a place to
fill in the world, and is
important in some respect,
whether [s]he chooses to be so
or not.
— *Nathaniel Hawthorne*

The worth of a state, in the long
run, is the worth of the
individuals composing it.
— *John Stuart Mill*

The public and private worlds
are inseparably connected.
— *Virginia Woolf*

Individuals and Society

One of the most basic relationships is that between the individual and society. Each of us is part of a social network composed of family, friends, school, the workplace, and other groups.

American writer Nathaniel Hawthorne points out that each individual has a purpose and an important role to play, whether or not it is deliberately chosen.

The philosopher John Stuart Mill takes this idea further by saying that the well-being and character of a collection of individuals determine the quality of the larger group: the state.

English novelist Virginia Woolf reminds us that we need to interact with others in order to discover our own purpose.

As you read the selections in this unit, reflect on the following:

1) To what extent do we conform to external rules?

2) Why do young people often rebel against convention, rules, and "the system"?

3) What do "others" have to do with *me*? In what ways are we all alike?

4) How can one be an individual within the context of society?

Before you read, discuss with the class your attitude to black-and-white photographs. Can black-and-white be as good as colour?

As you read, jot down the first few elements or features of the photograph that catch your eye.

Drum Major

Photograph by Alfred Eisenstaedt

Notes

Alfred Eisenstaedt (1898–1995) is known as "the father of photojournalism." He was born in West Prussia (now part of Poland), and his family moved to Berlin when he was eight. After Hitler came to power, Eisenstaedt moved to New York and became one of the first *Life* magazine photographers. His gift for capturing the spontaneous moment brought him, and his photographs, international acclaim.

You take it from here ...

Responding

1. Propose a Different Title   This image has been titled "Drum Major." Write down another title that you think suits it equally well. As a class, create a list of all the proposed alternative titles. Then, sort the titles into categories according to the features of the photograph they emphasize. In how many different ways was this photograph interpreted? Were some titles (or similar titles) suggested by more than one student? If so, why do you think that might be? Which were the most creative interpretations? Explain.

2. Write a Diary Entry   Taking the point of view of either the drum major or one of the children, write a diary entry in which you describe the incident captured in this photograph.

3. Write an Argument   In your estimation, was this scene deliberately staged by the photographer, or was it a spontaneous moment that he just happened to capture on film? What evidence in the photograph leads you to your conclusion? Write down your response and then compare your views with those of two or three other students.

4. Discuss Theme   In a small group, discuss why you think this photograph was selected for this unit. How does it relate to the theme of individuals and society?

Extending

5. Create an Advertising Campaign   Imagine that this photograph has been selected as the foundation for an advertising campaign. Work with a small group to choose a product or service that could be effectively promoted with this image. Develop a suitable slogan for a print campaign. Then, write a voiceover script for a 30-second television commercial for the same product.

6. Select Appropriate Music   Still working with the group you formed in Activity 5, review your campaign and then select a short segment of music that suits the photograph and the product it represents. Present your entire advertising campaign to the class.

7. Learn about the Photographer and His Work   Do some library and Internet research to learn about Alfred Eisenstaedt's life and work. View several of his photographs, and choose one that you find especially moving or interesting. Present the photograph to the class, providing some background information on the subject, analyzing the composition of the image, and explaining why you selected it.

Before you read, discuss with your classmates how important it is to dress the "right" way.

As you read, decide whether the characters and situation are realistic.

Zits

Cartoon by Jerry Scott and Jim Borgman

Notes

Zits, the popular comic strip about the life and times of 15-year-old Jeremy Duncan, began in 1997 and runs in over 1000 newspapers worldwide. It has been voted the Best Comic Strip twice by the National Cartoonists Society.

Jerry Scott, writer and co-creator of *Zits,* began his career by taking over the *Nancy* strip. He then co-created *Baby Blues* (which is based on his experiences with his second daughter) before going on to do *Zits.*

Jim Borgman, Pulitzer Prize-winning cartoonist, was raised in blue-collar neighbourhoods of Cincinnati. He was hired by the *Cincinnati Enquirer* one week after graduation to start work cartooning.

Jim Borgman and Jerry Scott

You take it from here ...

Responding

1. Respond Personally   Share with the class your response to this cartoon. Does the situation seem familiar to you? Do you think dress is an area of contention between most parents and teens? Is there any truth to the point the cartoonist makes in the final frame? Explain.

2. Read the Text   With a partner, take turns reading the dialogue aloud. Examine the lettering carefully, and discuss how the boldface and different font sizes of selected words helped you interpret the character's tone of voice.

3. Explain the Point   Imagine that you have to explain this cartoon to someone who simply didn't understand the message. Write an explanation of what is going on and what the creators want to say. As you write, keep in mind the theme of this unit: "Individuals and Society."

4. Improvise a Conversation   Working with a partner, improvise a conversation Jeremy and one of his friends might have once they leave the house. They might begin by discussing how their parents fail to understand the social importance of dress.

Extending

5. Create a Cartoon   Choose another topic that causes conflict between parents and their children, and think of a message you would like to send about this issue. Then, create a cartoon that delivers the message in a humorous way, and share it with the class.

> **PEER ASSESSMENT**
>
> As you view each cartoon, consider the following:
> - Does it make a clear point?
> - Does it succeed in delivering the message with humour? Explain.

6. Write a Poem   Clothing is just one means of expressing individuality. As a class, brainstorm other ways in which we express our personalities. Then, write a poem about individuality based on one or several of the means of expression identified by the class.

7. Perform a Skit   With one or two other students, prepare and perform a skit that portrays another familiar adult-teenager scenario focusing on the generation gap or communication problems.

Still Me Inside

But as soon as I walked into the room, all attention was focused on my head.

Narrative Essay by Mai Goda

Notes

Mai Goda wrote this essay when she was in high school. She is now a college student (majoring in philosophy) and a flutist for a Latin band. Now that she has, in her words, "'settled down' from those rebellious times in high school," her hair is back to its original colour.

"I need a change!"

And so on that single whim, I cut my long black hair, streaked it bright red and, to top it off, pierced my eyebrow. I had gone from dorky to punky in a week, and as trivial as it seems, this transformation has had a great effect on my life.

As long as I can remember, I had always been a good girl. In school, I got decent grades and never was in trouble. At home, I tried not to give my parents too much grief. But more than that, I had the "look" of a good girl. People always saw me as a quiet, studious, Asian girl. Friends' parents often asked if I played the violin or the piano. "No, the flute," I'd say, and they would nod, not surprised. Walking around with my long black hair over my face, I hid behind my image. I felt somewhat obliged to appease the stereotype imposed on me.

Needless to say, heads turned the day I walked into school sporting a new, short, bright-red hairdo. I enjoyed the reaction and attention I received from my friends and teachers. I didn't listen to my friends' warnings about people seeing me differently, people who frowned on a "rebellious punkster." After all, I was still the same person inside, so why should this change matter? I soon found out how naive I was.

One day, I was late for school and needed a pass from my vice principal. I was met by a surprisingly stern look. Writing one, his voice and stare were cold and condescending. Mistaking me for one of those punk delinquents, he left me with a warning: "Don't make a habit of it." Had I come late to school a week before, he would have said nothing. I was not used to this discriminatory treatment, and I felt angry, embarrassed, and somewhat defeated. Now when I went to the mall,

suspicious eyes followed me—store clerks keeping a cautious watch—but the worst was yet to come.

It was the night of our music recital for advanced students. For weeks I had prepared my piece and was excited. The room was packed with parents waiting to hear their children. But as soon as I walked into the room, all attention was focused on my head. As I sat waiting my turn, I felt the critical eyes of parents.

I performed well, but felt awful. Afterwards, I still saw those disapproving looks as they walked out with their children. I even overheard a friend being lectured on how she shouldn't colour her hair or pierce her face, and not to become "a punk like Mai." I was ready to go home feeling angry when my friend's father stopped me.

"You were very good tonight. At first I didn't recognize you," he said, looking at my head.

"Oh, yes, I look very different from last time, don't I?"

"Well, you played even better than last year. Look forward to hearing you again."

I went home feeling good, as if I had finally won a battle. Now the stern look of the vice principal, the suspicious stares of the store clerks and the disapproving eyes of my friends' mothers didn't bother me. I was still the same person inside, punky or not. There was nothing wrong with me; it was the judgemental people who had the problem. I regained my confidence.

I still get looks and stares, but they don't upset me. In a way, I traded in one stereotype for another, but this time I enjoy proving them wrong. People are surprised to see me getting good grades and applying to good colleges. They're surprised to hear me play the flute so well. And they are absolutely shocked to see me standing in front of the football field, red hair shining in the sun, conducting the marching band!

As for my red hair, I re-dye it occasionally to keep it bright burning red. It seems to give me the power to fight against the stereotypes forced on me, and gives me the confidence that I never had before.

You take it from here ...

Responding

1. Write a Script   Imagine that you are Mai Goda's friend and that she has just announced to you that she is going to dye her hair red and pierce her eyebrow. Write the script of your telephone conversation with her.

2. Discuss Stereotypes   One question posed in the introduction to this unit is, "How can one be an individual within the context of society?" When Mai Goda expressed her individuality by transforming her appearance, how did "society"—in the form of the vice principal, the shopkeepers, her friends' parents—react? What might explain their reactions? What preconceived notions (stereotypes) did they hold about Goda based solely on her outward appearance, both before her transformation, and afterwards? To what extent do such stereotyped notions present obstacles to achieving true "individuality" in society? Discuss your views with the class.

Extending

3. Analyze Teen Culture   Teens have categorized themselves according to preferred styles for generations (e.g., hippies, jocks). Working in a small group, compose a list of current groups or trends and create a profile for each one, describing its distinguishing features and its general attitudes and beliefs. Select a band/artist that represents both the music and the dress of each group. Consider how members of each group tend to be seen and treated by those in other groups and by society at large. For example, are they generally accepted? Respected? Feared? Are these reactions usually justified? Explain.

4. Write a Creative Response   Compose a short narrative or poem in which the main character undergoes an astonishing external transformation, which, in turn, affects how he or she is seen, and treated, by others.

Before you read, discuss the various meanings and connotations of the word "pose."

As you read, consider whether you would like to have the young woman as a friend.

The Pose

"Hey, she's real."

Short Story by Anwer Khan

God knows what got into her head. She abruptly broke her stride and slipped into Shandar Cloth Store. Then she opened the door of the show window and, deftly, removing the lovely mannequin, stood herself in the plastic dummy's place and assumed its pose.

It was evening. The street was packed with people, but they were so preoccupied as they went their way that none of them noticed what she had just done.

Why did she do it? She probably didn't know that herself. True, she was something of a daredevil in her childhood. But now she was a grown young woman, a college student, smart, sophisticated, urbane. Even the most daring boys at the college got cold feet walking with her. What she'd just done, well, it just happened. It was entirely unpremeditated.

Standing in the show window she felt a strange sense of comfort wash upon her. She was now, after all, a part of this bustling marketplace. She could also look closely at the place, the whole of it, standing in just one spot, without having to move. Walking as one of the crowd or while shopping, she never felt herself a part of the life around her—the buoyant, strident life, full of vigour and excitement.

Her tense body gradually became unstrung, and an unprovoked smile came to her lips. She quite liked it—standing with one foot slightly forward, the hem of her sari going over her head and then dropping down to wrap itself around the joint of her right elbow. She looked positively ravishing. She could stand in her new posture forever, she thought, overcome by a sudden impulse, although her knees had already begun to ache from the pressure.

She was just considering easing up on her heels a little when her eyes caught sight of a peasant who suddenly cut through the crowd on the sidewalk and came over to the show window and began gawking at her with eyes at once full of lust and wonder. His eyes seemed to say: Incredible! These craftsmen can be so skilful! How they make statues that look like real people!

It was good the glass panel stood between them, otherwise the country bumpkin would certainly have ventured to touch her.

The peasant perhaps wanted to linger on for a while, but the scouring glances of the passersby forced him to move on. As soon as he had moved away, she relaxed her feet a little. Even shook them a bit. But now her lips began to feel dry. "Just a little while longer," she told her lips under her breath, "and then I'll take you to a restaurant and treat you to a glass of ice water, followed by a steaming cup of some finely brewed tea." Her thirst let up a bit and she slipped back into her former pose.

She certainly had no wish to exhibit herself like this to the pedestrians. Perhaps the thought had never even entered her mind. Rather, it pleased her to think that she was now a full participant in the teeming life around her. It was a strange feeling. She had never experienced it before.

"Oh God!"—the expression came from the lips of two college girls—"how lifelike!"

Their voices, travelling along the glass panels and filtering through the holes in the steel strips holding the frame, came upon her softly, as if from a great distance.

The two girls gawked at her with admiration as they exchanged a few words between themselves, while she looked at them with tenderness. She was happy. Incredibly happy. No one had looked at her so appreciatively before. At least not in her presence. Like a kind and caring queen receiving the adulation of her subjects, she sustained her regal pose until the girls had once again melted into the crowd and disappeared from view.

"Let's see who comes next," she thought to herself.

Her feet had again started to protest. This time around, though, she sent them a warning, a rather stern one: Scoundrels, stay put! Can't you wait even a little? She wouldn't care a hoot about their protest, she decided.

She was still congratulating herself on her firmness when she caught sight of a cop who had just separated from the crowd and after taking a pinch of chewing tobacco from a box he held was rubbing it with his thumb. The moment he saw her, his hand stopped dead, his mouth fell open, and his eyes widened. She stared at the cop sweetly. The cop's eyelashes began to flap frantically; he rubbed the tobacco hastily, and stuffing it between his lower lip and teeth, practically stuck his eyes against the glass of the show window.

She was overcome by a powerful urge to laugh, but managed to stop herself with the greatest difficulty. Suddenly her feet began to itch

uncontrollably. There was even a slight, involuntary tremble. But the cop thought it was a mere illusion, or the effect of the tobacco.

The cop stared at her for a long time. He would withdraw a little, then come back and inspect her closely. This went on for so long that she began to tire. Is the idiot going to leave the place at all?—she wondered. She was feeling uncomfortable. She knew she couldn't go on standing in that pose. All the same, she also knew that she was safe inside the show window. Where would she find such protection outside?

Thank God the cop finally decided to leave, and she drew a breath of relief, loosened her hands and feet, straightened up her tense back, indeed even massaged it a bit. Night was approaching and the crowd had thinned down to a few swift-footed pedestrians.

Soon it will grow dark, she thought. She'd better get out of here while there was still some light. The cloth store must be emptying out. Somebody might see her getting out of the show window. She'd have to be very careful … and fast. And yet there was such comfort inside the show window! How she wallowed in that pleasure! Another ten minutes? Why not….

She was still mulling over this when she spotted her girlfriend Sheyama on the sidewalk. Right away she sprang into her former pose and held her breath. Sheyama threw an inattentive look in her direction and because her thoughts were elsewhere, the danger, luckily, was averted. The thought that some of her acquaintances might spot her here had not occurred to her until Sheyama came along. This was precisely the time when her older brother returned from work, she recalled with horror. He's already suffering from a heart ailment. What if he saw the family's honour exposed so shamelessly out on the street? Wouldn't he drop dead?

Two boys appeared in her field of vision. They were returning from school, their satchels glued to their backs. They looked with zesty curiosity and pasted their faces—eyes and all—flat against the glass.

"Hey, she's real," the voice of one of the boys entered her ear faintly. Once again she wanted to laugh.

"Punk—it's plastic," the other boy said. "Whoever uses a live model?"

"But she looks so real. Seems she'd open her mouth and start speaking any moment."

"That's because of the evening. In proper light, you'd see."

"Hi!" the boy said as he winked at her mischievously.

The other one broke into a gale of laughter. Then he too waved at her and said "Bye!" and the two walked out of her field of vision.

As soon as they were gone, she suddenly began to laugh, but just as suddenly, became very nervous.

A young man was looking at her with perplexed eyes from across the glass. When their eyes met, he smiled. She smiled back, if only to hide her trepidation. She quickly grabbed the plastic dummy, and tried to install it, pretending to be one of the store attendants.

The youth's eyes were still riveted on her.

Arranging the sari around the mannequin she looked at the youth from the corner of her eye to see who he was looking at. His eyes lingered briefly at the plastic figure, then bounced off it and became glued to her.

She backed up, supremely confident, opened the door to the show window and walked out.

None of the store attendants saw her go out, or if they did, she was so agile and so fast that they couldn't figure out what had happened. The doorman didn't notice as he was busy talking to one of the sales clerks.

Confidently she strode away, briskly but lightly, happy and satisfied. As though she'd just unloaded the entire pestering weight of her body and soul. After she had walked away some distance, she turned around and looked back. The youth was still staring at her, perhaps with wonder.

She quickly turned down another street.

You take it from here ...

Responding

1. Analyze Character   In one or two paragraphs, write a description of the young woman's personality, cultural background, and social class. Be sure to indicate what comments or details in the narrative helped you to form your opinions. Then, state whether she is the type of person you would like to befriend, and explain your opinion.

2. Discuss Motivation   With two or three other students, discuss the young woman's motivation. Why do you think she posed in the window in the first place? Why did she stay there so long?

3. Assess Point of View   We are told what the peasant and the cop are thinking. However, this is according to the young woman's point of view. Do you believe that she is correct in her analysis of their thoughts, or do you think the two men may have been thinking something entirely different? Choose one of these characters and write his version of the event.

Extending

4. Imagine a Sequel   Write a continuation of the story, telling about either the young woman's conversation the next day with her friend Sheyama, or the young woman's next encounter with the perplexed young man. Read your story aloud to a small group of students, and invite their reactions and comments.

> **PEER ASSESSMENT**
>
> As you listen to each sequel, consider the following:
> - Was the sequel written in a style consistent with that of the original story?
> - Were the characters realistic and engaging? Explain.
> - Which stories stood out as being especially creative and/or interesting? In what way?

5. Investigate Parallels   The myth of Pygmalion and the fairy tales "Sleeping Beauty" and "The Emperor's New Clothes" are all echoed in this narrative. As a class, choose one of these stories and discuss how it relates to "The Pose."

6. Tell an Anecdote   In a small group, share a personal story about a harmless, unpremeditated "daredevil" stunt you once pulled. What unwritten social rule did you break in doing so? What did you feel when it was over? A sense of accomplishment? Embarrassment? Both? Neither? Explain. (Note: Alternatively, you could choose to create a fictional anecdote—but make it realistic and have your listeners guess whether or not it's true.)

Mules

"You turn the key on, stupid!"

Short Story by Brian Fawcett

Notes

Brian Fawcett (1944–) was born in Prince George, British Columbia, and currently lives in Toronto. A former columnist for *The Globe and Mail*, he has also worked in the forest service, as a community organizer and planner, and as a teacher in maximum-security prisons.

"Dangerous Dan McGrew": popular dramatic poem about betrayal and a murder in a saloon, written by Canadian poet Robert Service

Francis the Talking Mule: character from, and title of, a 1950s TV comedy

truculence: hostility, argumentativeness

The day I turned 16 my father poked me awake at eight o'clock in the morning.

"Get up," he said. "We've got work to do."

I was still too sleepy to think straight, but the first thing that woke up was my sense of injustice. It was too early in the morning. He made matters worse by jerking all the covers off the bed. It was bad enough that my birthday wasn't celebrated as a national holiday. Now I was being forced to work. But as I awakened a little more, I noticed that my father was grinning instead of snarling, which was what he usually did if he found me lying around and he had work for me to do. I was about to tell him why I shouldn't have to do any work when he took my excuse away from me.

"It's your birthday. You're going to learn how to drive today."

Most kids think driving a car is one of the very best games, but I didn't think about driving at all, and when I did, it didn't come up as a game or as fun. Learning to drive meant having to go to work, and the only reason my father was teaching me was so I could drive his trucks and make all the weekend deliveries no one else wanted to do.

Until that morning, I hadn't spent more than about five minutes in my whole life thinking about learning to drive. The last time I'd practised driving was on a business trip with my father when I was 5 or 6 years old and he had an old Pontiac with an insignia on the dashboard which I used as an imaginary steering wheel.

Cars didn't interest me, and neither did anything else mechanical. Even when my parents had brought a Volkswagen back from a trip in Europe a few months before, I hadn't thought about driving it. I thought it was cute, and I liked to ride around in it, but that was about all. And now I was going to have to learn to drive *that* car, and *all* my father's trucks, and practically every automobile in the world. Some birthday present.

I stalled my way through breakfast, and my father began to glower openly. I stalled openly, but finally I realized that I had the rest of my life in front of me, and I couldn't hold out for another 15 minutes before my father created an uproar that might be even more frightening than having to learn how to drive.

The cute little car was parked in the backyard, but as I trudged down the stairs from the house it took on a definite air of menace. I walked over to the passenger side of the car and got yelled at, so I walked around the car as slowly as I could, checking all the fenders and the bumpers with exaggerated care. I got into the car, and my father wedged himself in on the other side.

"Now what?" I said, fingering the steering wheel and staring through the window at the once-friendly alley.

"What do you mean, now what?" my father hooted.

He'd been lecturing me for 15 minutes on the fine points of driving and I hadn't heard a word. "You turn the key on, stupid!"

"Which direction?" I asked, staring at him.

He reached over without saying anything and turned the key, holding it on until even I knew he should stop. I continued to stare at him. I don't think he'd realized I knew nothing about driving until that moment.

"Put your stupid foot on the clutch," he said.

I did, but I didn't press it in.

"Push it down."

I did.

"Put it into gear."

"What gear?" I said, gazing through the window.

"FIRST GEAR, YOU NUMBSKULL!" he roared.

He was really getting mad, so I decided I'd better pretend I knew what was going on.

"I guess I let the clutch out now, right?" I said, and let it out without waiting for an answer.

We lurched forward about 10 feet before it stalled.

"You have to give it some gas when you let out the clutch," my father said in a choked voice that also said he was about to strangle me.

"Oh. Right." I restarted the car, let the clutch out the right way, and we made it out of the driveway.

"Shift it!" my father roared.

"Shift what?" I hollered back at him, and whammed the shift lever back without depressing the clutch. Luckily the car stalled before the transmission exploded.

We tried it again, and again. About half an hour later we made it out of the alley. My father's troubles were just beginning, and I think he knew it. There was a wealth of things he assumed everyone knew about the mechanical universe, and I didn't know any of them. Just because I was supposed to push the clutch pedal down when I shifted from first to second didn't mean, as far as I could figure, that I had to do the same between all the other gears. So I didn't, and ground more gears, and got yelled at some more. Finally, he told me to stop the car, and he started from the beginning. After about four sentences, my head was reeling.

"So then after the horsepower and torque go through the transmission they're connected to the rear wheels through the universal joint …"

I tried to listen, but it was hopeless.

"Start the car again," he said when he was finished. "Do you understand how it works now?"

"Sure," I lied, and turned the key.

This time it went better. I lurched the car down the alley and steered it onto the gravel street without slowing down. I got yelled at for that. There were no cars coming so I couldn't see what I'd done wrong.

"You've got to stop at corners," he said.

"Why?" I asked. "You don't."

"I don't because I *know* how to drive," he snapped.

That didn't make a lot of sense, but I didn't say anything because I was busy stopping at the next corner.

"Why are you stopping here?" he asked.

"You told me to stop at corners."

"You don't have to stop unless there's a stop sign. You just slow down to make sure there isn't anybody coming."

"How about after I learn to drive?" I asked, trying to show how well I was listening. "I can drive straight through like you do, right?"

He glared at me and didn't answer. I had enough to think about to keep me going for several days, but I couldn't tell him that because we were headed up the street and the motor was making a lot of noise.

"Shift it!" he hollered.

"Oh, yeah. Sorry," I said, shifting it into fourth gear without a hitch.

He didn't seem to think that was very smart, so I shifted it back to what I thought was first and ended up in third. He appeared to approve, so I left it there.

We drove the car around the block about four times, and I was beginning to think it was pretty easy. My father was beginning to relax a little. I think he relaxed a little too much because he told me to pull into the alley when we were already past it. I did as I'd been ordered, and drove into a neighbour's front yard. My father started screeching again, so

I somehow found reverse and pulled back onto the street. I thought I'd executed the entire manoeuvre pretty well, but my father was shaking his head. He gestured toward the alley, and I drove into it.

It wasn't the end of the alley we'd come out of, and it was much narrower than it was supposed to be. What was worse, it made a complicated turn, and on the inside of the turn a malicious neighbour had sunk an enormous post to keep people from driving into the corner of his garage. For about a year, every time we'd driven into the alley my father had cursed the neighbour and his post, threatening to bring one of his trucks up and pull it out. But for some reason its presence must have slipped his mind, although I certainly was painfully aware of it. My father became aware of it again too when I cut the corner sharply and scraped the side of the Volkswagen along it.

"Stop the car," he screamed.

He got out to survey the damage. The running board was badly dented, and so were the front and back fenders. The back bumper had hooked itself on the post and it was pulled back about six inches from where it should have been. My father was frothing at the mouth.

Luckily for me he was undecided as to whether I was a complete moron for hitting the post or whether the neighbour was a complete moron for putting it there. By the time he'd decided, after some noisy debate with himself, that we were both morons, he'd cooled down a little, and ordered me in a tight voice to drive back to the house.

"I don't want to drive," I whined, going back to my basic stance on the entire matter.

"I don't care what you want," he shouted, his anger suddenly focused. "You're going to learn how to drive, even if it kills you, you bloody mule. And that's that!"

But that wasn't that, not by a long shot. I prepared myself to die, because I wasn't going to learn to drive. It wasn't worth it. It was already changing my life. I dreamed about driving—and about driving into things—and I thought about how driving was going to take away my freedom.

I'd discovered fairly early on in life that if I wanted to be left alone by all the things and people who had organized a conspiracy to get me to be like them, I had to find ways to make myself useless to them. As I grew older it became the one political understanding I'd gathered from the world around me that made sense: freedom means not having to work.

Up to this point, I'd been fairly successful at making myself useless and therefore free, but this looked like the end of all that. I was now going to be of use to my father.

It was a gloomy future. I liked being a kid, and every adult in the world seemed like a jerk. They'd built a jerky world and now they were going to force me to drive cars and trucks in it, and soon I would begin to act and feel like a jerk and one morning I would wake up and that would be it—no more fun, no fooling around, nothing but work and coming home and eating my jerky dinner with my jerky wife and jerky kids and talking about jerky things like money or how jerky my friends all were and then one day they'd drop their jerky bombs and blow us all to smithereens. It really was the end of the world.

The end came three days later. My father sent one of the drivers he knew I really liked to pick me up after school. Bud, the driver, spotted me coming out of the building, and beeped the horn of his empty truck. I ambled over without the slightest suspicion that it was a trap. I often went with him to make deliveries after school, and being picked up wasn't all that unusual. My father was prepared to go to any length to get me to work, and this truck was one of the ones I didn't mind. Actually, it was pretty cool getting picked up this way. Even better, Bud knew the words to what seemed like a million dirty songs. He even knew all the words to the dirty version of "Dangerous Dan McGrew," and that impressed me to no end. I walked up to the truck and asked him what was up.

"Get in," he grinned.

I headed around the truck.

"This side!" he yelled. "You're driving."

"No, I'm not," I said, and stopped where I was. "I don't know how to drive."

"You're sixteen now, aren't you?"

"Yeah," I admitted.

"Then you've gotta learn to drive. Get in."

I started for the passenger door.

"This side," he hollered.

I stopped again. "Why?" I asked, still stubborn.

"Because that's how things are."

"Just because things are the way they are doesn't mean that's the way they have to be, does it? Things are jerky."

"GET IN."

Bud didn't seem any more impressed by my logic than my father had been, so I reluctantly got in behind the wheel.

"Now what?" I asked.

He reached over and twisted the key to shut the motor off. "We're going to talk," he said.

"Sure," I said. "What's up?"

It was one thing not to listen to your father, and quite another not to listen to someone real, like Bud.

"Your dad says he doesn't understand you," Bud began.

"So what?" I asked.

It had never occurred to me that he wanted to understand me, or that he was supposed to. I began to coil defensively around the thought, but Bud saw it.

"No!" he said irritably. "Listen for once. You're just like a mule. As a matter of fact, that's what he said you were. You think whatever he says you should do is the opposite of what you're supposed to do."

I shrugged. I couldn't see anything wrong with being a mule. I liked mules. Francis the Talking Mule was one of my heroes. Mules were smarter than horses or donkeys, and when they could talk, they were smarter than people. The more I thought about being a mule, the more I liked it.

"So what?" I said. "What's wrong with being a mule?"

"Only one thing's wrong with being a mule."

"Oh yeah? What?" I imagined that I was flattening my ears against the side of my head and bridling back against the rope that held me.

"A mule isn't anything," he said, searching for some way to break through my resistance. "It isn't a horse and it isn't a donkey. It's a big nothing. All it can do is be ornery and fight back at everything."

"Yeah?" I said, caught halfway between pride and truculence.

"Yeah. And mules have to work just as hard as horses and donkeys anyway. Probably harder, because that's all they're good for."

"What's all that got to do with me learning how to drive?" Bud had succeeded in making me feel uncomfortable, and I was changing the subject.

"Driving is fun," he said. "You can go wherever you want once you learn. You can buy a car and do whatever you want. You're free."

"I don't want to do any of that junk," I replied, without feeling very confident about it any longer.

Bud was a person, and he was telling me the opposite of what I knew was true. He was right, but it was suspicious stuff he was saying.

"Besides," I quibbled. "I don't have any money."

"Save some. Go to work for your dad."

I'd heard that before and it didn't convince me any more now than it had in the past. Bud was just trying to get me to do work for my father.

"If I learn to drive, will you lend me your car?" I asked, grinning at my own sneakiness.

Bud hesitated. "Sure," he said. "If you learn how to drive properly."

I thought about that for a minute. Some of my friends already had their driver's licences, and one or two of them had bought old cars. Mainly, the cars gave all of us someplace to be on Friday night. I felt a heavier rope inching across my ears and I shrugged unconsciously. I would, I decided, go to work for my father exactly as often as I needed to in order to afford gas for Bud's car. Maybe, I thought, since we would all have to learn to drive, and we were all mules, or at least my best friends were, there was nothing to worry about. My dream would somehow remain safe from the wily schemes of ordinary men. I reached for the ignition key, twisted it, and the truck's motor started.

"Okay," I said. "What do I do?"

I did what Bud told me to, and twenty minutes later I knew I could drive. The next day I took my driving test with the same truck, and soon I was doing exactly what I'd most feared I would end up doing: all the weekend deliveries no one else wanted to do.

It was fun. Donnie and Artie often came along with me, and that made it even more fun. I started going to work every day, and I opened up a savings account so I could buy a car. I even began to get along with my father. He began to try to have conversations with me, and I would catch him looking at me speculatively, as if he were seeing the possibility of something unexpected and useful beneath the furry snout and long ears.

I wasn't very good at driving, and I demonstrated that in a series of hilarious car accidents during the next several months. I put the Volkswagen through the front window of a supermarket one afternoon after I'd impressed one of my friends with a thrilling zip-zap through the parking lot. I mistook the gas pedal for the brake pedal at the climax of this operation and almost zapped the manager of the store, who was one of my father's more important customers and knew exactly who I was. Two or three days later I ran over someone else's Volkswagen with one of my father's trucks as I rounded the corner of the town's busiest intersection. I'd seen someone I knew standing across the street and I'd stopped driving to wave at him.

My older brother, who was anything but a mule, was naturally skilled at every terror my father served up for him, and wouldn't let me near his new Chev convertible. He took it upon himself to give me a lecture about driving.

"Look, idiot," he said. "You've got to stop wrecking vehicles." He imitated my father's habit of never calling anything by its simple name. "These conveyances cost a lot of money."

"I'm not trying to," I pointed out. "Driving is hard."

He didn't think anything was hard, and he conceded my difficulty with a sniff of contempt.

"You'd better spend a couple of nights talking to the mechanic," he said, making it plain that the sessions weren't optional. "Maybe he can teach you what it's about."

The mechanic was a middle-aged man who treated my father's trucks as if they were his personal harem of exotic beauties. He wasn't enamoured of my gear-grinding antics, nor with me, but he obviously saw the opportunity to save his beauties from me, and spent several evenings showing me exactly the right way to treat a truck. He was showing me what *he* thought was perfection, but I gathered precisely three things from it all: when to shift up, when to shift down, and the idea that I was supposed to keep my foot pressed firmly on the gas pedal as long as those shifting points were not upon me. The accidents stopped, but the wreckage didn't cease. It merely took the form of destroyed transmissions and clutches, and worn out brakes.

Bud lent me his car right after the mechanic told him I knew all about how to drive. Later that night the police stopped me with eleven of my friends in the car. They'd clocked me at 55 miles an hour, and I didn't have the car lights on. I told the officer I hadn't been able to find the light switch, and then handed him a two dollar bill out of my wallet instead of my driver's licence, explaining that I'd just gotten it a few weeks before. He started to laugh, and had to let me go, but he phoned my parents about it.

Thankfully, he got my mother on the phone, and she took me aside the next day.

"Just what is it you think you're doing?" she asked.

It was a genuine question; not, as expected, the opening salvo of a lecture on my irresponsible behaviour. She'd maintained an amused silence throughout the previous weeks, and had even smiled while I was explaining to my father how it was that I'd come to make my unusual entry into the supermarket. I looked at her carefully, and flattened my ears slightly anyway.

"Driving Bud's car," I said, noncommittally.

"Well, you know, cars aren't everything in life," she said, almost as if she were discussing the matter with one of her friends.

"They aren't?" I was confused. I'd more or less decided that cars were everything in life. "What do you mean?"

She stared at me for a moment as if she were sizing me up for something, trying to decide who or what I really was, and whether or not it was worth imparting to me what she knew. Her amused silence over the previous weeks suddenly became a mystery to me. I prodded her impatiently.

"Tell me what you mean."

"You don't really want a car," she said.

"I don't?" This truly was mysterious. Everybody wanted a car, and here was my own mother telling me that I didn't want one.

"No," she said firmly, "it'd be much better not to have one. If you need a car you can use mine."

She was deeply enveloped in her mystery, and was gazing at the top of my head as if she could see the mule ears, or maybe she was looking beyond all that to some imaginary future she alone knew about. I interrupted her reverie. The rope was around my neck and I'd begun to like it.

"Why shouldn't I have my own car?"

She shrugged, and a more familiar vagueness appeared in her reply.

"Oh, well," she said. "They cost a lot of money. You save your money for something else."

I shook the rope and snorted, but she continued before I could think of anything to say.

"There's lots of things you can do," she said. "Don't get tied down with a car."

She reached across the table and, so help me, scratched me behind the ear and patted my neck. As she removed her hand, the rope went with it, and I glimpsed a kind of field in her eyes.

There was nothing there that I could see clearly. Some grass, maybe, and some blurry shapes in the distance. Certainly not what she imagined. I stood there for a moment looking, shook my mane a little, and asked her when I could borrow the car.

You take it from here ...

Responding

1. Analyze an Extended Metaphor   As a class, share your list of references to mules and discuss why the author chose this metaphor for his story.

2. Explain Motivation   Most teens look forward to receiving their driver's licence, and to the purchase of their first car. In a paragraph, explain why the narrator initially wants nothing to do with driving. What causes him to change his mind?

3. Interpret the Conclusion   As a class, discuss the mother's purpose in telling the narrator that cars are a nuisance. How does the narrator respond to her advice?

4. Write a Letter   How do you feel toward the narrator—sympathetic? Frustrated? Something in between? Write a letter to the narrator expressing your opinions and offering him advice.

Extending

5. Write a Personal Response   Write about a battle you have had with a parent or authority figure who asked you to do something you didn't want to do. How did you respond—were you uncooperative? Reluctantly cooperative? What was the outcome? On reflection, would you handle the situation differently now?

6. Write an Article   Write an article, directed at parents, about teaching teenagers how to drive. You might offer tips on how to approach the task and how to avoid personal conflicts—and perhaps some suggestions about when to call in a professional driving instructor instead.

Before you read, write a short description of the most special meal you have ever eaten.

As you read, consider whether your own feelings about inexpensive "matter-of-fact" meals like pizza have changed.

A Small Cheese Pizza

I wanted to know who he was.

Memoir by by Rachel Svea Bottino

Notes

Rachel Svea Bottino wrote this story when she was a high-school student.

It was an intensely cold November day with a biting wind. My mom and I entered the first restaurant we saw in a hurry to get away from the harsh weather. Mom ordered a pizza and I found a cozy booth near the heater. As I gazed around, I saw a homeless man sitting at a corner table. For some reason—I'm still not sure why—he intrigued me.

I studied him, absorbing every detail. Growing up, I was taught never to stare, but the temptation was overwhelming. Because of the way his knees grazed the bottom of the tabletop, it was evident that he was tall. His clothes were filthy. Even though he was wearing endless layers of clothing, he looked as though he weighed nothing. A mass of tangled hair, thick as a lion's mane, covered most of his face and a shaggy, knotted beard covered the rest. I focused on his eyes because they were the only part I could see.

His eyes were transfixed, almost hypnotized by the steam that curled up from the coffee cup sitting in the middle of the table. An employee came over and gave him a small cheese pizza, and what I saw next would change my whole perspective on life.

The man looked at that pizza as if it were the most precious thing in the world. He didn't touch it at first, almost like a person who has a priceless object he is afraid might break. He stared at that pizza as though it were made of gold. When he finally decided to eat it, he didn't grab a slice and devour it like we do. He ate unusually slowly, savouring every bite.

When we got our pizza, my mom placed it in the middle of the table and started eating. She couldn't see the man from where she was sitting and asked me why I wasn't eating. I nodded toward the man and she turned. When she saw him, she understood. That circular piece of dough in the middle of our table suddenly looked different. It was no longer just an inexpensive supper. People think of pizza as a matter-of-fact thing that has no significance whatsoever. But now, after seeing this man, something as simple as a small cheese pizza was suddenly so much more complicated.

I was drawn to this man not out of pity, but curiosity. I wanted to know who he was. I wanted to know what was going on in his mind. He is a human being, like everyone else, but is viewed as though he is incapable of having thoughts and feelings. When people look at him, they see a lost cause. But I saw a soul waiting to be found.

I watched him as he got up to leave. He finished the last of his coffee and headed toward the door. As the door opened, a gust of frigid air rushed into the store. Holding his collar tightly around his neck and bowing his head against the snapping wind, he walked through the parking lot and out of sight.

You take it from here ...

Responding

1. Speculate on Effect   The author says that the incident changed her "whole perspective on life." In what ways did her perspective change? In what ways do you think her behaviour also might have changed? Share your thoughts with a partner.

2. Present a Monologue   Prepare a monologue telling the story of the homeless man from his own point of view. How did he come to be at this particular restaurant? What was he thinking as he consumed his meal? What was his reaction to the girl who was staring at him from her booth? Perform your monologue for the class or a small group.

3. Debate Theme   The author argues that the homeless man "is a human being, like everyone else, but is viewed as though he is incapable of having thoughts and feelings." In a small group, discuss whether you believe she is correct in her assessment of other people's reactions.

Extending

4. Write a Description   Reread Bottino's description of the homeless man. Then, write your own brief description of an individual you have observed who stood out from the crowd. Work to make your sketch as detailed and powerful as Bottino's.

5. Write a Memoir   Compose your own reminiscence about a time when you suddenly became aware that something you took for granted (e.g., a warm home, sufficient food) was extremely precious to others.

6. Design an Advertisement   Use the situation described in this memoir to inspire a full-page advertisement that will encourage people to help those less fortunate than themselves. Before you begin your design, ask yourself the following questions:

   - What is the purpose of the ad? (To encourage people to support a particular charity? To raise awareness for a cause?)
   - Who is the target audience? (Students in your school? Business people in your community? The general public?)
   - Where would I place the ad to give it maximum exposure to the intended audience?

   Then, combine text and graphics to send a powerful message. Present your advertisement to the class or a small group, and invite reactions and comments.

   PEER ASSESSMENT
   - Was the ad compelling—would it persuade you to act?
   - Was the design effective—would it catch your eye in a newspaper or on a crowded bulletin board?

Helping Others Best Cure for Loneliness

What a change in attitude, brought about by a young fellow, his dog, and an old truck.

Memoir by Grant Nicol

"You say we are lonely who live out on the land, but I say it is you in the big cities who are lonely." Those words written by a Native elder living in the Northwest Territories came back to me as I crossed Stony Plain Road that hot morning in June.

The recent death of my mother combined with work pressures had cast a gloom over everything. I saw the city as a lonely place filled with indifferent people who had no time for anyone outside their own circle. Crossing the busy road and continuing south on 178th Street, these dismal thoughts stayed with me as I struggled with the black wave of depression that was my companion that morning.

I had left my car at Devonian Motors for repairs, which would take about three hours, so I decided to pass the time by walking to West Edmonton Mall.

The noise of traffic, the heat of the pavement, the smell of exhaust fumes, the frantic rush all around me increased my feeling of gloom and emphasized just how cold and hostile the city really was and how alone I felt.

Crossing the street at the entrance to the mall I was annoyed to find my way blocked by a battered old Ford pickup stalled in the middle of the intersection. The driver, a young blond fellow in faded blue jeans and T-shirt, was in quite a state. His face was flushed and sweating as he tried to start his vehicle.

Sitting in the front seat was his sole passenger, a big shaggy dog!

Like his master, the big brown mutt seemed worried and unhappy.

The young man was trying to ignore the drivers behind him who were now impatiently laying on their horns.

Moved by his predicament I asked: "Would you like me to go to a service station and have them send a tow truck?"

He had an open, honest face and his blue eyes looked straight at me.

"You know, it would start if I could just get it rolling," he replied hopefully. I was surprised to hear myself saying, "Get in, I'll try to push it."

At that moment a heavyset, important-looking fellow climbed out of the Caddy stopped behind. In an impatient voice he asked, "What's going on here?"

The young fellow looked nervous. "Mr. Important" was smartly dressed, with a diamond ring on his fleshy hand and an expensive-looking tan suit. I didn't like him! A bit testily I replied, "This young man cannot get his truck started, however it may start if we were to push it."

Then, ignoring him, I grabbed the truck box and leaned in on it.

To my surprise, "Mr. Important" grabbed the rusty tailgate and shoved right along with me. The truck moved. We were joined by another fellow whose car was stopped behind the Cadillac. Imagine the spectacle of three middle-aged men, two in business suits, running down 178th Street pushing a battered old truck!

I began to worry about "Mr. Important." His short legs were pumping along very fast and his face was wet with perspiration. The young fellow shouted, "I'll try her now!" He let out the clutch. The truck lurched, then sprang to life with a roar and took off down the street.

"Thank you!" the young man shouted out the window, looking back at us with a broad happy smile. Even big boofis the dog turned his shaggy head and looked back. He was grinning too!

We watched the heads of the young man and his dog bouncing along in the old truck as it rattled out of sight.

The traffic behind was strangely silent.

"Mr. Important," really a nice chap after all, turned to me, smiled and said "Thank you!"

Suddenly, the busy traffic became a happy bustling sound. The drivers were now warm, living human beings going about their business. They were part of me and I was part of them! What a change in attitude, brought about by a young fellow, his dog, and an old truck.

I discovered that morning that the best cure for big city loneliness was to start thinking of others and to lend a helping hand when needed.

You take it from here ...

Responding

1. **Write a Police Report**   This memoir is written in an easygoing, personal style. Play with the tone of the selection by converting it to a formal, objective summary of the event such as might be written by a police officer who happened to observe the traffic jam. Share your summary with the class. Discuss the changes you consciously made in content and in style as you retold the story.

2. **Consider Audience**   Several of the details in this selection establish the setting firmly in Edmonton. Working with a partner, identify each of these details, then discuss their impact on the story. How important is it for a reader to know these places? In your opinion, would the story be affected positively, negatively, or not at all if the specific references had been omitted? Explain your thinking.

3. **Debate Stereotyping**   Underlying this story is an implied prejudice against people who are overweight and who are obviously wealthy. Working in a small group, identify the words and observations that reveal these prejudices. Then, hold an informal debate as to whether these attitudes are common and whether they are in any way acceptable.

Extending

4. **Write a Memoir**   Think about the title of this selection. Has your own experience shown this to be true? In what other ways might helping others help us? Write your own memoir to illustrate the point: "Helping others is the best cure for loneliness [or unhappiness, or ...]," and then read it aloud to the class.

5. **Contribute to a Newspaper**   Many newspapers and magazines offer their readers opportunities to contribute personal stories; several even pay a small fee for those that are published. Investigate the opportunities that are available to you. Then compose and submit your own story.

TIPS

- Follow the guidelines carefully, paying special attention to word count.
- Read previously published stories to check appropriate topics and tone.
- Have several friends review your story before you submit it.

PEER ASSESSMENT

- Is the story interesting and easy to read?
- Does it make a clear main point, supported with additional points?
- Does it follow the publisher's guidelines (e.g., appropriate subject and length)?
- Is it free of grammatical and spelling errors?

Before you read, recall a moment when you were embarrassed by a small child saying something out loud that you wish he or she hadn't.

As you read, slow down so that you can picture the scene clearly in your mind.

Notes

Maxine Tynes (1950–) is a Black poet and teacher from Dartmouth, Nova Scotia, who traces her roots back to Black Loyalists. She has won the Dennis Memorial Poetry Prize, Milton Acorn People's Poet Prize, and an honorary Doctorate of Humane Letters from Mount Saint Vincent University. She has also worked as a freelance CBC broadcaster.

Reach Out and Touch

Poem by Maxine Tynes

baby girl, baby boy behind me on the bus
reach out
and touch the curly electric of my hair
your fingers dipped in the
brown skin magic of my neck
to see if it comes off
your mama
slapping hands away
hush-up of your questions
and wondering out loud
why it doesn't come off.
I turn and smile for you,
but you're already lost
in the silence and the fear that motherlove wraps you in.
I should have sat beside you
snugged my big warm self up close
held you while your mama juggled parcels.
then you would know it's o.k.

You take it from here ...

Responding

1. Identify Lessons   As a class, discuss the lessons the baby is being taught in the scene this poem describes. How might they affect the child's thinking and behaviour later in life?

2. Analyze Imagery   In your opinion, which image in the poem is the most powerful, intriguing, or unusual? To clarify your thinking, write a brief paragraph about your chosen image. Then discuss your ideas with the rest of the class.

3. Comment on Differences   This poem is about differences in skin colour and in age. Write a paragraph in which you explain Tynes's comments on these topics. How important to her is difference in skin colour? How important is difference in age? Explain your responses.

4. Recall Personal Experiences   Recall the first time you remember seeing an unusual adult—one who was differently coloured or dressed, or in some other way looked out of the ordinary to you. How old were you? How did you react? How did the adults around you behave? Share your recollections in a small-group discussion.

Extending

5. Change Perspective   Imagine you are the child in the poem, now grown up, and that something has caused you to recall the situation described in the poem. Write your own poetic or narrative version of the event from this perspective. Recall what you were thinking at the time, and how you felt—both before and after you were "slapped away" and "hushed up." You might describe how the event shaped your outlook later in life, and/or how you would react in a similar situation with your own children.

6. Create a Script   The narrator finishes the poem by stating what she *should* have done. Imagine that the narrator did, indeed, change seats and cuddle the baby. Write the script that would result from this action.

No Man Is an Island

Poem by John Donne

No man is an island, entire of itself:
Every man is a piece of the continent,
A part of the main.
If a clod be washed away by the sea,
Europe is the less,
As well as if a promontory were,
As well as if a manor of thy friend
Or of thine own, were.
Any man's death diminishes me,
Because I am involved in mankind;
And, therefore, never send to know
For whom the bell tolls:
It tolls for thee.

Notes

John Donne (1571–1631) was an English poet and a contemporary of Shakespeare. These words are taken from a meditation published as part of his religious writings.

You take it from here ...

Responding

1. Define Words in Context   Write what you think each of the following words means judging from its use in this selection. Compare your notes with those of a partner. Then use a dictionary to confirm any definitions about which you are still unsure.

main	diminishes
clod	send
promontory	tolls
manor	

2. Paraphrase the Poem   With a partner, reread the poem and, using the definitions from Activity 1, paraphrase it in your own words.

3. Explain the Title   Write a brief paragraph explaining what you think Donne means when he says, "No man is an island." Then write one or two additional paragraphs expanding on this thought. Do you entirely agree? Give reasons to support your opinion.

4. Discuss Theme   When Donne says, "never send to know for whom the bell tolls: it tolls for thee," he doesn't mean this literally. Discuss with a partner what lesson he is trying to teach. Write two or three sentences to explain this lesson. Then compare your explanations with those of the rest of the class.

Extending

5. Write an Anecdote   Imagine an everyday situation that illustrates the truth of this selection's theme. Use this as the basis for a one- to two-page anecdote.

6. Add an Illustration   Create a visual to illustrate either the anecdote you wrote in Activity 5 or the general theme "No Man Is an Island." Compile your completed works into a class anthology entitled "No Man Is an Island."

Notes

Paul Simon (1941–) is a New Jersey-born singer/guitarist/songwriter, best known as the driving force behind the popular singing duo Simon and Garfunkle. His solo career continues to flourish because of innovative albums such as *Graceland* and *You're the One*. "I Am a Rock" is on the album *The Sounds of Silence*.

I Am a Rock

Lyrics by Paul Simon

A winter's day
In a deep and dark December,
I am alone,
Gazing from my window to the streets below
On a freshly-fallen, silent shroud of snow.
I am a rock.
I am an island.

I've built walls,
A fortress steep and mighty,
That none may penetrate.
I have no need of friendship; friendship causes pain.
It's laughter and it's loving I disdain.
I am a rock.
I am an island.

Don't talk of love;
Well I've heard the word before.
It's sleeping in my memory.
I won't disturb the slumber of feelings that have died.
If I never loved, I never would have cried.
I am a rock.
I am an island.

I have my books
And my poetry to protect me.
I am shielded in my armour,
Hiding in my room, safe within my womb.
I touch no one and no one touches me.
I am a rock.
I am an island.

And a rock feels no pain;
And an island never cries.

You take it from here ...

Responding

1. **Discuss Metaphor**   In a class discussion, identify the literal qualities of rocks and islands. Then explain what the speaker means by saying, "I am a rock."

2. **Consider Mood**   *Mood* refers to the feeling a selection creates in the reader. In a paragraph, describe the mood of these lyrics, identifying specific words and expressions that contribute to it.

TIP
• Start by identifying lines that could be answers to someone's questions or comments.

3. **Role-Play a Telephone Conversation**   Working with a partner, role-play a telephone conversation between the speaker and a friend, using the ideas in these lyrics as your foundation.

4. **Offer Support**   Imagine you are a guidance counsellor or trusted teacher of the speaker. Write what you would say to the speaker in response to the sentiments expressed in this song.

Extending

5. **Develop a Script**   Imagine the speaker in this song meeting John Donne, author of the previous selection, "No Man Is an Island." Working with a partner, develop a script for the conversation you think might take place between them. Present your dialogue to the class.

6. **Illustrate the Lyrics**   Create a visual representation (e.g., a drawing or collage) in which you capture as many of the images from the lyrics as possible. Share your work with the class or in small groups.

PEER ASSESSMENT

As you view the illustrations, consider the following:
- Did the illustration successfully capture the mood of the lyrics?
- Which illustration made most effective use of the images in the lyrics? Explain.

The Carved Table

I'm seeing with my own eyes, she thought.

Short Story by Mary Peterson

Notes

Mary Peterson has written several short stories as well as a novel, *Mercy Flights*, published in 1985.

It was her second marriage and Karen sat at the round table in Marblehead with her new family, listening to their conversation and thinking of what her first husband would see, if he was there. He would notice, she thought, my new mother-in-law's enormous diamond, and he would see this new father-in-law's yachting jacket, he would be disgusted. Might even say, "What are you doing here? You'll lose your soul to these people."

There were six around the table: she and her handsome husband, his parents, and her husband's spoiled-looking older brother and his glossy wife, who tossed her fine red hair and laughed at the right times and made little asides to the mother-in-law while the men held forth. Karen envied that sharing. She envied her thoroughbred sister-in-law who did not take it all so seriously. She herself took it too seriously and she couldn't shake off the feeling that something was terribly wrong.

She touched the carved wood edge of the table with one hand and with the other she reached toward her husband, rested her hand on his knee. He was always quiet during the cocktail hour, but also he listened with an odd, fixed smile: one of complicity—mesmerized like a 12-year-old trying to learn the hard lessons of being an adult. When you were an adult you drank a lot; you kept up with your father in the drinking. This was difficult, since his father went to the bar for more bourbon often, and with each new drink he grew louder, and with each he had more to say and less that made sense. The man was well educated, she reminded herself, and certainly he knew much about banking, airplanes, and stocks. But also, he believed children on welfare should be allowed to die, so that we could purify the society. He believed in capital punishment. He believed we should step up the

arms race and show more muscle abroad. Wars are different now, she wanted to say. We have nuclear weapons. We need a different set of rules. She did not say these things. Neither did she say that his capitalism created in the minds of the poor a need: they saw the television advertising, they saw the consumption of goods. How could they have any dreams but the ones he himself had? No wonder, she wanted to say, the Cadillac sits outside the tenement, and at the market people buy junk food with food stamps. What do they know about beans and meat? They know what they see on television, in the magazines; they know the Mercedes they see *him* driving. Your capitalism, she wanted to say, is educating them in desperate ignorance. Your free enterprise system.

She did not say any of it.

Her first husband would be thinking and maybe saying these things. He would know that the people around the table were the enemy, the very same she and he had fought when they lived in Chicago and worked against the war in Vietnam. The same they had studied during the terrible sixties, the one they had hated.

"You're so quiet," her husband said, leaning toward her, giving her his hand. He was handsome and gentle and he didn't pontificate like his father and she loved him in spite of a score of things, and for a hundred others: not the least of them his stability, his good sense, his ability to be socially at ease with people, his open affection with her, the pure security of him.

"I was wondering," she said, "about the carving around this table." She tried to say it quietly, so the others wouldn't hear. "I know one of the wooden scallops was added, because one was broken, and I've been trying to guess if any of these—" and she ran her hand along the perimeter of the table "—is the new one. To see if it really fits so well."

"None have been added," he said. He seemed confused.

"You told me one was new. I remember."

"Karen's right," his father said. "One is new. I can't find it, either."

The other daughter-in-law and the mother had begun to play backgammon. They used an inlaid ebony board and when the dice were thrown they clicked like teeth. Her husband's brother had taken out an expensive cigar and was lighting it with great ceremony. He looked rich. His haircut looked rich and exactly right and his three-piece suit matched his shirt and tie exactly. He had a bored rich face and a sullen lower lip. You could not ask him a question because he would never answer it; he made light of everything.

The mother-in-law was beautiful and smooth-skinned and Karen had often watched her play with her grandchildren. She was the best of the family, but even in the best there was this other thing. In one game, the woman lined the children up to race. When they were ready, she broke away before she'd finished counting—she always won. "Your Grandmother lies," she told the children, laughing. One grandchild cried the first time she did it. The next time, the child who cried—a little girl—broke away early too.

Her first husband would have seen and understood all this, and although she didn't love him and didn't miss him, she respected his intelligence and he was more like her—shared with her a way of seeing. He would have observed her new husband's expensive suit, and her own diamond, and her own good haircut. But he's gone, she thought, and that's over. She released her new husband's hand. I'm seeing with my own eyes, she thought, and I mustn't blame it on anyone else. So now I must decide what to do.

You take it from here ...

Responding

1. **Examine Characterization**   Reproduce the following chart and, working with one or two other students, complete the columns by filling in all the words and details used to describe each individual. When you have finished, examine the completed columns one by one. Discuss how these details influence your attitude to each character.

Husband 1	Karen	Husband 2	Mother -in-law	Father -in-law	Sister -in-law	Brother -in-law

2. **Discuss the Situation**   The story ends with Karen saying, "So now I must decide what to do." Working in a small group, brainstorm the options that are open to her. Decide which one you believe she will take. Compare your response with those of other groups in the class.

3. **Extract Theme**   This selection does more than tell a story; it expresses a strong theme. In several paragraphs, explain the author's ideas about wealth and poverty. Do you find her arguments convincing?

4. Analyze Symbolism   Consider why this story is titled "The Carved Table." What is the significance of the table? Does it have a symbolic value? Why does Karen lie to her husband and say that it is the table that is on her mind? Share your thoughts in a class discussion.

Extending

5. Write Diary Entries   Complete several diary entries (at least three) written by Karen at different times in her life that can help explain the current conflict between her "old self" and the new social world she has entered. You might, for example, write one from when she was with her first husband, one while she was between the two relationships, and one when she first started to question her new husband's values in comparison with her own. How does she approach the question "Where do I fit in?" at these various stages of her life?

6. Script a Conversation   Working with a partner, write a short script for a conversation between Karen and her husband as they watch television one evening and see either (a) a news clip showing anti-poverty demonstrators clashing with police, or (b) an advertisement for a luxury automobile. Read your script aloud to the class.

Social Security

"Don't ask me to bend the rules."

Short Story by Norah Holmgren

Notes

persona: the character or personality we assume in public

social security: called social insurance in Canada, it refers to government-paid benefits such as the old-age pension or employment insurance

My mother and I were sitting in the Social Security office. It was on the eighteenth floor of an old building in the heart of the city, but I could still hear the swish swish of cars passing on the freeway below. If I stood up I could see them—long ribbons of them.

I don't live in the city anymore. The sight of 10 000 cars a day began to get me down. Where I live now, out in the country, I can distinguish each of my neighbour's cars by sound alone. In the evening when I come home from work the children can hear me coming closer and closer. In the morning when I hear the rattles and explosions of the Ford truck next door, I know it's time to get up.

My mother had asked me to come with her to Social Security. She wanted me to speak for her and hear for her. She speaks English perfectly and her hearing is unimpaired. She simply can't believe what is being said. If I came with her, she said, we could talk things over later and try to make sense of them. It would be too late then, but it's better to try to understand anyway, isn't it?

In the waiting room we were among the Mexican families, the slim, young Chinese girls, the Filipino men, the grey old German men, and the old Swedish ladies like my mother who had been cooks and maids and seamstresses and bakery clerks. The music of these languages rose and fell. The clerks had to shout over the din. When it got too noisy an armed guard would parade by us once or twice. We all had something in common: we were waiting for our names to be called.

The procedure was this: when we entered, a woman at the door questioned us about our business. If she couldn't turn us away, she gave us a number from 1 to 50. When that number was called, we turned it in and got a number from 51 to 99. When that number was called, our name was entered on a list. When our name was called, we could be shown in. We were told to expect to wait two or three hours for these transitions.

We sat side by side, not talking, observing the people in the room as they observed us.

When my mother's name was called, we stood up and were shown through a doorway into a vast room with rows and rows of desks. Our clerk beckoned to us. He was young, freckled, and dressed in a short-sleeved white shirt open at the neck and chest to reveal a spotless white undershirt. We sat down. I was going to do all the talking.

"I'm Mr. Sisk," he said.

"Ssss?" said my mother.

"Sisk."

"Yes," she said.

His last customer was still hanging around though he had clearly been dismissed. He was a good-looking, tall old man who was standing very straight. He ignored us. It was Mr. Sisk he wanted.

"Why can't you be reasonable?" he said. "I'm an alcoholic. You know me. I never should have told you I haven't been drinking lately. It makes no difference at all. You know that."

"No, that's what I don't know," said Mr. Sisk.

We watched unashamed.

"You don't want to know."

"You aren't drinking now. Maybe you don't need a treatment program."

"I can't hang on much longer without help."

"The rules are clear. The key words are *currently* and *presently* and *at this time*."

"Bend the rules a little. If I take a drink I'll be gone for months. Lost, lost, lost."

"Don't ask me to bend the rules."

My mother stood up. "The rules must be stupid and cruel," she shouted. "Who are they for?"

Mr. Sisk looked at her. He didn't speak, but his eyes were blinking rapidly.

He stood up and led the man away.

"I couldn't help it," my mother said. "Do you think it will ruin our chances?"

"I don't think we have any chances to be ruined."

Mr. Sisk returned. He had buttoned up his shirt and put his jacket on. My mother handed him the letter she had gotten from Social Security. He looked it over and said, "What's the problem?"

I said, "What does it mean?"

"It means we paid her too much money and now we have to get it back. We are going to suspend her payments until the money is made up. It will take nine months."

"Is there no alternative?" I said. "It isn't her fault you gave her too much money."

Mr. Sisk drew himself up in his chair. "We don't use the word *fault* here. She can fill out a hardship report, stating that she cannot live without her Social Security allowance." He found the form in his desk and handed it to me. I looked it over. Declare all your valuables. Declare all current sources of income. Declare possible sources of income. State names and address of family members. An inquisition.

My mother had a few old valuables. Her husband, my stepfather, had a pension. They could live without her money. It was just that she thought of her Social Security cheque as her own money, money she had earned by 40 years of labour, money she could spend on herself with a clear conscience, not that she ever did spend much money on herself.

I said to her, "We don't want to fill out this form. All of this is none of their business. It seems that they have the right to withhold your money unless you tell them how much your wedding ring is worth and everything else."

Mr. Sisk addressed my mother in a very loud voice. "Are you willing to fill out this form?"

"I'm not deaf," she shouted at him.

He shuffled his paper. There was a commotion at the next desk. A red-headed clerk was yelling at an old woman in black. "Come back when you're sober."

"I'm not drunk. I've had a little drink," she said.

"Sit down, then," the clerk screamed.

"Something about this place makes you want to yell," my mother said.

"It's because they think we're all deaf."

"I get so mad," my mother said. "Sure that woman had a little drink. Sometimes you get so mad, sometimes you get so fed up, you just take a drink."

We got up to leave. "If you get a cheque from us by mistake, be sure to send it to me," said Mr. Sisk.

"You're going to make more mistakes? What's wrong with you people?" my mother said.

I took her out to lunch. I tried to minimize the loss of her money.

She said, "Stop trying to cheer me up. You're making me feel terrible." We sat in silence then.

After a while she started to talk. "I've worked and worked," she said. I sat very still. I hoped she would tell me a story. She rarely spoke about her early life. I knew only the generalities: Dad was good, Mother was a martyr, times were hard, you wouldn't believe it.

"When I was eleven—that was during the war—not much food then, the whole family got the flu at one time. There were seven of us children. Dad and I were the only ones who didn't get sick. Oh, how we worked. We cooked, we cleaned, we did the chores. I was so tired at night, I fell asleep in my clothes. My youngest brother died of pneumonia and was buried before the doctor got to us. My mother cried for months and months about that. It was just me and my dad doing all the work. We made soup, we dug potatoes, we fed the chickens. Oh, how we worked."

I waited but she didn't go on.

"What made you think of that story?"

"Mr. Sisk. I'd like to show him what work is."

We got up to leave. "I'm lonely," my mother said. "I'd like to go see Alice. Will you drive me over?"

Alice was a friend of hers I didn't care for. "I'll drive you, I'll wait for you, but I don't want to come in and visit."

"I don't want you to. I want to talk about places you've never been, times before you were born. You'd just be in the way."

After I'd dropped her off, I went into a little park near Alice's house and sat down with a book. There were an unexpected number of people in the park. A large table stood under the trees with paper cups full of water on it. People were watching the path expectantly. Soon tired men and women came running into the park. As each one crossed a chalk line, the bystanders would applaud and cheer. Friends would come forward to hug the runners. The event repeated itself over and over. The applause and cheers didn't diminish; they increased.

My mother soon came limping up the path. Runners passed her on either side. She paid no attention to them. I wanted to stand and applaud her, whose every race had been run without applause, but she would have been angry.

"Why are you smiling?" she said. "Are you laughing at me?"

"No, I'm appreciating you."

"Alice didn't remember the flu of 1917, but she was glad to see me."

Later that evening when I was back in the country and the children were in bed, I wrote a little note to myself. I planned to read it every now and then. It said: "Develop a terrifying persona for when you are old and at the mercy of systems. Save your money so you can always be independent. Never look as though you could be hard of hearing."

This morning when I was cleaning out my desk, I found it. I laughed first, then I called my mother to say hello.

You take it from here ...

Responding

1. **Analyze the Structure**   Develop an outline of this selection, indicating each of the separate episodes and incidents. When you have completed the outline, decide what gives this story unity. In other words, what holds it together? Write a paragraph explaining your ideas.

2. **Role-Play a Conversation**   Work with a partner to understand Mr. Sisk's point of view. Role-play a conversation that takes place after work between him and either a colleague, a friend, or his partner on the day the narrator and her mother visited the office. What does Mr. Sisk have to say about the clients he has had to deal with that day?

3. **Discuss Relationships**   How would you describe the relationship between the narrator and her mother? How do they feel about and behave toward each other? In your view, is this a typical relationship? Or is it unusual in some way? Compare your views with another student's.

Extending

4. **Develop a Minor Character**   Choose one of the following characters the narrator and her mother see in the Social Security office, and fill in the details of his or her life and situation:

   - one of the "slim, young Chinese girls"
   - one of the Filipino men
   - one of the "grey, old German men"
   - one of the "old Swedish ladies ... who had been cooks and maids, seamstresses and bakery clerks"
   - the tall old man in Mr. Sisk's office who says he is an alcoholic
   - the old woman in black

   Develop a one-page description of the character's appearance and personality, his or her personal history, family and financial situation, education, job history, and so on.

5. **Examine Government Forms**   Working with a partner, search the Internet or visit government offices to collect examples of government application forms (e.g., pension/social insurance, immigration, grants, refunds, disability, benefits). How easy are these forms to complete? What types of information do they require? Do you think the questions asked are fair? As a class, discuss your overall opinions regarding these forms.

TIP

- A good place to start your search is at the Government of Canada Web site at http://canada.gc.ca.

Before you read, write down the images that come to mind when you think of a favourite relative.

As you read, make note of the shifts in time in the poem.

Notes

Noah C. Augustine is a young Native writer from Red Bank First Nation in New Brunswick. This poem comes from a book he wrote about the traditions of his grandfather and his nation. Augustine has also done suicide prevention work in the Native community.

Grandfather

Poem by Noah C. Augustine

In memory of Joseph M. Augustine, who passed away January 14, 1995.

From all your grandchildren

Standing by your bed at night
we listened to stories unfold
we've heard them several times before
yet, each seemed first-time told
Like when your father shot a moose
how everyone would share
or when your grandfather became a chief
and how he truly cared
You spoke of rivers deep and wide
and of the boats you built
you described the forests thick with life
now cut with little guilt
You taught us how to trap the beaver
and when to snare the rabbit
you amazed us with your skills and knowledge
things you did from habit

Now we stand in a hospital room
just days before your time
you're smiling, laughing and telling stories
your mind is in its prime
Then came the day you had to leave
they were waiting up above
So we formed a circle around your bed
and filled it full of love
You left the circle in a joyous way
with family and friends around
this had made it easier, Gramp
as we lowered you in the ground
You spent your time with each of us
our memories we do cherish
Your name continues to draw a smile
upon people of the parish
Today, we stand above your grave
death is a part of life
but there's little pain or sorrow, Gramp
'cause we know you're with your wife
Instead, we're filled with pride and joy
to honour a man like you
an honest man, so full of pride
a man so known to be true

You take it from here ...

Responding

1. Describe the Tone   In a small group, discuss the *tone* of this poem. What emotions does the author seem to be feeling? What emotions does the poem arouse in you as a reader?

2. Write a Character Sketch   The grandfather's stories and behaviour are clues to his character. Using the information in the poem, write a brief sketch of Joseph Augustine in which you describe his personality, values, and experience.

3. **Respond Personally**   In your journal, write about someone in your own life who makes you feel the way the poet feels about his grandfather.

Extending

4. **Research on the Internet**   Joseph Augustine discovered the Augustine Mound, an ancient archaeological treasure trove. Search the Government of New Brunswick Web site and other Internet resources for information on the location and importance of the Augustine Mound. As you research, take notes on your findings, and jot down two new questions that you would like answered. Share your findings in a general class discussion, and see if your classmates can answer some of your questions.

5. **Compose a Poem**   Write your own poem in tribute to a close relative. If there are other family members who feel the same way about this relative, you might invite them to work with you to compose the poem.

6. **Retell a Family Story**   Most families have stories that are passed down from one generation to the next. Think of all the stories that your caregivers—parents, grandparents, older relatives, and family friends—have told you. Choose one of these stories to tell to a group of your classmates.

TIP

- The Government of New Brunswick Web site is at www.gnb.ca.

TIPS

- Make the characters in your story come alive for your audience, describing their manner of dress, their voices, habits, and other features.
- Rehearse telling the story, watching for places where you can add dramatic effect by pausing or speeding up, or by varying the loudness and pitch of your voice.

After Baba's Funeral

"You must never forget your homeland."

Notes

Ted (Theodore) Galay (1941–) was born in Beausejour, Manitoba. He received degrees from the University of Manitoba and the University of British Columbia before settling in Vancouver, where he works as a playwright and professor of mathematics. His own ancestors came from Ukraine to Canada around 1905.

Taras Shevchenko (1814–1861): a Ukrainian poet and revolutionary for political independence

Ivan Franko (1856–1916): a Ukrainian poet and scholar

Translation of Ukrainian words

avo: look

diakuiu: thank you

hoitsi: come to me

idit zdorovi: goodbye, or keep well

Excerpt from a Play by Ted Galay

After Baba's Funeral *is a one-act play depicting how a Ukrainian family in a Manitoba town deals with the passing of their matriarch. The setting is the Danischuk kitchen, where Netty and Walter Danischuk (a couple in their sixties); their son Ronnie (a university student in his late twenties); and Netty's sister and brother-in-law, Minnie and Bill Horoshko, have gathered after coming from the cemetery. The following excerpt is the final scene in the play.*

NETTY: Well, they're gone now. First, Father. Then George. And now Mother. *Pause.* Father's funeral was the worst. You remember how it rained and all the cars were sliding into the ditches.

WALTER: Father Horetchko said he never saw it like that for a funeral.

NETTY: It was like … even God was crying for our father.

Pause.

MINNIE: How was Mother when she was at your place?

NETTY: Fine. You just had to sit with her.

WALTER: She was no trouble.

NETTY: But she wouldn't know who we were, sometimes, and she would ask me, "And where's Netty?" and I'd say—

RONNIE: Mom, you've told that story two times already.

MINNIE: Ronnie, be nice.

NETTY: So what if I have. It's so hard to listen to me? *Pause.* Never mind. You'll go Sunday, you won't have to listen to me any more. *She turns to* MINNIE. You look forward to your kids coming home and they treat you like dirt.

MINNIE: Nastia, don't upset yourself, he didn't mean it.

NETTY: Nobody cares how *I* feel. Nobody tries to understand. I don't know why Jack got so mad at me. I wasn't trying to show him up.

BILL: Netty, you always have to be the most important one.

NETTY: No, I wasn't trying to show them. But somebody had to do it and there was no one else.

RONNIE: You did it because you wanted to.

NETTY: Who else was there? Nobody else would take her!

RONNIE: Damn it, can't you be honest just once? You took her …

WALTER: Ronnie …

NETTY: *I took her because she was afraid!* She was afraid of being left! All right! I wanted to take her. She needed me. Nobody else needed me. And she was afraid. To be left. And I know how it is to be afraid of being left. I'm afraid now. Who's going to look after me when I'm sick? My mother and father have gone. My children have left me. Who will look after me?

Pause.

MINNIE: You have Walter.

Pause.

NETTY: What if he goes first?

WALTER *comes up behind* NETTY, *puts his hands on her shoulders.*

WALTER: You will manage, Netty. You always have. You always will.

RONNIE *moves in to the family. Pause.* NETTY *nods.*

NETTY: When Father used to go away to work, I'd say to him, "I'm afraid, how can I manage? And maybe you won't come back." And he would say to me, "You will manage, Netty. God will help you. And I will be back in the spring." He always came back.
Even when he was dying, he came back. They called us to the hospital, and when we came there, he said, "I was already halfway there, but I came back because I didn't say goodbye to you."

Pause.

MINNIE: Yes, I remember that.

WALTER: Are you all right, Netty?

NETTY: Yes. RONNIE *touches her shoulder. She looks up, squeezes his hand.* Yes, I'm all right. *They leave her. She turns to* MINNIE. Mother's trunk is here. Maybe there's something you'd like.

MINNIE: Nastia, you had her. You should take what you want first.

BILL: That's right. And Jack and Theresa.

MINNIE: Let Ronnie choose something.

NETTY: Ronnie doesn't want anything.

RONNIE: I think … maybe I would like to have something.

MINNIE: Sure. Let Ronnie choose what he wants.

WALTER: I'll get it out. We can look what's there. *He pulls the trunk over to a chair.* Netty, you take the things out.

RONNIE *positions the chair for* NETTY, *and remains by her as she takes things out.*

NETTY: Here's their wedding picture.

MINNIE: Oh, will you look at the costumes!

NETTY: And this is Father and his brother, in the old country, just before they came over. *Points to corner of photo.* See, nineteen-o-five.

RONNIE: Did Baba come then too?

NETTY: No, she came in nineteen-o-six.

MINNIE: Here's *our* wedding picture, Bill.

WALTER: Why don't you take it?

MINNIE: I'll take it for Joanie.

BILL: If I knew then what I know now. You're smart, Ronnie. Stay single.

MINNIE: Listen to him! He knows everything.

BILL: Too late. For me, it's too late.

MINNIE: Don't talk like that. I don't like you to talk like that.

NETTY: Here's some of Baba's kerchiefs from the old country. *Brings out kerchiefs.* This one she brought with her. *Holds one up.* These her brother sent her.

MINNIE: Did anyone write to him?

NETTY: Not yet. I'll have to. *Hands kerchief to MINNIE.* Take one for Joanie. I took one for Edie.

MINNIE takes them.

Look, her black dress she wore for the year after Father died. *Holds it up.*

RONNIE: *Pointing into trunk.* What's that?

NETTY: I don't know. *Pulls out two framed pictures, wrapped in an embroidered cloth.* Oh, Minnie, look.

WALTER: Taras Shevchenko and Ivan Franko.

NETTY: Father always read to us from their poems. They must be here too. *She digs and pulls out two books.* Here they are. Minnie, do you remember?

MINNIE: Yes. "You must never forget your homeland," he used to say.

NETTY: "And you must learn and be educated," he would say to us, "to keep up your tradition, and pass on to your children the stories and songs of their people."

MINNIE: Ronnie, you should have these.

RONNIE: Yes. I'd like to have them.

NETTY passes them over to him.

BILL: You'll have to learn to read Ukrainian.

NETTY: He knows. At catechism, he learned.

WALTER: What else is there?

NETTY: Just a quilt. *Pulling it out.* Baba made it herself. No. Minnie, will you look at that!

MINNIE: *As NETTY passes them to her.* Valianky! *They are high, felt boots.* She kept her *valianky*!

NETTY: I forgot about that. She kept them when they moved from the farm. You remember?

BILL: Baba in her *valianky*, going to feed the chickens.

RONNIE: Now I remember! He was making fun of Baba!

NETTY: What? Who?

RONNIE: Peter! That's why I wouldn't stay at Baba's. He laughed at her. He said she dressed funny, she talked funny. He even said she smelled funny!

BILL: What Peter?

WALTER: Kashka's boy. When they came out years ago.

RONNIE: So I wouldn't play with him. But I was ashamed and when Baba tried to hug me, I pushed her away and I wouldn't go to her. Because she did smell funny. And she was wearing *valianky*. Then I wanted to tell her I was sorry but I never did.

WALTER: She forgot long ago.

NETTY: It didn't matter.

RONNIE: Can I have them?

WALTER: *Looks at* NETTY. Sure.

He takes them and passes them over to RONNIE.

BILL: What do you want them for?

RONNIE: To keep my feet warm.

MINNIE: Well, old man, I guess we should be going. You have a long day tomorrow.

BILL: That's right.

WALTER: Well, it's good you could come.

MINNIE: You'll have to come and see us soon.

WALTER: Sure. *He exits to get* BILL's *coat.*

NETTY: We'll try, but since the accident, Walter doesn't like to drive.

MINNIE: Ronnie, while you're home, bring your Mama and Daddy for a visit.

BILL: Sure, you can drive them.

RONNIE: All right.

WALTER *re-enters with coat and helps* BILL *on with it.*

MINNIE: Good. Well, goodbye, Nastia. It's a sad day.

NETTY: Yes. *They kiss.* Goodbye. *Idit zdorovi.*

MINNIE: *Diakuiu.*

WALTER: Goodbye, Bill. *They shake hands.* Minnie.

MINNIE: Goodbye, Walter. And Ronnie. And don't forget, you come to see us.

RONNIE: We won't. Goodbye, Aunt Minnie, Uncle Bill.

MINNIE *and* BILL *exit.*

WALTER: Bill is looking good. Don't you think?

Pause. NETTY *touches his arm.*

NETTY: Yes. He's all right.

NETTY *takes off her apron and goes to the trunk.* RONNIE *stands near the chair.* WALTER *starts to clear the table.* NETTY *puts the things back in the trunk.*

Such a small box. To hold so many memories. *She closes the trunk and pushes it back to where it was.* I'm going to miss her. We only had her for a short time, but the house feels empty without her. She would sit here (*sits*), and she would l-o-o-k (*leans forward*) and she would say, "*Avo* ... look ..." *points toward* RONNIE. "... the little boy.... He's there." And she would reach out her arms and say, "*Hoitsi, hoitsi.*"

NETTY *reaches out her arms. Pause.* RONNIE *takes a step forward.* NETTY *lowers her arms.*

NETTY: Well, it's good you could come. Jack wanted to have one grandchild from each family for pallbearers. We wouldn't have had anybody if you hadn't come.

WALTER: Yes, it's good you could come.

RONNIE: Yes. It's good.

You take it from here ...

Responding

1. **Reflect on Reading Strategy**   As a class, discuss how well the "As you read" suggestion worked for you. Did it help you sort out the characters and follow the narrative? Explain.

2. **Identify with the Characters**   Often when we see characters on stage, we recognize aspects of our own friends and family in their behaviour. Which characters in this scene remind you of people in your own life? Discuss your response in a small group.

3. **Isolate Background Information**   Important background information is often buried in the speeches and comments of characters. Work your way through the dialogue in this excerpt to uncover important details about this family's past, and use the information to write a brief family history.

4. **Role-Play a New Scene**   Ronnie is considerably younger than the rest of the characters on stage. Working with a partner, role-play the conversation that might take place back at the university when Ronnie tells a close friend about what happened on his visit home.

5. **Write a Eulogy**   It is traditional at many funerals for a close friend or family member to give a eulogy for the person who has died. The eulogy takes the form of a tribute to the deceased, telling about his or her personal qualities and approach to life. Using the information provided in this excerpt, write a eulogy for Baba.

> **TIP**
> - Read some examples of eulogies before you start to write this one. One example is Justin Trudeau's eulogy for his father, "A Son's Eulogy," in Unit 5 of this text. Many other examples may be found on the Internet.

Extending

6. **Create a Memory Chest**   Baba's trunk contains objects from her life that were enormously significant for her. Choose a famous person or someone you know and admire, and describe 8 to 10 objects you would put into a memory chest for this person. Be sure to cover the entire course of the person's life, from the earliest days to the present. Present your list to a small group, explaining the reasons behind your selections.

7. **Prepare an Oral Report**   This play presents a number of words and traditions familiar to the many Canadians of Ukrainian origin. Working with a partner, investigate the history and presence in Canada of the Ukrainian people—or of another culture in Canada other than your own. Choose one aspect to focus on (e.g., history of settlement in Canada; how this group has contributed to the Canadian literary/art/music scene, or to other areas such as science, medicine, athletics), and prepare a brief oral report on your findings to present to the class.

> **TIP**
> - Consider using audio-visual aids—video clips, music samples, photographs—to enhance your presentation.

Reflecting on the Unit

Responding

1. Consider Youthful Rebellion   Why do young people often rebel against convention, rules, and "the system"? Take another look at "Zits," "Still Me Inside," "The Pose," and "Mules," and think about whether the main character is being rebellious in his or her actions or attitudes. Identify the character that you think is the most rebellious. In a small group, talk about your choice and support your decision.

2. Consider Impact   "A Small Cheese Pizza," "Helping Others Best Cure for Loneliness," and "Social Security" portray people in need. Choose one of these stories and write a personal essay describing the impression it made on you. Has it changed the way you view, and behave toward, strangers who have fewer advantages than you?

3. Write a Letter   As a class, define the word "alienated" and discuss how this applies to both the son in "Mules" and Karen in "The Carved Table." Then, working individually, write a letter to one of these characters offering advice on how to deal with these feelings. Base your advice on your personal experience, the experience of others you know, and on what you have learned as you worked through this unit.

Extending

4. Reach Out   The speaker in "Reach Out and Touch" yearns to make a simple gesture to help stop misunderstanding. As a class, brainstorm a list of ways in which individuals can begin to overcome barriers that can lead to prejudice.

5. Explore an Issue   In a small group, share a time when your rights as an individual were restricted because of the need to protect the rights of society (e.g., you had to turn off your cellphone at a theatre). Choose one situation and prepare a skit that depicts the scenario from both perspectives.

> **SELF-ASSESSMENT**
>
> The main focus of this unit is the relationship between the individual and society. Identify
> - the most thought-provoking things you encountered
> - what you found confusing
>
> Write your response as a personal journal entry.

To tend unfailingly,
unflinchingly, toward a goal, is
the secret of success.
– Anna Pavlova

Don't agonize. Organize.
– Florynce R. Kennedy

The readiness is all.
– William Shakespeare

Out in the World

This unit looks at situations you will encounter
as you move into the world, with practical information on goal
setting, money management, job hunting, and more.

As the words of celebrated Russian ballerina Anna Pavlova
remind us, goal setting is a necessary ingredient for success.

Lawyer and social activist Florynce R. Kennedy's words
have inspired many generations. Indeed, when one starts out
in life, it is important to be organized and to plan ahead.

The line from Shakespeare highlights the point that the
right attitude can contribute to success. If you prepare yourself,
you will readily cope with change and challenge as your
journey continues beyond high school.

As you review the selections
in this unit, keep the
following points in mind:

1) Common sense and
   common courtesy will
   take you far.
2) It is hard to do anything
   well without a goal and
   a plan.
3) Knowing your strengths
   and weaknesses is a
   good step toward self-
   improvement.
4) High-school graduation is
   only one step to a future
   of lifelong learning.

The Far Side

Cartoon by Gary Larson

Notes

Gary Larson (1950–) was born in Tacoma, Washington. He loved to draw when he was young, but loved science more. (The scientific world later honoured Larson by naming a louse and a butterfly after him!) The award-winning Larson cartooned for 14 years, retiring in 1995 to live in Seattle.

THE FAR SIDE® BY GARY LARSON

"Yoo-hoo! Oh, yoo-hoo! ... I think I'm getting a blister."

You take it from here ...

Responding

1. Respond to the Cartoon   What can you tell about the speaker in this cartoon? Has he been on the job long? What does he have to learn? How do you suspect his boss and his co-workers would respond? Discuss your views with a partner.

2. Consider Humour   Why do cartoons make people chuckle? As a class, discuss whether you find this cartoon humorous, and explain why or why not. Then, consider humour more generally. Does laughter come from personal experience? From a sense of embarrassment? From other sources? Give examples to explain your thinking.

3. Discuss Issues   In a humorous way, this cartoon reminds us that certain people may not be suitable for certain jobs. Discuss with the class what can happen if we ignore this fact—for example, when seeking work, or hiring new employees.

Extending

4. Write a Diary Entry   As the speaker in this cartoon, write a diary entry describing your first day on the job. Include your reflections on what happened, how you handled the challenges of the day, and how you feel about going in the next day. Then, write a second diary entry dated one year later describing how you helped a new employee get through his or her first day at your workplace.

5. Create a Cartoon or Collage   Imagine the worst possible job for you—a "nightmare" job that is completely unsuited to your needs and abilities. Then, imagine your dream job. Visualize details about the type of work you do, the people you work with, your work space, and so on. Create a two-part collage or cartoon contrasting these scenarios.

6. Write a Personal Response   Write a personal journal response in which you consider your own suitability—and unsuitability—for particular jobs or careers. Describe what plans you have in place, or might develop, to guide you in your search for a suitable job or career. Include some consideration of where you might seek further direction in this matter.

Ten Commandments of How to Get Along with People

by ANN LANDERS

LIST/ADVICE

Notes

Ann Landers is a widely known American syndicated advice columnist, with an estimated 90 million readers. Her advice covers a diverse range of topics.

1) Keep skid chains on your tongue; always say less than you think. Cultivate a low, persuasive voice. How you say it counts more than what you say.

2) Make promises sparingly, and keep them faithfully, no matter what it costs.

3) Never let an opportunity pass to say a kind and encouraging word to or about somebody. Praise good work, regardless of who did it. If criticism is needed, criticize helpfully, never spitefully.

4) Be interested in others, their pursuits, their work, their homes, and families. Make merry with those who rejoice; with those who weep, mourn. Let everyone you meet, however humble, feel that you regard him as a person of importance.

5) Be cheerful. Don't burden or depress those around you by dwelling on your minor aches and pains and small disappointments. Remember, everyone is carrying some kind of a load.

6) Keep an open mind. Discuss but don't argue. It is a mark of a superior mind to be able to disagree without being disagreeable.

7) Let your virtues, if you have any, speak for themselves. Refuse to talk of another's vices. Discourage gossip. It is a waste of valuable time and can be extremely destructive.

8) Be careful of another's feelings. Wit and humour at the other person's expense are rarely worth it and may hurt when least expected.

9) Pay no attention to ill-natured remarks about you. Remember, the person who carried the message may not be the most accurate reporter in the world. Simply live so that nobody will believe them. Disordered nerves and bad digestion are a common cause of backbiting.

10) Don't be too anxious about the credit due you. Do your best, and be patient. Forget about yourself, and let others "remember." Success is much sweeter that way.

You take it from here ...

Responding

1. React to What You Read   What do you think is the best piece of advice in this selection, one that you might adopt as a personal resolution? How could it change your life or the way you see yourself? Write your answer as a personal journal response.

2. Consider Audience   This selection appeared on a Web site that focuses on workplace issues. In a small group, discuss why it would be appropriate for that site's audience. For what other audiences might it be equally relevant?

3. Look at Sequence of Ideas   Consider whether these commandments seem to be presented in a particular order. Do they fall under specific themes or categories? Would you suggest any changes to the order? Would you leave out any of the 10 points or substitute different ones? Explain your answers to a partner.

Extending

4. Create Your Own List   Create your own "Ten Commandments" of advice for how to succeed out in the world—for example, Ten Commandments of How to Get and Keep a Job, How to Attract and Keep Good Employees, or How to Get Along with a Roommate. Add a paragraph explaining who your intended audience is, and how you chose a tone and writing style appropriate for that audience.

5. Add a Visual   Create a computer-formatted version of the list you wrote in Activity 4. Use a combination of graphics and varied fonts to present your text most effectively. Share your design with a small group, explaining the effect you wished to achieve and the audience it is directed to, inviting their comments.

> **PEER ASSESSMENT**
> As you read each list, consider the following:
> - Did the list offer helpful advice?
> - Was the design interesting and eye-catching? Did it present the text clearly?
> - Was the explanation of the design clear?

The Top 10 Best Ideas for Setting Goals

by HILTON JOHNSON

LIST/ADVICE

Notes

Hilton Johnson is president and founder of a virtual sales training and coaching organization in the United States.

You cannot pick up a book or participate in a training program today without the author or instructor teaching the power of goal setting. Yet most people today spend more time planning a two-week vacation than planning their lives by setting goals. It's been said that achieving goals is not a problem—it's *setting* goals that is the problem. People just don't do it. They leave their lives to chance … and usually end up broke by the time they reach retirement.

I thought that since this is such an important ingredient for [success], this was a good time to share with you some of the greatest thoughts about goal setting that I've discovered over the years.

So, here goes…. The Top 10 Best Ideas for Setting Goals:

1) **Make a List of Your Values**

What's really important to you? Your family? Your religion? Your leisure time? Your hobbies? Decide on what your most important values in life are and then make sure that the goals you set are designed to include and enhance them.

2) **Begin with the End in Mind**

Tom Watson, the founder of IBM, was once asked what he attributed the phenomenal success of IBM to and he said it was three things:

The first thing was that he created a very clear image in his mind of what he wanted his company to look like when it was done. He then asked himself how would a company like that have to act on a day-to-day basis. And then in the very beginning of building his company, he began to act that way.

3) **Project Yourself into the Future**

The late, great Earl Nightingale created a whole new industry (self-improvement) after a 20-year study on what made people successful. The bottom-line result of his research was simply, "We become what we think about."

Whatever thoughts dominate our minds most of the time are what we become. That's why goal setting is so critical in achieving success because it keeps us focused on what's really important to us. He then said that the easiest way to reach our goals is to pretend that we had *already* achieved our goals.

That is, begin to walk, talk, and act as though we are already experiencing the success we seek. Then, those things will come to us naturally through the power of the subconscious mind.

4) Write Down the 10 Things You Want this Year

By making a list of things that are important to you, you begin to create images in your mind. It's been said that your mind will actually create chaos if necessary to make images become a reality. Because of this, the list of 10 things will probably result in you achieving at least 8 of them within the year.

5) Create Your Storyboard

Get a piece of poster board and attach it to a wall in your office or home where you will see it often. As you go through magazines, brochures, and so on, and you see the pictures of the things you want, cut them out and glue them to your storyboard.

In other words, make yourself a collage of the goals that excite you … knowing full well that as you look at them every day, they will soon be yours.

6) Decide on the Three Most Important Things

Decide on three things that you want to achieve before you die. Then work backwards listing three things you want in the next 20 years, 10 years, 5 years, this year, this month, this week and finally, the three most important things you want to accomplish today.

7) Ask Yourself Good Questions

As you think about your goals, instead of *wishing* for them to come true, ask yourself *how* and *what you can do* to make them come true. The subconscious mind will respond to your questions far more strongly than it would statements or wishes.

8) Focus on One Project at a Time

One of the greatest mistakes people make in setting goals is trying to work on too many things at one time. There is tremendous power in giving laser-beam focused attention to just one idea, one project, or one objective at a time.

9) Write Out an "Ideal Scenario"

Pretend that you are a newspaper reporter who has just finished an interview about the outstanding success that you've achieved and the article is now in the newspaper. How would it read? What would be the headline? Write the article yourself, projecting yourself into the future as though it had already happened. Describe the activities of your daily routine now that are very successful. Don't forget the headline.

10) Pray and Meditate

As you get into bed each evening, think about your goal before you drop off to sleep. Get a very clear colourful image in your mind of seeing yourself doing the things you'll be doing after you've reached your major goal. (Remember to include your values.) And then begin to ask and demand for these things through meditation and prayer.

You take it from here ...

Responding

1. Discuss Practicality of Ideas   What idea did you choose as something practical that you could try? In a discussion group, find out what ideas other students chose. Which ideas seem to be the most popular? The least popular? Try to account for these trends.

2. Personalize the List   Carefully read through the list again and reorder the items to suit your personal goal-reaching strategies. Begin with the idea that you find most useful, and end with the least useful. Beside each, write a one- or two-sentence response, explaining the usefulness or potential of each idea.

3. Identify Ideas You Are Already Using   With a small group, discuss some goals that you have already accomplished in your life. Identify some strategies you used to reach these goals. Did you use any of the strategies listed in this selection, or similar strategies? Explain.

Extending

4. Create Your Storyboard   Following the suggestions in Idea 5, create a storyboard of the goals you hope to achieve in the next year, the next 5 years, and the next 10 years. Share your storyboard with a partner or a small group, explaining your goals and describing how you intend to go about achieving them.

> **SELF-ASSESSMENT**
> - What did you learn about your own goals in the storyboarding process?
> - Did you clarify how you can go about attaining them?
> - What next steps will you take toward attaining one of your defined goals?

5. Write Your Own "Ideal Scenario"   Use Idea 9 and create your own Ideal Scenario. Write it in the style of a newspaper article, including quotations from your own interview of yourself. Be sure to include a headline.

She could be a millionaire by the time she turns 25.

Teen Financier Gets Oprah's Attention

by COLETTE DERWORIZ

PROFILE

Notes

equities: amounts of money that a business is worth beyond what is owed on it

mutual fund: a financial fund that invests the pooled capital of its members in diversified securities

savvy: shrewdness; skill based on knowledge

Lesley Scorgie, 17, reads the business pages and checks the Internet as she plans her investments.

For Calgary teenager Lesley Scorgie, investing her money was a no-brainer.

Now her savvy investment skills have caught the attention of U.S. talk show host Oprah Winfrey.

Scorgie, a 17-year-old honours student at Dr. E.P. Scarlett High School, started investing in Canada Savings Bonds when she was 10. She soon diversified into mutual funds and equities, all with money she made working part-time jobs.

She won't disclose how much money she made, but as a condition of appearing on Oprah she had to show them financial statements proving she could be a millionaire by the time she turns 25.

"I am kind of shocked at myself that I can do that," Scorgie said Sunday. "It requires a lot of persistence and attention but it's totally achievable."

Scorgie and her mom were whisked off to Chicago last Tuesday to tape the Oprah Show, called Ordinary People, Extraordinary Wealth.

It features personal investment author Ric Edelman, and gives viewers eight secrets for "you" to become wealthy.

Scorgie saved money from babysitting and delivering flyers, and entered the world of investments full-force once she got her first part-time job at the Calgary Public Library.

"Something I learned in the first few months of having a job is that I really don't have a lot of things to buy. I don't have the financial commitments that an adult has," she said.

"It is a proven fact teenagers have more disposable income than adults."

She said the most difficult part of investing her hard-earned cash was getting people to take her seriously.

"It's horrible," said Scorgie. "It's such a pain, and you wonder why kids blow all their money because there is no one there to take you seriously when you say, 'I have $1000, can I invest it?'"

With supportive parents and a keen interest in the stock markets, mutual funds, and investing, Scorgie is on track to a worry-free future.

"I don't want people to look at me differently," she said, noting she hopes her story will inspire other youth to invest their money.

"People are finally respecting what I say. I have been saying this for so long, and it is so practical," she said. "You've got to save your money, you can't just blow it on lunch every single day.

"It is really important for kids to start investing when they are young, to have a secure financial future."

Scorgie plans to take business classes at the University of Calgary next fall.

You take it from here ...

Responding

1. **Discuss Reading Strategies**   Without looking back at the selection, make a list of points that you remember. Would you say that you remember most of the important points, or very few? What do you think determines what you can recall and what you ignore or forget when you read? Compare results and ideas with a partner.

2. **Discuss Reactions**   Discuss your opinion of this profile with your classmates. Did it get your attention? Why or why not?

3. **Consider Spending Patterns**   According to the selection, "It is a proven fact teenagers have more disposable income than adults." Discuss this statement in a small group. Do you agree with it in general? Does your own experience bear it out? Consider your own spending behaviour. For example, do you buy lunch every day? Do you buy your own clothes? Do you spend money each week on entertainment? In your opinion, do you spend a greater proportion of your money on "non-essentials" than most adults do? Explain.

Extending

4. Set Personal Financial Goals

    a) Make up a budget sheet for yourself, with spending categories such as "entertainment," "transportation," "clothes," "gifts," "miscellaneous," and "savings." To set some guidelines for future spending, estimate how much you have spent on each category in the past month, the past six months, and the past year. Note any big-ticket items you are saving for, as well as the amount of money you have in the bank, and money you expect to receive (from part-time jobs, gifts, allowances) in the upcoming weeks and months.

    b) Using the information you compiled in part (a), write an analysis of your current spending habits, and establish your spending and saving goals for the next year.

5. Research Money Matters   Think about how you would go about investing $1000. Obtain some basic information written for beginning investors, and begin to explore different investment options. For each option, consider the risks involved and the return you could realistically expect at the end of a year. Organize your findings into a brief written report.

> **TIP**
>
> • As a starting point, find books on personal finance in the library, or pick up some investor information at a local bank branch.

How to Make Yourself Save

FROM THE INVESTOR LEARNING CENTRE OF CANADA

TIPS

Notes

The Investor Learning Centre of Canada is a registered charity dedicated to providing non-biased, non-promotional investor information to Canadians.

Investor Learning Centre OF CANADA

GICs: guaranteed investment certificates

After dieting and trying to quit smoking, saving money is probably the hardest thing to do. Regularly saving a portion of your earnings seems like it should be simple, but it's not.

There are always emergencies that take up the extra money—like car repairs or dentist bills. Or there are temptations, like a nice dinner out on the town, or that antique chest of drawers you've been eyeing at the store down the street. While you work hard and deserve to treat yourself, the extra treats and unexpected expenses can derail even the best-intentioned savings plan.

The key to saving is really equal parts common sense and discipline. Here are a few tips to help you put away that extra bit of money each month—and still have enough money to treat yourself without feeling guilty.

Tip #1—Set realistic goals.

Ever looked at your salary and then at your paltry bank balance and sworn you would stash away at least a third of your next pay cheque? Many of us have, but few of us actually are able to meet such a tough goal. We just end up feeling rotten about ourselves, throw in the towel, and decide to try again next month. The truth is, you've got to be easier on yourself. Most savings plans fail because we set unrealistic goals for ourselves. If you're having trouble saving now, imposing a huge savings target isn't going to help.

The best strategy is to start small, with a target you know you can hit. Then once you get used to the reduced level of spending, you can gradually increase your monthly savings target. Pretty soon you'll be putting away more money than you ever thought possible.

Tip #2—Pay yourself first.

You may have heard of the old saying, "Pay yourself first." If you deduct your savings directly from your pay cheque or bank account, you are treating your savings like a bill you have to pay. The money is already gone so you can't be tempted to spend it. And you'll be surprised at how much money you've saved without even missing it. You can set up an automatic withdrawal plan that deposits money directly into a mutual fund, Canada Savings Bond, or even a special savings account. But remember to make your monthly withdrawal a realistic amount—about 10 percent of your salary. Start small because if you take too much money away from your monthly income, then you risk having to halt your savings plan to make ends meet.

Tip #3—Reduce buying on credit.

Buying on credit is extremely easy and many people have several cards—maybe two from banks or trust companies, one from a gas station, and a few from department stores.

There are many advantages to using credit cards. You don't have to carry around a lot of cash, and you can take advantage of bargains when your cash is limited. And then there are those emergency situations when a credit card saves the day.

But unfortunately, having credit cards at your disposal can also lead to bad buying habits. You can whip a card out and buy that new leather jacket before you pause to think about whether you can really afford it.

Now, maybe that new jacket isn't really a bad buy if you can pay off your credit card balance each month. But the truth is, many of us don't, and now you are incurring hefty interest charges. You end up spending even more money—money that you might have been able to put into a mutual fund or a savings account.

Tip #4—Don't forget to reward yourself.

Let's say you've embarked on a monthly savings plan and somehow managed to save a little more than you expected. Or you've saved up for a new bedroom suite, and you have a bit left over. Spend some of those extra savings. The positive reinforcement you will get from treating yourself will help you save successfully in the future.

Four tips to help you save

- Set realistic goals.
- Pay yourself first.
- Reduce buying on credit.
- Don't forget to reward yourself.

Prepare for cash emergencies

No matter how disciplined you are with your spending habits, cash emergencies tend to pop up when you least expect it and suddenly you are short on cash.

To make sure you are covered for these situations, it's a good idea to have some "liquid" funds that you can withdraw quickly. A rough guideline is to have the equivalent of three months' salary available in case of an emergency. Money in a savings account, Canada Savings Bonds, cashable GICs, or in a money market mutual fund doesn't fluctuate in value and you can get at it quickly.

You take it from here ...

Responding

1. Think about What You Read   Discuss with a partner what tip in the selection represents the best advice to you personally—now. Explain why. What tip(s) do you think you will follow in the future? Explain.

2. Discuss Rewards   Were you surprised by Tip 4? Write one or two paragraphs explaining the reasoning behind it, and how it takes human behaviour into consideration.

How to Make Yourself Save

3. Assess the Additional Information   The article clearly organizes four tips, using sub-headings and a summary near the end. What information is added as an unofficial fifth tip? How important is this information? Do you think it ends the article satisfactorily? Explain your opinion to a partner.

4. Identify Your Spending Habits   The ability to save money has much to do with controlling spending. In a reflective journal response, examine your spending habits and how they make saving easy or difficult for you. Also consider which tip from the article is most relevant to you.

Extending

5. Do the Math   Working as a class or in a small group, look up the current interest rate on a major credit card (e.g., Visa, MasterCard, American Express). Assume that a minimum payment equals 5 percent of the unpaid balance, including the interest. If you spend $100 a month on a credit card and make only the minimum monthly payment, what will your debt be at the end of a year? How much of this debt is interest charges? When you have finished the math exercise, discuss how it helped you appreciate the point made in Tip 3. Will this knowledge likely influence your choices in the future? Explain.

6. Discuss Credit   With a small group, share your thoughts on the ready availability of credit in our society. Do you believe it brings about more benefits than problems? Or do you think the reverse is true? Recall specific print and TV ads you have seen that promote credit cards and "buy-now-pay-later" schemes. Discuss the benefits these ads emphasize, as well as the responsibilities that go with buying on credit. What happens if you don't live up to those responsibilities?

7. Create a Spoof Ad   With a small group, find examples of some of the print and TV ads promoting credit cards or "buy-now-pay-later" schemes discussed in Activity 6. Choose one as the basis for a spoof ad showing the downside of credit. Present your ad to the class in the form of a role-played or videotaped TV commercial, or as a full-page print advertisement.

PEER ASSESSMENT

As you view each spoof ad, consider the following:
- Did the spoof ad make a strong statement about the potential pitfalls of credit?
- Was it humorous? Ironic?
- Was it creatively presented?

Banking and Saving
by Citizenship and Immigration Canada

WEB SITE ARTICLE

Notes

caisse populaire: French term for credit union

BANKING

How do banks work?

Essentially, banks and other financial institutions such as trust companies, caisses populaires, and credit unions provide

- a safe place to keep your money
- services to help you manage your money
- loans and mortgages

It is important to realize that financial institutions do not just hold your money in a safe place. They make money by

- investing your money, for which they pay you interest
- lending you money, for which they charge you interest
- providing you with credit, usually in the form of a credit card. The interest rate on credit cards on your unpaid balance is quite a lot higher than on a conventional loan.

How do credit cards work?

A credit card, usually provided by a financial institution or a department store, allows you to

buy things to a certain limit and then to pay the money over a period of time. In other words, you owe money to the credit card company. If you pay only the "balance now due" portion of the monthly bill, you are paying interest, but you are not paying off the debt you owe to the credit card company.

What do financial institutions offer you?

- **Safety.** All banks and most trust companies are regulated by the federal government to determine whether they are financially sound. All caisses populaires and credit unions and some trust companies are regulated by the provinces. All deposit taking institutions, other than caisses populaires and credit unions, are required to be members of the Canada Deposit Insurance Corporation (CDIC). CDIC insures eligible deposits to a maximum of $60 000.

- **Advice.** Banks tell you in advance what kind of account, loan, or mortgage you can receive. They usually give responsible advice, but you should check with more than one to find the accounts and services that are best for you. You do not need to sign any agreement until you are sure that you understand what it means.

- **Services.** All financial institutions offer packages of financial services. You should choose the type of account that you will use most. For example, an account that offers travellers' cheques, international credit cards, and foreign banking services may charge extra for each of these services.

When should you borrow money?

There are many good reasons to borrow money, such as furthering your education, opening or expanding a business, or buying a house. These are all investments that will likely provide a good return in the long run. You might also need a car, a computer, or other tools to help you with your business.

SAVING

Why, where, and how should you save money?

Most people budget to save some money each month, usually in a savings account in a bank, trust company, caisse populaire, or credit union. You can save for a number of reasons:

1) **Major purchases.** Before a reputable financial institution will lend you money for a house, a car, or to start a small business, it will usually require that you provide a down payment of up to 20 percent of the full cost from your own savings.

2) **Retirement.** If you contribute to a registered retirement savings plan (RRSP), you do not have to pay income tax on these savings until you use them. Many people contribute to such a plan at work through payroll deductions, especially if they do not have a pension plan. Your bank can tell you more about RRSPs.

3) **Emergencies.** To some degree you can insure against accidents, sickness, and loss of income, but it is a good idea to have savings put aside for the unexpected. Most financial advisors suggest you try to keep three months' salary in the bank.

4) **Specific longer-term family needs** such as your children's post-secondary education, which is not free in Canada.

You take it from here ...

Responding

1. Understand the Main Points   Working with a partner, identify the main points this article addresses. Which points did you identify as being important right now, and which will you likely need five years from now?

2. Discuss Text, Audience, and Purpose   Write a paragraph explaining each of the following:

- Where does this article originate? Where else could this information be found?
- Who is the target audience of this article? How can they benefit from it?
- What is the purpose of the article? Do you think it achieves its purpose?

3. Look at Format   Work with a partner to explain how the information in this selection is organized, identifying some of the techniques that were used to present the points in a clear, easy-to-read style.

Extending

4. Create a Brochure   Use the information in this selection as the basis for a brochure. Begin by identifying your target audience, and choose the tone and look accordingly. Edit the text and select appropriate visuals to accompany it. Produce the final layout.

5. Research Banks   Find out what banking institutions and services are currently available to you. As a group project, do a comparative study of at least three financial institutions (banks, credit unions) in your community. For each institution, collect information on services such as

- basic chequing and savings accounts
- Internet banking
- investment services
- public information seminars (on home-buying, personal financial planning, and so on)
- special services geared to teens and young adults
- student loans
- "teen" credit cards
- support for young entrepreneurs

Review the information as a group. Do all banks offer the same services? Are some more youth-friendly than others? Which would you choose to do business with, and why? Organize your information into a comparison chart or a written report assessing the relative strengths and weaknesses of each institution.

TIPS

Begin your search for information by doing one or more of the following:
- visiting the institutions' Web sites
- visiting the institutions in person
- checking the reference section of the library

Before you read, discuss with the class your own experiences with shopping online.

As you read, notice whether you are being convinced to shop online.

E-Commerce: What's in It for Me as a Consumer?

by the Canadian Bankers Association

INFORMATIONAL BOOKLET

Notes

For more information on electronic commerce, visit the Office of Consumer Affairs Web site at http://strategis.ic.gc.ca/oca.

While it's easy to get caught up in the hype surrounding e-commerce, not all consumers want to shop online. Some people prefer shopping in traditional ways, talking to sales staff and "touching" a product. Although e-commerce may not be for everyone, it does offer certain benefits:

- opportunities to browse, comparison shop, and make purchases on your own terms
- convenience—the store is always open on the Net
- an expanded marketplace—your shopping mall has gone global (you can purchase from a company in Paris, Tokyo, or San Francisco, all from the comfort of home)
- a wider product selection
- the ability to make informed decisions by gaining access to plenty of information and relevant links to other sites
- the potential for lower prices resulting from reduced supplier overhead costs and greater competition
- easier access to suppliers

BARRIERS TO BUYING ONLINE

Concerns of consumers who have never purchased over the Internet

Security	90%
Can't see or touch product	69%
Privacy of giving personal info	67%
Customer recourse	64%
Prefer other ways of shopping	59%
Too new/people aren't ready	16%
Hard to find what you're looking for	9%

Source: Deloitte & Touche E-Commerce Holiday Survey, November, 1999

WHY WE LIKE SHOPPING ONLINE

75%	Said shopping on the Internet saved them money
50%	Said it was more convenient
48%	Said there was more choice on the Internet
29%	Said it was more fun than traditional shopping

Source: Ernst & Young Internet Shopping Survey

Online Shopping Tips

✔ Know the merchant you're dealing with.
✔ Look for detailed product information.
✔ Read the contract's terms and conditions and print or save them.
✔ Check for quality assurance certificates or seals.
✔ Verify the merchant has a fair and clear complaints-handling process.
✔ Ensure you're comfortable with the merchant's purchasing process and that you know how to cancel your order.
✔ Make sure the merchant has a secure transaction system to protect your financial information.
✔ Review the merchant's policy for protecting personal information.
✔ Be on guard against mass-market e-mail.
✔ Educate yourself and your children about controlling personal information.
✔ Watch out for scams.

You take it from here ...

Responding

1. Assess Impartiality   Discuss the information in this selection with a small group of classmates. Does it provide both pros and cons about shopping online? Is the information slanted in any way? Has the information and the way it is presented influenced your own opinion about shopping online? Explain.

2. Examine Design Features   Work with a partner to examine the design of the selection. Make notes on the following:

   • What part of the design first catches your eye?
   • What information is the most reader-friendly?
   • What different types of fonts are used, and where? How do they affect readability?
   • Is the text easy to read quickly?

3. Consider Pros and Cons   As a class, review the two tables in this selection. Take a poll to see how many agree with each item listed (e.g., "Agree or Disagree: I don't like to shop online because I have concerns about security"). Are the percentages similar to those in the tables? If not, can you suggest reasons for the difference? Compare your own views on online shopping with those of other students in an informal class debate.

E-Commerce: What's in It for Me as a Consumer?   **401**

Extending

4. Comparison-Shop   Work with a partner to evaluate online and real-life shopping, comparing costs, time spent, and the overall experience. Begin by creating a shopping list of 10 items. Include groceries, drug store items, and one gift for a special occasion (e.g., a wedding, birthday, or graduation). Then, locate each item on your list, both online and in stores, and record the costs, including taxes. Write a short report on the experience, comparing the costs and relative time spent on each "shopping trip." Include your thoughts on the overall shopping experience: whether you found it more enjoyable to search for items online or in the real stores, stating why.

5. Think through Related Issues   The information in this selection is directed to consumers, with tips on how to shop online safely, and information on pros and cons from the consumer's perspective. As a class, discuss how e-commerce affects other groups, such as retailers, small-business owners, and their employees. What actions might they take to adapt in an age of e-commerce? After the discussion, work with a partner to design a brochure with advice for a different target audience.

6. Search for More Information   What are your consumer rights when you shop online? How can you make payments in a secure way? What are some other issues related to e-commerce? Do research to find additional information on this topic and report your findings back to the class.

Looking for Work Is a Search Campaign

by JANIS FOORD KIRK

WEB PAGE ARTICLE

Notes

Janis Foord Kirk is a career consultant and columnist living in Kelowna, British Columbia. Her columns have appeared regularly in *The Toronto Star* and the *Ottawa Citizen*. She has also written two books: *Surviving the Upheaval in Your Workplace* and *Survivability: Career Strategies for the New World of Work*.

A search for work is a campaign, a self-marketing campaign. Generally it unfolds in two distinct yet complementary and overlapping parts. There's a "planning" stage, followed by a "doing" stage.

The "planning" part includes labour market research, study, and self-assessment. Some of the tangible results from preparatory efforts like these are your personal profile, a list of 10 to 15 potential employers, and at least one well-targeted résumé.

You move into the "doing" stage once you begin answering advertisements, going on interviews, following up, and negotiating offers.

Somewhere in the middle of these two stages is a grey area, part planning, part doing. Here, you talk to people you know and conduct informational interviews, looking for leads, new contacts, jobs, and opportunities.

Because there's some confusion about the terms (most of them career management jargon) that define a search, here's a brief glossary.

Search:
At one time better known as a "job search." Nowadays, however, the successful completion of a search doesn't always result in a "job." Contract, consulting, and independent opportunities come up as readily. Work of this kind can nonetheless move you along your career path, especially if it adds experience, builds skills, and shows entrepreneurial effort.

The visible work marketplace:
Think of the want ads, employment agencies, recruiting firms. Most people look for work in this marketplace so competition tends to be stiff. By some counts, however, only about 25 percent of available opportunities are found here. Cover these bases diligently, but don't limit your search activities to this market.

The hidden marketplace:
Most opportunities are never advertised or placed with a recruiter, making this the largest

marketplace for work. The trouble is, it has no formal structure. You have to create one yourself. Do this by choosing a particular field or industry, researching its labour market, networking within it, and by building a list of potential employers including the name of the person who would be your boss.

Labour market research:

You'll need to develop, as well, a research file on the field itself. Visit libraries and information resource centres. Contact industry-specific associations. Check the Internet, look for industry and government studies.

Networking:

This occurs as you move out into your field, occupation, or profession to meet (and impress) people who may be able to help you in your search. Cast a wide net. Don't only contact people who may have a specific job for you. As important are industry intelligence and the names of people who work in the field. In other words, network for information, leads, and contacts as well as for jobs.

Contacts:

Contacts come in two different varieties. People already in your acquaintance: Friends, relatives, neighbours, associates, past employers and co-workers, and the like. Those who know and respect you will be willing to help, to pass on leads, and refer you to others in their acquaintance. A few will come to you, but most of the time you have to seek people out and ask for their help. As you do, be specific about your own goals.

People you meet in the course of your search. You can build your list of "contacts" (aka: your network) by attending association meetings, by volunteering, cold calling, or conducting informational interviews or advice calls.

Leads:

Concrete information about work and opportunities, as in: "I heard that XYZ company is expanding its sales force/moving/looking for an administrator."

Cold calls:

Calls you place to people you don't know, in organizations that you'd like to research or work for. The least effective cold call is to the personnel department asking about available jobs. The most effective is to the person who would be your boss asking about opportunities or, alternatively, for an informational interview.

Information interviews:

Some claim this technique is being overused, or misused. Still, when handled properly, it's a way to meet and impress people in your field and obtain information and referrals. While networking and researching, you'll hear and read about people who work in your chosen field. You may be able to elicit their help by calling and asking for information and counsel. If you decide to use this technique, prepare well and move cautiously. When you call, ask if the person has time to speak with you. (If not, ask about the best time to call back.) Ask for 20 minutes of his or her time. Try to arrange a meeting. Alternatively, book an appointment for a telephone interview.

Have a list of relevant questions. Stick to the 20-minute limit.

Advice call:
This is a variation on informational meetings. The approach is basically the same, but instead of asking specific questions, you give a quick overview of your background and goals, then ask for advice and counsel.

Referrals:
At the end of every meeting or call, ask for the names of others who might be able to help you. Referrals are potential new "contacts."

Follow up:
Touch base with everyone who helps you; thank them and tell how you've used the information and advice they've given you. Write a note, or leave a thank-you message on voice mail.

You take it from here ...

Responding

1. Practise Comprehension Strategies   Review the selection and extract the key information. Write it out as a series of concise point-form notes. Then, design and create a diagram that explains the main points of the search campaign and shows the points of connection among them.

2. Focus on a Statement   According to this article, the expression "job search" has largely been replaced by the broader term "search." With a partner, discuss the author's explanation for this. Will this information influence your own plans for searching for work? (Will you still look for a "job"? Will you consider other options?) Suggest one or two alternative expressions that would describe the search for work that goes beyond a "job search."

3. Write a Personal Response   If you already have experience searching for work, write a paragraph in which you explain what you have done that falls under the writer's categories of "planning," "doing," and "in-between." If you do not yet have experience, create a plan for your first work search, organized under these categories.

4. Consider Strategies for Organizing Information   This article offers sophisticated strategies for conducting a work-search campaign. With the class, discuss ways that you would organize, in an effective, businesslike fashion, the information or input that you receive at various stages of your own search campaign.

Extending

5. **Create a Personal Time Line**   To help you clarify your current readiness to enter the job market, create a time line showing when and how you will most likely do the various tasks involved in the job search. Take into consideration your career goals, when you intend to begin working, whether you plan to continue your education after high school, and whether you intend to balance school and work. Consider sharing your time line with a parent or guardian or a guidance counsellor who might offer further suggestions.

TIP

- At first, keep your focus on the fields you want to work in; don't limit your investigation to jobs you think you can do. Once you have identified several jobs related to these fields, you can start thinking about which ones you might explore further.

6. **Uncover the Hidden Marketplace**   As the article points out, most work opportunities are not advertised, but they can readily be found by anyone who goes looking for them. Choose one or two areas that interest you, and start digging to uncover "the hidden marketplace" of related jobs. For example, do you love movies, music, animals, sports, travel? Brainstorm a list of as many related employers and opportunities as you can (use the Yellow Pages and other directories available in the library and on the Internet to extend your list). Identify relevant associations and organizations, viewing their Web sites, reading their journals and newsletters, and even visiting them in person to request more information. Build a file of potential employers and job descriptions, which you can refer to when your work search begins in earnest.

Before you read, think about the saying, "You only have one chance to make a good first impression." Discuss with a partner what you would do to make a good first impression on potential employers.

As you read, decide whether you believe the young man in the picture will find a job that day.

In Search of Work

Photograph by Sally and Richard Greenhill

You take it from here ...

Responding

1. **Discuss Photograph Elements**   In a small group, answer the following questions, making comments about the photographer's choices:
   a) What is the approximate age of the man in the picture? Describe his appearance.
   b) Where is he? How much of the photograph focuses on him? Why do you think the photographer took the picture from this angle?
   c) Light and darkness allow us to "feel" a picture rather than just see it. What use is made of light and darkness in the picture? What do these elements suggest regarding our interpretation of the picture?
   d) Identify other elements or details in the photograph, and explain how they contribute to the viewer's interpretation.

2. **Assess the Photograph**   Write a paragraph explaining whether you think the young man in this photograph is likely to get a job that day. If he does, what kind of a job is it likely to be? Give reasons to support your opinions.

3. **Imagine Character**   Working with a partner, describe the type of person you think the young man might be. What sort of work might he be good at? What might he like doing? What jobs might not be suitable? Compare ideas with another student pair.

4. **Write a Stream-of-Consciousness Narrative**   Imagine what is going on in the mind of the young man, and write a stream-of-consciousness narrative expressing his thoughts and feelings at the time of the photograph.

Extending

5. **Role-Play an Interview**   Working in a small group, imagine that the young man enters the building and has an interview with one of the job counsellors inside. Take turns playing the role of the young man and the counsellor, experimenting with different interpretations of the characters and different outcomes of the interview.

6. **Create Photographs**   Working with a partner or small group, plan a series of three to five photographs you could take that could accompany the previous selection, "Looking for Work Is a Search Campaign." Produce the photographs, and prepare a presentation to the class in which you explain your choices and describe any challenges you encountered in the process of taking the photographs.

TIPS

- As you plan your photographs, keep in mind the purpose of each one—what story do you want to tell?
- To create strong images, choose a key focal point, and try to avoid including cluttering details.

The Job Hunt Preparation Checklist

by Human Resources Development Canada

SELF-HELP QUESTIONNAIRE

Notes

Human Resources Development Canada's **mission** is "to enable Canadians to participate fully in the workplace and the community." Information on the department's programs and services, including career information links and quizzes, can be found at its Web site at www.hrdc-drhc.gc.ca.

INTRODUCTION

This Job Hunt Preparation Checklist is designed to help you with your job search. It will also help with other areas you need to consider in making a transition to another job. This exercise will help you rate yourself in the various areas as well as give you some ideas about what you might try.

There are no right or wrong answers—only answers that are true for you now.

Use the following scale to choose the answer that most closely describes you.

never	rarely	sometimes	usually	always
1	2	3	4	5

Looking at yourself

I know how to determine what career options are available to me.

O	O	O	O	O
1	2	3	4	5

I can speak for at least 10 minutes about my skills, abilities, education, work, volunteer experience, and personal traits in relation to any job I apply for.

O	O	O	O	O
1	2	3	4	5

I can describe how my interests relate to the job I am looking for.

O	O	O	O	O
1	2	3	4	5

I am prepared to discuss my personal accomplishments with potential employers.

   ○   ○   ○   ○   ○
   1   2   3   4   5

JOB HUNTING PREPARATION CHECKLIST

Planning your job search

I use my homework site for job-seeking activities like writing letters, making phone calls, researching companies, and recording my activities.

   ○   ○   ○   ○   ○
   1   2   3   4   5

I schedule my time every week so I know in general when I will be job searching.

   ○   ○   ○   ○   ○
   1   2   3   4   5

I express a positive attitude of success in my job hunting activities.

   ○   ○   ○   ○   ○
   1   2   3   4   5

Before I apply to an organization, I research such things as what it does, how big it is, and what it offers.

   ○   ○   ○   ○   ○
   1   2   3   4   5

I know how to approach companies that are not advertising jobs but may have openings.

   ○   ○   ○   ○   ○
   1   2   3   4   5

I know how to develop a network of personal contacts to find out more about job opportunities.

   ○   ○   ○   ○   ○
   1   2   3   4   5

I am able to fill out employment applications accurately.

   ○   ○   ○   ○   ○
   1   2   3   4   5

My résumé is visually attractive and has a professional look.

   ○   ○   ○   ○   ○
   1   2   3   4   5

I know how to design my résumé for the job I am applying for.

   ○   ○   ○   ○   ○
   1   2   3   4   5

I take advantage of services offered by my Human Resources Development Canada Centre, and provincial and community employment resource centres (where available).

   ○   ○   ○   ○   ○
   1   2   3   4   5

Preparing for your interview

I feel very confident when I go for an interview.

   ○   ○   ○   ○   ○
   1   2   3   4   5

I know how to make a positive first impression.

   ○   ○   ○   ○   ○
   1   2   3   4   5

I am prepared to answer typical questions interviewers ask.

   ○   ○   ○   ○   ○
   1   2   3   4   5

I am prepared with questions to ask during the interview to show my interest in the position and in the company.

   ○   ○   ○   ○   ○
   1   2   3   4   5

As soon as possible after an interview, I try to review my performance.

   O   O   O   O   O
   1   2   3   4   5

Examining your options

I am aware of alternatives to an immediate job hunt, such as training or starting up a business.

   O   O   O   O   O
   1   2   3   4   5

If circumstances warrant it, I know what part-time jobs are available and where to find them.

   O   O   O   O   O
   1   2   3   4   5

I know how to upgrade my skills if necessary.

   O   O   O   O   O
   1   2   3   4   5

If I considered moving to find a job, I know where to find information that could help me in this situation.

   O   O   O   O   O
   1   2   3   4   5

Developing a realistic budget

I feel I have my finances under control.

   O   O   O   O   O
   1   2   3   4   5

I can identify the financial resources that are available to me during my job search.

   O   O   O   O   O
   1   2   3   4   5

I can determine my monthly cash needs during my job search.

   O   O   O   O   O
   1   2   3   4   5

I know how to prepare a budget to help me through this period.

   O   O   O   O   O
   1   2   3   4   5

When you have finished, add up your score. The higher the score, the better prepared you are.

You take it from here ...

Responding

1. Discuss Checklist Results   With a partner, discuss your responses to the checklist items. What ideas were new to you? In which of the five areas ("looking at yourself," "planning your job search," "preparing for your interview," "examining your options," and "developing a realistic budget") do you seem most prepared? On which specific items could you use more information or practice?

2. Reflect on Responses   Write a reflective journal entry dealing with your responses to three of the items.

3. Brainstorm Interview Questions   Working with a small group,
   a) consider the point "I am prepared to answer typical questions interviewers ask," and then brainstorm a list of typical interview questions. Then, individually, outline possible answers to at least five of them. Compare your answers with those of other students in the group.
   b) react to the point "I am prepared with questions to ask during an interview to show my interest in the position and in the company" by brainstorming a list of questions you might ask during an interview.

Extending

4. Present Yourself   One item states, "I can speak for at least 10 minutes about my skills, abilities, education, work, volunteer experience, and personal traits in relation to any job I apply for." Create a list, a diagram, a large web, or another organizer in which to gather information about yourself under each category. Then, develop a 7- to 10-minute speech about yourself, and present it to a small group as if you were at a job interview. When you have finished, invite feedback from the group.

PEER ASSESSMENT

As you listen to each speech, consider the following:
- Was the speaker confident, maintaining good eye contact and a firm voice?
- Was the tone professional and polite?
- Was the information in the speech relevant to the intended target audience?

5. Examine Options   One alternative to looking for an existing job is to create your own. Search the Internet, library, and other resources for information on what it takes to be an entrepreneur, and for details about programs for young entrepreneurs in your province and community. Choose one item (e.g., a Web site, a government brochure, an aptitude self-test) and present it to a small group of classmates.

TIP

- Identify your audience before you begin writing your speech. Imagine a specific employer and/or job, and target your speech accordingly.

TIP

- A good starting point is the Youth Employment Information page on the Human Resources Development Canada Web site at www.youth.gc.ca (or follow the links from the HRDC main page, www.hrdc-drhc.gc.ca).

Before you read, as a class, discuss what purposes are served by résumés.

As you read, think about what you can tell about this applicant based on the résumé.

Your Résumé

by HUMAN RESOURCES DEVELOPMENT CANADA

INFORMATION/RÉSUMÉ

Notes

Human Resources Development Canada's mission is "to enable Canadians to participate fully in the workplace and the community." Information on the department's programs and services, including career information links and quizzes, can be found at its Web site at www.hrdc-drhc.gc.ca.

The purpose of a résumé is to introduce you to employers. It highlights your qualifications, work experience, and education. The résumé is also a useful tool when you are filling out application forms.

Be sure to include the necessary basic information:

- Name, address, and telephone number— include an alternate number for messages.
- Educational background—include the dates you attended, and any diplomas, degrees, certificates, or awards that you received.
- Work experience—list your previous jobs with a brief description of duties, and include employer names and addresses.
- Volunteer work or extracurricular activities— include those activities that relate to the job you are seeking.
- References are optional. If you want to include them, list the individual's name, position, address, and telephone number.

Take special care when writing your résumé:

- Use simple words.
- Keep sentences short.
- Avoid long descriptions.
- Be clear when describing your duties.
- Use action verbs.
- Pay attention to presentation:
  - it should not exceed two or three pages
  - it should be neatly typed with no grammar or spelling mistakes

Before you begin writing your own résumé, you may wish to review Jodi's résumé.

Jodi Anson

432 Elm Street
Kendridge, BC
V4N 6A9
(604) 555-1351

Career Objective
A position as a Millwright or Industrial Mechanic

Work History
1997 to Present
Millwright, Butler Paper Company, Kendridge, British Columbia

As a millwright I gained experience with the installation, operations, and repair of stationary industrial machinery. My duties included analyzing work orders and specifications and deciding on the work that was required. I would inspect machinery, perform routine maintenance, and correct irregularities and malfunctions. I am competent with the use of hand and power tools such as lathes and grinders.

1986 to 1996
Industrial Mechanic, Edgewood Mining Ltd., Herman, Nova Scotia

I completed a four-year apprenticeship with Edgewood Mining. I worked as a mechanic's aid, where I helped with repairs, maintenance, and installation on industrial machines. My duties included calibrating, regulating, and repairing system parts. After six years, I was promoted to a team that specialized in diagnostics services. I gained experience using hand and power tools.

1984 to 1986
Service Station Attendant, BP Gas Station, Herman, Nova Scotia

In my capacity as service station attendant, I was responsible for serving clients at the gas bar. I performed minor service and maintenance such as washing the windshield, changing motor oil and antifreeze, as well as checking fluid levels and air pressure of tires. I also handled cash and sold car accessories such as windshield wipers, fan belts, and air cleaners.

Education and Training
1986 to 1990
Completed courses in industrial instrumentation technology and industrial machinery repair at the KAR Institute in Herman, Nova Scotia

1990
Completed a four-year apprenticeship program in which I got on-the-job training at Edgewood Mining Ltd. in Herman, Nova Scotia

1996
Red Seal trade certificate—Industrial Mechanic

Extra-Curricular Activities
Active in sports—golfing, baseball, fishing, and hockey. Enjoy working in the garden, fixing up old cars, and finishing basements.

References available upon request

You take it from here ...

Responding

1. Examine Style   This selection begins with a list of tips for résumé writers. Working with a partner, review these, and then re-examine Jodi's résumé. How closely does this example adhere to the instructions?

2. Discuss First Impressions   Discuss what you can tell about Jodi Anson based on this résumé. What first impression would a potential employer have of this applicant?

3. Consider Content and Format   As a class, discuss what information should go into a résumé. In what order should it appear? Have you seen organizational patterns for a résumé that differ from this one? Explain. If you have a résumé, compare it to this one: is the format similar? If it is different, in what way?

4. Discuss What to Leave Out   Make a list of personal information items that should be left off a résumé. For each item in your list, explain why it should not be included.

Extending

5. Create (or Recreate) Your Résumé   Use the guidelines in this selection to update your résumé—or if you do not have a résumé, to create one.

6. Have Your References Ready   Compile a list of people that you might use as character references and employment references. Make sure your contact information for them is current, and that you have asked their permission to use them as references.

Covering Letters

by Hastingscounty.com

WEB PAGE/COVER LETTER

Notes

hastingscounty.com is the Web site of the County of Hastings in Ontario. This information is from the site's Job Search Tips page.

COVERING LETTERS

A covering letter should always be sent with your résumé when applying for a job. The covering letter briefly describes the exact job you're applying for and why you're interested. If you're not writing about a specific job, specify the type of work you'd be interested in doing. You can highlight something in your résumé. You can even include information such as when you would be available to start, if you're willing to travel, and how the person could contact you for an interview.

John Doe
1 Shaw St.
Sometown, ON M4R 2Z1
(123) 555-9876

January 24, 2002

There are many ways to write a covering letter, but here's one example you can use as a guide.

John Doe
1 Shaw St.
Sometown, ON M4R 2Z1
(123) 555-9876

January 24, 2002

Ms. Francine Beck
Human Resources Manager
The Family's Stop Hotel
100 Main St.
Sometown, ON M6K 1P2

Dear Ms. Beck:

I would like to apply for the position of cook advertised in the January 20th edition of Sometown News and Times.

I have three years' experience working as a cook. All of my experience has been in a fast-paced environment. My ability to work well under pressure would be a benefit to an organization such as the Family's Stop Hotel.

My résumé is enclosed. Please phone at your convenience to arrange an interview. I look forward to your reply.

Sincerely,

John Doe

John Doe

You take it from here ...

Responding

1. **Discuss Purpose**   With a partner, discuss what purpose a covering letter serves. How well does this example fill that purpose, in your opinion? Explain.

2. **Examine the Components**   As a class or in a small group, review the features of a standard business letter, and then identify each feature as it appears in this letter. Consider also the information that is included in this letter, how it is organized, and the tone, noting how these are appropriate to a business—as opposed to a personal—letter.

3. **Expand on the Letter**   Think of three questions an interviewer might ask John Doe, based on this letter. Then, as John Doe, write an expanded version of this cover letter that includes the additional information.

Extending

4. **Create Cover Letter Templates**   Identify two jobs for which, given your interests and abilities, you could apply. Then, write the cover letters that you could send with your résumé to each job. You will be able to use these letters as templates for cover letters in the future.

5. **Interview an Employer**   Think of someone you know (or know of) who hires employees—someone who could offer practical suggestions about cover letters and résumés from an employer's standpoint. Ask if he or she will agree to a brief interview to share insights and advice for first-time job seekers. Prepare a list of questions and conduct the interview. Write up your notes and present them in an oral report to the class.

> **TIPS**
>
> The revised letter might include more details on
> - job experience
> - personal aptitude and interests as they relate to the job
> - your knowledge about the company and why you want to work there

Herman

Cartoon by Jim Unger

Notes

Jim Unger (1940–) was born in London, England. He came to Canada and began his cartooning career at the *Mississauga Times*. He later moved to Ottawa, where he began creating his famous *Herman* cartoons. He retired in 1992 after producing over 6000 cartoons in 18 years. Unger's original intended name for *Herman* was *Attila the Bum*. In 1990, *Herman* was selected as the first newspaper comic syndicated in communist East Germany after the Berlin Wall came down.

"The man we're looking for will be dynamic and aggressive."

You take it from here ...

Responding

1. Focus on Tone of Voice   With a partner, practise reading the caption as you think the speaker would say it. Suggest and practise other captions that would capture the situation.

2. Examine the Situation   Write two or three paragraphs analyzing the situation presented in the cartoon. In your analysis, consider the following questions: Why is the interviewee there? Does he really want this job? Does he need it? How do you suppose he got as far as the interview? What interview skills does he need to acquire? What do you suppose is the speaker's impression of him?

3. Look at Irony   In a class discussion, identify the obvious irony in the cartoon. Then, suggest some underlying ironies that are also illustrated here.

4. Analyze Humour   Write a one-page analysis of what creates humour in this cartoon. Refer to the choice of subject, facial features and body language, and how the artist emphasizes contrasts.

Extending

5. Present Skits on the Theme   Working in a small group, plan and present a skit or tableau on the theme of "Interview Don'ts." Present it to the class, or videotape and edit it to produce a humorous instructional film.

6. Role-Play an Interview   As a class, compile a list of 8 to 10 questions that might be asked by a potential employer at a job interview. Individually, take a few minutes to think about how you might respond to each question on the list. Then, work with a partner to role-play a job interview. In the role of the employer, the interviewer will ask any three questions from the list, and the interviewee will respond. Then exchange roles. After both partners have played both roles, share your comments and feedback on the process.

> **PEER ASSESSMENT**
>
> Did your partner
> - respond to your questions thoughtfully?
> - speak in a calm, confident manner?
> - manage to convince you that he or she was the person for the job?

Before you read, think about how you can make sure that if you have a reasonable complaint, it is heard and acted on.

As you read, note which ideas and strategies you have heard before, and which are new to you.

Methods of Complaining
by Alberta Consumer and Corporate Affairs

INFORMATION/COMPLAINT LETTER

Most often, complaints are made in person, by telephone, or they are written. No matter which way you choose to complain, there is some basic information that you should include in your complaint. Review the Complaint Information Checklist.

In-Person Complaints

The place to start with your complaint is with the seller or person with whom you originally dealt. Present yourself well and be polite. It's a good idea to bring along a witness. Describe your problem, and present your documentation. State what you want done about the problem.

If you don't get satisfaction, get the name of the person with whom you are speaking. Go home and write down the details of the meeting. These notes will be useful when you follow up your initial complaint by complaining to someone with more authority.

Telephone Complaints

Although telephone complaints are the easiest for you, they're the least effective method of complaining because it's often difficult to get through to someone who is in a position to assist you.

Before making a telephone complaint, gather all the related information. Call the business with which you have a complaint. Briefly explain your problem and ask for the name of a person who can assist you.

Introduce yourself and again describe your problem. Ask whether the person has the authority to do anything about the problem. If the answer is no, ask to be referred to someone who can help you. Keep a list of everyone you speak to and keep notes so you have a record of your conversations.

When you do speak with someone in authority, get a statement from them about what they will do and the time frame in which they'll do it. Before the end of the telephone conversation, review your understanding of what's been said so there will be no disagreements later.

Follow up with a letter to the person, outlining details of the agreement. Keep a copy of your letter.

Written Complaints

If they are done well, written complaints are the most forceful method of complaining. A letter should be neat, preferably typed, and short. If possible, keep it to one page. Send it by certified or registered mail so you have proof it was sent. Direct the letter to a specific person or at least to a specific job title. For example, to "Mr. Smith" or to the "Director of Customer Relations," not "To Whom It May Concern."

SAMPLE COMPLAINT LETTER

Type your letter, keep it short, keep a copy

Identify the date and location of the purchase

Send letter by registered or certified mail

Your address

Date

Write to a specific person

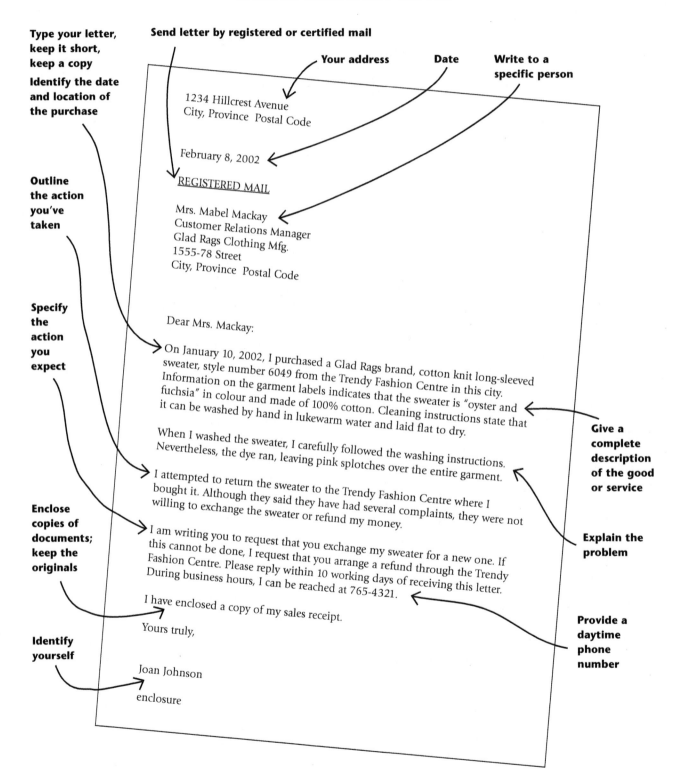

1234 Hillcrest Avenue
City, Province Postal Code

February 8, 2002

REGISTERED MAIL

Mrs. Mabel Mackay
Customer Relations Manager
Glad Rags Clothing Mfg.
1555-78 Street
City, Province Postal Code

Dear Mrs. Mackay:

On January 10, 2002, I purchased a Glad Rags brand, cotton knit long-sleeved sweater, style number 6049 from the Trendy Fashion Centre in this city. Information on the garment labels indicates that the sweater is "oyster and fuchsia" in colour and made of 100% cotton. Cleaning instructions state that it can be washed by hand in lukewarm water and laid flat to dry.

When I washed the sweater, I carefully followed the washing instructions. Nevertheless, the dye ran, leaving pink splotches over the entire garment.

I attempted to return the sweater to the Trendy Fashion Centre where I bought it. Although they said they have had several complaints, they were not willing to exchange the sweater or refund my money.

I am writing you to request that you exchange my sweater for a new one. If this cannot be done, I request that you arrange a refund through the Trendy Fashion Centre. Please reply within 10 working days of receiving this letter. During business hours, I can be reached at 765-4321.

I have enclosed a copy of my sales receipt.

Yours truly,

Joan Johnson

enclosure

Outline the action you've taken

Specify the action you expect

Enclose copies of documents; keep the originals

Identify yourself

Give a complete description of the good or service

Explain the problem

Provide a daytime phone number

You take it from here ...

Responding

1. Discuss Complaint Strategies   As a class, imagine several scenarios that would prompt someone to make a complaint. For each example presented, discuss the various strategies that could be used for dealing with the problem: in person, by telephone, and in writing. Which would you use first? If that didn't resolve the problem, which would you use next? Record your information in a chart.

2. Make Notes   Review the three methods of complaining, and, for each one, note what information you should record as you go through the process. In each case, explain why this documentation is important.

3. Understand the Tone   In a small group, discuss the difference between being reasonable and being unreasonable when making a complaint. In what ways does the tone of the sample complaint letter make its writer seem reasonable and controlled? Can you sense any frustration or anger in the tone? Explain. Suggest how the information might have been presented in a less measured way. How would the recipient likely respond to each version?

Extending

4. Let off Steam in a First Draft   An effective letter of complaint states the problem, but controls anger. Sometimes you may write more than one draft, using earlier drafts to get rid of your anger or frustration and then revising until you have a polite, effective letter. Write what could be the first (angry) draft of a complaint letter. Then, in a paragraph, discuss why your first draft may not get the attention that you want, while a later, more businesslike version, would.

> **TIP**
> - You could use the sample letter in the selection as the basis for this activity.

5. Create an Instructional Video   Work with three or four other students to prepare an instructional video demonstrating how—and how not—to make an in-person complaint. Devise a complaint scenario (e.g., you are returning a DVD player to the store because it won't work) and role-play it in two ways. First, have the person returning the item behave calmly and politely, according to the advice given in the selection. The person receiving the complaint will be polite as well. The second time, show how *not* to make an effective complaint, with an irate customer and an equally fed-up store employee. Script the two scenes (perhaps writing in a narrator's part), and rehearse them several times before taping your video.

What Kind of Driver Are You?

by the U.S. Department of Transportation National Highway Traffic Safety Administration

QUESTIONNAIRE

As drivers, we all bear some responsibility for the atmosphere on the nation's roads. Think you're a great driver? Test yourself with the situations below and find out.

Do you ...	Yes	No
Overtake other vehicles only on the left	O	O
Avoid blocking passing lanes	O	O
Yield to faster traffic by moving to the right	O	O
Keep to the right on narrow streets and at intersections	O	O
Maintain appropriate distance when following other vehicles	O	O
Provide appropriate distance after passing vehicles	O	O
Use headlights in cloudy, raining, low light conditions	O	O
Yield to pedestrians	O	O
Come to a complete stop at stop signs	O	O
Stop for red traffic lights	O	O

Do you ...	Yes	No
Approach intersections slowly to show your intention to stop	O	O
Follow right-of-way rules at four-way stops	O	O
Drive below posted speed limits when conditions warrant	O	O
Drive at slower speeds in construction zones	O	O
Maintain speeds appropriate for conditions	O	O

Do you ...	Yes	No
Use vehicle turn signals for turns and lane changes	○	○
Make eye contact and signal intentions where needed	○	○
Acknowledge intentions of others	○	○
Avoid unnecessary use of high beam headlights	○	○
Yield and move to the right for emergency vehicles	○	○
Refrain from flashing headlights to signal a desire to pass	○	○
Maintain proper speeds around roadway crashes	○	○
Make slow, deliberate U-turns	○	○
Focus on driving and avoid distracting activities	○	○
Avoid returning inappropriate gestures	○	○
Avoid challenging other drivers	○	○
Try to get out of the way of aggressive drivers	○	○

Do you ...	Yes	No
Refrain from momentarily using the shoulder to pass vehicles	○	○
Avoid stopping in the road to talk with a pedestrian	○	○
Avoid blocking the right-hand turn lane	○	○
Avoid taking more than one parking space	○	○
Avoid parking in a disabled space, if you are not disabled	○	○
Avoid letting your door hit the car parked next to you	○	○
Avoid inflicting loud music on neighbouring cars	○	○
Avoid driving when drowsy	○	○
Use your horn sparingly around pedestrians	○	○

Obtain your score by adding up the total number of "Yes" responses out of a possible 36.

You take it from here ...

Responding

1. Talk about Your Test Results   Share your test results with a small group of classmates. Were your scores similar? What do the results say about you as a driver? What items in the questionnaire made you stop and think? Explain.

2. Consider the Items   Still working in a small group, discuss the following statement: Being a "skilled" driver is not the same as being a "good" driver. To clarify the distinction between these ideas, review the items in the questionnaire and identify the ones that are most directly concerned with driving expertise, and those that are more concerned with common courtesy.

3. Discuss Road Rage   As a class, discuss the phenomenon of "road rage." Identify several items in the questionnaire that might directly lead to road rage.

Extending

4. Set up a Poster Campaign   Working in a group, create a list of "The Top Ten Tips for Good Driving." Then, design a poster campaign to publicize them.

5. Debate Issues   Poll the class on the following: "Agree or Disagree: People over 25 are generally better drivers than people under 25." Divide the class into "Agree" and "Disagree" camps, and hold an informal five-minute debate, giving reasons and, where possible, evidence to back up your opinion. Then, hold a second debate on this statement: "Agree or Disagree: Young women are generally better drivers than young men."

6. Create a Brochure   Compile a brochure aimed at young people in your community who are about to get a driver's licence. Include practical information such as how and where to apply for a learner's permit, lists of driving schools in your area, and tips on good driving practices.

TIP
• Check out government transportation department publications and Web sites such as www.youngdrivers.com for ideas on what to include in your brochure.

"It's always easier to walk away before you've paid."

Lemons for Sale

by Hal Karp

MAGAZINE ARTICLE

Notes

Hal Karp has written articles for *Reader's Digest* and other publications on a range of topics, including automobile safety and Internet privacy issues.

When Kathy Hirsch's pickup truck died last spring, the 23-year-old courier, whose livelihood depends upon having a vehicle, went shopping. At a used-car lot in Edmonton, she and her husband were surprised to find a 1989 GMC pickup with only 149 272 kilometres on its odometer. When the salesman explained the low mileage by claiming the truck had been in storage, they inspected and test-drove it, then bought it for $7702.

The following day, Hirsch took it in for new tires. When the mechanic put the truck on the lift, he found the suspension system was held together by a household hardware clamp, the drivetrain was leaking fluid, and the entire brake system needed replacing. Total cost—$1400.

Six days later, the fuel system and onboard computer failed. Hirsch shelled out another $1600. On the way home, she stopped to wash the truck. As soon as the water hit it, large patches of paint washed away. Frustrated and angry, she tried to return the vehicle to the seller—and was told, "Sorry, buyer beware."

When, a few days later, the driveshaft almost fell out, Hirsch decided to sue. While researching the truck's history, she uncovered the truth: In 1995 the truck's odometer was recorded at 203 000. Hirsch had to wonder: In the five years since then, how many more kilometres had the truck seen? A mechanical inspection confirmed the odometer had been rolled back, probably hundreds of thousands of kilometres.

Used Junk. Was Hirsch's experience uncommon? Hardly. The Automobile Consumer Coalition (ACC), a consumer-advocacy group based in Toronto, estimates that of the 2.2 million used cars sold each year, at least 1 in 10 has hidden damage or potentially hazardous wear.

Consumer advocates and police reckon that every year tens of thousands of vehicles suffer odometer tampering, or are totalled, rebuilt on the cheap, then sold as damage-free; and thousands more damaged cars cross the border from the United States, including vehicles with flood damage.

Carfax, a private firm with the most comprehensive database of Canadian vehicle histories—17 million vehicles, covering over

95 percent of what's on the road—has some alarming numbers. "One in ten vehicles we check has a problem in its registration history," says Carfax's Scott Fredericks. That's 1.7 million cars!

Last year, Basil Dumville, a 41-year-old commercial fisherman in Glenwood, P.E.I., went shopping for a pickup truck to tow his boat and trailer. When he found a local used-car dealer selling a 1991 Ford F150 with 148 892 kilometres on it, he thought he'd struck gold. He purchased it at book value: $7000.

Several days later, a mechanic determined that the truck's engine was shot and needed replacing. Then the heater, starter, and transmission developed problems. Finally the suspension started falling apart.

When the seller wouldn't take the truck back, Dumville's curiosity about his vehicle's past grew. Using its vehicle identification number (VIN)—a numeric fingerprint unique to each vehicle—he logged on to Carfax's Web site, carfax.com. For about $30, he discovered that his prized buy had been totalled and written off in New Brunswick in 1996. Yet the registration Dumville was given showed nothing of this.

Ron Giblin of the Insurance Crime Prevention Bureau (ICPB) in Toronto estimates that some 300 000 vehicles are totalled each year in Canada. Today in nearly all jurisdictions, these vehicles have their registrations branded as "salvage" or "irreparable" so future buyers know. But branding laws are relatively new and not retroactive. Dumville's truck slipped by because New Brunswick didn't brand it in 1997.

Some Canadian jurisdictions are still not branding their registrations. The Northwest Territories, for example, won't start until fall 2001, and in Ontario—home to 38 percent of the nation's cars—branding is only now coming into effect.

That leaves enough loopholes for unscrupulous auto rebuilders to take advantage. They purchase write-offs, fix them on the cheap, and find ways to erase or conceal the brand, hiding a past of severe damage. While most provinces do have an inspection system that allows for a write-off's registration to graduate from "salvage" to "rebuilt," *Reader's Digest* learned that obtaining a falsified inspection certificate is not difficult.

Del Huget, lead investigator for the Alberta Motor Vehicle Industry Council (AMVIC), says that fraudulent inspections are one of its biggest problems. And it's no different in the East, says a body-shop owner in Ottawa. Body shops supposedly repairing such cars are also licensed to inspect them. "It's not just the fox watching the henhouse," he says. "It's the fox *owning* the henhouse."

Det. Mark Barkley of the Toronto Police Auto Squad showed *Reader's Digest* a seemingly beautiful BMW that was actually made out of two different cars welded together in the middle. Said Barkley, "In a crash, vehicles like this are potential death traps."

To be safe, buyers should take these steps *before* they buy:

- Research the vehicle's history. Buy reports from both Carfax and your local registry. Also check the ICPB database of written-off and stolen cars, accessed online (icpb.ca) for about $10. Keep in mind that none of these sources covers vehicles that have never been branded; that's part of the problem.

- Closely examine the vehicle's body for uneven paint or body parts that don't line up. Do the doors, hood, and trunk open and close easily? Do the bumpers and fenders sit squarely?
- Have a qualified mechanic inspect the vehicle. Inspections cost anywhere from $50 to $150—and they're worth every penny. "Two thirds of the cars people bring us for inspection end up not being all they're supposed to be," says Gary Bourk, owner of Bourk's Ignition Ltd. in Ottawa.

Spin Doctors. RCMP Const. Bryan Dufresne believed that modern technology had eliminated odometer fraud. Then, three years ago, he met a woman who'd spent $3000 to buy a car and instead got a pile of junk that had clocked hundreds of thousands more kilometres than she was told. Dufresne decided to investigate.

Offenders, known as spinners, are everywhere, he says. "A pro can roll back an odometer in minutes, sometimes with just a screwdriver, sometimes with a power drill." Digital odometers are no different; laptops can reset them.

In Edmonton, a former employee of an auto auction house that serves dealers recalls a saying among fellow employees: "There are two kinds of vehicles at auction: those tampered with and those that are going to be tampered with." Says AMVIC investigator Del Huget, "There's potentially big money in spinning—$3000 to $6000 per vehicle, right into the seller's pocket."

Why is odometer fraud so rampant? Because vehicle histories nationwide fail to include easily accessible mileage records. You might record the mileage when registering your car, but that information is rarely entered into computer databases. Ontario's Used Vehicle Information Package, for example, includes a list of former owners and registration dates but fails to list mileage records. To avoid a spun car, investigators suggest consumers:

- Ask if the vehicle has maintenance records. If so, see if the mileage accords with the odometer. A car with no records should raise caution.
- Contact a local dealer who represents the vehicle's manufacturer and ask about warranty work done. See if records include mileage notations.
- Examine wear on the brake and gas pedals. Does it match the kilometres? Check out the tires. An average tire lasts 80 000 kilometres. If the odometer reads less than that and the tires look worn, be cautious.
- Check to see if the numbers on the odometer are lined up and snug. If they jiggle when you bang your hand on the dash, have an expert check for fraud.

BEWARE THE CURBSIDER

Last February, Edmonton police officer Bruce Edwards believed he was purchasing a 1998 Ford Windstar from a gentleman selling the minivan for his brother who no longer needed it. After taking the Windstar for a test-drive, Edwards paid $15 500 for it and drove off. On the way home, he noticed the dash appeared loose and soon discovered that the minivan's air bags had been deployed and not replaced. When he took it to the mechanic, he learned that the Windstar had been in a major collision.

Del Huget of AMVIC informed Edwards that he'd been taken by a "curbsider." These unlicensed used-car dealers sometimes acquire junk cars, then sell them from parking lots and curbs or through newspaper ads, pretending to be selling a personal vehicle. Huget's investigation revealed that Edwards's seller had sold six other junk minivans over the past year.

Curbsiders are prevalent nationwide. A recent Toronto-area study by the Used Car Dealers Association revealed 868 curbsiders, who were responsible for about 20 percent of all classified car ads.

To avoid being conned by a curbsider, experts suggest:

✔ When responding to an ad, say, "I'm calling about the car in the paper." If the seller responds, "Which one?" you might want to reconsider that vehicle or proceed with caution.
✔ Check the registration. Is it in the seller's name? If it is, ask when he acquired it. Never let the seller register a vehicle for you. This trick is to keep you from seeing the original registration, which may be branded.
✔ Be wary of a seller who won't meet you at his home. Edwards's curbsider insisted on meeting him at a local fast-food restaurant.
✔ Insist on having a qualified mechanic inspect the car. If the seller balks, you walk.

U.S. Lemons. Soon after Brad Perrigo and his wife, Anita, moved to Hamilton in August 1997, the young couple needed a car. In a local *Auto Trader* magazine, they found a fully loaded 1995 Mazda 626.

After a test-drive and inspection, Perrigo thought the vehicle was a true find. "It was immaculate," he recalls. The couple bought the sedan for $14 000. It came with a safety-standards certificate, showing it had undergone the pre-registration inspection required by Ontario law.

Days later the Perrigos discovered a compact disc jammed in the car stereo. When a local electronics shop got it out, they found more

than the disc. The stereo was full of sand. That was just the beginning.

The engine, brake, electrical, and exhaust systems soon began to fail. And over time, the once-immaculate Mazda developed a coat of rust, while the passenger-side power window crawled at a snail's pace. "It's like the whole car needs to be oiled," says Perrigo. That's because the Perrigos' vehicle was damaged in a Michigan flood.

Documents obtained by *Reader's Digest* show that six months before the Perrigos purchased the Mazda, it was written off as salvage in the States because it had been 84 percent damaged in a flood. Carfax records indicate that thousands of flooded vehicles from the States are cleaned up and resold. Unsuspecting buyers who purchase these waterlogged wrecks unknowingly risk injury and death. Lifesaving devices, such as brakes and air bags, no longer function as designed after a vehicle has been flooded up to the dash.

Flood cars aren't the only lemons coming north. Vehicles written off after collisions find their way here, too. Just ask Jeff Robinson of Oshawa. Two years ago the 25-year-old truck driver got stuck with a leased 1996 Chevy Blazer that spent more time in the shop than on the road.

When Robinson ran a Carfax check on his vehicle, he discovered it had been totalled in New Hampshire in 1996. His attempts to get out of the lease were unsuccessful. In the end, he spent over $12 000 for a vehicle he hardly drove.

Like the Perrigos' car, Robinson's SUV also had a safety-inspection certificate. Both buyers felt reassured by this document. Experts say they shouldn't have. Although many provinces require such an inspection before a vehicle can be registered, they guarantee little, explains Phil Edmonston, author of *Lemon-Aid: Used*

Cars 2001. "They don't even cover engines and transmissions," he says.

Is there any way to catch a lemon from the United States? ICPB's Giblin points out that government controls are somewhat wanting: Computer links existing between Canada and the States may not detect an imported vehicle's unsavoury history. As a result, thousands of junk cars are regularly imported into Canada. "They enter by the truckload," says Giblin. "A few days later, they show up on our roads with clean registrations."

Here's how to steer clear of a wet or wrecked U.S. lemon:

- A flood car may have a musty odour. Sellers often conceal this with air fresheners, so keep an eye out for those. Other signs include dash instruments that fail to work, or rust. And check out the carpeting. If it's newer than the car, there's probably a reason.
- Get a U.S. vehicle history from Carfax, whose database covers all of North America. Examine its history from your local registry. Does the car's birth year match the first entry? If not, ask where the vehicle came from.

Not all used cars are lemons, of course. Scott Wilson of the Alberta Motor Association (AMA) says, "Leasing has resulted in a high availability of three- and four-year-old cars." Thousands more source from fleets of company and rental cars. As a result, many excellent secondhand vehicles can be found.

The trick to getting one is to buy smart. Take the time to do it right, says George Iny, president of the Automobile Protection Association. "It's always easier to walk away before you've paid," he says. "Once you've given over the cash, you're limited in what you can do."

Remember Kathy Hirsch? After a lawsuit, she managed to get back most of her initial purchase price on the pickup. But that covered only debts she incurred to repair the vehicle.

The Edmonton mom is now stuck paying off the loan—$307 a month on a truck she doesn't have. And although she'll pay for another two years, she's relieved the 1989 pickup is no longer in her driveway. In her new truck, which she researched thoroughly, she can once again travel without fear.

You take it from here ...

Responding

1. Look at the Facts   Discuss the article as a class. Were you already aware of some of the information it presented? What details did you find most surprising? Why? Choose one of the points of interest you noted while reading, and bring it into the discussion.

2. Make Notes on Important Information   For your own use now or in the future, make notes on the following:

   - steps to take before buying a used vehicle
   - checking for odometer tampering
   - avoiding a curbsider con
   - researching an out-of-country vehicle

3. Examine Statements   Copy the following statements, and label each one either "Myth" or "Truth." For each statement, provide evidence from the text to support your choice.

- Modern technology has made odometers tamper-proof.
- Branding laws eliminate risk in buying used vehicles.
- A safety-inspection certificate will keep you from buying a lemon.
- Vehicle maintenance records are important.
- It is next to impossible to buy a reliable secondhand vehicle.

Extending

4. Develop a Consumer Checklist   Combine the information in this article with information from other sources to create an extensive checklist designed to help people buy used cars. Organize your checklist points into an attractive, user-friendly format, such as a booklet, brochure, or poster.

5. Do Consumer Research   Imagine that you are saving up to buy a car, and begin to explore your options. Check newspapers and dealerships and learn the range of current prices for specific models of new and used cars. Check consumer magazines and used-car buyers' guides such as the *Lemon-Aid Car Guide* (available in libraries or online at www.lemonaidcars.com) for advice on which cars are safest, which are most reliable, and which should be avoided. Based on your findings, identify what you would buy if you were looking for

a) a new car
b) a used car that is less than 10 years old
c) a used car that is more than 10 years old

Write a brief report explaining the criteria you used in making your choices.

6. Create a Radio Commercial   Working in a small group, write and produce a radio commercial for Carfax. Consider your target audience, essential information about Carfax (visit the Web site at carfax.com), and how best to use sound and voice to get that message across. Present your commercial to the class.

How to Inspect an Apartment

by Sandra Clockedile

INSTRUCTIONS/LIST

Notes

Sandra Clockedile is a librarian—and dedicated apartment dweller—in Fairfield County, Connecticut.

Inspecting your new apartment will document any pre-existing problems, and it will give you a chance to get problems fixed before you settle in. Ideally you should do this before moving any of your belongings in.

Here's how:

1) Get a pad of paper or notebook and a pen or pencil.

2) Check all the walls and ceilings: make a note of any dents, holes or cracks in the plaster; scuff marks that don't rub off; and tears, bubbles or peeling wallpaper.

3) Check all the floors: make a note of stains or discoloration in carpets; tears in linoleum; cracked or chipped tiles; and dents; scuffs or stains on hardwood floors.

4) Check all trim (including moldings, door and window sills and door and window frames) for stains, cracks, leaks, or other problems.

5) Check all electrical outlets and lights to make sure they are functioning; pay close attention to any 2- or 3-way light switches and dimmers.

6) In the bathroom(s): make sure all faucets (hot and cold) work without leaking; check for chips or scratches in fixtures and tile; check walls around the tub for "sponginess"; and check counter tops for dents, scratches, or stains.

7) In the kitchen: make sure all faucets (hot and cold) work without leaking; check for chips or scratches in fixtures and tile; check counter tops for dents, scratches, or stains; and make sure all appliances work and are clean.

8) Make sure all exterior doors and windows work, seal properly, and have functioning locks; be especially alert to evidence of water infiltration.

9) If you have a deck, balcony or patio, check it for chipped flagstone, warped or cracked boards, or problems with exterior siding.

10) If you have a storage area, make sure it is cleaned out and that the locks are secure.

problems, no matter how small; if he didn't, write a formal letter noting the problems you found.

13) Request that your landlord repair any problems you want taken care of as soon as possible.

TIPS:

1) Keep copies of all correspondence with your landlord.

2) Videotaping your walkthrough will provide a visual accompaniment to your written notes.

3) Have a friend help—four eyes are better than two.

11) Check all smoke and carbon monoxide detectors.

12) If your landlord gave you an apartment inspection sheet, complete it noting all

---

You take it from here ...

Responding

1. Respond to the Information   Discuss the information in this selection with a partner. What ideas would you not have considered before reading it? What do you think is the best advice it contains? Why?

2. Consider Reasons for an Apartment Inspection   In one or two paragraphs, explain why a renter should inspect a new apartment prior to moving in.

3. Make an Inspection Chart   Using the information in the selection, create a chart or template that could be used by a prospective tenant inspecting an apartment.

Extending

4. Research Landlord and Tenant Laws   As a class, review and discuss the landlord and tenant laws in your area. In your discussion, consider the following questions:

- What rights do renters have?
- What can landlords require of tenants?
- What can landlords *not* require of tenants?

5. Create a Visual   Create a cartoon or other visual that could accompany and draw a reader's attention to this list of instructions.

6. Compare Rents   Working in a small group, do a three-city comparison of apartment prices. Select three cities in different regions of Canada and check classified ads in newspapers and online sources to identify a range of prices for a one-bedroom apartment in each one. Then, select three apartments for each city, including at least one from the high end of the price scale. Create a chart showing the specific information revealed in each ad such as price, location, and amenities (e.g., laundry facilities, swimming pool). As a group, discuss your findings. How do you account for differences in price within each city? If you found differences in price from one city to the next, suggest reasons for these as well.

Reflecting on the Unit

Responding

1. Prepare a Speech   "Common courtesy and common sense will take you far." Prepare a five-minute speech expanding on this statement, using examples from this unit and one personal experience.

2. Express Goals and Strategies   What are your goals, and how will you achieve them? Choose two of the following areas explored in this unit:

   - employment
   - personal finances
   - buying an automobile/learning to drive
   - finding your first apartment

   In a personal essay, identify specific goals you wish to achieve in each of the two areas and describe the steps you will take to reach them.

Extending

3. Listen to the Experts   As a class, list topics covered in this unit about which you would like to know more. After selecting one topic to pursue further, invite a guest speaker to address the topic. Research the field beforehand to prepare a list of questions you would like answered. Discuss the information presented.

4. Create a Job Search Portfolio   Each job you apply for will require you to highlight certain skills and accomplishments. To prepare for your future work search, set up a portfolio containing transcripts and certificates, and personal information organized under headings such as "education and training," "work experience" (volunteer and extracurricular jobs), "skills: computer, leadership, other." Also, compile a list of contacts and references, and include résumé and cover letter templates. Add to your portfolio as you acquire new skills, experiences, and job contacts.

> **SELF-ASSESSMENT**
>
> The main focus of this unit is on situations you will encounter as you move into the world beyond high school. Identify
> - the most inspiring ideas you came away with
> - the most anxiety-provoking information you read
>
> Write your response in the form of a letter to the teacher.

alliteration repetition of consonant sounds in a line or series of words

allusion brief reference to a person, place, or event from history, literature, or mythology

analogy similarity in some respects between things that are otherwise dissimilar

anecdote short narrative used to make a point or introduce a topic

antagonist major character or force in that opposes the hero, or *protagonist*

assonance a partial rhyme based on similar vowel sounds; repetition of vowel sounds in a line or a series of words

atmosphere prevailing feeling created by the story

audience target readers, viewers, or listeners for whom a selection is intended

autobiography a person's life story, as written by himself of herself

bias a predisposition or personal inclination on a matter, which inhibits impartial judgement

biography a person's life story written by someone else

brochure pamphlet or leaflet giving descriptive or helpful information

caption words that accompany a photograph, picture, or cartoon

cause–effect method for organizing an essay; *cause* looks at the reasons why something came to be; *effect* is the result or outcome of an event or change

character sketch description of a character's or person's moral qualities or behaviours, including specific examples and quotations from the story

cliché stale, familiar phrase or pattern

climax highest point of emotional intensity, usually a turning point in the protagonist's fortunes

collage artwork made of selected pieces or a mix of various materials

compare to look at the similarities between two things, situations, or characters

complication event that starts or causes a conflict

conflict struggle between opposing characters or forces

connotation a meaning suggested by or associated with a word or thing, in addition to its literal meaning (compare *denotation*)

content the ideas and situations of a selection; sometimes called "the what" or subject matter

context specific situation in which a word is used; the personal or historical situation surrounding a person, character, or story

contrast striking difference distinguishing two things being compared

convention rule of writing or familiar pattern within a genre

cover(ing) letter letter accompanying a résumé, which often explains the applicant's special interest in or qualifications for a specific job

crisis moment of intense conflict

criteria various standards used to judge something

denotation something referred to; the literal meaning (compare *connotation*)

denouement the final resolution of a play or story plot

detail specific aspect or small part of the whole

dialogue a conversation between characters or people

diction   choice of words used by a writer or speaker

discrimination   negative action or attitude based on race, religion, age, or sex

draft   rough copy or first attempt

dramatic irony   occurs when what a character says or believes contrasts with what the reader or other characters know to be true

dynamic character   protagonist who undergoes a significant, lasting change

editorial   personal opinion or stand written on an issue of interest

e-mail   electronic mail sent between computers

endorsement   advertising technique in which a famous person recommends a product

episode   incident or event that is part of the narrative or plot

evaluation   judgement or assessment of someone or something

fairy tale   exaggerated made-up story for young children

falling action   section of a story following the climax

foreshadowing   a hint of events to come later

form   general term referring to the way in which a selection is put together, its "shape" or structure; sometimes called "the how" of the selection

frame   single, complete image in film, cartoons, or pictures; frame can also refer to the outside boundary of the image or what is contained within this boundary

free verse   poem that doesn't rhyme and has no regular structure

genre   type of text such as a poem, short story, or film

graphics   visual products of commercial design or illustration

idiom   an expression that uses language figuratively and reflects a specific context or culture

image   words that form vivid sense impressions for the reader

imagery   repeated pattern of words that form sense impressions for the reader

implication   indirect hint or suggestion

improvise   to make up spontaneously; to ad-lib a scene

irony   two or more contrasting or contradictory meanings

italics   sloping typeface used for emphasis

jargon   specialized language used within particular groups

juxtaposition   side-by-side or superimposed contrast for dramatic effect

logo   emblem or design used to represent and advertise a company or organization

marketing   planned selling and promotion of products or services

media   all-inclusive term referring to means of mass communication (e.g., television, movies, newspapers, radio, magazines)

memoir   an account of the author's personal experience

metaphor   direct comparison between two unlike objects

mood   feeling created in the reader by a selection

motivation   what causes a character or person to do something

myth   imagined traditional story used to explain something in a given culture

narrative essay   essay that tells a story, either a made-up one to illustrate a point or, more commonly, a true telling of actual personal or historical events

narrator   person or character telling the story

neologism   a new word or expression

onomatopoeia   words used in poems that sound like what is being described (e.g., hoot, clang)

pan   reference to a camera technique in which a camera slowly swivels on a tripod from one side to the other laterally

pantomime (or mime)   drama without words, acted through gestures, body movements, and facial expressions

parallel structure   usually refers to sentences that use a similar grammatical structure

paraphrase   to put a given text into your own words

parody   humorous imitation or take-off of something or someone's style

persona   the character or personality we assume in public

personal inventory (personal data sheet)   summary of information about a job applicant

personal response   refers to the reader/listener/viewer's response to a selection; it usually includes personal associations and previous personal experiences that relate to the selection

personification   technique of giving human characteristics to abstract, inanimate things or nonhuman creatures

plot   storyline or series of episodes

point of view   perspective from which a story is told. The three most common points of view in short stories are: (1) first-person narrative (uses "I" and the perspective of the protagonist directly); (2) third-person or limited omniscient narrative (uses "he" or "she" and presents the protagonist's perspective from "outside" the narrative); and (3) omniscient (story is narrated from several points of view and reveals the thinking of more than one character, or is narrated by an outsider)

précis   brief summary of a longer selection, usually the ideas of the selection

prejudice   hasty or automatic advance judgement of someone or something before fully experiencing or appreciating the person or thing in question

profile   piece of writing that reviews the life and or career of a person

proofread   to read for and correct mechanical (grammar, spelling, punctuation, capitalization) errors

pros and cons   arguments for and against an argument

protagonist   main character through whose eyes the story is told

public service ad (PSA)   print, TV, or radio ad serving a noncommercial community or humane cause or purpose

pun   play on words

purpose   reason the author wrote the selection

realism   refers to the use of qualities that make a selection life-like or believable

relevance   quality of a selection that relates it to the reader or audience

resolution   (sometimes called the *denouement*) occurs when a conflict is resolved or a mystery is explained

résumé   summary of basic personal information (name, address, telephone number) and information on education, skills, and experience gained through past employment, volunteer work, and hobbies; an important job-search tool

review   personal analysis or commentary, usually about a play, musical performance, movie, or book

rhetorical question   question to which no answer is expected

rising action   incidents taking place before the climax

sarcasm a form of wit that uses cutting, often ironic, remarks intended to wound

satire use of irony to ridicule an idea, person, or thing, often with the intention of causing social change

science fiction writing that speculates about the effects of technology, science, or the future on humans

sentence variety using different kinds of sentence structures to create interest for a reader

sequel an imagined follow-up to a story or poem

sequence order and arrangement of a selection

setting time and place of the selection

simile indirect comparison using "like" or "as"

situational irony occurs when what happens is different from what is expected or considered appropriate

skit humorous scene or dramatization

slang type of language used in casual speech; usually uses short-lived figures of speech in place of standard terms for effect

slogan short catchy phrase used in advertising

speaker person in a poem or play who is talking

spoof humorous dramatization making fun of something serious or well known

stanza (or verse) the "paragraph" of poetry

static character character who does not change

stereotyping use of a fixed view or familiar pattern

storyboard series of pictures used to help visualize a movie scene or to develop a cartoon

stream of consciousness in stories, the presentation of uninterrupted thoughts and feelings of a character

structure way in which a selection is organized

style the unique manner and approach a writer or artist uses in a selection

subconflict minor conflict often related to the main conflict

subtheme minor idea often related to the main theme

suspense reader's feeling of anxiety about the outcome of a situation

symbol something that stands for or represents something else

tableau a still-life dramatic composition used to present a scene or an idea

technology generally refers to mechanical or electronic arts, or the tools used to accomplish a purpose

text language of a selection; broadly used to refer to visual or electronic texts such as cartoons and films as well as print materials

thematic statement one-sentence statement that generalizes a story's message

theme central idea of a selection, which is often implied rather than directly stated

thesis main idea of an essay, found in the first paragraph

tone attitude of the writer or speaker toward his or her topic or audience

topic subject of a selection; what the selection is about generally at first glance

trait characteristic, usually expressed as an adjective in a character sketch

verisimilitude life-like quality possessed by a story

Web page a page from a Web site

Web site place on the World Wide Web consisting of a home page and other files maintained by a particular organization

TEXT CREDITS

UNIT 1

2: "Shape of Things to Come" from *Time*, Winter 1997-1998. © 1998 Time Inc. Reprinted by permission.

5: "The Fun They Had" from *Earth is Room Enough* by Isaac Asimov, copyright © 1957 by Isaac Asimov. Used by permission of Doubleday, a division of Random House, Inc.

9: "Supertoys Last All Summer Long" by Brian Aldiss from *Supertoys Last All Summer Long and Other Stories of Future Time*. Reprinted by permission of Little, Brown and Company UK.

18: From Wicks by Ben Wicks. Reprinted by permission of The Canadian Publishers, McClelland & Stewart Limited, Toronto.

20: "A Clone of Our Own" by Gunjan Sinha, *Popular Science*, Summer 2001. Reprinted by permission.

23: "Stem Cells Q & A" by Amina Ali and Owen Wood. CBC News Online. http://cbc.ca/news/indepth/background/stemcells.html. Reprinted by permission.

27: "Smart Shirt" by Priya Giri from *Life Magazine*, Fall 1998 Special Issue, p. 65. © 1998 Time Inc. Reprinted by permission.

29: "Risk" by Joanna Russ, © 1975 by Mercury Press, Inc. First published in *The Magazine of Fantasy & Science Fiction*, June 1975.

32: "When Cars Drive You" by Keith Naughton from *Newsweek*, January 1, © 2000 Newsweek, Inc. All rights reserved. Reprinted by permission.

36: "Logged on to the Guy Next Door" by Scott McKeen from *The Edmonton Journal*, September 11, 2000. Reprinted with permission of the Edmonton Journal.

39: "There Will Come Soft Rains" by Ray Bradbury. Reprinted by permission of Don Congdon Associates, Inc. Copyright © 1950 by Crowell Collier Publishing Co., renewed 1977 by Ray Bradbury.

46: "Fire and Ice" by Robert Frost from *The Poetry of Robert Frost* edited by Edward Connery Lathem, © 1951 by Robert Frost. Copyright 1923, 1969 by Henry Holt and Company, LLC. Reprinted by permission of Henry Holt and Company, LLC.

48: Words by Bruce Cockburn. © 1988 Golden Mountain Music Corp. (SOCAN) Used by permission.

51: From "50 Simple Things You Can Do to Save the Earth," Copyright © 1999 by the Earthworks Group, is published by the Earthworks Press, Berkeley, Calif. Reprinted with permission from the August 1990 Reader's Digest.

55: "Zoo" by Edward D. Hoch. © 1958 by King-Size Publications, Inc. Renewed © 1986 by Edward D. Hoch.

UNIT 2

60: *Zits* reprinted with special permission of King Features Syndicate.

62: "Deportation at Breakfast" by Larry Fondation from *Unscheduled Departures: The Asylum Anthology of Short Fiction*, ed. Greg Boyd. Published by Asylum Arts, © 1991. Reprinted by permission.

65: "Sporting that Strangely Piercing Look" by Sharon Lindores, *Edmonton Journal*, June 27, 1998. Reprinted with permission of the Edmonton Journal.

69: "Four Minutes That Get You Hired" by Connie Brown Glaser and Barbara Steinberg Smalley, condensed from *More Power to You*. © 1992 by Connie Brown Glaser and Barbara Steinberg Smalley, Warner Books, NY. Reprinted with permission from the August 1993 Reader's Digest and by permission of Little, Brown and Company, Inc.

74: © 1992 Farworks, Inc. Distributed by Universal Press Syndicate. Reprinted with permission. All rights reserved.

76: "Warren Pryor" by Alden Nowlan from *Selected Poems*, published by House of Anansi Press. Copyright © the Estate of Alden Nowlan. Reprinted by permission of Stoddart Publishing Co. Limited.

78: "The Hidden Songs of a Secret Soul" by Bob Greene. © Tribune Media Services, Inc. All rights reserved. Reprinted with permission.

81: "Assembly Line" by Shu Ting from *A Splintered Mirror: Chinese Poetry from the Democracy Movement* translated by Donald Finkel. Translation copyright © 1991 by Donald Finkel. Reprinted by permission of North Point Press, a division of Farrar, Straus & Giroux, Inc.

83: "For Laurie, truck driving paved her road to freedom" by Danielle Bochove, *Edmonton Journal*, September 6, 1992. Reprinted with permission of the Edmonton Journal.

87: "The World of the Stay-at-Home Dad" by Andrew Olscher, *Toronto Star*, September 23, 1993. Used by permission of the author.

91: Reprinted with permission from *Realm: Creating Work You Want*™, published by YES Canada-BC. Available online at http://realm.net and in print by calling 1-877-REALM-99. For more information, Phone: (604) 412-4144 E-mail: info@realm.net.

96: From *A Recent Future*. © James Keelaghan 1994.

99: "When choosing your path, follow your heart" by Elizabeth Newton, *Edmonton Journal*, August 30, 2000, p. G4. Reprinted by permission of the author.

103: "The dignity of work" by Charles Finn, *The Globe and Mail*, July 8, 1999, P. A20. Reprinted by permission of the author.

UNIT 3

108: Reprinted from *Magic City*. © 1992 by Yusef Komunyakaa, Reprinted by permission of Wesleyan University Press.

111: "Runyan's Vision? To Inspire the Best in Others" by Tom Barrett, *Edmonton Journal*, August 1, 2001. Reprinted by permission of the Edmonton Journal.

114: © 1971 Crown Vetch Music.

116: Herman® is reprinted with permission from LaughingStock Licensing Inc., Ottawa, Canada. All rights reserved.

118: "Just Once" by Thomas J. Dygard, copyright © 1995 by Thomas Dygard, from *Ultimate Sports* by Donald R. Gallo. Used by permission of Random House Children's Books, a division of Random House, Inc.

125: From *A Gathering of Spirit: A Collection by North American Indian Women*. © by Vickie Sears. Used by permission of Firebrand Books, Milford, Connecticut.

129: "On the Right Track" by Dorothy Chisholm first appeared in *Other Voices*, Fall 1990.

136: "Field of Dreams a Real-Life Gem" by Wayne Coffey, *New York Daily News*. © New York Daily News, L.P. Reprinted-reproduced with permission.

140: From *The Collected Poems of Langston Hughes* by Langston Hughes, copyright © 1994 by The Estate of Langston Hughes. Used by permission of Alfred A. Knopf, a division of Random House, Inc.

142: From *Why Don't You Carve Other Animals?* By Yvonne Vera. Copyright © 1992 by Yvonne Vera. Reprinted by permission of TSAR Publications.

146: Excerpted from *Beyond the Limits: A Woman's Triumph on Mount Everest* by Stacy Allison (with Peter Carlin). Copyright © 1993 by Stacy Allison and Peter Carlin. Reprinted by permission of the author.

151: "Out of This World" by Chris Hadfield,

Time, May 21, 2001. © 2001 Time Inc. Reprinted by permission.

156: "Four Who Make a Difference" by Jennifer Burke Crump. Reprinted with permission from the May 2001 Reader's Digest.

162: From *Coyote's Morning Cry: Meditations and Dreams from a Life in Nature* by Sharon Butala. Published by HarperCollinsPublishers Ltd. Copyright © 1995 by Sharon Butala.

UNIT 4

166: DILBERT reprinted by permission of United Feature Syndicate, Inc.

168: http://cbc.ca/news/national/rex/rex20010119.html. Reprinted by permission of the author.

171: Reprinted by permission of the author.

174: © 2000 by Farworks, Inc.

176: Reprinted by permission of the author.

186: © 2001 Sony Electronics, Inc. All rights reserved.

188: © Forest Stewardship Council.

190: © 2002 Lycos, Inc. Lycos® is a registered trademark of Carnegie Mellon University. All rights reserved.

194: "Buy Nothing Day Provokes Pause for Thought" by Liane Faulder, *Edmonton Journal*, November 27, 1997. Reprinted with permission of the Edmonton Journal.

197: "Television's Child" by Glen Kirkland from *The Reading Teacher*, Vol. 54, No. 5, February 2001. Reprinted by permission of the author.

200: Calvin and Hobbes © 1985 Watterson. Reprinted with permission of Universal Press Syndicate. All rights reserved.

202: From *Funny, You Don't Look Like One: Observations from a Blue-Eyed Ojibway*, Theytus Books, Ltd.

206: Reprinted with special permission of King Features Syndicate.

208: © 1993 The Boston Globe Newspaper Co./Washington Post Writers Group, reprinted by permission.

212: "Be specific when searching the web" by Andy Walker, Cyberwalker Media Syndicate, reprinted from *The Edmonton Journal*, January 25, 2001.

UNIT 5

218: © 1992. Reprinted by permission of the author.

221: © 1998 by Chrystia Chomiak. English translation © by Marco Carynnyk and Marta Horban, 1998.

227: From *Arguments with Gravity*, Quarry Press, 1996.

230: "A Son's Eulogy for His father" by Justin Trudeau. Reprinted by permission of Canadian Press.

234: From *The Imperfect Paradise* by Linda Pastan. Copyright © 1988 by Linda Pastan. Reprinted by permission of W.W. Norton & Company, Inc.

236: Excerpted from *Paper Shadows: A Chinatown Childhood* by Wayson Choy. Copyright © 1999 by Wayson Choy. Reprinted by permission of Penguin Books Canada Limited.

240: "Home Sweet Home" by Jennifer Aubrey Burhart from *Teen Ink 2: More Voices, More Visions*. © 2001 The Young Authors Foundation, Inc., d/b/a Teen Ink.

242: From *The Collected Poems* (1991). Reprinted by permission of the author and Sono Nis Press, Victoria, BC.

244: From *Between Ourselves: Letters Between Mothers and Daughters 1950-1982* ed. Karen Payne. © 1983, Michael Joseph Ltd. & Pelham Books.

247: Reprinted by permission of the author.

250: From *The Rebellion of Young David* by Ernest Buckler. © 1975 by Ernest Buckler. Reprinted by permission of Curtis Brown, Ltd.

256: From *The Road Home: New Stories from Alberta Writers*, Reidmore Books.

262: Kuroda Saburo, "Strangely Fresh" from Edward Luebers and Naoshi Koriyama, translators, *Like Underground Water: The Poetry of Mid-Twentieth Century Japan.* Copyright © 1995 by Edward Luebers and Naoshi Koriyama. Reprinted with the permission of Copper Canyon Press, P.O. Box 271, Port Townsend, WA 98368-0271.

264: From *Eskimo Poems from Canada and Greenland.* University of Pittsburgh Press. © 1973 English translation Tom Lowenstein.

UNIT 6

268: Reprinted with special permission of King Features Syndicate.

270: © 1927, Max Ehrmann. All rights reserved. © renewed 1954, Bertha Erhmann, Robert Bell, Melrose, Mass. USA 02176.

273: "Because You Waited" by Joan Bond From *Other Voices*, Vol. 9, No. 1, Spring 1996. Reprinted by permission of the author.

275: "Dogs and Books" reprinted with permission from Key Porter Books from *Close Encounters* by Christie Blatchford. © 1998.

278: "Fox Hunt," © 1993 by Lensey Namioka, from *Join In: Multi-Ethnic Short Stories by Outstanding Writers for Young Adults*, edited by Donald R. Gallo. For rights information contact Ruth Cohen, Inc., Literary Agent. Reprinted by permission of Lensey Namioka. All rights are reserved by the author.

286: From *Let The Drums Be Your Heart: New Native Voices*, Douglas & McIntyre. Reprinted by permission of the author.

289: © 1984 by Lisa Wilson Strick. Originally appeared in *Woman's Day Magazine*.

293: © 1940 Originally appeared in *New Yorker*. © 1951 by John Collier, renewed 1978 by the Estate of John Collier. Reprinted by permission of the Harold Matson Co., Inc.

297: From *Shall We Join the Ladies*. Reprinted by permission of McGraw Hill Ryerson.

300: Copyright © The Estate of Morley Callaghan.

309: "A Matter of Ethics" by Douglas Todd, *Vancouver Sun*.

314: "Death Watch" by Thomas Fields-Meyer, *People Weekly*, June 14, 1999, pp. 81-82.

317: © *Vancouver Sun*

320: "Thankful Just to Be" by Rick McConnell, Edmonton Journal, October 6, 2001. Reprinted with permission of the *Edmonton Journal*.

323: From *Still Me* by Christopher Reeve. © 1998 by Cambria Productions, Inc. Published by Random House, Inc. Reprinted with permission from the July 1998 Reader's Digest and by permission of Random House, Inc.

UNIT 7

333: © 2000 Zits Partnership.

335: "Still Me Inside" by Mai Goda, from *Teen Ink 2: More Voices, More Visions.*© 2001 The Young Authors Foundation Inc., d/b/a Teen Ink.

344: From *Domains of Fear and Desire: Urdu Stories*, ed., trans. Muhammad Umar, TSAR Publications, 1992.

343: From *My Career with the Leafs and Other Stories* by Brian Fawcett. Reprinted by permission of Talonbooks, Vancouver.

353: "A Small Cheese Pizza" by Rachel Svea Bottino, from *Teen Ink 2: More Voices, More Visions.* © 2001 The Young Authors Foundation Inc., d/b/a Teen Ink.

356: "Helping Others Best Cure for Loneliness" by Grant Nicol, *Edmonton Journal*, October 3, 1995. Reprinted by permission of the author.

359: From *Poetic Voices of the Maritimes: A Selection of Contemporary Poetry*, Lancelot Press.

363: © 1965 by Paul Simon. Used by permission of the publisher: Paul Simon Music.

365: "The Carved Table" by Mary Peterson, *Ploughshares*, Fall 1980. Reprinted by permission of the author.

369: From *The Available Press/PEN Short Story Collection.* © 1985 by the PEN American Center.

375: From *Let the Drums Be Your Heart: New*

Native Voices, Douglas & McIntyre. Reprinted by permission of the author.

378: From *After Baba's Funeral and Sweet and Sour Pickles*, Toronto: Playwrights Canada, 1981.

UNIT 8

384: © 2000 by FarWorks, Inc.

386: "Ten Commandments of How to Get Along with People" by Ann Landers, www.workplaceissues.com/pmtenc.htm

388: www.topachievement.com/hiltonjohnson. html. Reprinted by permission of the author.

391: "Teen Financier Gets Oprah's Attention" by Collette Derworiz, *Calgary Herald*, February 26, 2001. Reprinted with permission of the Calgary Herald.

394: Used by permission of the Investor Learning Centre of Canada and Alberta Capital Market Foundation.

397: Immigrant Services, Fact Sheet #5, www.cic.gc.ca/english/newcomer/fact 05e.html. Reproduced with the permission of the Minister of Public Works and Government Services Canada, 2000.

400: © Canadian Bankers Association 2000.

403: www.survivability.net/world-work/looking-work.htm © 1998 Janis Foord Kirk.

409: Human Resources Development Canada website http://www.hrdc-drhc.gc.ca/hrib/hrp-prh/pi-ip/career-carriere/english/products/takecharge/tc-12 e.shtml#1. Reproduced with the permission of the Minister of Public Works and Government Services Canada, 2001.

413: Human Resources Development Canada website http://www.hrdc-drhc.gc.ca/hrib/hrp-prh/pi-ip/career-carriere/english/products/takecharge/tc-32 e.shtml. Reproduced with the permission of the Minister of Public Works and Government Services Canada, 2002.

416: http://www.hastingscounty.com/Social Services/OW/looking.htm

419: © 1976 Universal Press Syndicate. All rights reserved. Herman ® is reprinted with permission from LaughingStock Licensing Inc., Ottawa, Canada. All rights reserved.

422: From *Consumer Complaints: A Self-Help Handbook.* © 1987 Alberta Government Services, Consumer Services Branch.

424: U.S. Department of Transportation National Highway Traffic Safety Administration http://broadcast.webpoint.com/wlvi/rd1qz.htm

427: "Lemons For Sale" by Hal Karp, *Reader's Digest*, April 2001. Reprinted with permission from the April 2001 Reader's Digest.

433: © by Sandra Clockedile (www.apartments.about.com), licensed to About.com, Inc. Used by permission of About.com, Inc., which can be found on the Web at www.about.com. All rights reserved.

PHOTO CREDITS

UNIT 1

Opener: All © Photodisc; 2: © Reuters New Media Inc./Corbis/Magma; 5: © Photodisc; 6: © P. Coll/Firstlight; 10: © Photodisc; 12: © Photodisc; 14: © Corbis/Magma; 18: CP Picture Archive/Judy Chreighton; 20: © Superstock; 24: © Photodisc; 27: © Kevin Fleming/Corbis/Magma; 29: © Corbis/Magma; 32-33: Graphic by Kiera Westphal, Christoph Blumrich and Stanford Kay – Newsweek; 36: © Photodisc; 39: © Photodisc; 41: © Photodisc; 43: © Photodisc; 44: © Photodisc; 46: © Photodisc; 49: © Corbis/ Magma; 52: Left: © Corbis/Magma, Right: © Photodisc; 53: Left: © Photodisc, Right: © Photodisc; 56: © Photodisc.

UNIT 2

Opener: (Clockwise from top left) © Corbis/Magma, © Photodisc, © Photodisc, © Photodisc, © Corbis/Magma, © Corbis/Magma, © Photodisc; 60: Courtesy Jim Borgman and Jerry Scott; 62: © Jim Piper/Superstock; 63: © Robert Maass/Corbis/Magma; 65: © Roger Ressmeyer/

Corbis/Magma; 66: © Adrian Weinbrecht/Stone; 70: © Photodisc; 71: © Photodisc; 76: © Photodisc; 79: Top: © Photodisc, Bottom: © Superstock; 81: © Superstock; 83: © Edmonton Journal; 84: © Edmonton Journal; 87: © Photodisc; 88: © Photodisc; 92: © Photodisc; 93: © Bettmann/Corbis/Magma; 96: © Raymond Gehman/Corbis/Magma; 99: © AFP/Corbis/Magma; 100: © Corbis/Magma; 104: © Marek Ciezkiewicz.

UNIT 3

Opener: © Photodisc, Middle: © Jamie Marcial/Superstock; 108: © Corbis/Magma; 112: CP Picture Archive/Doug Mills; 114: Left: CP Picture Archive/Nora Penhale, Right: CP Picture Archive/Ryan Remiorz; 119: © Corbis/Magma; 120: © Photodisc; 123: © Photodisc; 127: © Peter Finger/Corbis/Magma; 130: © Bob Krist/Corbis/Magma; 132: Corel; 134: © Photodisc; 136: Associated Press/Universal; 137: Associated Press AP; 138: © Bettmann/Corbis/Magma; 140: © Photodisc; 143: © Photodisc; 147: © Corbis/Magma; 148: © Galen Rowell/Corbis/Magma; 152: CP Picture Archive/Chris O'Meara; 153: © Corbis/Magma; 154: © Photodisc; 157: © Chick Rice; 159: © Karl Richter; 162: © Photodisc.

UNIT 4

Opener: (Clockwise from top left) © Photodisc, © Photodisc, © Corbis/Magma, © Photodisc, © Corbis/Magma, Centre: © Corbis/Magma, Background: © Corbis/Magma; 166: Courtesy of Scott Adams; 169: © Photodisc; 171: © Twentieth Century Fox/Photofest; 172: © AFP/Corbis/Magma; 177: © Columbia Pictures/Photofest; 178: Columbia Pictures/Photofest; 180: Touchstone Pictures/Photofest; 182: *AI Artificial Intelligence* © 2001 Warner Bros., a division of Time Warner Entertainment Company, L.P. and Dreamworks LLC; 184: Universal Pictures/Photofest; 192: Adbusters 2001 Days of Resistance Calendar. Used by permission of Robin Collyer; 195: Image courtesy of www.adbusters.org; 197: Courtesy of Glen Kirkland; 198: © Owen Franken/Corbis/Magma; 202: Courtesy of Drew Hayden Taylor; 203: From left: CP Picture Archive/Phill Snel, CP Picture Archive/Frank Gunn, CP Picture Archive/Edmonton Sun/Jack Dagley, © Bettmann/Corbis/Magma; 206: Courtesy Jim Borgman and Jerry Scott; 208: Courtesy of Ellen Goodman; 209: © Photodisc; 212: Courtesy Andy Walker; 213: Reproduced with permission of Yahoo! Inc. © 2000 by Yahoo! Inc. Yahoo! And the Yahoo! Logo are trademarks of Yahoo! Inc. 214: © Canada.com.

UNIT 5

Opener: All © Photodisc; 219: © James Marshall/Corbis/Magma; 222: © Firstlight; 224: © Trinette Reed/Corbis/Magma; 227: © Charles West/Corbis Stockmarket/Magma; 230: CP Picture Archive/Paul Chiasson; 231: CP Picture Archive/Fred Chartrand; 232: CP Picture Archive/Andy Clark; 234: © Corbis/Magma; 236: CP Picture Archive/Keith Beatty, Toronto Star; 237: © Todd Gipstein/Corbis/Magma; 241: © Photodisc; 242: © Photodisc; 245: © Photodisc; 248: © Richard Hutchings/Corbis/Magma; 250: © Photodisc; 252: © Photodisc; 253: © Photodisc; 257: © Bettmann/Corbis/Magma; 259: © Bettmann/Corbis/Magma; 262: © Photodisc; 264: © Richard A. Cooke/Corbis/Magma.

UNIT 6

Opener: Top left: © Corbis/Magma, All others © Photodisc; 268: Courtesy of Jim Borgman and Jerry Scott; 270: © Photodisc; 273: © Photodisc; 276: © Photodisc; 279: © Papilio/Corbis/Magma; 280: © Photodisc; 283: © Photodisc; 286: © David Samuel Robbins/Corbis/Magma; 290: © Corbis/Magma; 294: © Photodisc; 298: © Jonathan Blair/Corbis/Magma; 301: © Photodisc; 302: © Corbis/Magma; 305: © Photodisc; 309: © David Young-Wolff/Stone; 310: © AFP/Corbis/

Magma; 315: © Nikolai Ignatiev/Network/Saba; 318: © Michael St. Maur Sheil/Corbis/Magma; 321: © Photodisc; 324: CP picture archive/Daniel Hulshizer/Associated Press; 325: © Bettmann/Corbis/Magma.

UNIT 7

Opener: (Clockwise from top left) © Reuters NewMedia Inc./Corbis/Magma, © Phil Schermeister/Corbis/Magma, © Reuters NewMedia Inc./Corbis/Magma, © Reuters New Media Inc./Corbis/Magma, Background: © Photodisc; 330: Alfred Eisenstaedt/Timepix. From Life Classic Photographs, John Loengard, ed., New York Graphic Society Books, p. 52; 333: Courtesy of Jim Borgman and Jerry Scott; 336: © Photodisc; 338: © Photodisc; 340: © Richard Bickel/Corbis/Magma; 344: © Photodisc; 346: © Photodisc; 349: © Photodisc; 350: © Photodisc; 351 © Photodisc; 353: © Corbis/Magma; 357: © Photodisc; 359: © Photodisc; 361: Left: © Michael Nicholson/Corbis/Magma, Right: © Photodisc; 363: Top: CP Picture Archive/Mark Lennihan, Bottom: © Hulton-Deutsch Collection/Corbis/Magma; 366: © Photodisc; 369: © Ron Stewart/Superstock; 372: © Photodisc; 374: © Blake Woken/Corbis/Magma; 377: © Craig Aurness/Corbis/Magma; 378: © Photodisc; 379: Courtesy of the Heit family.

UNIT 8

Opener: (Clockwise from top left) © Photodisc, © Photodisc, © Photodisc, background: © Photodisc; 386: © Photodisc; 389: © Photodisc; 391: Dean Bicknell/Calgary Herald; 395: © Photodisc; 397: © Photodisc; 401: © Photodisc; 404: © Photodisc; 407: Reprinted by permission of Sally & Richard Greenhill; 409: © Roger Allyn Lee/Superstock; 413: © Photodisc; 416: © Photodisc; 424: © Photodisc; 428: © Photodisc; 434: © Joseph Sohm; Chromo Sohm Inc./Corbis/Magma